Selling Rights

D0139811

Selling Rights is a practical and accessible guide to all aspects of selling rights and co-publications throughout the world. The sixth edition of this authoritative handbook has been updated to include the changes which have taken place in technology, sales and distribution, and legislation in the United Kingdom and overseas, especially relating to web 2.0. *Selling Rights* covers the full range of potential rights, from English-language territorial rights, book club and paperback sales through to serial rights, translation rights, dramatization and documentary rights, and electronic publishing and multimedia.

Lynette Owen provides full details of the historical and legal background to rights, advises on aspects of negotiating licence contracts and explains how to get the best possible deal.

This fully revised and updated edition of *Selling Rights* includes:

- changes and proposed changes to copyright legislation in the United Kingdom, the European Union and elsewhere as a result of developments in electronic publishing and the impact of technology companies such as Google and Amazon
- the need to deal with the use of orphan works, the entry of more countries into membership of the international copyright conventions and initiatives to tackle electronic piracy
- developments in the area of parallel importation
- practical advice on rights management systems and on more efficient ways to promote and submit titles to potential licensees
- developments in the licensing of translation rights
- coverage of collective licensing systems for the use of extracts from copyright works
- initiatives to make copyright works more accessible to the reading impaired
- recent developments in e-publishing, such as the new e-readers, downloadable audiobooks, and the rise of the mobile phone
- important distinctions such as whether e-books constitute sales or licences.

Lynette Owen is Copyright Director of Pearson Education Ltd. She is the general editor of, and a contributor to, *Clark's Publishing Agreements: A Book of Precedents* (7th edition, 2007) and is the author of a number of practical handbooks on copyright and licensing for publishers in transitional and developing countries in central and eastern Europe and Asia. She regularly lectures on training courses both in the United Kingdom and abroad.

Selling Rights

Sixth edition

Lynette Owen

Routledge
Taylor & Francis Group

LONDON AND NEW YORK

First edition published 1991 by Blueprint
Second edition published 1994 by Blueprint
Third edition published 1997 by Routledge
Fourth edition published 2001 by Routledge
Fifth edition published 2006 by Routledge
This edition published 2010 by Routledge
2 Park Square, Milton Park, Abingdon, OX14 4RN

Simultaneously published in the USA and Canada by Routledge
270 Madison Ave, New York, NY 10016

Routledge is an imprint of the Taylor & Francis Group, an informa business

© 1991, 1994, 1997, 2001, 2006, 2010 Lynette Owen

Typeset in Goudy by Taylor & Francis Books
Printed and bound in Great Britain by
CPI Antony Rowe, Chippenham, Wiltshire

British Library Cataloguing in Publication Data
A catalogue record for this book is available from the British Library

Library of Congress Cataloging in Publication Data
Owen, Lynette, 1947-
  Selling rights / Lynette Owen. – 6th ed.
    p. cm.
  "Simultaneously published in the USA and Canada by Routledge."
  Includes bibliographical references and index.
  1. Authors and publishers–Great Britain. 2. Contracts–Great Britain. 3.
Copyright licences–Great Britain. I. Title.
  KD1340.O96 2010
  346.4104′82–dc22
                         2009053636

ISBN 13: 978-0-415-49692-6 (pbk)
ISBN 13: 978-0-203-86366-4 (ebk)

Contents

Acknowledgements and further reading

The following publications have provided invaluable background information when preparing the present volume, and may be of interest as further reading and as a source of more detail on specific aspects of copyright, licensing, contracts and the digital environment:

Chris Anderson, *Free: The Future of a Radical Price* (Random House Business Books, 2009).

Ken Auletta, *Googled: The End of the World As We Know It* (Virgin Books, 2010)

Association of American Publishers Rights and Permission Advisory Committee, The New and Updated Copyright Primer: A Survival Guide to the Copyright and Permissions Process (Association of American Publishers, 2000).

Susan Bielstein, *Permissions: A Survival Guide: Blunt Talk about Art as Intellectual Property* (University of Chicago Press, 2006).

Sven Birkerts, The Gutenberg Elegies: The Fate of Reading in an Electronic Age (Faber, 1995).

Sven Birkerts, Tolstoy's Dictaphone: Technology and the Muse (Graywolf Press, 1997).

Carole Blake, From Pitch to Publication: Everything You Need to Know to Get Your Novel Published (Macmillan, 1999).

Asa Briggs (ed.), Essays in the History of Publishing (Longman, 1974).

J.M. Cavendish and Kate Pool, A Handbook of Copyright in British Publishing Practice, third edition (Cassell, 1993).

Charles Clark, 'The Answer to the Machine is in the Machine' and Other Collected Writings, edited by Jon Bing and Thomas Dreier (Norwegian Research Center for Computers and Law, 2005).

Robert Darnton, *The Case for Books: Past, Present and Future* (PublicAffairs, 2009).

Denis de Freitas, The Copyright System: Practice and Problems in Developing Countries (Commonwealth Secretariat, 1983).

Denis de Freitas, The Law of Copyright and Rights in Performances, second edition (British Copyright Council, 1998).

Michael F. Flint, A User's Guide to Copyright, sixth edition (Tottel, 2006).

Julian Friedmann, How to Make Money Scriptwriting, second edition (Intellect Books, 2000).

Paul Goldstein, *Copyright's Highway: The Law and Lore of Copyright from Gutenberg to the Celestial Jukebox*, revised edition (Stanford University Press, 2003).

Hugh Jones, Publishing Law, third edition (Routledge, 2006).

Roy S. Kaufman, *Publishing Forms and Contracts* (Oxford University Press, 2008).

Lawrence Lessig, *Code: and Other Laws of Cyberspace* (Basic Books, 2000).

Lawrence Lessig, *The Future of Ideas: The Fate of the Commons in a Connected World* (Vintage, 2002).

Lawrence Lessig, *Free Culture: How Big Media Uses Technology and the Law to Lock Down Culture and Creativity* (Penguin, 2004).

Richard McCracken and Madeleine Gilbert, Buying and Clearing Rights: Print, Broadcast and Multimedia (Routledge, 1995).

Nicolas Negroponte, Being Digital (Hodder Headline, 1995).

Lynette Owen (general editor), *Clark's Publishing Agreements: A Book of Precedents*, seventh edition (Tottel Publishing, 2007, now Bloomsbury Professional).

William Patry, *Moral Panics and the Copyright Wars* (Oxford University Press, 2009).

John B. Thompson, *Books in the Digital Age: The Transformation of Academic and Higher Education Publishing in Britain and the United States* (Polity Press, 2005).

Alan Williams, Duncan Calow and Nicholas Higham, Digital Media: Contracts, Rights and Licensing, second edition (Sweet & Maxwell, 1998).

Ingrid Winternitz, Electronic Publishing Agreements (Oxford University Press, 2000).

Jonathan Zittrain, *The Future of the Internet and How to Stop It* (Allen Lane, 2008).

The ABC of Copyright (UNESCO, 1981).

Continuum's Directory of Publishing (Continuum, published annually).

International Literary Marketplace (Information Today, published annually).

Literary Marketplace (Information Today, published annually).

Writers' and Artists' Yearbook (A. & C. Black, published annually).

The Writer's Handbook, ed. Barry Turner (Macmillan, published annually).

Preface

Nearly four years have passed since the fifth edition of *Selling Rights* appeared and the intervening period has seen a number of developments affecting the sale of rights. In particular, the focus on the question of whether copyright is fit for purpose in the digital age continues at both national and international level and is of daily concern to the creative industries, including our own.

The continuing perception by a number of user groups, in particular the younger generations who have grown up expecting content of all kinds to be available quickly and free of charge on the internet, that copyright is an obstacle to access rather than a necessary framework for encouraging and rewarding creativity remains a cause for concern, and there are ongoing calls for open access to content from the academic community, many of whom are authors as well as consumers.

As usual, I have maintained the aim of the previous editions: that of a practical handbook for those working in the book industry, in particular rights staff working in publishing houses and literary agents, but also recognizing some readership from members of the legal profession with a particular interest in publishing rights. Again, the coverage assumes a main readership in the United Kingdom, but, as always, feedback from American and other overseas colleagues has been much appreciated.

I have also continued to maintain the overall structure of previous editions, with an initial chapter on the copyright background to trading in rights and recent developments in that area, the control of rights in literary works and practical aspects of the promotion and sale of rights, followed by individual chapters on different categories of rights sales. Some areas have undergone significant changes in recent years – in particular book club rights, where the stock supplied is now generally identical to that of the trade edition and where sales may be handled outside the rights department. This channel to market has inevitably been affected by the availability of books at heavily discounted prices from traditional booksellers, supermarkets and online retailers. First serial rights, once an area which could generate substantial income, have been affected by falling newspaper circulations and advertising revenue, the cost of taking newspaper content online and a trend towards seeking new readers by giving away items such as CDs and DVDs. Audiobooks have grown in popularity, with downloading of audio content on the rise as a result of the popularity of devices such as the iPod. In the more glamorous world of film and television, the last four years have seen a remarkable number of successful dramatizations based on published works, with more to come.

In the area of reprography and electronic licensing, I have aimed to maintain the distinction between the use of, or access to, extracts from published works versus the supply of the entire work in electronic form, either verbatim or enhanced in multimedia form. Collective licensing arrangements now recognize the demand for extracts of copyright works through scanning and digitization, and a number of licences have been extended accordingly to meet those needs. Since the last edition of this book appeared a new generation of dedicated e-reading devices have become available, with what appears to be a better chance of success. Of considerable significance to authors and publishers are the forays of technology companies into the digitization of published works, in particular the controversial initiatives undertaken by Google.

As in all previous editions, I have not attempted to provide model contracts, a range of which continue to be available in the collaborative work *Clark's Publishing Agreements: A Book of Precedents* (seventh edition 2007, Tottel Publishing, now Bloomsbury Professional) and in other more specialized volumes of precedents for electronic licensing. I have also continued to provide only general guidelines on financial terms for licensing: I remain conscious of anti-trust concerns not only in the United States but also within the European Union. In the case of permissions ('Anthology and quotation rights', Chapter 17) the Office of Fair Trading no longer permits registration of guidelines originally agreed and regularly updated between the UK Publishers Association and the Society of Authors. In the area of electronic licensing, the last ten years have seen many players retrench or withdraw, platforms collapse and new players and platforms emerge almost daily, which makes 'norms' in relation to payment models and financial terms far harder to establish. It remains the case that intellectual property rights are worth whatever a given licensee is prepared to pay for them at the time and much depends on the author, the property, the topicality of the content and the demands and indeed whims of the market. It is also true to say that there remain many differences in attitude and practice between educational, academic and professional publishers, on the one hand, and trade publishers on the other.

On the copyright front, the last ten years have seen both positive and negative developments. Increasing pressure on countries to become members of the World Trade Organization and to comply with the intellectual property obligations inherent in membership of that organization has resulted in many of the 'absentee' nations of the world signing up (at least in the legal sense) to membership of one or more of the three major international copyright conventions; only a handful of countries now remain out in the cold. It would, however, be foolish to assume that full-scale piracy or casual infringement of copyright are features of the past; electronic piracy is on the rise and affects both the trade and the academic sectors of our industry. Some is undertaken for commercial gain, some for ostensibly philanthropic reasons. Perhaps of equal concern have been the burgeoning movements which either oppose copyright altogether as a barrier to free access by the user, or which seek open access of one kind or another which inevitably impinges on the activities of publishers who have made major investments in their goal to provide added value when bringing copyright works to market. There has been renewed lobbying from some developing countries at the highest levels for exceptions to copyright for educational and academic use and special exceptions for the reading disabled; whilst the publishing industry must recognize the power of user demands, it must itself lobby to promote the value of the services it provides and the need to reward authors for the use of their creative output.

As always, developments on the political and economic front can affect the sale of rights both positively and negatively. The last two years have seen a major economic recession which has affected some markets particularly severely – Russia and the Baltic States are major examples. The People's Republic of China seems to have emerged relatively unscathed; the publishing industry there remains largely state controlled and some content remains sensitive. The issue of territorial rights continues, particularly between the Anglophone markets, and has added complexities as a result of the burgeoning market for e-books. Author societies and literary agents continue to lobby for higher rates of royalty for the electronic exploitation of literary works. One thing remains sure – the area of rights is never static.

As for previous editions, I have been fortunate to be able to call on a number of colleagues for advice on specific areas, and I would like to express my warm thanks to Georgina Bentliff of the Copyright Licensing Agency (CLA), David Bishop of the Publishers Licensing Society (PLS), Julian Friedmann of Blake Friedmann and Diane Spivey of Little, Brown.

Lynette Owen
London, March 2010

Chapter 1

Rights
The historical and legal background

This introductory chapter aims to set the scene for what follows by tracing the history of how the concept of copyright arose, some of the different copyright philosophies (including those of the United Kingdom and its major trading partners), and in particular the flurry of recent initiatives proposing copyright reform at international, multinational and national levels. To trade in intellectual property, it is essential that the work in question is protected by copyright and that a framework of mutual copyright protection is in place if the trading is to take place between different countries, perhaps with differing copyright regimes.

The rise of the UK publishing industry

In the United Kingdom, the publishing industry can be held to have been born when the University of Cambridge received a Royal Charter to print in 1534, followed by the University of Oxford in 1586. The first commercial publishing house was the family firm of Longman, founded in 1724, but the real burgeoning of the commercial houses, many of which still exist today under the umbrella of larger organizations, took place in the nineteenth century. This was the result of a variety of factors: an increase in population, the concentration of population in cities and the development of literacy. The latter part of the twentieth century saw a movement towards the consolidation of many formerly independent small and medium-sized publishing companies into larger groups, some of them part of multinational media corporations. The publishing cycle continues with the founding of more small independent publishing houses.

Copyright

The publishing industry – and by association the trade in publishing rights – is inextricably linked to the existence and recognition of copyright. Without copyright, it is doubtful whether many authors would have the incentive to be creative. Some authors may still be prepared to publish without reward, perhaps in order to make known the findings of their academic research and as a means of furthering their professional careers, and indeed the pervasive influence of the internet has led many would-be authors to post their writings online, and to self-publish, with varying standards of quality resulting. Others have chosen to become authors in an attempt to earn their living directly from their writing. Without copyright and the laws and systems that underpin it, there would be total freedom for literary works to be reproduced, translated, adapted and exploited in a variety of ways without any obligation to recognize the interests of the creator. For authors, this would affect both their moral rights – the right to be recognized as the creator of the work and the right to prevent derogatory changes to the work (rights that are separate from although linked to copyright) – and their economic rights, the right to receive a fair reward for the use of their work by others. As Dr Johnson (an early Longman author) remarked, 'No man but a blockhead ever wrote except for money'.

The 1990s were a period of extraordinary activity on the copyright front, largely as a result of the development of the digital environment and rapid growth of the internet as a global force, and this has continued on into the twenty-first century. At the time of writing, it is estimated that there are approximately 1.8 billion internet users worldwide, equivalent to about a quarter of the total world population. There have been ongoing national and international forums and conferences within the copyright industries, dialogue with players from other industries entering the field, changes and proposed changes to national and international legislation and treaties, and a number of high-profile court actions, all seeking to ensure the protection of content as radical changes were taking place in methods of delivery of that content. There remains a need to maintain the delicate balance between copyright protection and user access, with the requirements of the academic community a particular area of concern to the book and journal industry. The concept of copyright has never had a higher profile, both within the industry and at national and international governmental levels; it is under both scrutiny and attack as to its relevance in the digital world.

What is copyright?

Copyright is a form of intellectual property; other categories of intellectual property now include patent, trademark and design rights. Perhaps not surprisingly (although ironically in the light of the later copyright history of that country) copyright is first identified as a concept in China during the Song Dynasty (960–1279) when the Imperial Court issued an order banning the making of unauthorized printing blocks for reproduction purposes. A scroll printed during the Southern Song Dynasty (1127–1279) carries a notice specifying that reproduction is forbidden and that the printer had registered the work with the appropriate authorities.

In the Anglo-Saxon common law tradition, copyright is classified as a property right, which can be sold, assigned, licensed, given away or bequeathed. The countries of continental Europe, with their civil law tradition, follow a different philosophy, that of *droit d'auteur* (the author's right), which is perceived as a human right; it places far more emphasis on the rights of the creator, and limits the rights which can be transferred to others such as employers or authorized users such as publishers. It is not the purpose of this book to provide comprehensive coverage of the increasingly complex area of intellectual property rights (more detailed sources of information are listed at the front of this book in *Acknowledgements and further reading*, pp. vii–viii) and indeed some would contest that copyright is a property right, classing it instead as a regulatory system created by governments (a view recently expressed by William Patry in his *Moral Panics and the Copyright Wars*). However, it is vital that those directly involved in the licensing of rights should have a basic understanding of the concepts of copyright; they should also be aware of the different philosophies and terms of protection that prevail from country to country, and of the significant changes to legislation that are necessary to ensure continuing protection during a period of continuing and radical technological changes.

Copyright provides protection for what are often termed 'works of the mind'; it covers not only original literary works, but many other creative works, including music, recordings, films, art, sculpture and photography, as well as works in digital form such as computer programs and databases. The exact significance of the term 'literary work' may vary slightly from country to country, depending on the exact definition under domestic copyright law; in the United Kingdom it includes any original work in written form, including computer programs, compilations and certain types of database.

Copyright has both positive and negative aspects in terms of the power of control it conveys. Ownership of copyright in a work enables the owner to authorize other parties to make use of the work in agreed forms, often through licensing arrangements. Such use is subject to appropriate acknowledgement to the owner, and is usually on the basis of suitable financial recompense to the owner. Alternatively, copyright owners may choose not to authorize exploitation of the work if they feel that such use would be inappropriate or detrimental to the nature or commercial value of the work. Infringement of copyright through unauthorized use is almost always an infringement of statutory rights and may also be a punishable offence, which may be dealt with under civil or criminal law according to the nature of the infringement and local legislation in the country concerned. In most cases, the first owner of copyright in a literary work is the author. An important exception to this, specified in the copyright legislation of countries following the Anglo-Saxon tradition, is when a work is created in the normal course of the author's employment duties. Hence, full-time staff writers employed on composite works, such as encyclopaedias and dictionaries, do not normally retain copyright in what they produce; scientists employed by a pharmaceutical company do not usually control copyright in their research findings. In the United States, copyright in works 'made for hire' (i.e. works prepared by employees as part of their normal duties, or where the writer and the commissioning party have reached agreement on this basis) belongs to the commissioning party.

This is not the case in countries following the *droit d'auteur* tradition, where ownership of copyright is normally retained by the individual, but with the employer having an exclusive right to exploit the employee's work, perhaps for a certain number of years.

In countries following the Anglo-Saxon tradition of copyright, the author, as the usual first owner of copyright in a work, will usually decide whether to retain ownership or whether to assign copyright at the point when a contract is negotiated with a publisher. It is common practice in trade publishing (books designed for readership by the general public) that authors retain ownership of copyright in their own name and grant to their publishers exclusive licences to publish their books in designated forms and media for a designated period of time in a designated geographical market. In addition to these prime publishing rights, other subsidiary rights may be granted to the publisher for exploitation within the agreed markets.

In educational and academic publishing, it is more common for the author to assign ownership of the copyright to the publishing house, whilst continuing to receive payment for sales and other exploitation of the work; provision is usually made for the author to recover the copyright if the book is allowed to become completely unavailable in any format and if no valid sublicences are extant. The main reasons for copyright to be assigned in such cases will be covered in Chapter 2.

The duration of copyright protection varies from country to country and is covered by the domestic copyright legislation of the country concerned. In the case of the United Kingdom, literary works were long protected for the lifetime of the author and for a further period of fifty years from the end of the year in which the author died. As from 1 January 1996, this period was amended to seventy years *post mortem auctoris*, following UK implementation of a European Union directive aimed at harmonizing the period of protection in the member states of the European Economic Area (see *Copyright legislation in the United Kingdom* later in this chapter, pp. 16–25). The United States has now extended its period of protection for works created on or after 1 January 1978 to seventy years *post mortem auctoris* (see *Copyright legislation in the United States* later in this chapter, pp. 26–8). However, at the time of writing, many countries (including a number of highly developed countries such as Japan) still have shorter terms of protection, so one can never assume that there is a totally level playing field.

As the publishing industry has developed, a whole sector of publishing activity has grown up whose sole aim is to explore all the potential copyright possibilities of a book, and to make licensing arrangements for those rights to be exploited as widely as possible so that the book can reach a wider audience – in the original language wherever that language can be read, translated into other languages, or made available in other forms through media other than the printed page. It is this aspect of the publishing business that this book aims to cover.

The international copyright conventions

In 1886 the Berne Convention was established as a multilateral copyright treaty. Its aim was to establish minimum standards of copyright protection that would be complied with in the domestic copyright legislation of its member states. Its main features are that no formal procedures (such as registration) are required in order to secure copyright in a work, and that for the majority of creative works the minimum term of copyright protection is the lifetime of the author plus fifty years. At that time, the provisions of domestic copyright legislation in the United States, which had a shorter term of protection and included a requirement for a formal copyright registration procedure, made that country ineligible to join Berne.

In 1952, the Universal Copyright Convention (UCC) was established; its main features are a provision to allow for formal procedures such as registration, a minimum copyright protection period of the lifetime of the author plus twenty-five years, and a provision that every work will be regarded as complying with registration formalities if it carries the UCC copyright symbol ©, the name of the copyright holder and the year of first publication.

A further significant development of relevance to rights dealing was the introduction in 1971 of the Paris Revisions to the texts of both the Berne Convention and the Universal Copyright Convention. These revisions were introduced at the request of the developing countries, which felt that they did not have sufficient access on reasonable terms to rights in educational and academic works published in the more affluent countries. The provisions of Paris set out procedures whereby publishers in developing countries which have ratified the Paris text of the appropriate convention may apply for compulsory translation or reprint licences in essential books of this kind if they are unable to make contact with the copyright owner, or if they are refused a licence without adequate reason. Not all countries have ratified the Paris text of the two conventions;

the United Kingdom ratified the Paris text of the Universal Copyright Convention on 10 July 1974, and that of Berne only on 2 January 1990. It is an undoubted fact that more voluntary licences have been granted to publishers in the developing countries since the introduction of these provisions, if only to forestall the granting of compulsory licences by local authorities. This aspect of licensing will be covered in more detail in Chapters 12 and 16. By December 2009, the Berne Convention had 164 member states and the Universal Copyright Convention 100: of these, 98 states belong to both conventions.

The United States acceded to the Universal Copyright Convention on its inception in 1952, and thus for the first time gave formal copyright recognition to the copyright works of other member states, although the United Kingdom did not accede until 1957. The United States revised its copyright procedures in 1988 to enable it to comply with the require-ments of the Berne Convention; its membership of Berne took effect on 1 March 1989.

It is therefore only comparatively recently that mutual copyright recog-nition has been in force between the two largest producers of English-language books in the world. Many British authors, including Charles Dickens, found that their works were being published in this major English-speaking overseas market without permission or payment, since their books were considered to be in the public domain. The transatlantic traffic in unauthorized editions was not entirely one way: American authors such as Mark Twain were published without permission in Britain. On the other hand, there is much evidence of reputable American publishers negotiating for rights in British books and making payment for licences when there was technically no legal obligation for them to do so. Much of Virginia Woolf's business correspondence is concerned with arrangements for American editions not only of her own books, but of those of other authors published by the Hogarth Press, which she and her husband had founded.

The entry of other countries with major publishing industries into the international copyright fold was even more recent; the then Soviet Union joined the Universal Copyright Convention only on 27 May 1973, before which it had both translated and reprinted foreign works on a large scale.

The People's Republic of China acceded to the Berne Convention on 15 October 1992, and to the Universal Copyright Convention on 30 October 1992, after many years of utilizing foreign works on a vast scale, usually without permission or payment; Vietnam, which has also made liberal use of foreign works, joined the Berne Convention as recently as October 2004. Even now, membership of an international copyright con-vention does not necessarily operate retrospectively. When Russia acceded to the Berne Convention on 13 March 1995, it was with the proviso that foreign works first published before 27 May 1973 (the date of the Soviet Union's accession to the UCC) would remain in the public domain in Russia. Countries may also seek to impose reservations when joining; when Saudi Arabia joined the Berne Convention in February 2004, it did so with a general reservation on copyright protection for works 'contrary to Islamic law', a condition generally considered incompatible with Berne.

There had long been a need to update the Berne Convention, the stronger of the two conventions, in order to take into account the copyright implications of the digital environment. Following a number of meetings of the Committees of Experts on the Berne Protocol and New Instrument, a Diplomatic Conference of delegates from 160 countries was held on 2–20 December 1996 in Geneva under the auspices of the World Intellectual Property Organization (WIPO) with a brief to discuss 'certain copyright and neighbouring rights questions' aimed at strengthening the provisions of Berne, and in particular to take into account the impact of the new technologies. The intellectual property industries and creative organizations were represented at the conference, as were the hardware manufacturers, and 'passive carriers' such as the telecommunication industries and internet service providers.

Topics included whether acts such as digitization, temporary storage and ephemeral display should be included as part of the reproduction right; also discussed was the possibility of introducing a telecommunication right, and the question of whether there can be any 'fair use' exceptions to the use of copyright material in the electronic environment when the distinction between communication to public and private users is no longer realistic in the context of the internet. Other topics included a proposal for a *sui generis* right for databases (stemming from the 1998 EU Database Directive) and the need to prohibit encryption-breaking devices designed to circumvent electronic coding devices employed by copyright owners to protect their property.

On 20 December 1996 the Conference adopted two new treaties: the WIPO Copyright Treaty (WCT) and the WIPO Performances and Phonograms Treaty (WPPT). The WIPO Copyright Treaty contains a number of key points. Rightsholders have a new exclusive *right of communication to the public*, which includes communication by digital means. There is still a need to further define the word 'public', since electronic access via media such as the internet is normally undertaken by individuals. Regrettably, the Treaty does not include revised wording on the right of reproduction, but the conference endorsed a statement from the United States that Article 9 of the Berne Convention on the right of reproduction should be held to apply in the digital environment. A right of distribution is included in the Treaty, although this is limited to works in tangible form and allows contracting states to deal individually with the question of international exhaustion (for more detail, see *Territorial rights and parallel importation* in Chapter 9). The Treaty also permits each contracting state to provide for limitations and exceptions to the rights of reproduction, provided that these meet the requirements of the so-called 'three-step test' derived from Article 9 (2) of the Berne Convention: that they are special cases; that they do not conflict with the normal commercial exploitation of the work; and that they do not prejudice the legitimate interests of the rightsholder. This area remains the subject of some contention between rightsholders and users in the digital environment, and in the last two years there has been increasing pressure from the developing countries to introduce a broader range of copyright exceptions, in particular for educational use (see *Lobbying from the developing countries* later in this chapter, p. 35).

The Treaty requires contracting states to implement civil and criminal penalties for the circumvention of electronic protection systems (e.g. encryption systems and unique identifiers for copyright material). It extends protection for photographic works in contracting states from a minimum period of twenty-five years to fifty years from the date of their creation, and also confirms that computer programs and original databases are considered protected under the category of literary works.

The Treaty came into effect on 6 March 2002, after the thirtieth state (Gabon) had ratified the text. By December 2009, the WCT had seventy-one signatories, including the People's Republic of China; at the time of writing, the original fifteen EU member states have not yet signed and will only do so after they have all fully implemented the 2001 EU Directive on the Harmonization of Certain Aspects of Copyright and Related Rights into their domestic legislation (see *National, multinational and international copyright initiatives* later in this chapter, pp. 9–12).

The WIPO treaties, once their provisions are implemented by member states, bring those countries into line with the requirements of the World Trade Organization (WTO) Agreement on Trade-Related Aspects of Intellectual Property Rights (TRIPS). The WTO was established on 1 January 1995, and has the responsibility for administering new global trade regulations as agreed in the Final Act of the Uruguay Round of the General Agreement on Tariffs and Trade (GATT). The WTO administers a unified package of agreements to which all member states are committed; the GATT included important side agreements whose membership was limited to a few countries. All 125 members of the GATT automatically became members of the WTO on acceptance of the Uruguay Round, and the WTO currently has 153 members. The People's Republic of China is now in membership; at the time of writing Russia is not yet a member, but has recently ramped up the status of its application.

TRIPS is the most comprehensive multilateral agreement on intellectual property rights to date. It covers copyright and related rights (the rights of performers, producers of sound recordings and broadcasting companies), trademarks, industrial designs, patents, trade secrets and test data. TRIPS recognizes that problems arise from widely varying standards of protection and enforcement of intellectual property rights; as a minimum standards agreement, it seeks to apply basic GATT principles and standards of the international treaties to intellectual property in all member states by complying with the basic provisions of Berne and the more recent WIPO treaties. It requires member states to provide enforcement measures under both civil and criminal law. The agreement requires each member state to guarantee national treatment for the intellectual property of other member states (i.e. a standard of protection equivalent to that which it would accord its own nationals). The WTO Secretariat in Geneva provides facilities for the settlement of disputes. Developed-country members were obliged to comply with the provisions of TRIPS from 1 January 1996; developing countries had until 1 January 2000 to comply, whilst countries classified by the United Nations as 'least developed' had until 1 January 2006. Countries classified as having economies in transition had until the year 2000 to apply if they were able to meet three requirements: that they were moving from a command to a free market economy; that they were planning reform of their intellectual property system; and that there were special problems in implementing revised intellectual property laws and regulations.

All countries were required to offer national treatment to the works of other countries, regardless of their date of entry into compliance. During 1999, many countries amended their national legislation in order to comply with TRIPS requirements, but actual compliance is dependent on enforcement measures and implementation of satisfactory penalties for infringement. As far as the book industry is concerned, problems range from systematic mass photocopying of textbooks and journals, undisclosed overruns by printers, full-scale piracy and exporting of English-language reprints to other markets, unauthorized translations (which are harder for copyright owners to detect) and digital piracy, which has been massively facilitated by the all-pervasive influence of the internet.

National, multinational and international copyright initiatives

The last fifteen years have seen the establishment of many national, multi-national and international forums for the discussion of new issues on intellectual property rights arising from the development of the new technologies. Discussions have included whether copyright in its present form provides an adequate protection for the framework of those rights, whilst many users have questioned whether copyright now represents a barrier to the dissemination of content (see *The anti-copyright movement, open access and other initiatives* later in this chapter, pp. 28–35). A number of major discussion documents have been issued, and new legislation has been introduced at both multinational and international level which has resulted in a major impact on the domestic intellectual property legislation of individual countries.

In the United States, what was then termed 'the information superhigh-way' was given considerable attention during the Clinton administration, with Vice-President Al Gore giving a number of well-publicized speeches on the topic. In 1995, a working group under the chairmanship of Bruce Lehmann, then Assistant Secretary of Commerce and Commissioner for Patents, issued a report entitled *Intellectual Property and the National Information Infrastructure*, which supported the role of copyright in regulat-ing the digital environment and recommended various amendments to US domestic copyright legislation. Many of its recommendations were later incorporated in the 1998 Digital Millennium Copyright Act (DMCA – see *Copyright legislation in the United States* later in this chapter, pp. 26–28).

In July 1995, the European Union issued a *Green Paper on Copyright and Related Rights in the Information Society*, which perhaps raised more questions than it answered; however, it did recognize the substantial investment necessary to develop new works and services in the digital environment, and the need for adequate protection of that investment through copyright and related rights. The Green Paper was widely circu-lated for comment by interested parties, and was followed by proposals intended to harmonize certain aspects of intellectual property legislation within the EU. These included a wide definition of reproduction rights to include acts such as digitization, storage and temporary display; a right of communication; and proposals for legislation to protect anticopying devices.

The result was the EU Directive 2001/29/EC on the Harmonization of Certain Aspects of Copyright and Related Rights in the Information Society, which came into force on 22 June 2001. This required member states to implement its provisions into their domestic copyright legislation, bringing them into line with the requirements of the WIPO treaties. Of particular concern were provisions for limitations on copyright, as the legislation of many continental countries has more liberal provisions for 'fair dealing' than the United Kingdom.

The Directive included a reproduction right, a right of digital transmis-sion and a right of communication to the public, and required member states to provide remedies against the circumvention of technical systems of protection and identification of copyright material. It was recognized that at the moment there is a lack of harmony on moral rights provisions between EU countries, and it is not impossible that a further directive on moral rights may follow in due course. On the question of territoriality and par-allel importation, the general rule in the EU has been that the first sale of a copyright product in one country with the consent of the rightsholder exhausts the rightsholder's right to prevent resale elsewhere within the EU.

The implementation of the EU Directive has resulted in substantial changes to UK domestic copyright legislation (see *Copyright legislation in the United Kingdom* later in this chapter, pp. 16–25).

The EU has already issued a number of directives for implementation in member states: Legal Protection of Computer Programs (1991); Rental and Lending Rights (1992); Copyright in Satellite Broadcasting and Cable Retransmissions (1993); Harmonization of the Term of Protection of Copyright (1993); Legal Protection of Databases (1996); E-Commerce (2000); and Anti-Counterfeiting and Enforcement of Intellectual Property Rights (2004), the latter designed to crack down on infringements in member states. The European Union was of course expanded significantly in May 2004 when Estonia, Latvia, Lithuania, Hungary, Poland, the Czech Republic, Slovakia, Slovenia, Malta and the Greek territory of Cyprus became members, followed by Bulgaria and Romania in January 2007.

In June 2008 the EU High Level Expert Group set up under the then i2010 European Digital Library programme (now Europeana – see *Digital libraries* in Chapter 23) agreed a Memorandum of Understanding on Self-regulating Codes of Practice for Orphan Works (works for which the current copyright owner is unknown), although libraries have continued to press for a complete copyright exception for orphan works. This would be difficult to implement across twenty-seven EU member states and a wide variety of creative industries; if implemented, it would involve a renegotiation of the 2001 Copyright Directive.

The latest major EU initiative after the 2001 Directive on Harmonization of Certain Aspects of Copyright and Related Rights in the Information Society has been its *Green Paper on Copyright in the Knowledge Economy*, published on 16 July 2008. The Green Paper raised a number of questions, including whether there should be guidelines for contractual arrangements between creators and authorized users of their works such as publishers; whether there should be guidelines for model contracts for other types of copyright arrangement; whether there should be copyright exceptions for libraries and archives and for users with reading disabilities; whether there should be more precise rules defining what acts end users may or may not undertake when making use of copyright content; and the copyright position of user-created content (see also *Social networking and user-generated content (UGC) sites* in Chapter 23). The paper also raised the issue of how to deal with the use of orphan works and whether that issue should be dealt with by amending the 2001 Directive or by a separate Statutory Instrument.

In November 2008 the UK Publishers Association (PA) lodged a detailed submission in response to the Green Paper, outlining and providing examples of a number of initiatives already in hand to deal with many of the issues raised, in particular the existence of collective licensing schemes (see Chapter 23), a licensing scheme and other initiatives to meet the needs of the visually impaired (see Chapter 18) and the ARROW initiative to facilitate the use of orphan works (see Chapter 23). The PA urged the Commission to avoid any prescriptive regulations and guidelines for copyright contracts and stressed that any exceptions should be subject to the provisions of the Berne 'three-step test'.

In May 2009 the EU confirmed there had been over 350 submissions commenting on the Green Paper. In August 2009 the Commission announced proposals for drafting regulations which would make it easier for users to access more out of print and orphan works. In October 2009 the Commission issued a Communication aimed at consultation with European publishers to tackle the 'important cultural and legal challenges of mass-scale digitisation and dissemination of books', as a prelude to a full-scale review of Copyright in the Knowledge Economy in 2010. This initiative was announced during the course of revisions to the controversial Google Settlement in the United States (see Chapter 23), from which non-UK European titles were now being excluded. The Commission also promised an impact assessment on the digitization of orphan works, commencing with a public hearing in Brussels on 26 October 2009, with a full report to follow.

On 22 October 2009 the EU (in the form of DG INFSO and DG MARKT) issued what it termed a 'reflection document' entitled *Creative Content in a European Single Digital Market: Challenges for the Future*. This paper also addressed the impact of new technologies on the creative industries and the involvement of companies such as mobile phone operators, internet service providers (ISPs), telecom companies, search engines, online retailers and social networking services. The paper addresses issues for the music, audiovisual and video games industries as well as the publishing industry, where it terms the online distribution of literary works 'still a nascent market' and refers obliquely to the Google initiative in the United States (see *The rise of Google* and *The Google Settlement* in Chapter 23). The paper refers to achieving 'a Digital Single Market without borders for rightsholders and the consumer'. It lists various Commission initiatives; highlighted are the need for access to content by individual consumers and commercial users, the need for protection of the interests of rightsholders, and proposals such as extended collective licensing, a 'streamlined pan-Europe and/or multi-territory licensing process', the need for freely accessible information on copyright ownership and licences and the possibility of 'a more profound harmonisation of copyright law', with mention of a 'European copyright law' to achieve a truly unified legal framework across the twenty-seven member states. The paper also addresses collective rights management systems and the need for more collaboration with ISPs to fight digital piracy. The Commission intends to 'continue to take a pro-active role in order to ensure a culturally diverse and rich online content market for consumers, while creating adequate possibilities for remuneration and improved conditions in the digital environment for rightsholders'. The UK Publishers Association has prepared a submission in response to the Paper.

Copyright recognition between countries

There is no such thing as an international copyright law. It is important to remember that even if two countries both belong to the same international copyright convention, the level of copyright protection in those two countries will not necessarily be equal. Membership merely ensures that certain minimum standards are set, but the provisions of domestic copyright legislation are paramount, and local enforcement may be inadequate, to say the least. A classic case of discrepancy in protection between countries remains the works of George Orwell, under present UK copyright law still firmly in copyright in the UK until the end of the year 2020, seventy years after his death in 1950. From 1976, Orwell's work passed into the public domain in the then Soviet Union, since Soviet domestic copyright legislation then offered protection for twenty-five years *post mortem auctoris*, the minimum requirement for a country belonging to the Universal Copyright Convention. Works such as *1984* and *Animal Farm*, long banned in the Soviet Union for political reasons, were published as soon as censorship was relaxed in the late 1980s without any payment required. In 2004 Russia extended its term of protection to seventy years *post mortem auctoris*, but at the moment Orwell's works remain in the public domain there, since they were first published before 27 May 1973.

While most countries in the world now belong to the Berne Convention, the Universal Copyright Convention or both, and many have also now ratified the newer WIPO treaties, there are still some absentees: Taiwan (precluded because of its continuing ambiguous political status), Afghanistan, Myanmar (Burma), Iran, Iraq, Angola, Burundi, Eritrea, Ethiopia, Mozambique, Sierra Leone, Somalia and Uganda.

Changing political circumstances in the 1990s also resulted in copyright anomalies created by the break-up of states that previously belonged to one or both conventions (e.g. the former Soviet Union, Czechoslovakia and Yugoslavia). Each new state had to introduce its own domestic legislation to a sufficiently high standard to apply for membership of one or more of the conventions; at the time of writing, only one former Soviet republic (Turkmenistan) remains outside membership of any convention; it has a bilateral trade treaty with intellectual property components with the United States, but compliance has been unsatisfactory.

When dealing in rights, it is therefore vital to be aware of the overall copyright picture, since it is only against a background of mutual copyright recognition that publishers can conduct satisfactory international business.

Unauthorized usage and piracy

The original act of publication seemed at first a simple one: to make an arrangement with an author to write a book, to take the manuscript and turn it into book form in its language of origin, and to sell that book in that form as widely as possible in the markets where it could be read. Even at a comparatively early stage in publishing history, however, problems arose. Samuel Richardson, master of the epistolary novel, was a victim of piracy as early as the mid-eighteenth century when the second part of *Pamela* and the whole of *Sir Charles Grandison* were reprinted in Ireland (not then subject to English copyright law) from sheets of the legitimate editions stolen from the printers.

A century later, Charles Dickens was outspoken in his condemnation of the unauthorized reprinting in the United States of his works and those of other leading authors such as Sir Walter Scott. Although that country had introduced its first federal copyright law in 1790, there was no reciprocal arrangement for the protection of works from other countries. Dickens became an ardent activist for the mutual recognition of copyright.

The establishment of the international copyright conventions represented the first step towards providing a framework for copyright recognition between member states, although the conventions have by no means eradicated the misuse of works protected by copyright in their country of origin and elsewhere. This misuse continues to take place both in countries that officially subscribe to the concept of copyright through membership of one or more of the conventions (in which case it is classified as piracy) and in countries that remain outside the framework of membership (unauthorized usage). The result of both types of abuse has been the loss of billions of dollars to the copyright industries over the years; the exact figures are difficult to quantify, as many examples (particularly in the remoter countries) do not come to the attention of the copyright owners or the appropriate copyright authorities.

The International Intellectual Property Alliance (IIPA) was founded in 1994 as a coalition of trade associations representing major creative industries in the United States, the largest exporter of intellectual property in the world; revenue from those industries is now estimated to generate over 11% of US annual GDP (as compared with approximately 6.4% of GDP in the United Kingdom). Apart from the publishing industry, these include powerful lobbies from the music, film, television and software industries, where the United States dominates the world market. The most recent figures available from the IIPA are for 2007 and estimate losses to the US book industry through piracy, photocopying and unauthorized internet usage in forty-eight key countries at $529 million; other sources estimate 2008 figures at $580 million for the USA and £150 million for the United Kingdom.

IIPA maintains a detailed register of the copyright status of countries worldwide which is regularly updated; it comments on proposals for national copyright reform, and regularly recommends whether or not countries with inadequate intellectual property legislation or a poor track record in protecting copyright should be maintained on or added to the US Special 301 Watch List (301 refers to the relevant section of the 1988 US Trade Act). Countries that fail to comply with their obligations as members of the international conventions or as signatories to bilateral treaties covering copyright may then be subject to lobbying and international trade pressure (e.g. the occasions on which the United States threatened to remove 'most favoured nation' trading status from the People's Republic of China unless that country improved its record on the protection of intellectual property). In 2007 the United States lodged a formal complaint to the WTO concerning China's failure to enforce intellectual property rights; in August 2009 the WTO disputes panel found that major Chinese restrictions on the importation and distribution of copyright-related products including films, DVDs, music, books and journals were inconsistent with China's WTO obligations and called on the Chinese authorities to allow US companies to partner Chinese enterprises in joint copyright ventures.

In its February 2010 Special 301 Report on Global Copyright Protection and Enforcement submitted to the US copyright authorities, IIPA named Paraguay for the 306 monitoring list (306 refers to a section of the 1974 US Trade Act), ten countries for the priority watch list (including Canada, India, Indonesia, the People's Republic of China, Russia and the Philippines, as well as several Latin American countries) and twenty-four countries for the watch list (including Brazil, Egypt, Greece, Hungary, Israel, Italy, Malaysia, Pakistan, Poland, Romania, Spain, Thailand, Turkey, Vietnam and many of the former Soviet Republics). The IIPA stresses the importance of implementing copyright protection in every country to TRIPS standards, and urges the need to implement the WIPO treaties. It warns of the increasing tendency for piracy to be linked with international crime syndicates, and has flagged a substantial increase in the level of internet piracy.

In the United Kingdom, a cross-industry alliance against piracy and counterfeiting was launched in July 1999, bringing together the publishing, music, audiovisual, software and brand manufacturing industries. The aim of the alliance is to lobby Parliament to introduce tougher penalties for intellectual property infringement, and to strengthen the hand of the enforcement agencies. On a practical note, the UK Publishers Association has long worked together with the Association of American Publishers (AAP) and with local publishers associations in the countries concerned to target key areas of piracy, collecting data, organizing police raids and taking legal action; apart from the piracy of obvious trade bestsellers such as J.K. Rowling's *Harry Potter* series, piracy of English-language teaching materials and academic textbooks is rife in markets such as Turkey, India, Pakistan, Thailand and China. Infringement takes the form of full-scale commercial piracy, printers running on extra copies of authorized printings, large-scale photocopying of whole books, digital piracy of complete books both in the original language and in translation, and passing off local works under the names of well-known western authors, or the unauthorized use of brands such as that of the Harvard Business School.

The rise of internet piracy, where the texts of entire books are available for download, has been significant in the last few years. Key offenders have been Scribd (www.scribd.com, described as a 'social publishing site' and which more recently has started to reach agreement with key publishers for the use of their content), RapidShare (www.rapidshare.com), Docstoc (www.docstoc.com) and Megaupload (www.megaupload.com), and there are many more. Some are file-sharing/hosting sites, whilst others (for example Sweden's The Pirate Bay site prior to the 2009 legal action against it and its purchase and transformation into a legitimate site – see *Some lessons from the music industry?* in Chapter 23) are torrent sites which do not themselves host content but provide an index to enable would-be users to locate the content they require elsewhere. In the week of publication of Dan Brown's latest bestseller *The Lost Symbol*, the entire text was available, unauthorized and free, from at least fifteen websites, with over 100,000 downloads in two days. Although bestselling trade titles are obvious targets, publishers are now finding the complete contents of academic textbooks available from a wide variety of sites such as TextbookTorrents (www. textbooktorrents.com). Forced to take down seventy-eight files for Pearson Education titles in July 2008 following the threat of legal action under provisions of the US Digital Millennium Copyright Act, the site reported that the publishers 'are acting on extremely shaky ground' but that it was were not in a position to fight the takedown notice. The site closed in October 2008 but has since resurfaced under new ownership. It no longer offers unauthorized downloads but appears to offer access to the purchase of low-price reprint editions of textbooks licensed for sale only in designated developing countries (see Chapter 12).

In January 2009, the UK Publishers Association launched its Copyright Infringement Portal, enabling member publishers to log details of online infringements and to serve notice and takedown against the infringing sites. The portal also allows users to see if the sites they report have also infringed the rights of other member publishers. The service is free to PA members and is also available to UK non-member publishers in return for an annual subscription related to the size of their turnover. The site has also been made available to member publishers of the Association of American Publishers via the AAP website.

Copyright legislation in the United Kingdom

There is a lengthy history of copyright protection in the United Kingdom. A form of protection existed under the Licensing Act of 1662, which granted perpetual protection to anyone who registered a work with the Stationers' Company. In effect, this created a monopoly for the stationers themselves; their justification was that the system prevented the publication of seditious works.

The Licensing Act expired in 1694 and the stationers pressed for further legislation in the hope of reinstating perpetual protection. However, their requirements were not entirely met by the first official Copyright Act in the world, the Statute of Anne in 1709; this established copyright as a personal property right and provided for a term of protection of twenty-one years from the date of publication in the case of works already published and fourteen years in the case of works not yet published, renewable for a further fourteen years if the author remained alive at the end of the first period. For the next sixty-five years, the provisions of the Act were frequently circumvented in practice and via lawsuits, until in 1774 the provisions were enforced by a House of Lords decision in the case of *Donaldson v. Becket*, which affirmed the common law and statutory rights of the author. This was followed by the Copyright Act of 1775 and the Copyright Act of 1814, which extended protection from fourteen to twenty-eight years and then for the lifetime of the author if he or she was still alive at the end of the twenty-eight-year period.

This was followed by the Act of 1842 and then by the Act of 1911, which extended protection for the first time to the lifetime of the author plus fifty years, although any assignment of copyright by the author was valid for only the first twenty-five years of that period, after which rights reverted to the estate. The 1956 Copyright Act also provided protection for the lifetime of the author plus fifty years, and this period was carried forward into the current Copyright, Designs and Patents Act 1988, which came into force on 1 August 1989. Computer programs were accorded more specific protection under the Copyright (Computer Programs) Regulations 1992.

The move towards harmonization of legislation within the European Union led in 1993 to the issue of Directive 93/98/EEC on the duration of copyright and authors' rights; this required the then member states of the European Union (Austria, Belgium, Denmark, Finland, France, Germany, Greece, the Irish Republic, Italy, Luxembourg, the Netherlands, Portugal, Spain, Sweden and the United Kingdom) and the European Free Trade Association (EFTA) countries (Iceland, Liechtenstein and Norway) to amend their domestic intellectual property legislation if necessary to extend the duration of protection for copyright works to seventy years *post mortem auctoris* for all works still in copyright in a single EU member state on 1 July 1995 (only Germany already had this term of protection for literary works). In the United Kingdom there was consultation with the copyright industries and the creative societies, followed by a Statutory Instrument known as the Duration of Copyright and Rights in Related Performances Regulations 1995 (SI No. 3297), which came into force on 1 January 1996.

The extension of the copyright period in the United Kingdom had complex implications. Not only did it extend the term of protection for works still in copyright; it also revived copyright protection in the works of many major authors, including James Joyce, Virginia Woolf, Thomas Hardy, D.H. Lawrence, John Buchan, Sir Arthur Conan Doyle, H.G. Wells, Rudyard Kipling and Beatrix Potter. Copyright in the works of authors who died between 1925 and 1945 was likely to be revived, provided that those works were still protected by copyright in another European Economic Area (EEA) member state as at 1 July 1995 – in effect, Germany (which already had a seventy-year period of protection) and possibly France or Spain. Ownership of the extended or revived copyright in the United Kingdom lay with whoever owned it immediately before 1 January 1996 or before the work entered the public domain, although any exclusive licences in place at those points should continue to be honoured.

Anyone who took steps to publish a public domain work in good faith was considered to be the holder of 'acquired rights' and could continue to publish under a 'licence of right' if they had already made a commitment to publish the work in question as a result of arrangements made before 1 January 1995 or had manufactured copies before 1 July 1995. Arrangements made before 1 January 1995 might include the commissioning of new editors for the work, placing a print order or (arguably) announcing a new edition. Valid holders of acquired rights were required to give notice of their intention to publish (or to continue to publish) to the owner of the revived rights, and to pay reasonable royalties or other remuneration to that owner. The question of what might constitute reasonable remuneration was open to some argument; since under the new system no such arrangement could be exclusive, users could maintain that any royalties rates paid should be lower than those payable for an exclusive licence. Any disputes on the question of revived copyright between owners and users could be taken to the Copyright Tribunal; on a less formal basis, the UK Publishers Association also offered a mediation service, in consultation with the Society of Authors.

A further Statutory Instrument came into force on 1 December 1996: the Copyright and Related Rights Regulations (1996, No. 2967). This contains a number of different provisions. Regulation 9 amends Section 18 of the 1988 UK Act (on the 'issue of copies of a work to the public') in somewhat ambiguous language; it appears to reinforce the provision for free movement of goods within the EEA, which would prevent British publishers from taking action against parallel importation of US open market editions into the United Kingdom from an EEA country (see Chapter 9).

Regulation 10 extends rental and lending rights to all literary, musical and dramatic works, films and sound recordings, and to most artistic works. Regulation 11 then (as a derogation from the 1992 Rental and Lending Directive) exempts from the lending right loans by most educational establishments, and also the present UK Public Lending Right scheme, which is entirely an author's right (see Chapter 3).

Regulation 16 introduces a so-called 'publication right'. This gives a new publication right to anyone who first publishes a previously unpublished work that has entered the public domain. Publication is defined as 'any communication to the public', which could include public exhibition (e.g. of an unpublished manuscript). The new right is in effect equivalent to a copyright, except that it runs for a period of only twenty-five years from the end of the year in which the work is first published. First publication must take place within the EEA, and the publisher must at that time be an EEA national. There are no moral rights in the work.

The 1988 UK Copyright, Designs and Patents Act introduced the full concept of moral rights for the first time into UK copyright law; they had long been established in the domestic copyright legislation of many countries in continental Europe (French *droit moral*).

Moral rights include the right of paternity (the right of the author to be clearly identified as the creator of the work), the right of integrity (the right of the author to object to derogatory treatment, i.e. to prevent any distortion of the work that would be damaging to their reputation) and the right to prevent false attribution of authorship. Under UK law, the key moral rights of paternity and integrity do not apply to computer programs, computer-generated works, employee works, works written for publication and published in a newspaper, magazine or similar periodical, and works written for publication in encyclopaedias, dictionaries and other collective works of reference.

The 1988 Act requires that authors must formally assert their right of paternity in writing; this may be covered by a provision in the head contract between author and publisher, or by a statement printed on the title verso of the book itself. At the time of writing, the UK government is consulting with the publishing industry on whether there is an ongoing need for active assertion of the paternity right. Moral rights are personal to the author and the author's heirs, and are thus a separate right from the actual copyright in the work; under UK law they generally endure throughout the period of copyright protection of the work, although there is also provision for them to be waived. This is not the case in countries with the *droit d'auteur* tradition, where moral rights are normally inalienable and perpetual. In the former socialist countries, legislation (even when recently revised) often provides for the state to take over responsibility for the administration of moral rights if there are no remaining heirs of the author to undertake this task.

The moral rights of an author are directly relevant to the licensing of literary works; if the author has not waived his or her rights, there will be an obligation for the licensor to ensure that any licensees respect these rights in terms of proper acknowledgement of the author, and preservation of the integrity of the work. It should, however, be remembered that there is one particular area of licensing where the right of integrity cannot be guaranteed, that of film and television rights (Chapter 21) and, by implication, some merchandising rights if these are handled via the film or television company (Chapter 22). Insistence on the right of integrity could well affect the licensing of electronic and multimedia rights (Chapter 24).

The Copyright and Rights in Databases Regulations 1997 were introduced from 1 January 1998, implementing EC Council Directive No. 96/9/EC; this created a new category of copyright work and also a subsidiary database or *sui generis* (free-standing) right in recognition of the rights of database creators. Databases had previously been covered by UK copyright law as compilations, but it was necessary to implement new legislation because continental copyright laws view creativity rather than 'sweat of the brow' as a prerequisite for intellectual property protection. The *sui generis* right is a property right rather than copyright, and also covers computer-created compilations such as telephone directories. Under the new Regulations, databases (whether in electronic or other form) are protected from unauthorized extraction and reuse for a period of fifteen years from the end of the year in which the database was completed. If the database is subsequently updated and the revisions are viewed as substantial, the fifteen-year period can be extended accordingly. Some fair dealing for educational and academic purposes is permitted.

A further EU directive of relevance to publishers, the E-Commerce Directive COM (1998) 297, was due for implementation by member states by 17 January 2002; in the UK, this was partly implemented by passing the Electronic Communications Act 2000. This provides rules regarding the liability of intermediaries such as service providers, and allows for electronic signatures to be legally recognized and admissible in court; it also provides for the establishment of a register of approved providers of cryptography support services.

At the time of writing, the most recent major revision to UK copyright legislation remains the implementation of the EU Directive 2001/29/EC on the Harmonization of Certain Aspects of Copyright and Related Rights in the Information Society. There was considerable discussion of the proposed changes amongst the copyright industries; key elements of the Directive include a transmission right and the right for copyright holders to use encryption and identifier systems to protect their works. It was implemented in the United Kingdom not through full-scale redrafting of the 1988 Copyright, Designs and Patents Act, but via a Statutory Instrument (SI 2003 No. 2498), the Copyright and Related Rights Regulations. These came into force on 31 October 2003; key elements include clarification that copyright protection extends to the digital environment by widening the definition of the term 'broadcast' in the 1988 Act to be technologically neutral and to include the supply of content online (the 'making available' right).

The SI also includes legal protection for electronic rights management systems and confirms that there are new criminal penalties for the circumvention of technological protection measures (TPMs – see Chapter 23). It also clarifies the permitted exceptions to copyright protection and, in particular, places tighter restrictions on fair dealing (see *Fair dealing in Chapter 17*), making it clear that this is permissible for research and private study, criticism and review and news reporting but that it does not extend to commercial use of any kind. Once implementation of the Directive was completed, the United Kingdom was in a position to ratify the WIPO treaties (see *The International copyright conventions* earlier in this chapter, pp. 5–9) but can only do so when all other member states have fully implemented the requirements into their domestic legislation.

The 2004 EU Directive on Anti-Counterfeiting and Enforcement of Intellectual Property Rights was due for implementation by member states by April 2006; it covers only civil remedies for copyright infringement, but there are separate proposals for criminal sanctions. The United Kingdom implemented the Directive on time, with some other member states implementing later.

On the purely domestic front, no formal registration procedure is required to establish copyright protection in the United Kingdom; however, publishers have long been obliged by statute to supply one copy of each of their print-on-paper publications to each of the six deposit libraries (the British Library, the university libraries of Oxford and Cambridge, the National Libraries of Scotland and Wales and – an anomaly – the library of Trinity College Dublin). The Legal Deposit Libraries Act 2003 extended the requirement to deposit non-print works; however, at the time of writing publishers are still depositing offline and hand-held works under the Voluntary Code of Practice 2000 while the libraries review their facilities for accepting and storing online content such as databases and websites and how they will deal with regular updates of such products.

In order to maintain copyright protection as widely as possible, it has been necessary for successive Acts to take into account developments in new technology that affect creative works; for example the increasingly sophisticated nature of copying machines and the progressive development of technology and new platforms for such widely varying media as film, television, DVDs, computer software, and in particular the all-pervasive influence of the internet. All these are of direct relevance to the publishing industry, since all could take as their source a literary work. In 2006, a review of the overall framework of intellectual property (IP) protection and management was undertaken under the chairmanship of the former editor of the *Financial Times*, Andrew Gowers. The resulting 142-page report in December 2006 was considered generally favourable by publishers and included statements such as 'IP rights, which protect the value of creative ideas, are more vital than ever' and the UK copyright system 'must take tough action against those who infringe IP rights at a cost to the UK's most creative industries'. Also included was a statement that 'getting the balance right (i.e. between rightsholders and users) is vital to driving innovation, securing investment and stimulating competition'. Key points also included the need to promote increased public awareness of IP rights (with funding for a campaign to this end) and an improved UK Patent Office, to be renamed the United Kingdom Intellectual Property Office (UKIPO). The report favoured limited private copying, including proposed exceptions for format shifting and for distance learners and moderated virtual learning environments (VLEs) to use limited extracts of copyright material provided that no licensing scheme was available. Also proposed was an exception for caricature, parody and pastiche. The report highlighted the need for better access to orphan works (the British Library has estimated that 40% of all print works could be classified as orphan works), the regulation of digital rights management (DRM) systems (see Chapter 23), recommended penalties of up to ten years imprisonment for online infringement of copyright, to match those for physical infringement, and the establishment of a new strategic and advisory body for IP policy (SABIP), on which the creative industries would be represented. The UK Publishers Association filed a detailed submission in response to the report, stressing in particular recent extensions to existing licensing schemes for the educational sector via the Copyright Licensing Agency (CLA – see Chapter 23) and that some exceptions might not be compatible with the Berne three-step test. There were also concerns about format shifting (except between devices legitimately owned by the same user) and a view that there was no need for a specific exception for caricature, parody and pastiche in what the PA referred to as 'the land of Monty Python'. Following consultation with interested parties, the aim of Gowers has been for a final consultation with a draft Statutory Instrument with responses due by March 2010.

In January 2009, UKIPO issued a consultation paper entitled *Copyright – The Future: Developing a Copyright Agenda for the Twenty-First Century*, which again raised the question of whether copyright is still fit for purpose in the digital age. The paper confirmed the wish of the UK government to encourage and enable the creative industries to continue developing innovative business models and licences for the fair and flexible use of content, and to receive fair remuneration for such use. It is also essential for government to enforce copyright legislation to minimize the risk of infringement when publishers put content online, and to introduce copyright exceptions only where there are no clear licensing solutions available. In turn, publishers need to adapt to changing circumstances, issue clear and effective licences to meet user needs, and to support collective licensing for secondary usage for educational, research and professional purposes.

The UK Publishers Association submitted a detailed response in February 2009, stressing throughout that 'digital is different', particularly in terms of potential for infringement. The need for usage to comply with the Berne three-step test was reiterated. A suggestion in the paper that the licence system might need to be 'simplified' was answered in some detail with reference to collective licensing, 'best practice' licences such as those available from NESLI (see Chapter 23), technical initiatives such as the Automated Content Access Protocol (ACAP – see Chapter 23) providing access to rightsholder and licence information. In answer to the issue of authentication of works reference was made to existing identifier systems such as the ISTC and DOI (see *Identifiers* in Chapter 23).

Following publication of a preliminary report in January 2009, in June 2009 the government issued its Digital Britain report. A substantial proportion of the report covers the need to improve internet coverage and bandwidth in rural areas of the United Kingdom, and confirms that digital competence will become a core element of the National Curriculum for schoolchildren. Only Chapter 24, 'Creative Industries and the Digital World', is directly relevant to issues within the publishing sector. The report restates that government recognizes the economic importance of the creative industries and that creativity should continue to be rewarded in the digital world and that public policy should be extended to include interactive content. The report highlights the problems of unauthorized peer-to-peer (P2P) file sharing and other copyright infringements; the need to establish self-regulating agreements between rightsholders and ISPs, and for a detailed code of practice for notice and takedown, with ISPs to maintain records of repeat infringers which could then be divulged to rightsholders on receipt of a court order. The proposal was mooted to create a Rights Agency to act as a broker between the creative industries and ISPs to combat illegal file sharing, and that if such an arrangement failed to produce a 70–80% reduction in infringements within two years OFCOM would be given powers to impose a code and to oblige ISPs to introduce technical protection measures such as restricting bandwidth to known offenders.

The report raised the issue of fair dealing (albeit under the misnomer of the US term of fair use), with a proposal for a future consultation on exceptions for areas such as distance learning and archiving, two issues already raised in the Gowers Review and where government intends to consult on the draft text of a Statutory Instrument. The issue of orphan works was raised again, with a proposal for legislative reform to establish commercial schemes to handle such usage, and a need for would-be users to employ adequate due diligence to first try to locate the rightsholder and to retain payment until a missing rightsholder can be identified. There was also a recommendation to extend Public Lending Right (PLR, see *Public lending right: an author's right* in Chapter 3) to audiobooks and e-books.

Tougher proposals from government published on 25 August 2009 proposed strong measures for restricting internet access to repeat infringers; this brought a negative reaction from ISPs, who feel that persuasion rather than coercion is the way to deal with infringement. Government has since commented that it now considers the proposed delay before requiring the imposition of technical measures too long. In its submission on the report, the UK Publishers Association expressed concern that the proposals risked politicizing the issue of relationships with ISPs in the run-up to the next general election, and urged that OFCOM and the government should have joint powers to take action against infringement.

Following further consultations with the creative industries and another submission from the Publishers Association, on 28 October 2009 came the reading of the Digital Economy Bill, with the aim of implementation by April 2010 before the general election. The Bill included provision for a 'three strikes' policy which would lead to the suspension of some internet services to persistent offenders. Other proposals included better access to orphan works and the possibility of file sharing between friends and family. Also included were proposals that government should produce model contracts to strike a fair balance in copyright dealings, and should also aim to standardize the ways in which copyright exceptions are dealt with in contracts.

The final Bill was published on 20 November 2009, and has encountered objections from internet companies including Google and Facebook as well as from some writers and agents. ISPs would have an obligation to send notifications to their subscribers linked to online copyright infringement and maintain records of such notifications, which could be made available to rightsholders on an anonymized basis on request; rightsholders would then have to obtain a court order to access detailed data if they wished to take legal action against the infringers. The Bill confirms that OFCOM will have powers to implement technical measures to restrict or withdraw internet access from infringers if the ISP notification procedure does not substantially reduce levels of infringement.

The Bill also provides for an increase in the current limit for criminal (as opposed to civil) infringement of copyright from £5,000 to £50,000 per offence. It also gives the Secretary of State (of whichever government department is responsible for IP matters at the time) powers to amend the 1988 UK Copyright, Designs and Patents Act with the aim of reducing online copyright infringements. The Secretary would also have powers to implement regulations to authorize a licensing body to license the use of orphan works, and to require that fees be set aside for such usage. The Bill also makes provision for extended collective licensing by enabling the Secretary to permit collecting societies to assume a mandate to license the use of works and collect fees on behalf of rightsholders who have not mandated that organization, unless they have specifically opted out of doing so. These new provisos would be subject to safeguards, including codes of practice for collecting societies. The Bill proposes that Public Lending Right would be extended only to those digital works accessed on site in a library, with one loan per copy held in the library concerned rather than multiple access. The Bill was passed on 7 April 2010 but omitting provisions for extended collective licensing and orphan works.

Hot on the heels of the Digital Economy Bill in October 2009 came a paper from the Department of Business, Innovation and Skills entitled *Copyright – The Way Ahead: A Strategy for Copyright in the Digital Age* and setting out the current government's views on achieving a fair copyright system in the United Kingdom, supporting investment by the creative industries, providing a fair reward for creators and allowing consumers to benefit from the digital age through 'non-commercial use of legitimately purchased copyright works' and access to out of print titles and orphan works. The government also seeks improved access to copyright works for educators and researchers and a simpler system of copyright access for businesses. The paper stresses that government is aware that there is difficulty in dealing well with technological changes and that it does not want to see the potential benefits of new technologies circumscribed by copyright, or the copyright system undermined by new technologies. Its stated aim, after consultation with the creative industries, is to work to improve the current copyright system. At the time of writing, a report on how this might be done is expected from SABIP (see earlier in this section, p. 22) during the course of 2010. Government favours a pan-European approach to copyright exceptions for the digital age and repeats its wish that there should be guidelines on how copyright contracts should reflect copyright exceptions. It also plans to establish a working group to develop model contracts and contractual clauses that achieve a fair balance between the rights of creators and authorized users such as publishers. It seeks a clear distinction at EU level between commercial and non-commercial use of copyright material and mentions again file sharing between family and friends. A proposal is mooted for 'pre-commercial use' of copyright material by small and medium-sized enterprises (SMEs). The paper repeats the need for extended collective licensing as flagged in earlier reports and legislation to facilitate the licensing of orphan works. The paper also states government's intention to investigate the establishment of voluntary registries of copyright works in the aftermath of the US Google Settlement (see Chapter 23). In particular government wishes to support the creative industries in developing business models appropriate for the digital age, and to support initiatives to reduce online copyright infringement. At the time of writing the UK Publishers Association is preparing yet another response to this paper. Rarely has copyright come under so much scrutiny in so short a period of time.

Copyright legislation in the United States

Copyright legislation was enacted in a number of individual states prior to the War of Independence (1775–83); federal legislation was first introduced in the Copyright Act of 1790. More recent legislation includes the Copyright Act 1873, amended by the Chace Act in 1891; the 1909 Act, amended in 1912, 1914 and 1919; the 1947 Act and the 1976 Act, which came into force on 1 January 1978. That Act was amended when President Reagan signed on 31 October 1988 the Berne Convention Implementation Act (BCIA), finally enabling the United States to accede to the Berne Convention on 1 March 1989 (see *The international copyright conventions* earlier in this chapter, pp. 5–9).

The BCIA amended some of the formalities that had hitherto been a feature of American domestic copyright legislation, in particular the formal requirement that a copyright notice be printed inside a work to maintain copyright, and the requirement for deposit and registration of works with the Library of Congress. However, it is still a requirement that works first published outside the USA and published in the USA via distribution or licensing arrangements should be deposited with the Library of Congress; it is also a prerequisite for US works and foreign works from non-Berne countries to be registered if a copyright suit is filed in the USA. Registration is also still advisable for foreign works from Berne countries, as this will support the copyright owner's claim for statutory damages in cases of infringement.

The position on copyright protection for some UK titles that had entered the public domain in the United States has altered since 1 January 1996, when the United States introduced revisions into its domestic copyright law to comply with certain provisions of the Uruguay Round of the GATT (see earlier in this chapter, p. 8). These revisions have permitted some titles originating in Berne or WTO member states that had entered the US public domain through technicalities such as failure to re-register with the Library of Congress, but which were still protected in their country of origin, to enjoy the remainder of the term of protection to which they would have been entitled if they had never entered the public domain. Up until 31 December 1997, US protection for these 'Restored Copyrights' was secured by filing a Notice of Intent to Enforce with the US Copyright Office; since that date publishers can serve direct notice on any US publisher which has been publishing a work on the basis of its public domain status; the US publisher then has twelve months in which to dispose of any existing stock.

The United States has long had a complex system relating to the term of copyright protection. For works published before 1 January 1978, a period of copyright protection of twenty-eight years from the date of first publication applied, followed by a second term of twenty-eight years if the copyright owner re-registered with the Library of Congress. For works published from 1 January 1978 onwards (the date on which the 1976 Act came into force) and for older works unpublished on that date, the period of protection was fifty years from the end of the year in which the author died. Works 'made for hire' were protected for seventy-five years from the date of first publication.

The current period of protection for new works in the United States is seventy years *post mortem auctoris*, bringing the United States into line with the period of protection currently prevailing in the United Kingdom and other EU countries, and ensuring reciprocal protection for US works in those markets. The extension was the result of the Sonny Bono Copyright Term Extension Act, which came into force on 27 October 1998. It has been referred to informally as the 'Mickey Mouse Protection Act' as it came into force at a time when the Disney character was in danger of falling into the public domain. This Act also extended the term of protection for works made for hire from seventy-five to ninety-five years from first publication or 120 years from the date of creation, whichever expires first. There was undoubtedly a powerful lobby for an extended term of protection from major players in the US intellectual property industries, in particular from the film industry.

Protection for works still in their first twenty-eight-year term of protection as at 1 January 1978 is extended to a total of ninety-five years from first publication. Protection for works in the second twenty-eight-year term as at 27 October 1998 is also extended to a total period of ninety-five years from first publication. Unlike the revival of copyright following the implementation of the Duration Directive in the United Kingdom, any work that had fallen into the public domain as of the end of 1997 will remain so.

Earlier legislation had permitted US authors or their heirs to terminate prior transfers and assignments during a period of five years beginning fifty-six years from the date when the original copyright was secured; the Bono Act allows for a further five-year period to do so, starting seventy-five years after the date that copyright was first secured; it also permits executors and administrators to arrange for this if no heirs survive.

In 2002, the validity of the Bono Act was challenged in the US Supreme Court through an action (*Eldred v. Ashcroft*) brought by a coalition of website and reprint publishers specializing in public domain works; they were represented by Lawrence Lessig, professor of law at Stanford University and a prominent advocate for the relaxation of copyright restrictions (see *The anti-copyright movement, open access and other initiatives* later in this chapter, pp. 28–35). The action claimed that the US Congress did not have the authority to enact the extensions; however, the Act was upheld by a ruling of the Supreme Court in January 2003.

The United States introduced the WIPO Copyright and Performances and Phonograms Implementation Act 1998 (the 'WIPO Act') from 28 October 1998 as part of the Digital Millennium Copyright Act (DMCA). In particular, this implements Article 11 of the WIPO Copyright Treaty and Article 18 of the WIPO Performances and Phonograms Treaty (see *The international copyright conventions* earlier in this chapter, pp. 5–9). It adds a new provision to US copyright legislation by recognizing the need to prevent the circumvention of technological devices to protect copyright works. It does not, however, provide added protection for databases, where proposed legislation encountered resistance. Also not included was proposed legislation to overrule a decision of the US Supreme Court that the doctrine of 'first sale' removed the right of copyright owners to prohibit parallel importation of competing editions of copyright works (see *Territorial rights and parallel importation* in Chapter 9). Another relevant section of the Digital Millennium Copyright Act, the Online Copyright Infringement Liability Act, limits the liability of service providers for copyright infringement in certain circumstances; they must have policies for terminating the access of subscribers who repeatedly infringe copyright, and not interfere with protection measures used by copyright owners. The introduction of the Digital Millennium Copyright Act enabled the United States to ratify the WIPO treaties. There are still no moral rights enshrined in US copyright legislation, with the exception of those for artistic works; otherwise, they are held to be covered by Section 43 (a) of the Lanham Act.

Orphan works have been a continuing issue at international, multinational and national level and a report on the topic was published in January 2006 by the US Copyright Office. This proposed an amendment to the Digital Millennium Copyright Act to specify that if a would-be user of a copyright work had made reasonably diligent efforts to locate the copyright holder but without success, the user should enjoy the benefit of limitations on the remedies which the copyright holder could obtain against the user if the owner appeared at a later date. The Orphan Works Act was proposed to Congress in May 2006 and finally passed into law in September 2008 amidst some controversy.

The anti-copyright movement, open access and other initiatives

The concept of copyright has not always enjoyed unquestioning support, even from authors; Mark Twain once opined, 'Only one thing is impossible for God; to find any sense in copyright law on the planet'. To this he added, 'Whenever a copyright law is to be made or altered, then the idiots assemble'. A century later, Nicholas Negroponte, founding director of the MIT MediaLab, stated in his 1995 book *Being Digital*: 'Copyright law is completely out of date. It is a Gutenberg artifact. Since it is a reactive process it will probably have to break down completely before it is corrected.' The debate has continued in an era where the internet has had a massive impact on consumer views about access to content.

So has copyright had its day? Publishers would claim that it remains essential in that it is intended to serve the public interest, to stimulate creativity, to encourage investment in the development, production, promotion and distribution of the end products which result from 'works of the mind'. But do we say all this because we believe it, or because we are desperately seeking to justify our own existence? Copyright has sometimes been referred to as a 'compensation culture', but neither copyright legislation nor the creative industries can remain static – both must react to the changing world around us, and in particular to the fast-moving technologies which have led the public – and in particular the younger generation – to expect instant (and preferably free) access to a wealth of content, be it print based, visual, audio or audiovisual in nature. Publishers must be aware of the needs of their customers and concentrate on bringing value to content as justification for their financial reward. It is surely preferable for copyright to be a regime which facilitates access through voluntary licensing rather than being perceived as an obstacle and subject to statutory licences imposed by governments.

What challenges are now being posed to copyright and to the creative industries which have hitherto relied on copyright to underpin their businesses? They come on many fronts and in many forms. Most extreme are the factions who argue for the complete abolition of copyright, although the music industry – perhaps the creative industry which has been under the most high-profile attack in recent years from initiatives such as P2P file sharing – has belatedly fought back against the erosion of its business, with some increasing success (see *Some lessons from the music industry?* in Chapter 23).

Copyleft

The Copyleft movement encompasses a group of licences which can be applied to software, documents, music and art. Using a reversed version of the familiar copyright symbol, Copyleft supports the philosophy that anyone who receives a copy or a derivative version of a work can use, modify or redistribute the work or derivative versions of it, thus discouraging users who might seek to develop a proprietary version for commercial use. In this, Copyleft represents the exact opposite of the traditional concept of copyright.

The movement was born in the 1980s when Richard Stallman, a computer programmer, created the GNU General Public Licence (GPL) for software, the first Copyleft licence. Copyleft licences do not ignore copyright; creators wishing to make their work available on Copyleft terms must first gain, defer or assign copyright holder status. By granting a Copyleft licence, they deliberately give up some of the rights which normally follow from copyright, including the basic right to control distribution of the work concerned. For many people, Copyleft facilitates the use of copyright to subvert the traditional restrictions it imposes on the dissemination of content, and here it has become a tool in the current political and ideological debates on intellectual property rights. Copyleft licences have sometimes been referred to as viral licences because any works derived from a Copyleft work must themselves be Copylefted. Copyleft had its origins in the world of software, but its influence has inspired the Creative Commons licences. Further information on Copyleft can be found on the website www.gnu.org/copyleft.

Creative Commons

Creative Commons is not strictly an anti-copyright movement; it is a model which originated within the US academic community with a view to promoting ideas and resources and allowing creators to make their works available for use free of charge under specific conditions. It took its inspiration from the Free Software Foundation's GNU General Public Licence (see *Copyleft* earlier in this chapter, pp. 29–30). The movement claims that 'Creative Commons works within the copyright system to help reduce barriers to creativity'. The movement was first established in 2001 with support from the Center for the Public Domain; it is now based at Stanford University. There are currently six different licence models which can be applied to literary works, music, photographs, films and websites, but not to computer software; there are some facilities to 'mix and match' conditions from the range of licences. The most restrictive licence (Attribution) allows users to download a work and share it provided that the creator is credited and that a link is provided back to the creator; no commercial use is permitted and no changes may be made to the content. At the opposite end of the spectrum, the most liberal model is a Public Domain licence which permits any type of use and which in effect renounces all claim to copyright. The licences were originally drafted under US law but UK versions are now available (www.creativecommons.org). A further suite of licences is currently in preparation.

The use of Creative Commons licences is likely to be of interest to those who genuinely wish to share their work as widely as possible, without complex formalities but retaining some credit for their creativity – in effect using the slogan 'Some rights reserved' as opposed to 'All rights reserved'. However, there are some negative aspects: creators will not receive feedback on who is using their work, and if the content is made available under a form of licence which permits using the work as the basis of a derivative work, there is no real protection for the moral rights of the original creator, and hence no redress if the work is used as part of a derivative work which might become subject to legal action. Creative Commons licences can be granted for the full term of copyright, which could prove problematic for the reputation of the original creator if the work continues to be used by a third party when it has become out of date. The granting of a Creative Commons licence would also preclude the possibility of the creator granting an exclusive commercial licence for the same material at a later date.

An alternative scenario is 'Founder Copyright', which allows creators to limit their copyright protection to fourteen or twenty-eight years (harking back to the early terms of copyright protection in America) by assigning copyright to Creative Commons in exchange for a licence for the required term, after which the work will pass into the public domain. This could result in problems for a work with little perceived initial value which subsequently becomes commercially valuable.

In a case of practising what he preached, Lawrence Lessig, professor at Stanford Law School and a founding father and director of Creative Commons, has made a number of his books – including *The Future of Ideas*, *Free Culture: How Big Media Uses Technology and the Law to Lock Down Culture and Creativity*, *Code: Version 2.0* and *Remix: Making Art and Culture Thrive in a Hybrid Economy* – available via various types of Creative Commons licence.

The open access movement

Of key concern in recent years to academic, and in particular scientific, technical and medical (STM) journal, publishers has been the open access (OA) movement. The Joint Information Systems Committee (JISC) has provided the following definition of open access: 'Open Access occurs when full-text journal articles, plus other research information ... are made freely available online. One approach to achieving Open Access relies on researchers depositing their papers or data in a digital repository from which they can be freely accessed.' It should be noted that the definition refers to free access, but not to free reuse, in contrast with the philosophies of Copyleft and Creative Commons described earlier in this chapter (pp. 29–30 and 30–1).

There are aspects of copyright which remain of key importance and which cannot be dispensed with in an open access environment. In particular, it is crucial for academics as authors of scientific research papers to be credited as the authors of their work as a key requirement for academic advancement. They are also concerned to preserve their moral rights in terms of the integrity of the content of their work; the provenance and reliability of the work are also of key importance to readers. A further copyright issue is who actually owns copyright in the work; recent years have seen moves from academic institutions to claim copyright ownership in works produced by their employees as part of their normal duties, particularly if the use of university facilities has been involved, whilst the provision of funding from research bodies has become a major issue in the open access debate.

What developments have taken place so far? The movement started to gain pace in 2000 when an advocacy group in the United States under the name of the Public Library of Science distributed an electronic open letter urging scientific publishers to hand over all research articles from their journals to public online archives free of charge within six months of first publication; this initiative was a reaction to the slow progress by PubMed Central, a free electronic full-text archive of research articles set up by the National Center for Biotechnology, in securing access to material from journals. A petition signed by some 29,000 academics stated that the signatories would no longer write for, sit on editorial boards for or purchase journals from publishers who failed to comply. Unsurprisingly, this initiative met with resistance both from commercial publishers and from learned societies dependent on income from their journals. Both foresaw that subscription income from journals would decline and that researchers could seek to bypass the conventional publishing process altogether, depositing their work directly online. Against this, publishers argued that the added value they provide through peer review, the selection of material of the highest quality, publication under the brand name of an established journal, and the delivery and search facilities in which they have invested all justify their claim to a share of revenue from the journals business.

Despite this, a number of STM publishers embarked on open access publishing models, in some cases on an 'author-pays' basis, whereby either individual authors, their research funding organizations or their academic institutes on their behalf pay a fee for publication of their articles, which are then made freely available online; fees have often been waived in cases of economic hardship and in particular for authors from developing countries. Some journals have been established on an entirely open access basis, whilst others include some articles published traditionally and others on an author-pays basis. At the time of writing it is still estimated that under 10% of global academic journal content is available online free of charge. Some of this content is made available via projects such as HINARI, which makes hundreds of biological science journals from over seventy publishers available free of charge or at low cost to 137 developing countries, or AGORA, which provides a similar service for journals in the fields of agriculture, food science and nutrition.

By 2003 the debate had heated up, with proponents of open access arguing that traditional subscription-based publishing restricted access; they put forward the moral argument that knowledge should be freely available, the economic argument that academic library budgets were increasingly stretched (journal subscriptions from the major twelve publishers had risen by up to 50% since 2000) and the political argument that since taxpayers in effect fund scientific research they should be entitled to free access to that research.

By the end of the year, the UK Parliament had set up a Science and Technology Select Committee Inquiry into Scientific Publications, with the focus on pricing and availability of journals within the scientific community and on whether open access was the solution to the problem. Submissions were prepared by a range of interested parties and evidence was given to the inquiry by key journal publishers, learned society publishers, librarians, academics, research funding bodies and supporters of open access. There was detailed discussion of the subscription model versus the author-pays model, with publishers supporting the former as upholding editorial independence and claiming that the author-pays model dilutes quality. The question was also examined of who should pay – the academic author, the academic's institution or perhaps a pharmaceutical company funding that academic's research work – and the effect the latter type of funding would have on editorial independence.

The Select Committee's report of July 2004, *Scientific Publishing: Free for All?*, appeared to give implicit rather then explicit endorsement to the principle of open access and supported further testing of the author-pays model. It did not, however, urge compulsory publication in open access journals of material by academics funded by government bodies, but suggested instead that such material should be deposited in institutional repositories. In the aftermath of the report, the Department of Trade and Industry came out clearly in favour of the publishing industry, with legislative support or funding for testing the author-pays model flatly rejected by the government. Despite this, by 2009 the number of open access journals had continued to grow; there are approximately 3,500 journals which are fully OA, but with the exception of those included in BioMed Central, Hindawi and the Public Library of Science programmes, relatively few are amongst the top-ranking journals. There are now requirements from funding bodies such as the Wellcome Trust and the National Institutes of Health in the United States that research produced with their backing must be made available on an open access basis. In 2009 the US Congress endorsed the latter requirement as compulsory.

OA journals are listed in directories such as the *Directory of Open Access Journals* (DOAJ) and *Open J-Gate*. Prominent OA journals include the *British Medical Journal* (BMJ – which has subsidized its initiative through the sale of summaries) and the *Journal of Medical Internet Research*. It has been estimated that 14.6% of the journals listed in the DOAJ operate on the basis of some form of Creative Commons licence. The debate on OA remains heated and polarized. January 2009 saw the publication of a report from the UK JISC entitled *Economic Implications of Alternative Scholarly Publishing Models: Exploring the Costs and Benefits*. The report supported

OA as the most cost-effective model, encouraging its extension from journals to book publishing. Comment from the UK Publishers Association highlighted the fact that the report minimized the contribution of publishers and that in an OA environment there was inadequate funding to pay for the value added by publishers.

In March 2009 Professor Roland Reuss published the Heidelberger Appell (the Heidenberg Pamphlet) castigating the various forces he felt were posing a threat to 'the freedom of literature, art and science' – and highlighting in particular the OA model for science publishing and the Google Library project (see *The rise of Google* and *The Google Settlement* in Chapter 23). His views were repeated during a lively session on the Google Settlement at the Frankfurt Book Fair in October 2009.

On 20 May 2009 a joint statement from the International Publishers Association (IPA), the International Association of Scientific, Technical and Medical Publishers, and the International Federation of Library Associations and Institutions (IFLA) called for a more rational, evidence-based debate on OA. Their statement encouraged the piloting of new business models whilst flagging the fact that different academic disciplines and publishing traditions would undoubtedly lead to different approaches and models.

The Adelphi Charter

An interesting recent initiative has been the Adelphi Charter in Creativity, Innovation and Intellectual Property, which seeks to set out new principles for copyright and patents and calls for a balance between permitting access to the ideas, learning and culture of others whilst recognizing and rewarding creativity and investment. The Charter argues for reasonable terms of protection for copyrights and patents, that the needs of developing countries should be taken into account and that a wide range of policies, including open source software licensing and open access to scientific literature, should be considered. However, this should be in the context of consultation and discussion to assess the balance between access to content and the rights of creators and developers. The Charter (which can be found at www.adelphicharter.org) has been drawn up by an international group of artists, scientists, lawyers, politicians, economists, academics and business experts.

What about 'free'?

It is perhaps worth mentioning here (in the aftermath of so many references to the expectations of users that content should be accessed free of charge in the digital age) the 2009 book *Free: The Future of a Radical Price* by Chris Anderson (author of the bestselling *The Long Tail*). Whilst not proposing a direct attack on copyright, Anderson posits a number of business models, in some cases facilitated by the online marketplace, which enable businesses to trade creatively, offering items for free whilst making real or perceived gains elsewhere. A very early example was that of Gillette, which in the early years of the twentieth century bundled its razors with other products, whilst making its profits on the sale of razor blades. In more recent times, coffee machines are installed in offices free of charge and profit comes from selling the companies concerned expensive coffee sachets. Mobile phones may appear to be free of charge, with profits made from the sale of monthly user packages. Search engines such as Google (see Chapter 23) may offer free access to 'snippets' of literary works, with their revenue coming from attendant advertising. Newspapers are increasingly offering free books, CDs and DVDs as an incentive to attract new readers (see Chapter 14 for the negative impact this has had on the sale of serial rights). These are interesting models and ones which the publishing industry has started to adopt in recent years in varying forms (e.g. offering free downloads of chapters of new books from their websites, to encourage sales).

Lobbying from the developing countries

A recent and perhaps less welcome initiative has been the lobbying of WIPO by a number of developing countries (Chile being amongst the most prominent) to include in its development agenda free access to educational and academic material. This is to some extent a resurrection of the issues raised in the late 1960s which led to the introduction of compulsory licensing provisions in the context of the 1971 Paris Revisions to the Berne and the Universal Copyright Conventions. Those provisions did, however, spell out strict procedures which must be followed before such licences can be granted and (although this aspect has been much misunderstood by the developing countries) provided for payment to be made for such licences. The current initiative seeks completely free access, and at the time of writing the International Publishers Association is lobbying strongly against proposals for WIPO treaties on minimum copyright exceptions (in particular for educational purposes) and on access to copyright material for visually and reading-impaired people (VIPs and RIPs – see also Chapter 18).

The development of rights business

Until the mid-twentieth century, the trade in publishing rights was comparatively modest; most houses on both sides of the Atlantic and in western Europe did not conduct sufficient business to justify full-time rights staff. Correspondence in the files of the older publishing houses reveals that when such deals were struck, they were handled by a wide variety of people ranging in level from the head of the house to anonymous clerks. It was only in the 1950s that the volume of business began to increase sufficiently to warrant special attention, and even then in many cases the work was handled by the managing director's secretary. It is perhaps for this historical reason that the majority of staff involved were women, and indeed women still tend to dominate the field on both sides of the Atlantic.

The sale of rights in literary works developed in the twentieth century for a variety of reasons apart from the fact that mutual recognition of copyright made negotiations both possible and financially worthwhile. Improvements in international communication, both in terms of travel and through the media, have led to a far greater awareness of the cultural and economic life of different countries. Thus a writer who becomes established in one country may now well be of interest to the reading public in a variety of other countries. This cross-border awareness is particularly strong in western Europe, and there has been much speculation on why so few continental (or indeed any foreign-language) books are successful in translation in the United Kingdom; historically, they have represented only 3% of total output, although this figure has started to improve in recent years with the publication of popular translations of crime fiction by writers including the Russian Boris Akunin and Swedish writers Stieg Larssson and Henning Mankell. It is also noticeable that relatively few books cross the Atlantic (in either direction) to become bestsellers in both major English-language markets of the world.

An early example of the increase in interest in foreign literature was the popularity in the 1980s of the 'magic realism' novels by Latin American writers. In the early 1990s, there was a brief, if rather short-lived, interest in writers from central and eastern Europe as those countries became more accessible to the west, and there is now some interest in writers from mainland China. Publishers such as Penguin and HarperCollins have initiated active programmes to publish translations of modern Chinese fiction, such as Jiang Rong's bestselling *Wolf Totem*.

Economic developments have also affected the rights market; perhaps the most obvious example is the significant rise in book prices in the developed countries, which makes such books increasingly beyond the reach of the poorer countries. The key areas here are school and university textbooks; the countries concerned are those that have long used western books, perhaps because they were former colonies and therefore had educational systems based on that of the mother country. In the case of the United Kingdom, Commonwealth countries have been major export markets for British educational and academic titles, whilst French publishers exported substantial quantities of books to Francophone Africa. As prices have risen, mass importation of large quantities of the original edition has become more and more difficult for the developing countries, resulting in a huge increase in the number of applications to reprint low-price editions in the countries concerned. In some countries, provisions have been introduced into domestic legislation (some in line with the Paris Revisions and some not) to enable publishers there to obtain compulsory reprint or translation licences for books needed for educational purposes that are considered too highly priced in the original edition. This development has had an inevitable impact on the licensing policy of textbook publishers in the wealthier countries, and is covered in more detail in Chapters 12 and 16.

Perhaps one of the most important developments in publishing in the twentieth century was the birth of the mass-market paperback when Allen Lane published the first ten Penguins on 30 July 1935. It was not the first time that the concept of a cheap reprint series had been tried; examples appeared as far back as the seventeenth century, while in the nineteenth century the increase in travel and literacy led to a surge in the number of 'library' or 'classics' series of reissues in the United Kingdom, and the very successful Tauschnitz series on the Continent. Penguins were perceived as something different; at 6d (2.5p) per copy, their appearance initially provoked a storm of protest from booksellers, who felt that cheap editions could only harm business. There was reaction too from some authors (including George Orwell), who felt that the level of their royalties would be reduced. In fact, history shows that the reverse happened. As the Penguin list expanded, it had a significant social effect in that it brought classics of both fiction and non-fiction within the reach of young people and the working population, who had previously thought that the ownership of books was beyond their class as well as their pockets. For several decades, the name of Penguin was used as a generic term for a paperback edition, although a host of other paperback imprints arose, in particular in the 1960s. The commercial value that now attaches to this sector of publishing is huge, and in rights terms once commanded substantial sums; however, in recent years licensing has largely been abandoned in favour of 'vertical publishing', where the same publisher first publishes a hardback edition and then, after an interval of about a year, the cheaper paperback version. Another area of licensing which has declined substantially in recent years has been that of book clubs, mail order operations which have been severely affected in the United Kingdom by the removal of fixed book pricing and the easy availability of books at discounted prices through the major bookshop chains and through online retailers such as Amazon. At the time of writing, the future of Reader's Digest is unclear, which may affect the sale of digest and condensation rights (see Chapter 15).

Despite a decline in some areas of rights, perhaps the most interesting development has been the expansion in the different types of rights that can be sold over the years. Historical files in publishers' archives may reveal merchandising arrangements for soft toys based on children's books from around the turn of the century (for example, Florence Upton's

Golliwogg character), and applications for film options in the 1930s. However, few people could have imagined forty years ago that today it would be
possible to license rights for the adaptation of a science fiction novel into a
computer game, for a famous author to be heard reading his own book on
an audiobook downloaded to an iPod, for a legal book to be available on
an electronic database for retrieval by a busy barrister, for medical data to
be easily accessible to a doctor on his ward rounds via a personal digital
assistant (PDA) or the display on a mobile phone, for students and academics to be able to access online collections of books and academic journals from a PC, laptop or dedicated reading device, or for the
merchandising revenue from a book-based film to exceed the box-office
takings. The increasing sophistication of copying machines and the ease of
access to them continue; as yet, only part of this giant reproduction usage
is under control in various countries through central licensing agencies.
Electronic copying is on the increase, and the exponential growth of the
internet has brought with it both opportunities and threats in terms of
the use of copyright material, as new players have sought to enter the
content market. The story of Google (see Chapter 23) is a dramatic example
of the impact of a technology company on the publishing industry, and
that saga is by no means over.

Many of these developments have been positive in that they have
potentially widened the market for the exploitation of literary works in a
variety of forms. To ensure suitable levels of protection, however, the new
media must be taken into account in the formulation of new intellectual
property legislation at both national and international levels. The wise
publisher seeking to sign up an author will ensure that this aspect of
the wording of the head contract is discussed with considerable care
to cover various possible forms of electronic use by the publisher himself
or via the medium of licensing to third parties, and how the author will be
remunerated for different types of use. The contract should aim to cover
not only rights that exist now, but also those that may come into existence
in the future.

Chapter 2

The publishing contract
Who should control the rights?

The question of who should hold control over the rights in a literary work remains a vexed one, and there is frequently a divergence of opinion between authors and publishers, between publishers and literary agents and a divergence of practice between trade publishers and academic publishers.

There is little doubt that in almost all cases the first owner of the copyright in the work is the author. It is he or she who has written the work, and it is a condition of copyright that the work should be original. As Daniel Defoe argued, 'A Book is the Author's Property, 'tis the Child of his Invention, the Brat of his Brain'. As mentioned in Chapter 1, the chief exceptions to the ownership of copyright by the author under the provisions of UK copyright law are works written during the course of an author's regular employment activities; US copyright law also makes provision for the copyright in 'works for hire' to belong to the commissioning party. In most cases, however, the author is the first owner of the copyright and hence in a position to choose whether to retain ownership or to pass it over in some way to another party. The two most common situations are retention of copyright by the author and the granting of exclusive publishing rights for a defined market, or full assignment of copyright.

Retention of copyright

In trade publishing, it is common practice for the author to retain ownership of the copyright in their own name. The author then grants to a publisher (or to several publishers in different markets) an exclusive licence to publish the book in a particular form in a designated territory. The author may or may not choose to grant to each publisher other rights in addition to the prime publishing rights in that territory.

An example might be an author who makes two separate arrangements for publication of a book in the English language: one with a British publisher and one with an American publisher. Each publisher will have a list of specified geographical territories in which to sell an edition of the work, with prime geographical territories as exclusive to that publisher and

additional territories as non-exclusive (the 'open market'), where both editions may be sold. Each publisher might also have been granted the right to
sublicense specified rights within their exclusive geographical territories;
perhaps mass-market paperback rights, book club rights and serial rights
for extracts in newspapers and magazines. One publisher might in addition
have been granted the right to license translation rights throughout the
world – or both may have been granted the right to license translation
rights in the countries within their exclusive geographical territories.
Alternatively, the translation rights may have been withheld for the author
(or, more likely, a literary agent acting on behalf of the author) to sell
separately. For a well-established author, rights such as film, merchandising
and television rights, and first serial rights (prepublication extract rights
licensed to newspapers and magazines) are often not granted to the
publisher but are handled by the author's literary agent. Other rights which
may be retained include sound and video recording rights and electronic
rights, although the exact definition of the latter category remains the
subject of ongoing debate, especially as new opportunities for exploitation
arise in the electronic environment; in particular, developments such
as the re-emergence of dedicated electronic reading devices, applications
for mobile phones, digital audio downloads, podcasting and the
digitization of content by non-traditional players such as Google and
Amazon (see *Search engines, online retailers and others: threat or opportunity?* in
Chapter 23) mean that a much broader range of rights now needs to be
considered and more carefully defined (see *Who should control electronic and
multimedia rights?* later in this chapter, pp. 45–9.

The package of rights negotiated between agent and publisher will depend
on a variety of factors – in particular the amount of money required by the
agent versus the amount of money on offer from the publisher; the ability
of the publisher to promote and sell the work in a wide range of markets
(a key consideration for multinational groups with publishing and marketing facilities in all the major English-speaking markets) and the ability of the
publisher to handle other rights. An agent may need to balance the possible
benefits of a single deal with a multinational versus the advantages of
separate deals with smaller publishers in individual markets, and in particular whether the author benefits more from receiving separate advances
and full royalties on separate editions rather than a share from sublicensing
arrangements. *From Pitch to Publication* by agent Carole Blake (Macmillan,
1999; second edition in preparation) provides excellent information on the
role of the literary agent and the author–agent relationship.

Assignment of copyright

Here, the publisher seeks an assignment of copyright and in so doing
acquires full ownership, including all publishing rights and subsidiary rights

in the work for the duration of copyright, unless there are reasons to return all rights or some to the author before the end of that period. In most cases the author receives an advance and royalties on sales of the original edition plus a share of any subsidiary rights income. This is therefore a very different type of arrangement from the outright purchase of copyright by publishers that was common in the late nineteenth and early twentieth centuries, when an author received a once-and-for-all payment for the copyright. A particular area of publishing where ownership of copyright by the publishing house is common is that of dictionaries, directories and encyclopaedias; here material may be compiled by in-house employees (hence categorized as employee works under UK copyright law) or by freelance writers commissioned to write individual sections; in such cases an outright fee would normally be paid to each contributor.

Assignment of copyright is also relatively common practice in educational, academic and professional publishing; although it is occasionally regarded as invidious, there are frequently practical and justifiable reasons for it. The first and most important reason is that books published by this sector of the industry are subject to frequent piracy (the translation, reprinting or unauthorized internet use of the book in its original language in a country that is a signatory to one or more of the international copyright conventions) or to the publication of unauthorized editions (the same types of usage, but in countries that do not recognize copyright through membership of the conventions).

Over the years, academic houses in the United Kingdom, the United States and continental Europe have been forced to enter into expensive legal action in areas of the world such as Asia, Latin America, Turkey and Greece in order to defend rights in their publications. In such cases, the main defence hinges on the ability to prove the ownership of copyright. Where the publishing houses themselves own the copyright through assignment from their authors, the cases have proved easier to defend; in a number of cases where copyright had been retained by the author, defence cases collapsed if the author had died or could not be located to take swift legal action against the offenders. The problem is particularly acute in the case of major textbooks where the original author has died and successive editors have revised the book over the years. Clear assignment of copyright to the publisher, with new contracts prepared for successive editions, will normally provide an adequate defence.

Another factor in this sector of publishing is the large number of multi-author works that are published. It would be impractical, to say the least, if it were necessary to consult all 204 contributors to a major surgical reference work each time the publisher wished to make a licence agreement. In the case of such works it is common practice for each contributor to assign copyright in his work to the publisher; a single outright payment may then be made to each contributor, with the overall editor receiving the advance against a modest royalty percentage on sales. It has also been common practice for publishers of academic journals to require an assignment of copyright from each contributor, although this remains an area for heated debate and is linked to the fact that journal publishers do not normally pay contributors for their articles. Publication in an accredited peer-reviewed academic journal has long been recognized as essential for academic advancement.

In practice, the question of ownership of the copyright is a matter for discussion at the earliest stage of negotiation between author and publisher, and the position agreed must be clearly specified in the head contract between the parties. In addition, it is incumbent on the publisher to discuss any other rights that are being requested, because these should be granted only if the publisher has adequate facilities to exploit them. Some authors or their agents may wish to include a clause in the head contract requiring the publisher to use its best endeavours to actively exploit the rights granted. The Minimum Terms Agreement conditions accepted by some UK publishers provide for this and for the approval of all major rights deals by the author. If assignment of copyright is requested, the reasons for this must be carefully explained. The view of assignment as theft of an author's birthright is inaccurate; any contract between an author and a reputable publishing house will enable the author to request the return of the rights if the publisher breaches the contract or ceases to use the rights granted, although digital storage, electronic publishing and the increasing availability of books via print-on-demand raise the question of when a book is 'available' and when it is really 'out of print'. Given the difficulty of predicting unit sales in this environment when a book reaches this stage of its life, the return of rights once income falls below an agreed level in any two accounting periods may be a more realistic criterion.

Equally important is for the publisher to be sure that it is contracting with the correct copyright owner. In recent years there has been a move on the part of the universities to claim that they should own the copyright in works produced by members of their faculties. Here much will depend on the circumstances; for example whether the work was undertaken in working hours and using facilities provided by the institution, or in the academic's own time at home. There may also be complications if the work arises as a result of research funded by an outside body such as a pharmaceutical company. Authors themselves should have a clear written arrangement with their employers or any outside bodies in cases of this kind before contracting directly with publishers. It should also be remembered that the 1988 UK Copyright Act introduced provisions for the moral rights of the author, and the question of assertion of the right of paternity or any waiver of moral rights (partial or total) should be discussed at the contract stage.

For more detailed discussion and examples of publishing contracts, whether those between author and publisher or those between publisher and licensee, readers are referred to *Clark's Publishing Agreements: A Book of Precedents*, seventh edition, edited by Lynette Owen (Tottel Publishing, 2007, now Bloomsbury Professional).

Division of proceeds from rights sales

What rights will be granted to the publisher in addition to basic publishing rights in an agreed territory, and what will the author receive from the sale of rights? These aspects must also be discussed when the head contract is first negotiated, either directly between the author and the publisher or between the literary agent (acting on behalf of the author) and the publisher. In principle, whoever is to handle specific rights will expect to retain a share of the proceeds from the sale of such rights as payment for the work involved in placing them; the proportion to be retained and the proportion to be paid to the author will reflect a number of factors.

In the past, literary agents retained a standard percentage from all income as commission for their work; the traditional figure was 10%. Agents may now retain 10% or 15% on the prime publishing arrangements with a publisher, but perhaps 20% on foreign-language sales, where in some cases a local subagent may be involved who will also require commission. The clientele of a literary agent may range from a first novelist in whom the agent has faith, to a well-established author with many bestsellers to their name; it is of course on the latter that agents depend for the bulk of their income, and this enables them to cover the running costs of the agency. If it is the publishing house that is to handle the rights, there may be other considerations. The publisher is of course making a major investment in publishing the book in the first place; the level of risk involved will vary from project to project, and the publisher's share of any rights income will offset the investment.

If the book is by a major author with a long and successful track record, the publisher may have had to acquire it at auction in competition with other publishers, making a substantial advance payment. Much of this may have to be justified by the onward sale of rights to newspapers, an American house and foreign-language publishers if such rights are within the publisher's control. Alternatively, if the author is completely unknown, the publisher is taking a risk and investing with the hope that the author will become established – but this may not happen until several books by the same author have appeared.

Other high-risk areas are in educational and academic publishing, for example the publication of a short-run academic monograph, albeit at a comparatively high price. The finance required to develop a completely new science course for secondary schools or a major new undergraduate medical textbook in a core subject can be enormous, and such projects face a highly competitive market and incur substantial development and design costs. In such cases, the sale of rights can help to offset a major investment.

It is therefore likely that there will be a wide range of practice in the way that rights income is divided between publisher and author. In trade publishing, it is common for the author to receive a higher proportion of the income from rights sales: 90% is not uncommon for the sale of prepublication rights to newspapers, while the split on translation rights could be as high as 80% or even 90% for a major author. On paperback licences or reprint licences to the American market, the author could receive between 50% and 90% of the proceeds, and special arrangements will also be made to cover deals where the publisher sells rights in the form of a coedition; this might involve the sale of printed copies in the English language to a book club or an American publisher, or it may entail the sale of printed foreign-language editions to overseas coedition partners. In such cases, the author may receive a royalty based on the price received per copy, particularly in the case of book club deals where margins are very small and the payment of a full UK author royalty would make the deal unviable. In educational and academic publishing, it is customary for the publisher to retain a larger proportion of the proceeds from rights sales; a common division would be 50/50 between author and publisher for both translation and reprint rights, although this might be increased to 60% or 75% in favour of a well-established author.

There are two main reasons for the difference in practice between trade and academic publishers. First, the range of rights that can be sold in academic books is far smaller; second, the rights income generated is usually modest in comparison with trade publishing. A reasonable return is required if the publisher is to maintain full-time staff to handle rights business. On the other hand, educational and academic publishers are particularly dependent on being able to retain the loyalty of good specialist authors, and the sale of rights may persuade such authors to continue writing for them. Some academic authors are keen for rights sales to be pursued that may be far from lucrative and may even result in a net loss. An example might be for arrangements for an Urdu translation of a midwifery textbook, where the author is more concerned that the book should be available in a local language where it is needed than about the income from such a licence. The rights revenue from such an arrangement will probably not cover the cost of the attendant paperwork, but the author will be satisfied. The economic argument is reinforced by the fact that few literary agents would be prepared to run a business based entirely on the proceeds of placing rights in educational and academic works.

The contrast between rights deals for trade and academic titles could perhaps be illustrated by contrasting a competitive auction conducted by telephone for translation rights in a new novel by a bestselling author with an application for low-price English-language reprint rights in an academic textbook from a developing country, perhaps involving a print run of 1,000 copies. The former could generate a six- or even seven-figure income up front. The latter might produce a total income of only a few hundred pounds during the life of the licence, but it might well require prompt action, complex legalized documentation, and an awareness of local legislation in order to prevent piracy or a compulsory licence being granted and hence loss of control of the book in the market concerned. This is of course an extreme example; some licences for well-established textbooks to more affluent countries may be lucrative, especially if a book has been translated regularly through successive editions. In such cases, the author might well wish to renegotiate the fee split on rights deals when a new contract is negotiated for providing an update of the book.

Who should control electronic and multimedia rights?

The debate on who should control these rights continues, particularly in the light of the now all-pervasive reach of the internet and the advent of e-books. Publishers have long argued that verbatim electronic rights, i.e. the reproduction of the work electronically without the addition of audio and video components and other adaptations, should lie with the publisher, since to license them separately would result in a directly competing edition, and many publishers might well wish to make the work available in this form themselves either direct from their own servers or via intermediaries such as bookshop chains or library aggregators. It will be important to define clearly in the head contract which arrangements will be treated as sales on a royalty basis and which as true licence arrangements, with the author receiving an agreed share of rights revenue. The Society of Authors has recommended a royalty of at least 25% of net receipts for e-book sales for trade titles; they and a number of literary agents also recommend that electronic rights should be granted for a period of two or three years and be subject to review as the market develops. Much may also depend on the form and purpose of publication (commercial and revenue generating, or promotional), whether the work forms part of a larger overall work and whether the author is required to undertake additional work to assist the publication in electronic form.

There was initially a perception on the part of some authors and agents that electronic publishing is a cheap option for publication, since it involves few or no manufacturing and inventory costs and low distribution costs. This leaves out of the equation the substantial costs incurred by the publisher in digitization, and in some cases the very high costs of maintaining a large body of content (e.g. back and current issues of academic journals) in a form suitable for direct supply to customers from its own server, and providing back-up and troubleshooting services to those customers. Perceptions are beginning to change now that the major trade publishers have embarked on mass digitization of their content; in January 2006 a meeting was held between the UK Publishers Association, the Society of Authors and the Association of Authors' Agents to discuss how digital rights should be covered in contracts; both sides recognize that changes in attitude and practice will be needed to take advantage of new digital opportunities and seek voluntary guidelines. There have also been related discussions between agents and trade publishers on whether rights in a work should revert if a book is no longer available in print form but still exists in electronic form or can be supplied through the publisher's own print-on-demand programme, a channel of supply long provided by academic publishers when print sales no longer justify keeping a small amount of stock in the warehouse. Publishers have suggested that their performance might better be judged by a minimum level of revenue to the author in a given accounting period, but as yet this area remains unresolved.

Some authors (particularly in the computer book field) are keen to post advance extracts from their next books on their own websites to invite comments from colleagues and potential readers. Others may wish to make extracts or the entire book available for teaching purposes on an intranet at their own academic institution. Any such plans should be discussed in advance between author and publisher in terms of the copyright implications and the potential effect on subsequent sales of the book of posting large amounts of material in this way. The author–publisher contract should certainly specify clearly what types of use the author is permitted to make of his own work in both print and electronic form.

The publisher might well wish to license the storage of a copyright work by electronic means to a third party, e.g. a document supply centre, to enable that centre to deliver copies of selected material either in hard-copy form by mail or fax, or by electronic means if the licence allows for this. Another form of licence could be a site licence to an academic institute or a consortium of such institutes, to enable staff and students to browse and print off material. These are only two forms of electronic reprography (see Chapter 23). There is also the question of allowing material to appear via search engines such as Google or via the websites of electronic retailers such as Amazon, uses viewed by such companies as promotional but which may impact on the original edition and which Google in particular has sought to extend to more commercial usage (see *Search engines, online retailers and others: threat or opportunity?* in Chapter 23). If publishers are to participate in such programmes, they need to be sure that they control the right not only to license the whole work electronically but also to allow others to use extracts and to undertake electronic marketing; the question of third party copyright material embedded in the text also arises.

There could be other uses which fall into the category of subsidiary rights; for example a licence to a third party to include part or the whole of a work in a large electronic database available either on CD-ROM or online. Other subsidiary rights that should be the subject of licence arrangements if undertaken by third parties are digitization, screen display, performance (e.g. if screen display takes place in front of a number of people, as in a lawyer's office when clients are present), transmission, networking, downloading, storage, the printing out of hard copy and the possible manipulation of text, either by changing it or by using it as 'cut and paste' in the context of other materials – this has implications for the right of integrity in the work.

The last fifteen years have seen the advent of e-books in the form of downloading works via websites such as those run by Amazon on to a variety of devices such as laptops, PDAs such as PalmPilots and now 'smart' mobile phones; the first generation of dedicated reading devices such as the RocketeBook and Franklin's eBookman did not prove success-ful, but the advent of new devices including the Sony Reader, the Amazon Kindle and the iRex Iliad have opened up new possibilities. This area is discussed in more detail in Chapter 24. The question of whether this type of publishing constitutes a primary publishing right or a subsidiary right is a vexed one and the topic still provokes debate. Most publishers hold that it is a primary publishing right, using alternative channels for delivery of the content of the book, and, if controlled elsewhere, could have a damaging impact on sales of the main edition. It might then follow that the author should receive a similar royalty percentage on the price of the electronic version as for the print version, rather than a share of a subsidiary rights royalty, even if the e-book is delivered via an intermediary such as Amazon, Waterstone's or an aggregator supplying collections of e-books to libraries. Pricing policies for e-books versus print editions have varied from publisher to publisher, with some charging a higher price for the electronic version (on the grounds that this has the advantage of searchability) and others charging a price one-third to one-half lower than that of the print edition.

For electronic publishing or licensing in forms that involve the addition of illustrations, animation, sound effects, music, video clips or an inter-active facility (including for enhanced e-books), the control of rights should be a matter for negotiation between the author (or author's agent) and the publisher. The high cost of multimedia development has meant that relatively few publishers have entered this field, and indeed some who did so have withdrawn from it altogether. Some publishers may still wish to enter into an alliance for investment and development with an outside partner such as a software house. As with all rights, control best lies with whoever is in a position to exploit those rights actively and in the interests of both parties. Again, a solution may be to grant the rights to the publisher for a specified and relatively short period of time (e.g. two or three years), to be retrieved if the rights have not been exploited.

If electronic rights are to be included in the head contract, there should be careful discussion on whether these will permit the publisher either to exploit those rights directly or to license them to third parties, or both. The publisher could be granted electronic publication rights allowing them to

> produce, copy, publish and sell, perform, display, broadcast and transmit the Work, whether in whole or in part, adapted or abridged, on its own or in combination with another work or works, together with any accompanying sounds and images, in any electronic form and to license the foregoing rights in electronic versions of the Work.

Use of the material in electronic form by the publisher will be subject to rates of payment that are either specified in the contract (in which case it is advisable to provide for review at regular intervals to ensure that the terms remain in line with current trade practice) or are left to be agreed when the exact nature of the electronic exploitation is known (for example only part of the work may be used as part of a larger electronic project).

The division of licensing revenue from electronic rights may be specified in the head contract, in which case it will be wise to define different types of licensing which might justify different divisions of revenue, depending on the financial model involved; an alternative would be to leave the division to be agreed with the author when the exact form and extent of the licensing usage are known.

It will be necessary to include a definition of the term 'electronic form', and this might read as follows:

> Electronic form shall include, but not be limited to, off-line electronic storage and information retrieval systems of a digital, optical or magnetic nature including (by way of example and not limitation) floppy disk, CD-ROM, DVD, ROM-card, compact disk, video, integrated circuit; mobile and hand-held devices; online transmission by satellite and other means of telecommunication; and any other electronic means of reproduction, publication, dissemination and transmission, whether now in existence or hereafter invented.

The range of rights will have to be regularly reviewed in the light of new developments.

It can be seen that the financial arrangements for electronic and multimedia rights may vary considerably, according to whether the publishing house itself publishes a product or products in electronic form, whether it will enter into a joint venture or whether it will license to an independent licensee. Much will also depend on whether the work concerned forms the main basis of the electronic product or only a small part of a larger product. The terms should also take into account whether the author is required to undertake additional work to assist with publication in electronic form. This remains a rapidly changing area where the author should be fully consulted on the potential exploitation or adaptation of the work in non-traditional form.

Publishers should not ignore the continuing implications of an important case in the United States, *Tasini v. The New York Times Co.*, where in October 1999 the Second Circuit Court of Appeal overturned a 1997 District Court ruling that publishers had the right to reuse full-text articles by freelance newspaper writers in online databases or CD-ROMs without seeking explicit permission from these authors. This has particular implications for publishers of encyclopaedias and reference works who may have employed writers to produce material for publication in print-on-paper form only. Publishers should never assume that electronic publishing rights are implicit in their contracts; if there is any doubt on older contracts, it is vital to reach agreement with the authors concerned. With new players entering the field, it is also advisable to check whether any rights already granted cover new forms of exploitation; for example, if audiobook rights have been granted to the publisher, does this cover the electronic downloading of audiobooks via websites such as Audible (see Chapter 20)?

Author approval of rights deals

Should the author always have a contractual right to approve rights deals before they are finalized? Here, practice may vary between different sectors of the publishing industry, from publisher to publisher and indeed from author to author.

In educational and academic publishing, the requirement for formal authorization from the author before a traditional rights deal can proceed is comparatively rare. Such a requirement could prove impractical, particularly in the case of works with many authors and licences that may have to be negotiated quickly in order to forestall piracy or the granting of a compulsory licence. The publisher may well be the copyright owner through an assignment arrangement; even if copyright has not been assigned, full control may have been granted on sublicensing arrangements.

Many academic authors have published with the same house over the years and trust the rights department to license only if they have negotiated the best deal possible. It is nevertheless a courtesy to inform the author in advance when a rights deal is about to be concluded; if there are any particular problems such as essential corrections or updating, these can then be picked up before the deal is finalized. Even if full control of licensing has been granted, it is always wise to consult authors over any new and unorthodox forms of licensing, for example granting an organization such as the

Copyright Licensing Agency (CLA) an extension of their existing mandate to grant a new kind of licence (see Chapter 23).

UK publishers who support the Minimum Terms Agreement (usually in the trade sector) agree to consult authors on all rights deals with the exception of anthology and quotation rights, book club rights, reprographic rights and rights licensed to charitable organizations for the use of the reading impaired (the visually impaired and people with physical disabilities affecting their ability to read). They also agree to supply copies of contracts for finalized licence deals to the author.

Even if the publisher does not support the Minimum Terms Agreement, some major authors are in a position to write into their contracts that all or some types of rights deal are subject to prior approval. Some such authors may in addition specify designated publishers whom they wish to publish their work in particular countries. In the case of translations published under licence, some major authors may require the right to specify designated translators. This is perhaps understandable in the case of literary writers, whose style may be difficult to capture in translation. Criteria may be somewhat different in the case of a translation of an academic book, where the prime concern is to have a translator who is not only competent linguistically but also well qualified in the subject matter of the book. In both sectors of publishing, there may be justification for requiring the right to approve the text of a translation at manuscript stage. This requirement could also apply to any licence where the text of the book may be altered – perhaps in the context of a newspaper serialization, or in an edition with adaptations for a specific market. Such requirements for approval must be incorporated into the contractual arrangements and will be covered in more detail in the relevant sections of this book. The introduction of moral rights, including the right of integrity, into UK copyright law places an obligation on the UK publisher to extend similar requirements to licensees, unless the author has agreed to waive his or her moral rights. It should, however, be remembered that the copyright legislation of the countries of continental Europe and many other countries does not permit the waiver of moral rights.

Chapter 3

An expanding range of possibilities

The range of rights that can be licensed has continued to expand over the years, reflecting wider trading between different countries as political and economic circumstances change, new channels of book supply and the development of new technologies with potential for exploiting the written word in a variety of ways – the extraordinary expansion of the internet (including social networking sites such as Facebook, MySpace, BeBo, Twitter and allied sites such as YouTube and SecondLife) and the advent of new platforms and new forms of publication such as e-books and down-loadable audiobooks are probably the most significant developments in the last twenty years. On the other hand, some more traditional areas of licensing have contracted, in particular the licensing of paperback rights to independent licensees (now largely replaced by vertical publishing within the same group); book club rights (whose importance has dwindled in the face of discounting by traditional booksellers and supermarkets); first serial rights, and to some extent the granting of low-price reprint rights (replaced in some markets by direct supply of the original publisher's own edition at a special price). With the increasing number of multinational publishing groups, intercompany licensing continues to expand.

In the past, rights attaching to literary works were often divided for the sake of convenience into volume rights and subsidiary rights, but these distinctions are becoming increasingly blurred, particularly with the diverse forms of electronic publishing and licensing.

Volume rights

These traditionally included the rights which were included in the package granted to the original publisher, either to exploit themselves under their own imprint or to license on to others (for example to an American publisher, to a book club, to a large-print publisher, to a publisher in a developing country for a low-price reprint, to a foreign-language publisher). Such rights are traditionally licensed on an ongoing royalty basis, although the original publisher might choose to manufacture copies on a royalty-inclusive basis for a US publisher or a book club, or a foreign-language publisher if the book in question is heavily illustrated; however, the viability of overseas coedition sales is affected by exchange rates.

In addition to these rights, a publisher acquiring rights for an agreed sales territory would also expect to control additional rights to be paid for on an outright fee basis – digest and condensation rights, anthology and quotation rights, one-shot periodical rights, second serial rights, single-voice readings on radio and television, and reprographic reproduction rights to allow the reproduction of text in media such as photocopying and scanning.

Subsidiary rights

A number of other rights have not automatically been included as volume rights – these include first serial rights, dramatic, film and television rights, and merchandising rights. These may be granted to the publisher in addition to the rights listed above, but it is increasingly likely that they will be retained by the author (or more probably the author's agent) for direct handling.

The question of control of electronic rights has been a vexed one, although recently there has been more convergence in thinking between publishers and agents. In particular, the advent of e-books with the facility to download a complete text from a website onto a computer or a hand-held device raises the question of whether this is a licence or simply an alternative form of delivery to the end customer, and hence a sale. Most publishers understandably favour the latter view and believe that such rights should be included in the publishing package, with the author receiving a full royalty on revenue derived from this method of supply. It is the choice of the customer whether to purchase a printed copy in a book-shop, whether to order a printed copy via an electronic bookseller such as Amazon, or whether to download a direct reproduction of the book onto a laptop, a PDA, a dedicated reading device such as the Sony Reader or the Kindle or a mobile phone. However, the licensing of a book for adaptation into a multimedia product involving the addition of images, sound or an interactive facility is a quite different scenario and is likely to be the subject of negotiation (see Chapter 2).

Categories of rights

As in previous editions, the following checklist cannot pretend to be exhaustive, as the range of rights continues to expand and alter. Chapters 9–24 examine each of these categories in greater detail.

English-language territorial rights

These rights may be licensed to an independent publisher if the original publisher will not itself be distributing the book in its language of origin throughout the world; alternatively, a large multinational group may license its subsidiaries to produce local editions at a time and price to suit market circumstances.

For English-language books, key markets are the United States, Australasia, South Africa and Canada, which is increasingly perceived as a territory that can support its own editions of trade titles independently of the British Commonwealth or the United States. Deals may be handled either as coeditions manufactured by the original publisher if exchange rates favour this, or as reprint licences with books manufactured by the licensees in the markets concerned. Other languages where licensing in this way may occur are Spanish and Portuguese.

Book club rights

These are rights licensed to a book club operation, which will normally offer books to its members primarily through the medium of mail order, at prices representing a substantial saving on the publisher's recommended retail price. In the UK, book club sales have been substantially affected by discounting in bookshops and supermarkets following the demise of the Net Book Agreement. Books are either provided to the clubs as physical stock, manufactured by the publisher, or through a reprint licence with the club manufacturing its own copies. Paperback book clubs may sell specially produced paperback editions not comparable with any edition available in the trade. Book club deals are now often handled by sales rather than by rights staff.

Paperback rights

Traditionally these were licensed by a hardback publisher to an independent paperback house which would manufacture its own copies, and such licences do still occur if the original publisher either has no paperback imprint or feels that a mass-market house could maximize sales. However, many books are now acquired for both hardback and paperback publication within the same publishing group ('vertical publishing'). Paperback books are published in a variety of formats.

Reprint rights

These can cover a variety of different circumstances; the acquisition of hardback rights from an original paperback publisher, perhaps to service a small library market; the revival of a long out-of-print title by licensing it to a specialist publisher; the licensing of a special low-priced 'promotional' edition some time after publication of the original hardback edition to reach a wider market; the licensing of a low-priced edition of a textbook to a developing country. Also included here would be educational rights, where the text of a work is reprinted for use in schools with the addition of editorial material such as a critical introduction and notes; also large-print rights, where books are reprinted in large type for the partially sighted.

Serial rights

These consist of first serial rights (extracts licensed to newspapers or magazines, which start before publication of the book itself) and second serial rights (extract rights beginning after publication of the book).

One-shot periodical rights

These cover the licence of an entire book (normally a novel) for inclusion in a single issue of a newspaper or magazine. They are relatively rarely granted because of their potential impact on sales of the book itself.

Digest and condensation rights

These cover the right to publish the work in summarized form in a magazine such as *Reader's Digest*, or to publish the work in condensed form, as in a compendium edition of several novels.

Translation rights

These cover the right to translate the work into another language and publish it within an agreed sales territory. Deals may be done on the basis of a coedition printed by the original publisher for each licensee (particularly appropriate for books with full-colour illustrations) or a licence involving local manufacture by the licensee. Where appropriate, a translation licence may also include the right to sublicense other rights in the language concerned, for example paperback rights, book club rights, serial rights and so on.

An associated type of rights is bilingual rights, where the original text appears alongside the translated text. This may be appropriate for dictionaries and some categories of language teaching material; some scientific publishers also produce highly illustrated books (e.g. medical atlases) with parallel text in several languages which can then be distributed in the appropriate markets.

Strip Cartoon or picturization rights

These cover the right to publish an existing publication in the form of a strip cartoon or series of photographs, with the story told in captions or speech bubbles.

Anthology and quotation rights

Commonly referred to in the book trade as 'permissions', these cover the right to reproduce text or illustrations from one copyright source in the context of another work, in print-on-paper or electronic form.

Rights for the reading impaired

These cover the right to produce a version of the work in Braille or Moon (both tactile systems for the blind), recordings on special cassettes, enlarged screen display and voice activated versions for computer use. Reading-impaired users may also include those with dyslexia or with physical disabilities which affect their ability to read in the traditional way.

Audiobook rights

These are the right to produce a work in recorded form, abridged or unabridged and either as a single-voice reading or in dramatized form. Audiobooks are now increasingly produced as CDs rather than as cassettes, and there are now services for downloading them electronically, e.g. via Audible.

Single-voice reading rights

These cover the right to read from the text of a work in undramatized form on radio or television. This area is now starting to be affected by podcasting, where it is now possible to download broadcasts via a computer and hence to transfer the recordings to an MP3 player such as an iPod.

Dramatization and documentary rights

These cover the right to perform the work in dramatized form on stage, radio, television or film. The range of rights required by licensees is also being extended to include podcasting and the downloading of audio and video content to platforms such as mobile phones, iPods and other MP3 players.

Reprographic and electronic reproduction rights

These include the right to reproduce the work on a medium such as microfilm or microfiche, by photocopying or by electronic means for electronic access and retrieval. Activities such as document delivery and the use of extracts from copyright works may be undertaken either in print-on-paper form or electronically, either by direct licence from the copyright owner or via a reproduction rights organization (RRO) such as the UK Copyright Licensing Agency (CLA).

Electronic publishing and multimedia rights

These include exploitation of a work either verbatim or with the addition of enhanced content through a variety of storage and retrieval systems of a digital, optical or magnetic nature, fixed offline electronic media such as CD-ROMs or cards for use with hand-held devices such as PDAs, or the online provision of content in full or in part to a variety of platforms over the internet or via satellite and other telecommunication systems.

The area of e-books has developed significantly in the last fifteen years. A distinction needs to be made between a dedicated offline product (e.g. a dictionary or encyclopaedia in CD-ROM form) and the downloading from a website of the verbatim text of a book on to a laptop, PDA, dedicated reading device or mobile phone, which is likely to be regarded as a primary publication right rather than a sublicensed subsidiary right. There is also the question of electronic rights granted to companies such as Google or Amazon (see Chapter 23) who may wish to undertake the digitization of entire books, but to make only brief sections available to users via their search facilities, or to actively sell content in whole or in part to users.

Merchandising rights

These cover the licensing of copyright characters or designs for reproduction on items such as wallpaper, stationery, ceramics, household goods, clothing or for exploitation in toy or electronic game form. Characters may also be licensed to endorse services such as snacks, fast food and drinks. The concept to be licensed may originate from a book, syndicated cartoon strip, film or television show, or perhaps from a toy which will then generate books where the character is featured. The inclusion of these rights may be a vital element in a film or television deal.

Publisher's right

This right has increasingly been introduced in the domestic laws of individual countries with varying duration (in the United Kingdom, twenty-five years from first publication). This is a separate right in the typographical design and layout of a work, which has an innate value quite distinct from the copyright content of the work. Thus, if a licensee wishes to reproduce the original typographical layout of the work and this is still protected by copyright, the original publisher may charge a separate fee for this use, which is not shared with the author since it represents a contribution towards the design and typesetting costs incurred when the work was first published.

Public Lending Right: an author's right

The right of an author to receive remuneration for the loan of his or her work from public libraries is personal to the author, with the publisher receiving no share from this revenue. The scheme was introduced in the United Kingdom in 1979 after considerable lobbying from authors (www. plr.uk.com). Authors must register their works for inclusion in the scheme. Loan records are compiled each year from a selection of public libraries, and grossed up to arrive at statistics for an annual payout. At the time of writing, the government-allocated Central Fund from which payments are made is £6.8 million, a reduction from previous years; the rate per loan in 2009 was maintained at 5.98 pence. The maximum annual payment to any one author is currently £6,600. The top-earning authors are understandably authors of popular fiction for adults and children; in the period 2008–9 the most-borrowed authors were James Patterson, Jacqueline Wilson, Daisy Meadows, Nora Roberts, Josephine Cox, Danielle Steel, and Francesca Simon; the list also includes Janet and Allan Ahlberg, Ian Rankin, Enid Blyton, Roald Dahl, Alexander McCall Smith, and Agatha Christie.

In August 2009 the Digital Britain report from the UK Department for Culture, Media and Sport (DCMS) suggested an extension to Public Lending Right to include non-print items such as e-books and audiobooks. The initiative has been supported by the Society of Authors, but was contested by the UK Publishers Association on the grounds that the extension could lead to unauthorized copying at a time when these new versions are still in their infancy and the subject of considerable investment from publishers.

Chapter 4

The rationale behind rights sales

It might be assumed that if a range of different rights has been granted to an agent or publishing house to handle, those rights should be exploited as widely and as promptly as possible. In most situations, this is indeed the case; however, the rights seller should always bear in mind that licensing is only one aspect of the overall promotion of the book and its profitability for the parties concerned; any rights strategy should be carefully planned and coordinated with other sales and marketing activities to maximize the benefits for both author and publisher.

The role of rights in the publishing process

The importance of rights in the overall book publishing process will vary according to the type of book in question. In the case of most educational, academic and professional works, the books are not conceived with the sale of rights in mind. They are designed to fulfil a need in the English-speaking market, and in the case of textbooks they are designed primarily for the curriculum in the country of origin. In the United Kingdom many academic publishers also rely heavily on sales of tertiary-level books to Commonwealth countries, and to European countries where the ability to speak English is high. In some subject areas they may also seek to compete with American publishers in the US market, although if they have no American subsidiary or regular distributor it may be necessary to license American rights.

Books at primary and secondary school level are more likely to require modifications if they are to be used in English outside the United Kingdom, in order to tailor them to the local curriculum. If the British publisher has overseas subsidiaries with a publishing function, they may be prepared to adapt major projects in this way, or the British publisher may seek a local licensee who is prepared to undertake the adaptation work. More commonly, American or Australian school publishers develop their own textbooks with local authors who are familiar with the local curriculum. This is often also the case with foreign-language publishers, although some may be prepared to undertake adaptation work if they feel that the basic concept of a textbook or course is something which they cannot acquire locally.

For school books, the sale of rights is usually an extra; it is rarely crucial to the decision on whether to commission the work in the first place. Extra revenue from rights is nevertheless welcome, and authors are usually delighted to know that their books are being used more widely. In some cases, the sale of rights may be the only way to access a particular market, particularly in translation. The revenue may, however, be very modest. Illustrated reference books for school libraries may have wider potential.

In trade publishing, the overall importance of rights may be very different. Initial investment in a project may be substantial, either because the advance payment required to secure the rights is high, or because the book has a high investment element in terms of picture research, the commissioning of artwork and photographs and colour origination costs. In either case the prospects for rights sales may be a crucial element in deciding whether the project will be viable. In order to defray the initial outlay, it may be necessary to set up arrangements for an American deal, a book club deal, serial rights and foreign-language rights, and a publisher's rights department may be called on to quantify the revenue that will be generated from such licences in advance of any firm commitment to the project. This information may then be a major element in a competitive bid for a project that is being auctioned by an author's agent or by an overseas publisher. However, much will depend on the bundle of rights that is on offer; there is an increasing tendency for authors' agents to restrict the package both in terms of geographical territory and the range of rights granted.

If production costs are high, the viability of the book may depend on coordinating a large coprinting for a range of partners in order to reduce the unit production cost of the book; if these deals do not then materialize, the overall profitability of the book may suffer. In such cases, the sale of rights is crucial, although in some cases not all the deals will be coordinated with the first printing and much will depend on whether exchange rates allow the licensor to quote acceptable prices to licensees. It may be that the initial coprinting will consist of copies for the original publisher, an American publisher and a book club, while foreign-language coeditions may be undertaken as a separate printing. These aspects will be covered in more detail in later chapters.

In recent years, it has become apparent that an active and successful rights operation, working in harmony with company strategy, can contribute very significantly to the overall profitability of a company, especially in the trade publishing sector. In particular, the retained profit from deals which do not involve manufacturing costs will go straight to the bottom accounting line, although the cost of manning a rights operation (including staffing, travel, promotion costs and investment in a computer-ized record system) must also be taken into account. Rights income should never be compared directly with sales turnover; the correct comparison is retained profit from rights deals against the profit element of direct sales. Oddly, the United Kingdom has never had complete industry figures for the number and value of publishing rights sales; in 2004 the UK Publishers Association backed an initiative to collate more accurate data from publishers and agents and the Department of Trade and Industry funded an initial pilot scheme. The scheme has been extended but the figures submitted have been far from complete.

The exact financial status of a rights department may vary from publisher to publisher; some may be run as profit centres, others may report to a specific editorial division or imprint. Some are run as group service departments whose revenue is allocated as 'other trading income' to the editorial division or imprint which generated the book in question, and whose overhead costs are then shared by those client editorial operations.

To sell or not to sell

There are, however, occasions when it is advisable in the overall interests of both the author and the publishing house not to sell certain categories of rights, or at least not to sell them without giving very careful thought to the implications of the sale.

At a basic level, the question arises when an author, or an agent acting on behalf of an author, first seeks a publishing house for the book in the original language. In the case of the English language, we are fortunate to have two major markets: on the one hand, the United Kingdom and its long-established export market to the Commonwealth; on the other, the United States, with a domestic population five times greater than that of the United Kingdom. Some categories of book may not be suitable for both markets; school books rarely cross the Atlantic, except with considerable modifications, while other titles are restricted in terms of their topic, scope or coverage, or even by the style of writing and visual design. For a book that does have potential in both markets, the immediate question for an author or agent is whether to grant world English-language rights to a single publisher on one side of the Atlantic, on the understanding that they will have access to the market on the other side through a parent or subsidiary company, local distributor or through the sale of rights; or whether to seek from the beginning to make separate arrangements with publishers on each side of the Atlantic, with agreed exclusive sales territories and some sharing of territories (usually known as the open market). There could also be an argument in some cases for licensing individual English-language markets such as Canada or Australasia separately.

For any author or agent faced with this question, a number of factors must be taken into account before deciding which rights to grant. The market for an academic book may be too small to justify two or more separate English editions, but the market for a trade title may be much larger.

The first task should be to assess the suitability of the publisher or publishers concerned. Many publishers on both sides of the Atlantic are now part of multinational media conglomerates, and as a result they already have facilities for selling the book in both markets without resorting to sublicensing to an outside house. To offer such a publishing house only its traditional domestic market may be a major disincentive for it to take the book on. Even if the associate company on the other side of the Atlantic is not appropriate for the book in question, many publishers have long-standing links through licensing with appropriate partners, and the same may apply to publishers who have no associate transatlantic companies. It is therefore essential when placing a book for the first time to establish how the book would be marketed outside the domestic market before a decision is taken on whether to place the book separately in other markets.

In the past, the right to sublicense paperback rights was included in the package of rights granted to the original hardback publisher. A more likely scenario now is for a publisher to bid to acquire hardback and paperback rights, and for the paperback edition to be published by a paperback imprint within the same publishing group ('vertical publishing'). If no such facility exists, a hardback publisher may choose to bid for a property in tandem with a paperback house.

It is crucial for an author or agent, when approaching a publishing house for the first time, to make a realistic assessment of whether the publisher has the experience and resources to handle rights such as US rights, paperback rights, serial rights, translation rights and other key rights, or whether they are best withheld and sold separately. Agents may wish to hold back first serial and translation rights, which they often place through a network of subagents overseas; they may also wish to hold back rights such as film, television and merchandising rights if the agency has special expertise in those areas.

It should, however, be remembered that the total package of rights offered to a hardback publishing house will certainly affect its decision on whether to take the work on at all. A publisher with an established and active rights department will normally seek to acquire as wide a range of rights as possible, and to withhold key areas may result in a negative decision.

The control of different rights in the same book by different parties requires careful consideration, as problems can arise if plans are not carefully coordinated, for example if there are separate British and American editions with both publishers having access to open market territories.

If serial rights are retained by the author's agent rather than by the original hardback publisher, the question of timing must be discussed so that the schedule for prepublication extracts provides maximum publicity value for the book. It is also vital to ensure that any sale of US serial rights does not prejudice timing and any confidentiality requirements for a UK deal. The sale of translation rights also requires careful thought on timing. The release of a Dutch translation very soon after publication of the original English-language hardback edition, for example, could have a detrimental effect on sales of an early export edition of the UK paperback edition in the open market. On the reverse side of the coin, Dutch trade publishers may be reluctant to pay substantial sums for translation rights if an early English export edition is to appear in their market, where there is a high ability to read English.

Many educational and academic authors approaching publishing houses direct will have neither the time nor the experience to handle rights negotiations. In such cases it is common for authors to grant the full range of rights to the publisher. Rights staff in such houses should be aware of some situations where it is dangerous to sell rights without full consultation with direct sales colleagues. The thoughtless sale of translation rights in an undergraduate textbook in a key subject area in Scandinavia or the Netherlands could well destroy hard-won adoptions of the English-language edition in universities and colleges in those markets. The same could apply to the licensing of, say, a Hindi edition of a major medical textbook in India, traditionally an excellent export market for British academic publishers (although pricing concerns may now make it advisable to supply special low-price student editions or to license low-price reprint rights to a reliable partner there). Copy for copy, the original publisher will always receive a higher return from the sale of the original English-language edition (the price of the book less export discount) than from the sale of a licensed edition (the publisher's retained share of the royalty). An overall decision may depend on whether the licensed edition will sell in substantially higher quantities. There is therefore a real need to think through the implications of licensing translation rights in countries where the ability to read English is high, and a particular need for care if translation rights are not within the control of the publishing house.

The other key area requiring extreme caution is that of requests from developing and emerging countries to produce low-price English-language reprint editions in their markets, particularly of English-language teaching materials and major academic textbooks. It is vital not to grant such licences automatically without careful discussion of the sales implications. There may well be better ways to service the very real need for cheap books in these markets, through subsidized schemes if these are available or special low-price editions produced by the original publisher. This complex area is covered in more detail in Chapter 12.

Intercompany licences

It is important to remember that the consolidation of much of the publishing industry in the United Kingdom, the United States and Europe into large multinational groups inevitably impacts on the rights market. If a publishing group controls world rights in a book in all languages, it may choose not to grant licences to external partners, but instead to publish the book itself in a variety of forms and languages through its own constituent companies. While English has increasingly become the *lingua franca*, particularly in academic publishing, the need for editions in local languages has not yet disappeared. From the 1990s onwards, a number of British academic publishers commenced foreign-language publishing activities in Europe, either through the acquisition of existing companies or by establishing subsidiaries, paths pioneered by the larger American publishing houses such as McGraw-Hill, Harcourt, John Wiley and Prentice Hall. However, few houses have either the inclination or the capacity to publish translations of all their titles; the tendency is to concentrate on key texts in designated subject areas, which inevitably has some impact on relations with independent licensees. Few trade houses have embarked on this policy, although further afield Penguin embarked on a small Hindi publishing programme in India in 2005.

The financial policy on such licensing varies from company to company. In some cases, subsidiaries pay commercial rates as if they were independent licensees; in other cases, rights are transferred on preferential terms, often as a means of building up the list of a newly established subsidiary. If the latter course is to be followed, it is wise to consider the implications for the author and perhaps take a policy decision on special rates of payment to authors for 'internal' licences.

A number of European publishing groups have followed the reverse path to markets outside their own language areas. Most of the leading scientific and legal publishers in Germany and the Netherlands have published extensively in English for many years and have established branches in both the United Kingdom and the United States. Publishing groups such as Bertelsmann and Holtzbrinck have acquired companies or set up subsidiaries on both sides of the Atlantic. All these developments impact on rights possibilities.

Chapter 5

Selling rights
Who and how?

Who should handle rights?

The ideal answer is specialist staff, whether they are employed by a literary agency or within a publishing house. As outlined earlier, the importance of selling rights has increased greatly since the 1960s, although their importance has also inevitably been affected by such developments as vertical hardback–paperback publishing, multilingual publishing within the same publishing group, and increasing restrictions on the range of rights granted to publishers by agents, particularly in the trade sector.

The employees of a literary agency are by definition specialist staff. Their individual areas of responsibility may be divided by function (for example translation rights, film rights) or by author. Within a medium-sized to large publishing house, a specialist rights department is advisable, even if it starts as a single person with a computer and a simple record-keeping system. The optimum size of a rights department will depend on the size of the list and the range of possible rights to be sold, as well as the perceived importance of the rights function to the company. In a very small or very new publishing house, it may well be impossible to devote the entire time of even one member of staff to the rights function, and in such cases rights deals may have to be handled on an *ad hoc* basis by staff whose role is primarily in editorial, promotion, sales or perhaps production work. However, as the scale of rights business expands, it will be important to dedicate more time and resources to proactive work in this area. Whoever handles the rights, it is important for them to have access to key contractual information on what rights are available to handle, and also whether rights sales may be complicated by the fact that the work includes third party copyright material for which permission may be limited to the original edition and would have to be recleared for onward licences; this information can be complex and is normally held in the location of first publication of the book concerned; it may have some bearing on whether it is wise to depute overseas staff (e.g. sales staff in the local office of a multinational) to have responsibility for offering rights in their territory without detailed background knowledge on the rights status of each title.

What skills are required?

The skills are many and varied, and often difficult to find in a single individual!

1 Both intuitive and informed judgement on the saleability of a project in a variety of forms and markets are very important. This can be a particularly critical skill in trade publishing, where rights deals are a major part of the publishing process and where the views of rights staff may be a key element in shaping the content and design of a project. An ability to adapt to new circumstances is essential, particularly as new media and new markets offer additional licensing possibilities.

2 A detailed knowledge of the range of projects that are to be handled enables the requirements of a wide range of individual customers to be met – the larger the list, the greater the need to home in quickly and accurately on suitable titles.

3 The ability to develop detailed and up-to-date knowledge of key licensing markets. This may involve regular reading of appropriate publications on the economic and political circumstances of particular markets, meeting licensees from those markets either on their home territory or at international book fairs, and updating one's knowledge of developments in new media.

4 A real flair and enthusiasm for the sales process is essential, although selling techniques will inevitably vary, depending on the nature of the product, the target market and the personalities of both seller and buyer. The same rights manager will probably have to operate quite differently when dealing with an American publisher and a Chinese publisher; strong and appropriate negotiating skills are essential.

5 Although not all areas of rights require linguistic skills, those rights staff working in appropriate areas should be able to speak some foreign languages (including American English) at least to the extent of using appropriate publishing terminology!

6 An ability to deal effectively with a variety of authors and agents as well as a wide range of staff at all levels within one's own publishing house – from a chief executive to a shipping clerk. This requires excellent communication skills.

7 A good knowledge of both editorial and production processes is important; the latter is particularly vital when dealing with coedition projects.

8 Sound numeracy skills are essential; financial calculations may often have to be undertaken in busy or stressful situations.

9 Rights staff must be able to conduct a wide range of negotiations simultaneously, each at a different stage, without losing control. Prioritizing workload is vital.

10 An ability to form a clear overview of a project in order to dovetail rights deals without conflict between the interests of different licensees and without negatively affecting direct sales of the original edition.

11 An ability to tie up all aspects of a deal with a watertight contract is essential; a genuine enjoyment of detailed contractual work is rare.

12 Also vital are an excellent memory, a good head for detail and an ability to organize systems (and junior staff, if these are available); these enable staff to cope effectively with a complex workload, some of which will inevitably consist of routine and boring procedures.

13 As with most office jobs, keyboard skills and an ability to deal with databases are now essential for rights staff.

14 Rights work usually involves seasonal pressure, with the majority of book fairs concentrated in the spring and autumn each year. Considerable patience, diplomacy, physical and mental stamina, and adaptability will allow the same rights person to move from the comparatively leisurely pace and gastronomic delights of Bologna in March to the less than perfect physical conditions of Moscow or Beijing in September, closely followed by the rigours of Frankfurt in October. The working conditions may vary but the role of the rights person is the same – to achieve rights sales on the best possible terms to appropriate partners.

15 It is important to be able to report effectively on rights activities: to authors, authors' agents and internally within the publishing house to relevant staff and management.

The combination of such qualities – the outgoing side required for selling, the eye for detail required for contractual work and the organization necessary to keep a rights operation going – is rare, and the pool of publishing staff specializing in rights work is relatively small; in the United Kingdom, and to some extent in the United States, the field is still largely dominated by women. This is less the case in literary agency work.

Training

Training is usually acquired 'on the job', although an increasing number of professional publishing courses at colleges in the United Kingdom (in particular Stirling and Napier universities in Scotland, Oxford Brookes University, Anglia Ruskin University, Kingston University, City University in London, the London College of Communication and University College London) now include a rights element, usually taught by bringing in rights specialists from outside. The UK publishing industry runs a large number of training courses for its members through the Publishing Training Centre at Book House in London (45 East Hill, London SW18 2QZ; tel. 0208 874 2718; www.train4publishing.co.uk). Courses specifically designed for editorial, marketing and direct sales staff sometimes include a brief rights component so that the role can be understood in relation to other publishing functions. The Centre also runs a regular three-day course on Selling Rights two or three times a year, with tutors drawn from rights departments, rights consultancies and literary agencies. The majority of delegates come from UK publishing houses, but overseas delegates are also welcome. The Centre also offers a one-day course on Publishing Contracts, which is very relevant to rights staff; a two-day course entitled 'Staying within the Law', which provides a basic introduction to copyright, key points of UK and EU legislation and some coverage of rights and permissions; a one-day course on 'Permissions for Profit', and a one-day course on 'Digital Licensing Agreements', covering both the acquisition and outward licensing of rights.

Publishing Scotland (137 Dundee Street, Edinburgh EH11 1BG; tel. 0131 228 6866; www.publishingscotland.org) also runs occasional courses on copyright, contracts and licensing.

There are no formal qualifications available for rights staff since the demise of the National Vocational Qualification (NVQ).

A number of courses on copyright and licensing have been run for overseas publishers (in particular in the People's Republic of China, the countries of central and eastern Europe and more recently the Arab world) under the sponsorship of organizations such as the British Council, the Soros Foundation, the organizers of the Frankfurt and London Book fairs and the International Publishers Association; some have been accompanied by handbooks in the local language. The courses are tailored to meet local needs and are run in the countries concerned.

Chapter 6

Tackling the task

Essentials

Basic record keeping

No matter how small a rights department may be initially, the mainstay of any such operation must be a centralized system on which to record the exact status of each project and where it is being offered.

It may well be possible for a person handling a very small list to have in their head the details of where each project is on offer or sold, but this will be of little use if they are away from the office or fall ill before a major book fair.

Types of record system vary, but the basic aim should be the same: to provide quick access to a summary of what is happening on each title in each market (including any restrictions on the rights which may be sold, either territorially, by a limited period of time or by category of rights). It should also provide a summary of all the titles sold or on offer to each rights customer – in effect, a profile of that customer's areas of interest and buying pattern. The record system may also give details of the percentage of each category of rights income to be paid to the author, either direct or via an agent.

If the records are to be kept on a manual system of record cards, this will involve a double-entry system for data; thus, if a book is submitted to a Danish publisher for consideration for translation, the details of that submission will have to be entered on the record card relating to that title, and on the record card relating to the Danish customer. The title record is essential to provide a concise overview of activities on that book – vital if the author should telephone and ask for a progress report, or enquire about activities on rights in a particular market. The customer profile is invaluable when preparing to meet that customer face to face.

Most literary agents and publishers have introduced computerized record systems of rights transactions, and these have revolutionized the maintenance and retrieval of data. If linked to a collection of basic letters on file with a mailmerge facility, such a system can transform routine procedures such as sending out proofs, reading copies or electronic files for consideration, chasing for decisions, following up on overdue contracts and payments, and identifying licences that are due to expire.

A rights database could consist of a simple spreadsheet system produced in-house, but there are a number of specialist systems available, with varying degrees of sophistication in terms of reporting options and bolt-on facilities. In the United Kingdom, a reasonably priced rights record system package is available from Bradbury Phillips International Ltd (www.bradburyphillips.co.uk); this is perhaps more suited to a small to medium-sized publishing house or agency than to a large academic house. Additional packages are available for royalty accounting and permissions management. An alternative system – which can deal with rights acquisitions as well as sales – is That's Rights! (www.thatsrights.com); this also offers facilities for royalties management. There is also the Brighteye International Rights Database (www.brighteye.ltd.com), which covers the promotion and sales processes, including both coedition and licensing deals. A number of companies producing publishing software solutions include rights as part of their facilities. Focus on Publishing Software offers an integrated publishing and accounting system which includes a rights management module (www.focusservices.co.uk), as does VISTA, whilst the SAP All-in-One Publishers Portfolio (www.ciber-uk.com/media/publishing) includes SAP IPM (Intellectual Property Management). At the time of writing Onix is planning to launch a rights module (www.booksonix.com).

A more expensive alternative covering a broader span of publishing requirements and connecting related in-house departments might be the Klopotek CR & R (Contracts, Rights and Royalties) system, which offers an integrated package covering contract production (head contracts and licences, with a range of templates held on file which can be customized), rights management and royalty administration for both the original editions and licence arrangements (www.klopotek.com).

Some of the larger houses have either developed their own computerized systems in-house or have used outside consultants to develop a specially designed system, usually an independent network with a workstation for each member of the department; such systems can also be linked to the main company system for access to up-to-date information on publishing programmes and schedules, publicity material, costings, stock levels and so on.

A well-designed computerized system has a considerable advantage over a manual system in that data on each procedure need be entered only once, and can then be retrieved either by title or by customer. Reports can be run to show negotiations at key stages to facilitate chasing procedures, e.g. for decisions on options or submissions, agreement on suggested financial terms, the return of contracts, and the remittance of key payments such as an advance or lump sum on which the validity of the contract depends.

The more elaborate systems can provide detailed customer profiles for use at book fairs and other meetings; information can include the names and list the responsibilities of key contacts, brief details of deals already finalized, listings of titles on offer or under negotiation, and details of titles where the customer's interest has been logged for books not yet published or on offer elsewhere. Complex systems can also provide analyses of rights sold by licence type, time period, language, territory, readership level and subject classification. Standard letters (e.g. submissions, option reminders, etc.) can be run and mailmerged with the customer address base. The question of whether a rights database should also contain full financial information on rights transactions will depend on whether accounting records are to be maintained in the rights department itself (common in smaller companies); in a larger company it may be preferable to design the rights system to link up with the database of the section of the royalties department administering licence revenue. Such a link (on a read-only basis) enables rights staff to check whether expected income has been received, and can also assist royalties staff to allocate revenue which may have come in from a licensee without sufficient identification data.

If the system can run on a laptop, it can easily be transported to book fairs or on sales trips, although the mobility of a system requiring simultaneous access and facilities for on-the-spot data entry by several rights staff at a book fair may be more complex.

It is difficult to provide precise guidelines for setting up a computerized rights database, since the exact requirements may vary considerably according to the needs of the rights department or literary agency. For example, a system for publishers who normally have full control of all rights in their publications will not require a facility for listing out the ownership of each individual rights category, whereas a publisher or literary agent who is authorized to handle only a limited range of rights may well need this facility. Those publishers who operate almost entirely on an option basis (i.e. the majority of educational and academic publishers) may find a 'queueing' facility useful, so that when a number of publishers are interested in acquiring rights in a particular language, the optimum option sequence can be listed and adjusted automatically if the first publisher in line declines the book. Reporting requirements may vary considerably; large publishers may need to report by imprint, by editorial division or perhaps by series or subject category (e.g. the rights status of all computer titles in a particular market).

The exact needs of the rights operation will have to be taken into account and discussed in great detail with whoever is responsible for designing the system. It is also likely that a number of problems will only emerge during the process of loading real data and testing whether retrieval can be achieved in the required form; provision for this (both in terms of time and cost) should be built into any computerization project.

A word of warning: once a rights system has been computerized, the whole operation will depend on both hardware and software functioning properly at all times. Malfunction of either can result in paralysis of the rights function, with very little possibility of retrieving data for a large list by manual methods for, say, a book fair or sales trip. Data should be backed up at the end of each working day. The likely life of hardware should be taken into account when budgeting for purchasing or leasing, and a full maintenance service for both hardware and software will be crucial. Client publishers should also consider whether they wish the database to be downloadable on to laptops for use by one or more staff at book fairs or on sales trips (see Chapter 8).

Some thought should also be given to upgrading the system to provide more capacity, allow for new reporting requirements, and take into account new operating systems and software as soon as these become available. A decision should also be taken on whether this can be done only by the external provider (with the attendant cost implications) or by the client company itself. Most rights systems are now Windows-based.

Staffing

In a small company, the rights operation may consist of only one person, perhaps not working on rights full time, who may also be responsible for their own keyboarding and clerical work. At the next stage, it might consist of two people, one to undertake the rights selling, and an assistant who may have a partly secretarial or clerical role but who may also handle routine tasks such as sending out reading copies and maintaining record systems. For a larger staff it will be necessary to decide on the best division of labour.

Some rights departments and agencies choose to divide the selling by geographical area, giving each person a designated sales territory. This can work well when there are strong linguists in the department, since they can then operate in areas where their language skills are appropriate. It is also a method commonly used by publishers who specialize in the coproduction of editions of illustrated books for overseas publishers, since such customers usually merit regular sales visits outside the major international book fairs. This method of organization has the advantage that the staff concerned come to know their own markets very well. A disadvantage may be that all the staff have to be familiar with the entire list, and that no one person has an immediate overview of the rights situation on a particular book worldwide.

Another method of dividing the workload is by function, with one member of staff specializing in translation rights, another in book club rights, another in serial rights, and so on. This approach can obviously be justified only if the list handled has adequate work in each area to justify the full time of each person.

Yet another method, particularly in operations where the list is very large, divides the workload by subject category, level or perhaps by imprint in the case of publishing groups where each imprint has a distinct identity. This has the advantage that staff are not required to operate across a huge list without adequate time to get to know a broad range of different types of customer well. They can concentrate on particular areas of the list in detail, but handle the rights in those titles worldwide and thus have an overview of each title without having to consult colleagues.

A further scenario, used by some multinationals, is to have rights units located in each key geographical area, e.g. the United States, Canada and Latin America; Europe; the Middle East and Africa; and Asia, with each rights operation handling product originating from the group worldwide but only dealing with licensees within their designated geographical territory. This has the advantage of local market knowledge but perhaps less detailed knowledge of product originating elsewhere within the group and any attendant contractual or permissions problems which might affect licensing.

All these methods have both advantages and disadvantages; as a rights operation expands, it is wise to review the structure and division of the workload regularly to achieve maximum efficiency. It is generally preferable for rights to be handled by staff operating in the publishing location from which the book originates as all the necessary information is readily to hand and authors can be given a speedy overview of licensing activities on their books.

The sales function

The sale of rights is usually carried out through a mixture of what might be termed active and passive selling; the proportion of active to passive selling will vary according to the staff resources available, the importance of rights to the publishing operation, the nature of the list and the range of rights available to be sold. The majority of licences will result from active selling, and this reinforces the need for allocating adequate staff and time to the function.

Passive selling

Some rights activities are by their nature passive, for example anthology and quotation rights (Chapter 17) and rights for the reading impaired (Chapter 18). In addition, some rights business may be generated without specific effort by the staff, through the status of the author or of the publishing house itself (university presses are the most obvious example of this). A considerable amount of rights business is also generated by what might be called the grapeshot technique of mailing catalogues, rather than undertaking specific activities on behalf of a particular project. In recent years, many publishing houses have also made their complete catalogues available on their company websites; if information is added on how to contact rights staff, this can prove a very valuable additional promotion tool for both new titles and backlist. Some publishers also produce selective rights guides of key new titles, either seasonally or for specific book fairs or sales trips, and these lists may also be made available on the company website or on a dedicated rights website.

Active selling

This may start with a variety of activities to acquire market awareness.

1 General market research on:

    (a) economic/political/financial status of individual markets

    (b) tastes in reading in different markets

    (c) differences in educational curricula in different markets

    (d) sociopolitical and cultural differences that may affect saleability in different markets

    (e) gaps in the market

    (f) the pace of new technology development in different markets and how this may provide licensing opportunities

2 Specific market research on:

    (a) individual publishing houses and their specialisms, local status and track record

    (b) individual decision-makers and their tastes

    (c) the purchasing power of possible licensees

    (d) their reliability in terms of production quality, translation quality if relevant, ability to hold to publication schedules, marketing abilities and payment record – as a general rule, new customers should be asked to provide references from other publishers with whom they have dealt and/or their bank

    (e) their ability to exploit any additional rights requested, e.g. electronic as well as print rights.

The sources for this information will vary according to the type of licence for which research is being undertaken, but they will include reference directories such as _Literary Marketplace_ (listing publishers, book clubs and literary agents in the USA and Canada) and _International Literary Marketplace_ (similar listings for the rest of the world). Both are published annually by Information Today and are available as print volumes (2010 prices US$309 and US$259 respectively, plus shipping) and online (subscriptions currently range from US$399 per year for access by one user to US$1,381 per year for access by ten users). Print and online packages are also available (contact custserv@infotoday.com). Other sources include national book trade directories such as the annual *Directory of Publishing*, covering the publishers in the United Kingdom and Ireland, published by the Continuum International Publishing Group (2010 price £100); the trade press in the United Kingdom, such as *The Bookseller* and the daily online news service, *BookBrunch*, and in major markets abroad (e.g. *Publishers Weekly* in the United States and the *Börsenblatt* in Germany); the general press both in the United Kingdom and abroad; specialist publications where relevant; the catalogues of potential licensees; attendance at book fairs both in the United Kingdom and overseas; the catalogues of those book fairs; and any databases listing individual exhibitors such as the *Who's Who* available for Frankfurt and Bologna (originally available as print publications, but now available online to registered exhibitors). Two annual publications, the *Writers' and Artists' Yearbook* (A. & C. Black) and *The Writer's Handbook* (Macmillan Reference Publications), provide listings of national and regional newspapers and magazines (useful in connection with serial rights) and of film and television production companies.

The aim of rights staff must be to build up a relevant corpus of knowledge that will assist them to target potential licensees quickly and accurately.

Assessing the project

Against this general background of the market, the rights seller will then have to make an assessment of each project to be placed; the factors involved will vary according to the type of rights in question. These will probably include:

1 The range of rights available to be sold; this will necessitate checking the head contract with the author in the case of a project already commissioned, or ascertaining which rights are likely to be granted in the case of a project still under consideration.

2 The optimum combination of rights to be sold; the interests of some potential licensees may conflict (e.g. book club and paperback publishers on occasion) and this should be taken into account when planning a rights campaign. Will the sale of some rights conflict with sales of the original publisher's edition in the United Kingdom or overseas?

3 The status of the author or authors in the domestic market, in the English-speaking market and elsewhere.

4 Is the content of the book suitable for other markets? Could it be modified if necessary to make it more suitable for a particular market, by either the author, the original publisher or the licensee?

5 The presentation of the book – length, format, design, number and types of illustration, binding, production quality and price – plus any technical problems that might affect its production, either by or on behalf of the licensee (for example English lettering directly on illustrations, which may pose problems if the book is to be translated).

6 The timing of the original edition in relation to the requirements of any licensees; will advance sales material be ready at an appropriate point in the year, in time for key book fairs or sales trips, for example? If the original publisher is to coprint copies for partners such as book clubs or overseas licensees, will those copies be ready on time to meet required delivery dates? This is particularly important in the case of books that have a seasonal market, such as a major trade book for the Christmas gift market or an academic textbook which must be available in good time for the start of a new academic year.

7 In the case of coeditions, can the books or sheets be manufactured and supplied at a price appropriate to the market in question, and can protection be built into the deals to guard against any fluctuation in exchange rates during the course of the deal?

Timing

When the project has been assessed, a marketing plan should be devised for each project with rights potential, but the timing and exact nature of such a plan will vary considerably according to the rights available for placement, the type of book and its potential for licensing. For example, an academic book that will be distributed in all English-language markets worldwide by the original publishing house may have few rights possibilities other than the sale of translation rights. As such a book may not be heavily illustrated in colour, it follows that there is little potential for coprinting the foreign editions.

This may well mean that foreign publishers will want to make their assessment of the book on the basis of finished copies, or perhaps at page proof stage. On the whole, it has been rare for such books to be assessed at manuscript stage, but nowadays it is possible to send PDF files of the manuscript as e-mail attachments; it is preferable to wait until these are in final form. However, careful thought should be given to whether these should be sent to untried customers in markets where piracy may be rife. The provision of advance material for assessment must be costed against the likely revenue that may be generated by the sale of rights; in the past it would have been uneconomic to order ten extra sets of page proofs for an academic monograph, but the provision of electronic files is a fast and cheap alternative method of supplying material ahead of publication. However, it is often the case that translation rights for such a book may be finalized in the months following publication of the original edition, unless the content of the book justifies simultaneous publication.

On the other hand, the sale of rights in a new novel by a major author with an international reputation will involve extensive planning by rights staff, often in advance of final acquisition of the book from the author's agent. A detailed rights plan with an assessment of the revenue that will be generated from rights sales such as book club, paperback and translation deals (and US and serial rights if these form part of the package on offer) may well play a crucial part in a competitive bid for a book at auction. For such titles, deals may be lined up well before the completion of the writing process.

A handsome full-colour book on a topic such as art, gardening or cookery may involve substantial origination costs and may necessitate multiple coedition deals in order to offset that investment. Permissions will have to be secured and paid for to enable any illustrations belonging to outside copyright holders to be reproduced in licensed editions. Early visual and textual material will have to be shown to potential partners in order to assess the scale of interest and hence the viability of the project; despite the availability of electronic files, potential buyers often still prefer to see this material in tangible form. Commitments on coedition sales are needed at the earliest possible stage of production to avoid aborting the project after a substantial investment has been made.

Specific rights promotion methods are covered in more detail in Chapter 7.

Option, multiple submission or auction?

Linked to the question of timing is the method of submission, and here much will depend on the type of book, the status of the author, the topicality of the subject, the potential market for the book and the type of rights that are to be placed.

On the academic and educational side, it is a tradition to grant potential buyers options, and this method is still extensively used, especially when placing translation rights. An option is an exclusive period of time during which a potential licensee can assess a project; the period of the option may vary, but for academic titles it is likely to be three months. The justification for this system is that time will be required to obtain one or more academic reports on the project from specialists in the field, to research whether there is a need for the book in the market, whether any adaptations are needed and to identify a suitable specialist translator. To submit the same book simultaneously to several different publishers would necessitate each of them spending time and money on seeking academic advice (perhaps from the same specialists) and in undertaking research, with no guarantee of obtaining the rights at the end of these procedures.

Attempts to dispense with the option system in this field of publishing have therefore been rather unsuccessful, although it is possible to reduce the option period if there is strong interest from several different publishers seeking rights in the same language. Alternatively, it is possible to grant one publisher an option and to send material on the book to competing publishers, provided that it is made clear to them that they are not at the head of the queue. In the past, since many academic publishers made their assessment on the basis of a finished copy of the book, multiple submission proved very costly if the book in question was expensive. However, the provision of electronic files is now a cheaper alternative.

The golden rule is to make quite clear to potential licensees exactly how the project is being handled. In the case of books with coedition potential, the aim is usually to place rights well in advance of first publication by the original publisher; assessment must be made on the basis of advance material. The option system is therefore likely to be inappropriate, as the pressure of the production schedule requires that decisions must be received from potential licensees by a specific date in order to coordinate orders in time to join the initial print run; there is no time to move down a queue of interested parties. If material is submitted simultaneously to several publishers seeking the same rights, it is vital that each party is aware of this.

The technique of multiple submission is much more commonly used in trade publishing and reflects the wider choice of potential buyers available. Publishers who receive material on a multiple submission basis may be invited to submit 'blind best bids'. This method of selling is more expensive in terms of needing multiple copies of proofs or reading copies; an alternative could be to supply partial or complete electronic files of the work, although this in itself raises questions of security if large numbers of customers are supplied with the complete work in digital form, especially in territories where piracy is rife.

In recent years, the use of the 'auction' in placing rights in major projects has increased considerably. The technique is used particularly in placing major English-language rights such as the sale of US rights by a UK publisher (or vice versa), paperback rights or first serial rights. It is also a technique used for translation rights and by literary agents when placing territorial rights.

The ground rules for an auction may vary from project to project, so it is vital that each participant is fully aware of the conditions under which the auction is being conducted. For example, a major project to be auctioned at Frankfurt might be run on the basis of an outline, manuscript, sample material or simply the news that a major author or personality will be writing a book. Selected publishers are approached, given the information or material, and then briefed on the terms of the auction and the deadline for submission of bids. All aspects of the required offer should be specified in advance: advance payment, royalties and any subsidiary rights to be included in the deal. Further requirements may be introduced, particularly if the book is highly topical or a new book by a bestselling author. These may include a guaranteed level of promotional activity for the book (perhaps including television advertising).

A title with auction potential may be the subject of a pre-emptive bid from one publisher, either prior to the commencement of the auction process or at the initial stage of the auction. If this bid is accepted, the seller is taking a calculated risk that the offer will be higher than any other bids received or anticipated.

The level of bidding in an auction can be dictated in different ways. The seller may indicate in advance a price below which initial bids ('openers') are unlikely to be accepted. Alternatively, a 'floor' may be set, perhaps by the seller but more commonly by one participant, who by so doing will secure 'topping' rights, i.e. the right to better the best final offer by an agreed percentage (ideally 10%, but 5% may be accepted).

Outside the context of book fairs, an auction may be conducted by tele- phone or e-mail. The auction should be prefaced by a 'closing letter' announcing the terms, with a requirement that all bids be submitted on a specified date by a specified time. If the contents of the book in question are sensitive, there may be a requirement for participating publishers to sign a confidentiality agreement. The first round may consist of blind offers, with none of the participants being aware of what other bids are in hand or where they stand in the bidding stakes. In the next round, participants will be informed of the highest bid made and will be required to submit higher offers. If competition is strong, an auction may run through several successive rounds before the result is announced, with a specified bidding sequence (for example, the highest bidder in the first round bidding last in the second round). The final round should take into account any participant with 'topping' rights before the final offer is accepted and full details are confirmed in writing, either by the seller or by the winner of the auction. The unsuccessful participants should then be notified.

The author's preference may be crucial in selecting the winner. If author approval is to be the deciding factor, this should be made clear when setting out the terms of the auction. It is not necessarily the highest financial bid that is the best offer; the decision could well be based on the overall package offered, which would take into account the nature of the winner's list and the overall commitment to this particular project.

It is important to remember that if a floor is set by one publisher and no better offer is received, the floor price must be accepted. There have been several well-publicized cases of projects where no publisher was prepared to offer more than the floor price (in some cases not even that); in other cases, the organizers of the auction have been accused of 'hyping' up the floor price to unreasonable levels. Certainly, sales of some projects auctioned amid much publicity for astronomical sums have subsequently failed to justify the initial outlay. In some cases, large commitments of this kind have contributed to the bankruptcy or subsequent takeover of the purchasing publisher. In other cases, the initial investment has been recouped almost immediately by the selling on of rights such as serial or translation rights. While an auction is perhaps justified in the case of a new book by a well-established author or a book by or about a well-known public figure, it has been increasingly used for books by relatively unknown authors. It is a technique which should be used sparingly and with care if unrealistic spending is to be avoided; a publisher 'bitten' in this way may be more cautious in returning to bid in the next auction, particularly if there is a feeling that the project was oversold.

Negotiating the terms

Returning to less heady deals, once a potential licensee has seen sufficient material to express firm interest in a project, the negotiating process will start. The aim is to reach agreement not only on the financial terms of the deal, but also on other aspects such as the timescale in which both parties will fulfil their obligations, any modifications which the licensee may wish to make for its edition, the duration and territory to be granted, and provisions for procedures in the case of dispute between the parties or termination of the contract; in the case of major projects, there may also be a commitment to a level of promotion spend for the licensed edition. It is important to think through all aspects of the deal as thoroughly as possible at the negotiating stage in order to avoid misunderstandings or confrontation at a later date; a deal that is felt to be unfair by one party is never satisfactory. It is of course difficult to provide definitive rules for negotiating terms, since much will depend on the project in question, the type of licence to be granted, the market required, the bargaining powers of licensor and licensee, and market conditions at the time. Some basic guidelines are provided in later chapters covering specific types of licence.

Tying up the contract

Whether a rights deal is large or small, the contract covering the arrangement is crucial. It is not enough to clinch a spectacular deal at a book fair or over the phone at the end of an auction; each side must feel that the contract reflects fairly their understanding of the arrangement. The deal is not finalized until the contract is signed by both parties. That said, there have been many cases over the years where contracts have been signed with insufficient attention to detail, and shortcomings only became apparent when a dispute arose between the parties. As for previous editions, this book does not attempt to provide sample contracts, since this ground is covered elsewhere in *Clark's Publishing Agreements: A Book of Precedents*, seventh edition, edited by Lynette Owen (Tottel Publishing, 2007, now Bloomsbury Professional); there are also other more specialist publications on areas such as electronic and multimedia licences. Any model contract should, however, be viewed only as a starting point, since each contract should be tailored to suit the individual circumstances of the deal.

In recent years, licensees in some countries have stated that licence contracts must be available in their local language as well as that of the licensor; Russia, Poland and the People's Republic of China are examples, although the policy seems to be somewhat inconsistently applied. Many licensors will be reluctant to sign such contracts without having the translated text checked for accuracy. If the rights seller has substantial business in these countries, it may be worthwhile having a licence template prepared in the language concerned, with the variable aspects of the contract (name of author, title of book, financial terms, publication date) inserted on a supplementary sheet which can be completed in English or numerically.

Liaison with other departments

Publishing rights staff need to be constantly in touch with other departments within the publishing house. These may include the legal or contracts department if this is separate from the rights department; the appropriate editorial department; the production department; direct sales staff; publicity staff; the royalty accounting department; and the warehouse and shipping department. Finalization of a successful rights deal could involve contracts staff if licence contracts are not prepared within the rights department itself; the editorial department for information, and for communication with the author if this is not the direct responsibility of rights staff; the production department if coprinting or the supply of duplicate production material is involved; direct sales staff so that they are alerted to the licensing of a book in their territory; publicity staff for building a dossier on the success of the project; royalty staff, who will need to create a financial record for the licence in order to pass on the author's designated share; and the warehouse and shipping staff if the deal involves the supply of physical goods.

Monitoring the payments

Since one of the main purposes of granting a licence is to generate income, it is vital to ensure that all payments are made promptly and accurately. Responsibility for monitoring rights income may vary from company to company; ensuring that key payments such as advances or lump sums are made will probably fall to rights staff, since the validity of the licence contract will hinge on payment being received within an agreed timescale.

In large companies, subsequent royalty accounting may well be monitored by a separate royalty accounting department, which will maintain an ongoing record of all payments received from each licence, chase overdue payments and pay authors an appropriate share of rights income in accordance with the provisions of each head contract. In a smaller operation, all monitoring and chasing procedures may be carried out by rights staff themselves. If monitoring is carried out by a separate department, it is vital that rights staff are informed of any overdue payments to avoid further deals being contracted with licensees who are not fulfilling their earlier obligations.

Record keeping of this kind may be maintained manually on record cards or on an electronic royalty system, with entries made each time payment is received. For a royalty-based deal, a cumulative record should be maintained of sales of the licensed edition, indicating when royalties on sales justify the initial advance and further payments become due. A basic computerized royalty accounting system is available from Bradbury Phillips (see *Basic record keeping* earlier in this chapter, pp. 68–71) and royalty facilities are also available from other suppliers. Larger publishing companies may have accounting for subsidiary rights income as part of their overall computerized royalty system, and it is always wise to check with the appropriate department what basic details are provided to an author when financial statements are sent out. For example, does an author's statement show only the payment being made, or does it also provide details such as sales figures for licensed editions?

The terms of the head contract will dictate whether the author's share of all rights income is paid out immediately on receipt, held until the normal accounting date or offset against the initial advance paid to the author by the original publisher.

In recent years, there has been an increasing tendency for licensees to require invoices as well as licence contracts in order to remit payment; this may apply not only to advances and lump sums but also to regular ongoing royalty payments. It should never be assumed that because a royalty statement has been submitted payment is on the way. Countries that often require invoices are Italy, the countries of central and eastern Europe, Russia and the People's Republic of China. Some publishers may require the invoices to be stamped and signed by the licensor; any such requirements should be checked with the licensee.

In many cases, the payment remitted by a licensee may be subject to deduction of withholding tax at source. The exact rate of tax depends on the fiscal regulations of the country concerned and on the current status of tax relations between the countries of both parties to the contract. Foreign licensees may ask a UK licensor to complete an exemption form or provide an annual certificate of residence, which will enable the licensee either to remit the full amount, if there is a double taxation exemption treaty in force between the two countries, or to reduce the rate of tax deducted. Queries on tax matters of this kind are the responsibility of the Inland Revenue (Centre for Non-Residents, Fitzroy House, P.O. Box 46, Nottingham NG2 1BD; tel. 0115 974 2000).

UK companies that pay corporation tax should normally be able to offset withholding tax deductions of this kind against corporation tax, provided that adequate supporting documentation is provided by the licensee; authors should therefore be paid their share of subsidiary rights income on the amount due prior to any tax deduction at source. Any publishing operation which has legal status as a charity (this would include the university presses of Oxford and Cambridge) is not liable for corporation tax and therefore cannot reclaim tax deductions on licence income.

Some countries have started to impose other types of tax on royalties remitted abroad. The People's Republic of China imposes a business tax of 5% on all such payments prior to the deduction of a further 10% withholding tax and the business tax cannot be recovered by the licensor. Other countries (for example Russia in 2004) have started to impose VAT on royalties remitted abroad. To avoid deductions being made from the expected amounts, licence contracts should be worded to ensure that advances, royalties and lump sums are remitted net of any VAT due in the country concerned, i.e. the licensee must pay such tax over and above the amounts specified in the contract.

Accounting statements from licensees should be checked for accuracy (e.g. correct calculation, progression to higher royalty rate, etc.) and any apparent anomalies queried promptly. Some may be explained by local regulations (e.g. different tax status between state-owned and private companies in some former socialist countries) or by fluctuations in the rate of exchange at which payments have been calculated if the contract specifies payment in a currency other than sterling; this is particularly common in countries with an unstable currency. It may be helpful to introduce a system to remind licensees in advance of when royalty statements are due and to supply each licensee with a new certificate of residence each January rather than wait for them to request one.

A regular chasing procedure should be set up to pursue overdue payments, and this is of course much easier with the assistance of a computerized system which can be programmed to run regular reports indicating when advance payments, lump sums or regular royalties remain unpaid. If chasing procedures are handled by a separate accounting department, it is common to send two chasing letters on overdue royalties and then refer the matter to rights staff to establish if the licence expired when the licensed edition went out of print or if the licence is still live, with the licensee in breach of the accounting obligations. Rights staff may wish to take steps to confirm formal termination of a licence that has expired, or to threaten termination if payment is overdue.

Internal reporting

In a larger publishing company, rights staff may be required to report regularly on rights deals achieved and on cumulative earnings against annual rights budgets, as well as to track revenue for their own purposes. Reporting is greatly facilitated by a computerized system. A well-designed system should enable reports to be run by imprint or publishing division, by language, by territory, and to produce detailed individual title reports when required. Even if reporting is not a formal requirement, a monthly or quarterly summary of rights sold will prove useful in addition to liaison on individual deals with appropriate editorial, promotion and sales staff.

Chapter 7

Rights selling

A range of methods

The sale of rights involves a number of different techniques, which will vary according to the nature of the product and the required result. Internet facilities and e-mail have greatly facilitated the promotion and sale of rights.

General promotion by mail: catalogues

On the print front, a certain amount of blanket sales information can be sent out in the form of catalogues. Potential licensees must receive regular and appropriate information and also have some sense of the publishing profile of the seller.

Many trade publishing houses produce a single catalogue, either annually or (more commonly) twice yearly to cover new titles to be published during the spring and autumn (fall) seasons; some may also include a brief listing of backlist titles. Publishing groups with a variety of imprints, each with a distinct market identity, may produce individual catalogues for each imprint. Publishers of trade titles, particularly those which are highly illustrated, are likely to produce full-colour catalogues. Educational and academic publishers may produce a large range of individual subject catalogues annually, containing both their backlist and front list titles (the latter flagged as 'NEW'); some may produce seasonal catalogues as well. Many academic catalogues are produced in black and white. Some rights departments may choose to produce selective rights guides featuring key new titles, perhaps produced for individual book fairs or seasonally.

It is crucial to build up a mailing list of appropriate customers, subject-coded where appropriate, which should be updated regularly to reflect any changes of contact name or address or any expansion of subject interest. If the customer is a large publishing house, it may be necessary to send different catalogues to a range of its commissioning editors, according to their specific fields of interest. Some overseas publishers employ scouts in the United Kingdom to identify suitable titles, and these should also be added to mailing lists where appropriate.

In large publishing houses, mailing lists would normally be held on computer as part of a larger overall mailing system, and the actual despatch of catalogues will be handled by a specialist department or perhaps contracted out to a mailing house. In smaller organizations, it may be necessary to maintain the mailing list on computer in the rights department itself, and for the catalogues to be packed and despatched from the department.

If all or most rights for the titles listed in a catalogue or rights guide are controlled by the publishing house, it is usually unnecessary to produce any form of annotation to accompany the mailing, although a covering letter can be inserted encouraging customers to reply to the relevant member of staff.

An alternative is to print details, appropriate contact names, or the name of the department, inside the catalogue itself. If, however, certain or all of the rights in a substantial number of titles contained in a catalogue are controlled by outside parties such as literary agents or another publisher (where, for example, a British publisher has acquired rights from an American or a foreign publisher), it will save considerable time to include a printed rights list with each catalogue, listing the titles in question, the rights situation and the names and addresses to which application should be made, or to annotate the catalogue entries with this information. Multinational publishers whose catalogues include titles originating from overseas companies whose rights may be handled separately may wish to indicate this with a coding system directing rights applicants to the appropriate rights department.

Some publishers use the technique of listing against a catalogue entry either the rights that have already been sold or the rights that are still available. However, as the lifespan of a catalogue may be six months or a year, the availability of rights can alter considerably during that period, making such information rapidly out of date.

Catalogues remain key tools for rights promotion (see *Online promotion and rights sales* later in this chapter, pp. 86–7).

Specific promotion: advance information and promotional material

For many categories of book, interest can be aroused by sending a specific and detailed information sheet; e-mail attachments have largely replaced mail and fax for this activity. This is particularly appropriate for specialized academic titles, as the material can be targeted to potential licensees with a particular interest in the topic and level of the book. Acquisitions editors in this field often welcome detailed information on specific titles in their key subjects, as it spares them scanning through much larger catalogues which may have little or no description of the contents of individual titles. A quick and convenient way to promote by e-mail is to send a targeted promotional letter including the URL (Uniform Resource Locator) of the description of the book on the company or dedicated rights website – this enables a potential licensee to click straight through to the relevant description without having to access and search what may be a large website.

This type of promotional material may, however, be less appropriate for a novel, which can be covered in a brief catalogue entry; further assessment would then involve a synopsis and some sample material. For an illustrated children's book, the style of illustration is crucial; in such cases, more elaborate sales material such as slides, colour photocopies of artwork, a dummy containing sample spreads or a printed-up section of the book (a 'blad' – brief layout and design) may be required well in advance of publication, and original artwork may be taken to book fairs. Sample graphics can be sent as attachments to e-mail. In the case of books where rights are being promoted after publication of the original edition, favourable reviews or press feature coverage can be of great assistance.

Advertising

A further form of promotion that might be considered is the use of paid advertising. *The Bookseller* offers rights promotion sections prior to key book fairs such as Frankfurt and Bologna, and *Publishers Weekly* also includes special pre-fair feature sections.

Online promotion and rights sales

Websites

Websites have increasingly provided useful additional channels for promoting rights for both publishers and literary agents. Many educational and academic publishers make available the full contents of all their catalogues on their central company website. The main purpose is to promote books for direct sales with facilities for buyers to order online. However, if control of rights in most titles lies with the publishing house, there may be no need to create a separate rights website; it may be sufficient to list contact names in the rights department for potential licensees. The ease of use of a company website will depend on its size and complexity in terms of the handling of rights. For example, a multinational company website may contain entries for books published on both sides of the Atlantic, but rights may be handled separately by UK and US rights departments; in such cases, the title entries need to be coded accordingly so that enquiries are correctly directed.

An alternative would be to create a dedicated rights department website with contact details, including the electronic equivalent of a selective rights guide or guides featuring key new titles with rights potential, perhaps with details of which rights are available and which already sold. A website of this kind requires regular updating to keep pace with rights sales and to take down older titles and replace them with newer candidates.

A dedicated rights website may prove particularly helpful for trade publishers and agents, who can then add referral details for titles or categories of rights not controlled by them; publishers who have embarked on this exercise state that this saves considerable administrative time on enquiries which have to be referred elsewhere.

It should, however, be borne in mind that to dispense totally with print catalogues in favour of online information can be extremely counter-productive; a print catalogue is a publisher's 'calling card' and is likely to remain so for the foreseeable future. Print material is particularly important when approaching a potential new customer for the first time; to refer a new contact to a website which may be large, time consuming and awkward to search is not a great selling point. Many customers also prefer to have print information to retain for reference and also to mark up for items of interest, perhaps during or after first contact at a book fair. A paper catalogue certainly provides better opportunities for serendipitous browsing than a large website.

Online rights trading

The majority of day-to-day business is now handled by publishers and literary agents by e-mail and this has greatly facilitated communication with licensees in countries where postal, fax and telephone services are unreliable.

Over the last fifteen years there have been a number of initiatives aimed at offering services to rights sellers and buyers through the medium of the internet. The Frankfurt Book Fair offered a Rights Exchange service, enabling rights sellers to post details of available titles on the book fair website in advance of the fair and for some time afterwards; this service was discontinued, but Frankfurt now offers a community platform and Rights Catalogue service. Registered Frankfurt exhibitors can contact each other via the fair website and there are facilities to register even if the publisher concerned is not physically present at the fair itself. The London Book Fair also offers a rights promotion service via its Exhibitor Website packages; the Silver Package (compulsory for all stands over 5 square metres) enables the exhibitor to upload details of five titles for which rights are available, plus a link to the company website; The Gold Package (compulsory for all stands over 40 square metres) allows the exhibitor to upload an unlimited number of titles for which rights are on offer, plus a link to the company website. Exhibitors can update and change information throughout the year (see Chapter 8 on book fairs).

The year 1999 saw the launch of several commercial online intermediary rights trading services, in particular RightsCenter Inc. (www.rightscenter. com). Based on an idea from John Brockman, the New York literary agent, the service enabled sellers to upload on to a secure network their material, including catalogue copy, author information, sample text, graphics or the full text of the work, on the basis of a fee per title. Chosen potential licensees then received an e-mail alert to inform them that information was available on the site. RightsCenter still exists, but now offers a Film Rights Directory service which lists film and television rights in literary properties available for sale.

Also started in 1999, Subrights.com formally launched its service at the London Book Fair in 2000. Its services were restricted to the book market and to titles already contracted for publication. Publishers and agents could list as many titles as they wished and could upload blurbs, graphics and full text in PDF format. The service charged a commission of 8–10% of any subsequent rights sales income concluded with the help of the system. However, in November 2000 Subrights.com announced that it was closing down, owing to lack of sufficient support.

A number of other online rights trading ventures were established at around the same time, all promoting as their major advantages the speed of contact and the saving of time and money involved in copying and sending out material in paper form. However, several key factors discouraged publishers and literary agents from taking up these intermediary services on a viable scale: large houses were daunted at the work involved in uploading and updating data on large numbers of titles; those in a directly competitive market, in particular academic publishers, were concerned about security aspects, in particular the release of early information which might be accessible to direct competitors. The move to making promotional material available online and the possibility of supplying manuscripts or proofs as PDF files has enabled publishers and agents to communicate electronically themselves without the need for an intermediary. Perhaps most importantly, face-to-face contact and telephone calls remain at the heart of rights trading. Despite this, in 2007 Francesca Spranzi established what she terms a virtual book fair as a cost-effective way for small publishers to market their titles internationally. The site is free to browse; publishers wishing to offer titles currently pay £5 per book per week for listing a small format title (up to 10,000 pixels) or £10 per title per week for listing larger titles (up to 20,000 pixels). For more details, see www. bookfaironline.net.

Online news services

A useful online news facility (rather than a trading service) of interest to rights sellers remains PublishersLunch (www.publisherslunch.com), a free daily e-mail service which enables publishers to post news of significant rights deals or offerings; it is part of the PublishersMarketplace service (www. publishersmarketplace.com), which provides a more detailed service for a monthly membership fee of US$20. It is mainly used by UK and US trade publishers and agents. The UK weekly book trade journal *The Bookseller* also runs a daily online service for subscribers which includes information on key rights deals, as does the daily *BookBrunch* service (www.bookbrunch.co.uk): headlines are accessible by all, but a subscription of £30 for three months, £55 for six months or £99 for twelve months gives access to more detailed content. Useful information is also available from the daily e-mail services from *Book Trade News* (www.booktrade.info) and *Publishing Perspectives* (www.publishingperspectives.com); users can currently register free of charge.

The use of subagents

Intermediaries can, however, play a significant role; many literary agents and some trade publishers favour the use of subagents to place rights in overseas markets. This can be particularly useful when the lists are large, the authors are major international figures and the sums involved are correspondingly high. The knowledge and range of contacts of the local agency, plus its immediate presence in the market, may enable it to negotiate a better deal than one handled at a distance. Key countries where agents are often used are Japan (the Tuttle-Mori Agency, the English Agency, Japan Uni and the Asano Agency are major players), Spain and Latin America (Carmen Balcells and International Editors Co.), Italy (EULAMA and Agenzia Letteraria Internazionale), Israel (the Book Publishers Association of Israel and the Deborah Harris Agency), Korea (Eric Yang, IPS and Shin Won) and Taiwan (Big Apple Tuttle-Mori and Bardon). In markets where there are several agencies, it is important to be clear on what basis they may handle rights – whether they have a clear and exclusive brief for an entire list (in which case it would be wise to agree an initial period of time for the arrangement, to be extended by agreement) or whether they handle individual books on a title-by-title basis. Chapter 6 dealt with the question of options versus multiple submissions; in the world of subagents, it is generally very counterproductive to offer the same project to several agencies in the same country simultaneously in an attempt to force them to compete to drive up terms; it will inevitably result in duplicated effort and eventual bad feeling.

In the countries of the former Eastern Bloc, it was normally necessary to conduct business through the state literary agencies. Since the political changes in the region, the monopoly of such agencies has been removed. A few of them (including RAO in Russia) still exist in much reduced form, acting as legal advisors to local authors and in matters of copyright reform, and as collection agencies in areas such as performing rights.

In the early 1990s, some western publishers who were not in the habit of visiting the region chose to subcontract licensing to specialist subagents such as Jovan Milankovic (Prava i Prevodi) in Belgrade, particularly for fiction and popular non-fiction titles. This was perhaps appropriate at a time when publishers in some countries had difficulty in remitting hard currency payments, and where the publishing industries passed through a period of transition and volatility as state-owned publishers were privatized and new private publishers sprang up daily and often disappeared equally quickly, in some cases leaving substantial debts unpaid. Publishers from the region now travel far more extensively to international book fairs, but some western publishers still choose to use the services of subagents on the grounds that they can better assess the reliability of new licensees; there is also an economy of scale in markets where the revenue from each individual licence may still be modest by western standards. Prava i Prevodi is still active in the region; the London-based Andrew Nurnberg Agency has also extended its range of overseas offices from Russia to include Bulgaria (this office also handles licensing to Serbia, Kosovo, Macedonia, Albania and Romania), the Czech Republic (also handling the Slovak Republic and Slovenia), Hungary (also handling Croatia), Latvia (also handling Estonia and Lithuania) and Poland.

Agencies such as Big Apple Tuttle-Mori and Bardon Chinese Media Agency in Taiwan have extended their activities to deal with publishers in mainland China since that country joined the international copyright conventions. Big Apple Tuttle-Mori have an office in Shanghai. There are also a number of state-owned copyright agencies in the main cities and many provinces, set up to assist mainland publishers to secure rights from abroad. The Andrew Nurnberg Agency also has offices in mainland China (Beijing) and Taiwan.

Agents may also be employed in the United States, particularly for major authors, where the rights income generated can be very substantial. However, the use of agents is not really to be recommended in the case of titles involving coprinting, since the procedures for such deals are complex and require regular and direct contact between the coedition partners.

At the risk of generalizing, literary agents in the United Kingdom and elsewhere have traditionally been less interested in handling rights to educational and academic works than in trade titles, for valid economic reasons. The revenue generated from the sale of rights in such titles is often relatively modest, and this affects the commission earnings on which the agencies must operate. Rights in such titles can usually be handled more effectively by rights departments under the umbrella of the original publishing house. This applies to a certain extent to the use of subagents abroad, where it is often preferable to undertake one's own market research and promote rights direct.

In Japan, a direct approach to a publishing house may nevertheless result in a response or indeed an offer coming back through a subagent. This may be because the Japanese publisher is unsure of its ability to conduct the correspondence in English. Where the initial interest has been generated by a direct approach from the original publisher, it is usually possible to negotiate for the agency to take 10% commission only from the Japanese side rather than from payments remitted to the licensor.

Face-to-face selling

While much rights promotion work is undertaken by mail, e-mail and telephone throughout the year, there is no substitute for a face-to-face encounter in which the would-be seller can gauge the reaction of the potential buyer. Such meetings take place at those book fairs which lend themselves to rights selling; in the United Kingdom between original publishers and potential local licensees such as book clubs, paperback houses, newspapers and magazines, or visiting publishers from overseas; and during sales trips by staff to overseas markets outside the context of book fairs. It is generally true to say that it is these meetings that are the lifeblood of rights selling, and many a deal can be finalized quickly if there is a good personal rapport (often built up over a number of years) between seller and buyer. However, it would be foolish to pretend that all such meetings are enjoyable, and at major book fairs such as Frankfurt staff can sometimes be seen closeted in earnest or even explosive conversation with customers whom they may well wish they had never met. Fortunately, such encounters are few in comparison with those with regular customers, who may well become personal friends over the years.

Book fairs and sales trips are covered in detail in Chapter 8.

Book fairs and sales trips
Preparation, survival and follow-up

Book fairs

Book fairs provide an ideal opportunity to undertake market research, to meet new contacts and to see existing customers to sort out any problems, to finalize pending deals and to discuss possibilities for future collaboration.

More than thirty book fairs are held each year. At present, the key events with a rights emphasis are:

1 The Bologna Book Fair, now held annually in late March and specializing in children's books and educational books (www.bookfair.bolognafiere.it).
2 The London Book Fair, now held annually in April; recognized as an extremely important rights venue, although still smaller and more restricted in range than Frankfurt. (www.londonbookfair.co.uk).
3 The Jerusalem Book Fair, held every two years in February; originally a meeting point for American and Israeli publishers but now more international (www.jerusalembookfair.com).
4 The Prague Book Fair (now under the name of Bookworld), held annually in May and probably more useful for trade than for educational and academic publishers. (www.bookworld.cz).
5 The Warsaw Book Fair, held annually in late May; the largest book fair in central and eastern Europe; exhibitors are now mainly from Poland, although publishers from some other countries in the region also attend (www.bookfair.pl).
6 BookExpo America (BEA), formerly the American Booksellers Association (ABA) Convention, held annually in late May or early June. Traditionally it alternated between New York and other US cities, but is now being held in New York up to and including 2012, which makes it attractive to overseas visitors also wishing to visit key US publishers in their home city. It is primarily intended as a showcase for new American publications to the American book trade, but it is

also used as a rights forum by American, Latin American and some overseas publishers. In 2009 it was announced that the duration of the 2010 show would be reduced to two days (www.bookexpoamerica. com).

7 The Liber exhibition in Spain, held annually in late September or early October and alternating between Barcelona (in even-numbered years) and Madrid (odd-numbered years); a useful marketplace for the sale of rights to the Spanish-speaking countries, but now held very close to the dates of Frankfurt (www.liber.ifema.es).

8 The Beijing International Book Fair, once a biennial event but now held annually at the beginning of September. A key opportunity to meet a wide range of mainland Chinese publishers, including many regional publishers who may not travel to western book fairs (www.bibf.net/ bibf/index.jsp).

9 The Moscow International Book Fair, also once biennial but now held annually during the first half of September. In Soviet times, this was a large event with participants from all the Republics; it is now more Russocentric, with relatively few foreign exhibitors (www.mibf. ru/english). There is also a smaller non-fiction book fair in late November/early December.

10 The Frankfurt Book Fair, the largest of all, held annually in October and covering all countries, all subjects and all levels of publication (www.frankfurt-book-fair.com).

The last twenty years have seen a plethora of new book fairs spring up, particularly in the countries of central and eastern Europe and also in regions such as Latin America, the Middle East and Asia. Although many of them are billed as international fairs, a number have developed into more local events, with the prime activity of direct sales by local publishers at discount to the visiting public. In central and eastern Europe, there are annual fairs in Budapest (April), St Petersburg (April), Bucharest (early June) and in the Baltic Republics (February/March, with the fair location circulating between Vilnius, Tallinn and Riga).

In Europe, following German reunification, the Leipzig Book Fair was overhauled and repromoted as an opportunity for east/west meetings; it is held annually in March. In 1996, the Belgrade Book Fair was revived following several years of political turmoil in former Yugoslavia; it is now held annually in October. The Salon du Livre is held annually in Paris in March. The Turin Book Fair is held in May, while in Sweden the Göteborg Fair is held in late September/early October; on the business side, all of these events are of prime interest to booksellers and librarians, and as the general public are admitted they tend to have a cultural rather than a rights trading focus, featuring many author events. Thessaloniki (held in May) is now being promoted as a Balkan rights event.

In the Middle East, the Cairo Book Fair is a regular event in January, but the Abu Dhabi International Book Fair, now coorganized with the Frankfurt Book Fair and held in March, is being promoted as a pan-Arabic rights venue. The Sharjah Book Fair was relaunched as an international event in November 2009.

In Latin America, the book fairs in Buenos Aires (April/May) and Guadalajara (November/early December) also tend to concentrate on direct sales and trading between Spanish-language publishers and booksellers, although Guadalajara is now actively promoting its possibilities as a rights trading venue. The Tokyo Book Fair (held annually in July) has not yet fulfilled its promise as a rights venue; Taipei (February) has proved more successful. The Seoul Book Fair (May) concentrates more on domestic sales than on rights. In mainland China, attempts from 2001 onwards to establish a Shanghai rights event seem unlikely to succeed in overtaking the annual Beijing event. The year 2006 saw the first Cape Town Book Fair, now held every June, although it is not yet clear whether this will develop as a pan-African rights trading forum.

Rights staff with appropriate projects to sell may wish to consider attending media fairs such as the Monaco Cinema and Literature International Forum (April) MIPCOM (MIPTV/MILIA) in Cannes (October) and the Online Information exhibition in London (late November/early December); the Frankfurt, London and BookExpo America events also now devote more space to electronic publishing and film and television rights. January 2010 saw a two-day Digital Book World conference in New York; it is unclear as yet if this might become an annual event. Frankfurt offers an annual Forum Film and TV event and the London International Book Fair (LIBF) now offers a service enabling publishers and agents to submit details of three titles for inclusion on the LIBF website with a view to making contact with film and television producers.

The question of which fairs to attend may be affected by a number of factors: the emphasis of the fair itself; the type of publishing in which one is involved; whether or not the company as a whole is committed to licensing in a particular market; the potential for rights sales; and (of course) the time and financial resources available to rights staff. Book fairs are expensive events, and a new fair is always difficult to assess from a rights perspective after only one visit; anyone considering attendance at a fair for the first time would be well advised to read press reports of any earlier fairs and canvass opinion from rights colleagues in other companies who have attended the event. A recession inevitably affects book fair attendance as publishers have to prioritize events.

Frankfurt remains the key event in the book fair calendar, since it covers all areas of publishing and attracts exhibitors worldwide; publishers from those countries with limited hard currency resources seeking to attend a foreign book fair will almost certainly choose Frankfurt (7,314 companies exhibited there in 2009). Bologna remains essential for publishers of trade children's books, although it has attracted some educational publishers as well. The fact that most foreign buyers tend to visit the London Book Fair 'on the hoof' without stands (and sometimes without notice in advance) can be frustrating, as this ties British rights staff to their stands. Rights business has nevertheless increased substantially over the last few years, and London is now rated as the key rights forum after Frankfurt. It moved to its present venue in Earl's Court in 2007 following a controversial initiative by Frankfurt to set up a rival event in central London.

The plethora of new fairs in central and eastern Europe in the 1990s was initially attractive to western publishers unfamiliar with those markets; however, they have proved expensive to attend and national rather than international in scope; they also concentrate more on domestic sales than on rights. More publishers from the region are now able to attend fairs such as Frankfurt, Bologna and London, although visits to local fairs of this kind can sometimes provide a useful introduction to a national publishing industry.

Many book fairs now feature a different country or region each year as the guest of honour (for the London Book Fair, the Market Focus feature), with a large exhibition of publications accompanied by author appearances, seminars and cultural events. This can prove a valuable introduction for rights sellers to markets they have not yet tackled, as such events usually attract a larger number of publishers from the featured country or region than would normally attend the fair concerned. If new contacts can be established, it may then justify a visit to the market concerned to follow up on leads. Some book fairs (e.g. Abu Dhabi) run 'matchmaking' events, where visiting publishers can meet up with local publishers with similar areas of interest.

Ways in which to investigate the usefulness of attending a fair without the full expense of an individual stand might include taking a small area as part of a national stand if this can be organized by the appropriate publishers' association (the UK Publishers Association runs a Turnkey service at a number of overseas fairs); sharing a stand with another publisher; taking space in the fair's rights centre if this facility is available to publishers (some fairs restrict access to agents, or charge higher rates for non-exhibiting publishers to use the facility); or attending without a stand, perhaps for only the key initial days of a fair. With pressure on time and financial resources, it is important to be selective.

The pace of each fair varies according to its size and character. At Frankfurt, timetables have become increasingly regimented and most participants now arrive at the fair with a diary fully booked with appointments every half hour throughout the day; business may extend into breakfast and evening meetings or functions. Ironically, although the final Monday of the fair was cancelled from 2004 onwards, many trade

publishers and literary agents now arrive several days before the fair commences and conduct business from their hotels. The atmosphere of Liber is
considerably more relaxed; the working day starts late, breaks lengthily for
lunch and then continues late into the evening in true Mediterranean style.
Middle Eastern fairs also have a long afternoon break, and some have
periods when only women visitors are permitted. The eastern European
and Asian fairs are smaller and in most cases organization has improved;
their size can be more convenient for rights staff visiting a market for the
first time and wishing to scan stands to gain an impression of the range and
standard of local publishing. The working day at the Beijing Book Fair
tends to end relatively early (4.30 p.m.) to allow exhibitors to attend early
evening functions outside the fair.

It is essential to prepare carefully for any book fair, whether one is a
newcomer or an old hand. As rights business builds up, the amount of time
and effort required for preparation will increase, although experience will of
course make it easier to judge the best form in which information and sales
material should be prepared.

Some publishers may wish to take advantage of advertising selected titles
in special pre-fair issues of trade publications such as *The Bookseller* or
Publishers Weekly (see *Advertising* in Chapter 7).

Several book fairs now offer online rights information services enabling
publishers to post details of rights available on a website before, during and
after the book fair itself. The Frankfurt and London fairs both piloted
such arrangements in 1997; the Frankfurt website (www.book-fair.com)
contains a catalogue of exhibitors, the Frankfurt Rights Catalogue (some
18,000 titles listed in 2009) and a *Who's Who* of key individual publishing
staff. The website also enables registered exhibitors to network and to
make appointments online; the services are available throughout the year.
London offers a year-round rights promotion service as part of its Exhibitor
Website programme which enables publishers to list a full company profile,
contact details and general product description plus a link to the exhibitor's
own website: in 2010 the Silver Package (for all stands over 5 square metres)
was priced at £250 plus VAT and permitted five titles to be listed; the Gold
Package (for all stands over 40 square metres) was priced at £300 plus VAT
and allowed details of an unlimited number of titles (which can be regularly
updated).

There is also the year-round service www.bookfaironline.net launched by
Francesca Spranzi with small publishers in mind, which lists titles on the
basis of a weekly fee per title (see also *Online rights trading* in Chapter 7).

Prearranging appointments

As mentioned earlier, the trend for major rights fairs is now towards pre-
booking all key appointments to save time while attending the event.

The timing for sending appointment letters by e-mail or by mail will vary according to the fair in question and the number of customers to be seen, but for a publisher with well-established contacts it is advisable to make contact by e-mail approximately eight to ten weeks in advance of the major fairs such as Bologna, London and Frankfurt. The most effective invitation will include the names of rights personnel attending, together with dates of attendance if they will not be at the fair throughout. The letter should also give the stand number and hall location; it is far preferable to give a suggested date and time for an appointment and the name of a specific member of staff who will handle the appointment rather than simply asking the customer when they would like to come, which will result in a plethora of requests for appointments on the morning of the first day.

If one is approaching a publisher for the first time in advance of the fair to request an appointment, it is essential to make clear the purpose of the appointment, that is, to sell rather than to buy rights (unless one is in a position to do both). If the letter is sent by mail, it is helpful to include some brief information about the publishing house and a copy of the current catalogue or concise information about a particular project to be discussed; brief information could also be appended to an e-mail. This will enable the recipient to assess whether an appointment will be worthwhile. There is little point in a meeting if lists are not really compatible, if the project offered competes with an existing title or if the publisher approached has a policy not to purchase rights. If possible, it is preferable to target a named individual editor if the appropriate person can be identified from a publishing directory such as *Literary Marketplace* or *International Literary Marketplace*; print publications such as the Frankfurt and Bologna *Who's Who* were not normally available in advance of the fairs themselves. Both are now available online to registered participants; Frankfurt ceased to produce a print version after 2008.

It is important to avoid sending too much unsolicited material to a new contact, either in terms of the number of titles or material on a single project. Brief information is preferable and usually adequate to line up initial interest.

It is traditional for the rights seller to operate from his or her stand and for potential buyers to move from stand to stand. This is logical, since the seller has at hand the range of books to be shown, catalogues, advance information and sales material. However, if one is starting out to sell rights for the first time, particularly with a new or relatively unknown company, it is inevitable that some difficulty may be encountered in persuading potential buyers to visit the stand 'on spec'. It may then be necessary to start off by visiting potential buyers, carrying books and sales material around the fair and returning to base at regular intervals. This can be extremely tiring and awkward if one is operating solo, but it may be the only way to make contacts until a range of regular partners has been established. If a small publishing house is unable to afford the cost of an individual stand, it is vital to try to prearrange some physical base, either through participation in a group stand or through the good offices of a fellow publisher, where personal belongings can be stored and messages taken. Some fairs provide communal meeting facilities in the form of a rights or agents' centre in return for a fee; however, it is important to check in advance who is allowed to use such facilities; the London Book Fair originally precluded the use of its centre by publishers not exhibiting at the fair, although it has since relaxed this restriction.

At some events it can be difficult to persuade potential buyers to visit the stand of the seller; this may be because they are small publishing houses with limited staff resources which are needed to man their own stands. In such cases, it is a courtesy to visit the stand of the buyer, but it will then be necessary to allow adequate transit time, particularly at a large fair such as Frankfurt.

Timetable

At major book fairs such as Frankfurt it is best to assume that no publisher will have more than half an hour to spare for an appointment, and in some cases even less time will be available. A draft timetable can be worked out on this basis and marked up as appointments are confirmed.

A number of factors may have to be taken into account when planning the timetable; for example, at Frankfurt many German (and increasingly other) publishers return home on Friday and hence are not available for the weekend days of the fair; others may choose to come on the weekend days only, in order not to lose working days in their offices. Publishers whose accommodation is located far from the city centre (often those from the less affluent countries) may be unable to attend appointments at the very beginning of the working day; those working 'on the hoof' without a permanent exhibitor pass may not be able to enter until after a designated time and may have to navigate lengthy security queues so cannot attend pre-9 a.m. appointments.

On the other hand, exhibiting publishers from countries with a tradition of an early start can usually be relied upon to turn up for breakfast meetings or stand appointments at 8.00 or 8.30 a.m. Publishers with a traditionally late lunch hour, such as those from the Latin countries, may not be available for appointments over that period. Those likely to have a busy round of early evening receptions may be reluctant to stay at the fair itself after 5 p.m. Publishers of staunchly Catholic persuasion may be absent from the fair on Sunday morning to attend a service, whilst the timing of Frankfurt in a month in which several major Jewish religious days occur has long been a bone of contention and can affect attendance at the fair; this has led to the organizers taking these considerations into account when planning fair dates. Many trade publishers and literary agents now arrive in

Frankfurt ahead of the first working day of the fair and arrange appointments in their hotels.

As one builds up regular contacts, it becomes possible to take all these factors into account, and also to identify those customers who are punctual and reliable and those who are not. In a busy schedule, a no-show can be extremely frustrating, whilst buyers who are newcomers to the fair may genuinely underestimate the distances involved in getting from stand to stand. For those rights sellers with a long working day, it is strongly recommended that the last appointment of each day should be with a congenial rather than a problematic customer.

Evenings may be spent in a variety of ways; at major book fairs (and in affluent times), large publishers may host receptions or formal dinners for customers. Other attendees may rely on less formal networking opportunities. Whilst parties can provide genuine opportunities for getting together with potential customers, and are often a medium for hearing about projects, publishing trends and moves within the industry, it goes without saying that it is inadvisable to start the following day at the fair with a sore head.

Information on established or potential customers

It is extremely useful to prepare a data sheet for each publisher to be seen, and this can be used as the basis for the meeting. If one is starting out to sell rights for the first time, the sheet may contain no more than the name of the publishing house, its country of origin, the range of subject interests plus the name of a possible individual contact; this information can be gleaned from sources such as *Literary Marketplace* and *International Literary Marketplace*, or added from the *Who's Who* of the fair once these data become available. As contacts are established, the sheet can be expanded to incorporate details of rights deals finalized, books under consideration and interest logged in future projects. Information may consist simply of a statement that rights have been sold or may include much more information, such as the financial terms agreed, the date the contract was sent out and returned, and other key stages in the negotiation.

To this information can be added notes on outstanding points or problems to be discussed during the meeting, such as technical specifications for duplicate production material, the provision of coedition prices or outstanding royalty payments. It may also be wise to include a list of projects recently submitted but rejected, in order to avoid reoffering them, and also perhaps a note of key new projects which may be of interest.

The larger the scale of rights business, the less practical it becomes to rely on memory and the more vital to have the relevant information available in printed form. Well-organized information of this kind has often proved its worth in times of crisis; if a member of the rights staff falls ill and cannot attend a book fair or has to return home early, there is at least some chance that a colleague can stand in and ensure that key points can be covered with major customers.

The advantage of a computerized rights database (Chapter 6) is that if the system is appropriately programmed, much of this customer information can be selected automatically, superfluous information can be deleted, and last-minute information added by word-processing and taken to the fair in printed form. An alternative may be to take a laptop with the database loaded onto it either in full or in edited form; however, this can make for rather less spontaneous meetings if the rights seller is constantly tapping a keyboard to access relevant information. There is also a need for access to a power point or regularly recharged batteries, particularly if work is actually to be processed at the fair (e.g. options recorded or sales finalized). If the updated data are required by other rights colleagues working in parallel at the fair, the laptops will have to be networked *in situ*, making port-ability a problem. The question of whether firm options or commitments should be logged on the database at a fair (rather than noting interest) is complex; it is usually unwise to do so if there is any possibility that several rights staff could generate interest in the same book from different custo-mers in the same market, or to commit on a title early in the fair if a better prospect expresses interest later during the event. It is also perhaps a truism to say that a busy rights person operating at full capacity at a book fair is likely to be fully occupied conversing and taking notes meeting by meeting, and to have little spare time to devote to 'housekeeping' of this kind. Whilst some rights staff choose to enter notes on a laptop rather than in a notebook of some kind, this can be restrictive if (as may happen) a custo-mer darts away from the meeting table to locate a book seen on the other side of the stand – with a manual notebook, one can follow the customer without drastically interrupting the flow of the meeting!

With a manual record system in the office, customer information would have to be transcribed by keyboard or by hand into some portable form such as a ring-binder, small card index, notebook or personal organizer. Much will depend on the amount of data required for each book fair. As the customer information will be used as the basis for each meeting, the ideal situation is when the preparatory notes of both seller and buyer correspond exactly!

Whether one works from a laptop, PDA, a ring-binder or a notebook, it is vital to guard the material with one's life. The loss of any such item during or (worse) at the end of a book fair would be a disaster.

Information on rights sold or on offer

When preparing for a book fair, it is also wise to put together a list of rights already sold or on offer, or where interest has been logged for projects still in preparation. This can be done in several ways.

Publishers in the trade sector are perhaps more conscious of working six months ahead, selling the spring list at fairs held during the preceding autumn and dealing with the autumn list during the spring fairs. Some carry a 'sales sheet' for each title in the current list, with details of the rights position in each language or market. Others maintain a system of inserting a sheet in each display copy listing the rights situation on that title. A preferable method may be to produce a listing of titles, perhaps organized alphabetically by author surname, and showing (language by language) all titles for which rights have been sold, are under negotiation or on offer, or for which future interest has been noted. It may also be decided to integrate details of titles where interest will have to be referred if control of the rights lies elsewhere.

Again, an appropriately programmed computerized rights database should be able to generate such listings automatically; the alternative is to transcribe the data from manual records. Having such information at a book fair (whether in manual form, as a printout or on a laptop or PDA) means that it is possible to answer enquiries on the status of rights in a particular title for a particular market as it stood immediately before the start of the fair, although discussions held during the course of the fair may of course alter the situation. It is usually advisable to instruct any rights staff remaining in the office during the book fair to hold off from processing any interim enquiries until they can be coordinated with interest shown at the fair.

Sales information and material

The material used at a book fair varies greatly according to the publishing house, the type of publication, the scale of rights business and the stage that each project has reached. For an academic list, it is usually appropriate to work on the basis of complete subject catalogues showing both new titles and backlist, individual information sheets, synopses, finished books and perhaps proofs or sample pages of major projects, particularly if illustrations are a key feature (for example in a medical textbook). Pictures of cover designs are usually of less significance in this sector, and in some cases may be purely typographic. Some academic publishers may also produce selective rights guides of key new titles. Never assume that a full and adequate supply of catalogues or rights guides will arrive safely at a stand if they are to be shipped there; it is a wise precaution to carry a working set in one's hand luggage.

If the rights policy is to log interest well in advance of publication, it may also be worth carrying very early information on each project as soon as it has been commissioned. This could consist of a copy of the in-house editor's proposal form justifying publication, although it may be necessary to remove certain confidential features such as the unit cost of the book, projected sales and its gross profit forecast. It should also be remembered that in some sectors of publishing (particularly that of STM) potential licensees may also be direct competitors in the English language, particularly in markets such as Germany.

It is important that any sales information be carefully classified by subject, and indeed by subspeciality, so that when a customer visits a stand the seller can quickly home in on specific topics of interest. It is a feature of certain areas of publishing (particularly in medicine and science) that, even if a project is some years in the future, potential buyers may be prepared to express interest and wait to receive more detailed information and material as the project progresses.

In the case of general publishing, publishers tend to produce annual or biannual catalogues featuring new titles, perhaps with a brief listing of backlist titles. For advance material, much depends on the type of book in question. For books where artwork or photographs are a key feature – and particularly where the basis of the rights business lies in printing coeditions for overseas partners – it may be essential to invest in elaborate and expensive presentation material: slide packs, sample spreads, 'blads' (sample printed sections – brief layout and design), proofs, visual material of covers and interiors scanned for display on a laptop, or dummy books to show both bulk and appearance. Sample material may show actual pages originated well in advance of the main project, or may be mock-ups to show typical illustrations accompanied by random text, sometimes in printer's dog Latin but designed to show the intended layout of the book. For key markets it is wise to have multiple sets of such material, which can be borrowed by the potential customer or available to several rights staff operating simultaneously, perhaps in different geographical territories. However, any rights operation dependent on coedition business may involve some retrieval and juggling of material.

In some cases, it may be possible to take original artwork to a book fair, perhaps even in the care of the artist if they are well known. While the original artwork can undoubtedly be impressive as a sales tool, one should also be aware of the high risk involved in transporting such material to a book fair, having it on the stand or walking round with it to visit potential customers. There have been many cases where valuable artwork has disappeared for ever during a moment of inattention, and the regular loss of original artwork at the Bologna Book Fair was a major factor in publishers voting some years ago that children should not be allowed to attend the event on trade days. Slides, colour photographs or colour scans of the artwork may not be as stunning, but their loss will certainly be less devastating. Visual material may of course be shown on a laptop (or even on a mobile phone – useful for showing cover designs), although customers do still seem to prefer to see 'hands on' material and samples they can retain.

Other useful material for children's books may include soft toys of the character featured in the book, cardboard models, showcards or dumpbins featuring the characters, while for well-established characters or designs a display of the items licensed for merchandising can provide an attractive background as well as an incentive to potential licensees.

For publishers specializing in coeditions, it will be necessary to arrive at the book fair armed with a range of accurate manufacturing prices, which will allow for negotiation on the basis of the product required (a same-language edition with a simple change of imprint, for example, or a full change of language for a translation), quantity, binding, packing and delivery requirements. Prices for duplicate production material should also be taken if this is likely to be a key element in the rights deal; increasingly, such material is being provided in the form of electronic files, so prices and available specifications for these are essential, although the mark-up on the prices can be problematic in some markets (see Chapter 25). If customers are likely to require duplicate film, prices will be needed for duplicate positive or negative film, with cover film specified separately.

Survival

The physical conditions in which book fairs are held may vary from the superbly efficient facilities of Frankfurt and the civilized location and gourmet delights of Bologna to situations that are frankly grim, although conditions in some of the worst locations have improved somewhat in recent years. The Warsaw Book Fair is still held in the Palace of Culture, an oppressive pile in the Stalinist Gothic tradition in which exhibitors sweat as temperatures outside rise, air vents fail to give relief and the marble floors reduce all but the fittest to hobbling their way round the rabbit-warren layout of the building. Exhibition equipment and general facilities have, however, been considerably improved. The Bucharest and Beijing fairs are both held at times of year which are likely to produce temperatures in the nineties, conditions which are not improved by the exhibition facilities: Beijing moved back to rather more modern facilities in 2005. Moscow finally built a new pavilion for the 2009 September fair.

A particularly annoying feature in some of the central and eastern European book fairs is advertising for seminars, book launch events and new publications, broadcast within the exhibition area. This is often so loud and so frequent that it can completely drown out the business conversations of exhibitors unfortunate enough to have stands in the immediate vicinity of the loudspeakers. At Beijing, some Chinese publishers of children's books and language teaching materials also broadcast loudly from their own stands.

Sadly, many book fairs offer opportunities for organized theft, ranging from the loss of handbags or briefcases containing vital travel documents (a particular problem in countries like Russia and China where it is advisable to carry a passport as an identity document) to the loss of laptops, PDAs and mobile phones. If there are no lockable storage facilities on the stand, particular care is needed and it is advisable to take photocopies of travel documents and the relevant pages of passports (including the relevant visa pages) and keep them back at the hotel in case of mishap.

Publishers attending the Moscow and Beijing book fairs should be warned that to obtain palatable refreshments at the fair during the course of a busy schedule can still be problematic, although there have been some improvements. However, in some venues floor coverings and trailing electrical wiring remain death traps for the unwary, while ablution facilities still range from the dubious to the unspeakable. Some iron rations and a supply of toilet paper may still be a wise precaution.

In locations with more sophisticated facilities, the policy on lunch breaks may vary. Some publishers may aim to take a short unencumbered break away from their stand; others may build lunch meetings at restaurants inside or outside the fair into their schedules. Some large trade publishers may conduct some of their meetings in hotel suites rather than at the fair itself, and at fairs such as Frankfurt and London many such meetings now take place in the days immediately preceding the fair. Some of the larger houses provide basic refreshments for both staff and visitors on their stands; others may be dependent on using snack-bar facilities in the exhibition halls as and when time permits. A working day completely without sustenance is unwise, however busy the schedule. For rights staff visiting a fair 'on the hoof' rather than with comfortable stand facilities, it is vital to pace oneself and to take occasional breaks where one can sit down, rest or take stock of the day's business.

In earlier years, communication with the outside world from eastern Europe or China was unreliable or non-existent. Communications are now hugely improved, and western-run or joint-venture hotels usually have direct international dialling facilities and business centres, and many now provide internet access in one's hotel room. It is advisable to buy a local SIM card for mobile phones to obtain local rates rather than connections for local calls via the UK. A BlackBerry or similar phone with e-mail facilities can prove useful when travelling, although to date they do not cope well with large e-mail attachments and can prove very expensive.

The price for these improvements has been a massive rise in the cost of hotel accommodation and services generally, including reliable transport, interpreters and eating facilities. In Russia and some countries of central and eastern Europe, the huge rise in the general crime rate makes it advisable to stay in a good western-run hotel with security facilities. China, once a safe country for foreigners, is now less so and it is essential to be streetwise.

Conducting business

The two main benefits of any book fair are the possibilities for undertaking market research and the opportunity to hold meetings with potential buyers.

Market research

A book fair provides a showcase for the wares of a wide range of publishers. The main constraint in undertaking market research is time; in an ideal world, rights staff should be able to allow adequate time for visiting the stands of other publishing houses to assess whether they may be potential new customers. When building up rights business from scratch, it is vital to invest time in this way in order to identify a nucleus of appropriate contacts.

The technique here is to obtain a copy of the fair catalogue, preferably in advance of the fair if this is possible. A limited number of copies of the Frankfurt Fair catalogue are sent to exhibitors in advance by post, whilst the catalogues of other fairs may be available only the day before the fair opens or perhaps only when the fair starts. Some book fairs offer their catalogue in online form. The fair catalogue is the starting point from which to identify publishers whose subject interests appear to be compatible, and thence to visit their stands to study the range and style of publications on display. If the fair in question issues a listing of key individuals attending (e.g. the Frankfurt and Bologna *Who's Who* databases), an appropriate contact name can be identified. A quick visit to a stand can provide an instant means of eliminating unsuitable publishers from the initial list of possible contacts; for example, a visit to a publisher listed in the fair catalogue as publishing veterinary books may reveal that in fact the books published are on pet care for owners rather than on canine surgery. Accuracy of description may depend on the publisher when they compile their own catalogue entry, or may be limited to a restricted number of subject categories to be ticked on the catalogue entry form.

In other cases, the broad subject area may be compatible but the approach may differ; for example, a publisher listed as specializing in architecture may publish glossy studies on the work of individual architects rather than practical books on the design of shopping malls or the use of computer-assisted design in architectural projects.

On the other hand, several hours invested in visiting stands may identify publishers with lists that are compatible in both content and style; in such cases, an appointment can be sought or a catalogue or information left on the stand, together with a business card and details of where one can be located, with a mobile phone contact number if available. Rights staff with busy schedules may find that they are confined to their own stands throughout the day and the only time they have available to look at the stands of likely new contacts is immediately after the doors of the exhibition halls have opened. The tragedy of 9/11 massively reduced the number of American exhibitors at Frankfurt in 2001 and security is now tight; however, it is possible for card-carrying exhibitors to enter the fair buildings from 7 a.m. and to spend some time browsing before the core schedule of the day begins.

If it is impossible to arrange an appointment for any reason, a follow-up letter can be written after the fair; major book fairs have now become such overwhelmingly busy events that random callers cannot always be accommodated. If an appointment request is refused, it is always helpful to try to find out the reason. If the publishing house in question rarely acquires rights from outside, it may not be worthwhile persisting in trying to make contact either at the fair or afterwards. If the person responsible for acquiring books in the area in question is not attending the fair, it is important to obtain a name and contact details so that an approach can be made by mail or e-mail; if they are simply not on the stand at the time a call is made, or occupied with another appointment, it may be possible to arrange an appointment for later in the fair if a schedule is available at a central reception desk; if not, it is important to establish whether a return call to the stand is worthwhile.

It is a sad fact that unannounced callers at book fair stands are not always welcomed, and cold-calling can be very disheartening, particularly if one is starting out in selling rights and working for a small and perhaps little-known house. A first visit to a book fair should be a learning experi-ence, which can be built upon by correspondence during the intervals between fairs so that the range of genuine contacts can be increased from year to year.

Appointments

The main purpose of an appointment is to discuss any outstanding problems, finalize deals that are pending and discuss potential new business, hence the importance of having ready to hand all necessary details of both customers and title availability.

A typical conversation might begin with agreeing financial terms for a project that had been under consideration before the fair (to be followed by the preparation of a contract after the fair); providing sample material and coedition prices for a full-colour project; taking details of specifications for duplicate production material required by the customer so that an accurate price can be obtained from the printer; and selecting appropriate titles from the forward programme that may be of interest. The importance of selecting *relevant* titles cannot be overemphasized; all too often potential buyers can be discouraged by overkill if too many projects are shown that are simply not appropriate for their list or their market. As relationships are built up, it becomes easier to home in on likely titles more quickly and accurately. However, as face-to-face contact with some customers may take place only once a year at a book fair, it is always worth asking even regular customers if they have plans to diversify into a new area, or if they are looking for a book on a particular topic to fill a gap in their list.

In some areas of publishing, much will depend on the personal taste of the buyer, and a skilled rights seller often knows by instinct that a particular novel or children's book will appeal to a specific individual editor. In academic publishing, the sale of rights is far less dependent on the personal taste of seller and buyer. Here, the criteria will be the academic status of the author, the topic covered by the book, whether it fills a gap in the market, the main features that might make it preferable to a local book or a competing English-language book, and whether it can be transferred to the buyer's market without the need for major adaptations.

Sales technique

Style of presentation

It is impossible to provide definitive rules on sales technique; each individual has his or her own personality and this will inevitably influence selling style. There may, however, be some basic differences in approach between trade and academic publishers. For example, if seeking to place rights in an exciting new political thriller by a well-known author, the key issue may not be the personal view of either seller or buyer on the quality of this particular story or the writing style of the author, but the almost certain commercial prospects for the book given the author's previous track record. In such cases, discussion of the merits of the work could well be dismissed in favour of financial discussions. If, however, the work on offer is a promising debut novel by a young unknown author, much will hinge on the seller's ability to communicate personal enthusiasm for the material, in terms of both content and style.

This personal involvement would hardly be appropriate in the case of a multi-volume handbook on head and neck surgery or a book on the technology of welding. Here the seller's main aim should be to communicate why the project fills a gap or is superior to any existing book on the market. The seller needs to be well informed on the range of coverage of the book, whether the author is a major authority in the field, whether new technology or new procedures are covered, and why the book is superior to any competing books on the topic, either published or imminent. It is obviously impossible for the seller to be a qualified expert in a range of disciplines across an academic list, but it is vital that key technical terms are understood so that they can be explained, perhaps in simplified terms, to a potential customer who may not understand the English terminology.

It is essential for sane survival in the world of rights selling that one has faith in the quality of at least a substantial part of the list one is handling. It would be foolish, however, to assume that only good books can be sold. Excellent literary quality is not necessarily a guarantee of saleability, and some of the most successful books in past years have been notable for their appeal to the lowest common denominator rather than for their stylistic merits. However, it is sometimes better to avoid a sale that may later backfire in the form of ill will from the buyer. If one wishes to build up long-term relationships with licensees, it is vital not to oversell a project to the extent that the buyer is misled. Memories are long in publishing, and a reputation for overkill or sharp dealing will undoubtedly follow a rights seller even if they move from company to company; the range of potential customers in any given country is not limitless. Given a project that may be less than perfect but that may nevertheless be highly saleable, it is far better to emphasize its saleability than to offer it as a literary masterpiece.

Although the techniques of multiple submission and auction are valid methods of operation, it is vital that potential buyers are fully aware of the terms of operation. The long-term detrimental effects of misleading potential buyers into offering more than they had intended, by implying that high competing offers have already been received, far outweigh the immediate financial benefits, since the ill will generated will affect future business.

On a more mundane note, it is usually easier to conduct an appointment taking notes by hand than to attempt to hold a conversation whilst tapping on a keyboard.

Language ability

Earlier chapters have broached the question of language ability. English is now widely spoken in many countries, and regrettably this has become an excuse for lack of linguistic ability among many British and American business staff in many areas of industry. Although it is technically possible to operate in English alone, fluency in one or more foreign languages is usually a huge advantage when selling rights. If several people are involved in selling rights, much will depend on how responsibility has been allocated. For example, if responsibility has been divided geographically, there may be no need for members of staff selling to the United States, Commonwealth countries, the Netherlands or Scandinavia to be strong linguists. However, if the sale of translation rights worldwide is a key part of the rights business, it is certainly preferable to have staff with a range of complementary language skills. French, German, Italian and Spanish are probably the most useful, and it should be remembered that even if seller and buyer do not speak each other's native tongue, there may well be a third language which is common to both; for example, an Argentinian publisher may speak French, a Brazilian publisher German, and so on. It is an excellent idea to keep a note of the optimum language of communication for each customer, and to transfer those details to the customer information prepared for a book fair. This means that, even in the midst of operating a busy timetable, the correct language can be selected immediately when the customer appears on the stand, or an appropriately qualified member of staff allocated to the appointment.

Fluency in the customer's language can be a major selling point, particularly if it is a less obvious language such as Russian or Mandarin. It is worth remembering that while the Italians and the Spanish may find brave attempts to speak their languages amusing or even charming, the French and the Germans do not, and it is wise to avoid attempting to communicate in those languages unless you have a good degree of fluency. Some overseas publishers speak excellent English but conduct a ritual whereby they will speak English when in England but expect negotiations to be conducted in their own language in their own country. It was once advisable to employ interpreters at book fairs such as Moscow or Beijing; but most publishers in those markets now have representatives who speak excellent English. As a general rule, it is always preferable to say clearly what is intended in one's own language than to risk misunderstandings by inadequate attempts to speak the language of the customer.

Book fair events

Although the prime purpose for rights staff visiting a fair will always be to promote and sell rights, it should not be forgotten that book fairs may also provide the opportunity for other meetings and events of interest. The presence of many publishers in one location provides an opportunity for specialist group meetings, such as the meetings of the International Association of Scientific, Technical and Medical Publishers (STM) immediately before the Frankfurt Book Fair and immediately after the London Book Fair, as well as the open and committee meetings of the International Publishers Association. The London Book Fair runs a Writers' Seminar and (in association with the Publishers Association) a half-day Back to Basics rights workshop on the Sunday afternoon preceding the book fair, the Chairman's Breakfast event on the first day of the fair (highlighting key industry concerns), as well as many seminars, events and the presentation of awards during the book fair itself. Book fairs which feature a country of honour (in the case of London, their Market Focus feature) have a number of events relating to that country during the fair, as well as attendant cultural events which may be held outside the fair premises. In 2009,

Frankfurt offered some 500 events; some precede the opening of the fair, such as the new Tools of Change conference (run in partnership with O'Reilly Media), which covered topics such as the Google Editions programme, peer-to-peer piracy, digital rights management (DRM) and the regular Rights Directors Meeting. Other events took place at the Education Forum, in the Film and Media Rights Centre and in the Weiss'raum, a new feature which explored new models in the digital arena; there was also a seminar on latest developments in the Google Settlement. Regular features are the Anti-Piracy Breakfast (run with the IPA, PA and AAP) and a number of events spotlighting specific markets under the banners of Have a look at ... and Meet ...

Other fairs may hold events which focus on the book trade in their national markets and related events such as the awarding of a particular book prize.

Follow-up

Prompt and efficient follow-up after a book fair is crucial. There is little point in making strenuous efforts to drum up interest in a project at a book fair if the potential buyer then has to wait weeks or even months to receive any further information or material. The speed of follow-up will, of course, depend greatly on the size of the list that is being handled and the number of customers seen at a fair, but it is wise to set oneself a comparatively tight deadline. If a hundred appointments need to be followed up, it should be possible to complete this work within two or three weeks of the end of the fair.

A follow-up letter by e-mail or post should confirm any discussions held on specific deals such as the suggestion of financial terms, confirmation of terms agreed, and technical matters such as the supply of coedition sample material and prices or of duplicate production material. For new negotiations, publishers should be told if they now hold an option on a project and, if so, the expiry date and the form of material that is being submitted for consideration. If the project is being offered by multiple submission, this should be made clear to each party.

If several rights staff are operating simultaneously in a given subject area, it is possible that there will be some overlap of interest in the same project from competing publishers in the same country or language. In such cases it is unwise to allocate firm options during the fair itself; rather it is preferable to log interest, compare notes immediately after the event and then allocate options in the optimum sequence; customers do not normally object to this method provided that the *modus operandi* is explained to them. After all, it makes no sense to grant an option to an Italian publisher simply because he expresses interest on the first day of the fair if the most appropriate Italian buyer is not seen until the third day of the fair.

If a project is not yet published, each customer should be made aware of what system will be operated once material becomes available. Some publishers reserve future options in the optimum numerical sequence and each publisher is then informed of their place in the queue. Others prefer to reserve only the first option and to inform competing publishers that their interest has been noted and that they will be informed if the rights become available.

Follow-up correspondence should be accompanied by any promised information or material. These could include catalogues, selective rights guides, information sheets, synopses, sample chapters, copies of the manuscript, sample illustration material, coedition prices, proofs, electronic files or reading copies; much material can of course now be supplied as an e-mail attachment, speeding up the decision process. If any items are not yet available, an estimated schedule should be provided.

A reputation for providing a prompt and efficient follow-up service after a fair can often make a crucial difference to rights business. If a company is notoriously tardy in dealing with customers, potential buyers may prefer to go elsewhere, particularly in competitive markets where alternative books may be obtained from other sources.

It is important not to discard the fair catalogue after each event. It can be used to target by correspondence potential additional customers who were not seen during the fair. While some catalogues employ broad classifications (e.g. textbooks, children's books), the Frankfurt catalogue is particularly useful for its detailed breakdown of subject interests, while the *Who's Who*, now available online throughout the year, provides an invaluable listing of individual key staff.

Real or virtual book fairs?

With the immediacy of e-mail and the telephone, is there any longer a need for real book fairs? Whilst such facilities undoubtedly spread the rights workload more evenly throughout the year, the demise of the majority of commercial online rights trading services (see Chapter 7) would seem to confirm that there is still no real substitute for a face-to-face meeting with a customer; at the major fairs, personal relationships can be established and customers seem psychologically 'primed' to buy. There is an added advantage if a book fair is held in a market in which the rights seller wishes to expand its activities; the fair itself, visits to local bookshops and publishers' own offices give a far better flavour of the local book trade than meeting in a third country. 'Real' book fairs are likely to be around for the foreseeable future and personal contact is at the heart of successful rights trading. It is ironic that after Frankfurt chose to cut its final working day of Monday, many trade publishers and literary agents started to arrive in Frankfurt several days ahead of the fair to conduct business from their hotels.

Sales trips

Much of the information provided here on preparation, sales material and follow-up procedures applies equally to rights sales trips outside the context of a book fair. These can be undertaken as solo trips, or perhaps as part of a trade mission such as those organized by the British Publishers Association to countries such as China, Taiwan, Japan, India and Mexico. These missions have provided excellent opportunities for sales and rights staff to participate in communal meetings with the local book trade, as well as to hold individual business meetings; they are often a good way to visit an unfamiliar market for the first time.

When planning a sales trip, it is wise to give the publishers to be visited as much notice as possible. When organizing appointments, it is also advisable to check on factors that may affect their availability, e.g. normal office hours, public holidays, religious festivals, dates of key sales conferences, etc. It will save a great deal of time if a map of each city to be visited is obtained in advance, and if one aims to visit publishers who are located in the same area on the same day. This can be particularly effective in locations such as New York, Tokyo, Moscow or Beijing, where careful planning can avoid much loss of time zigzagging around the city in a taxi.

The method of transport chosen for a trip will vary according to destination; for western Europe, there may be advantages to travelling around by car, particularly if several cities are to be visited and if heavy materials have to be transported. This will, however, necessitate some familiarity with street systems and parking facilities in the cities concerned. For trips to the United States it is usually simpler to travel from city to city by plane.

The question of whether to expend time and money on a sales trip will depend on the potential value of the likely rights business; in some countries the publishing industry is concentrated almost entirely in one city (e.g. in Paris and Tokyo) or in two main centres (e.g. for China, in Beijing and Shanghai; for Russia, in Moscow and St Petersburg). In other countries the industry is widely spread (for Germany, in Berlin, Cologne, Munich, Stuttgart, Heidelberg, Düsseldorf and Frankfurt; for Italy, in Rome, Milan, Bologna, Turin and Florence), so that a comprehensive trip may involve visiting several locations.

A key point to remember when planning any sales trip is that unless there is a possibility of access to office facilities in the destination city – in which case some material can be shipped ahead and the office used as a daily base – everything required for the trip will have to be carried. Even with an office base, varied material may have to be carried around each day. This could include multiple copies of catalogues, proofs, reading copies or heavy dummies – publishers still seem to prefer to see tangible material rather than onscreen information. This may call for a strong back, appropriate carrying cases (preferably with built-in wheels) and ready access to taxis. For the less heavily loaded, it can be productive to use public transport, particularly if the local metro system is efficient. Some cities now provide metro signage in English as well as the local language; others do not.

In countries where the language (and perhaps the script) is unfamiliar, it may be wise to ask customers to e-mail maps of their office location, identifying key landmarks. For a city such as Tokyo, adequate extra journey time must be allowed to accommodate the odd system of street numbers and building references, whilst in cities such as Moscow, Beijing and Shanghai distances can be considerable and transport facilities unreliable; the massive increase in ownership of private cars in both Russia and China has led to regular gridlock. The official costs of car hire and the rates charged to foreigners by taxi drivers can be exorbitant; experienced visitors may prefer to make private arrangements through a trusted contact and hire drivers by the day so that they are waiting to provide transport from appointment to appointment. A list of the names and addresses of contact companies should be taken in the local language/script, together with telephone numbers so that the customer can be contacted if it proves difficult to locate their address.

An alternative may be to arrange to hold some appointments at the hotel, if a business meeting facility, comfortable corner of the lobby or restaurant is available. This needs to be balanced against the undoubted benefit of seeing customers *in situ*.

In some countries, telephone facilities can still be highly inefficient and frustrating. In places it may still be advisable to have interpreting facilities available; an existing contact may be able to recommend suitable services, although these are often expensive. In Japan, a literary agent or local subsidiary company may be able to advise or assist.

If there is no access to office facilities, a hotel room will have to serve as an office, and seasoned travellers aim to identify a hotel in each location that can provide good facilities such as telephone, e-mail access via a laptop modem, a reliable message service and a business centre. A good customer in the city may be able to recommend a suitable hotel in a convenient and safe location at a reasonable price.

For those countries where the US dollar is the favoured foreign currency (e.g. in central and eastern Europe, Russia and China) facilities for cashing travellers' cheques may be limited and it is wise to take a suitable supply in cash, including small notes for tipping. Some countries will only accept recent and undamaged notes, so this should be checked with the bank. Since safety is now a prime concern in some of these countries, it is unwise to be seen emerging from an exchange kiosk with substantial amounts of cash. Some hotels provide machines in the lobby for exchanging dollars into local currency. In many locations it may be advisable to keep valuables and copies of key travel documents in a hotel safe.

It is wise to take a good supply of business cards and items such as a calculator, spare notebook, stapler, etc. It is also advisable to have several copies of a compact listing of the customers to be visited, with addresses and telephone numbers (in the local language where relevant); floor numbers are also helpful when visiting American publishers located in high-rise buildings. One copy should be carried in a pocket or handbag for ease of access when moving round from appointment to appointment. A mobile phone which works worldwide, perhaps provided with a local SIM card, will prove invaluable; a BlackBerry or similar phone will be useful to receive e-mail and/or text messages. A PDA or laptop computer may be useful for notes in preparation for follow-up letters and a report on the trip. Although such activities are probably best confined to hotel rooms, rights staff have been observed typing away on trains, in airport lounges or on planes.

It may be necessary to contact the home office during sales trips, although the frequency of contact may depend on the type of list handled. A coedition publisher may need to be in regular contact by phone or e-mail in order to confirm orders received during the trip or to obtain further data on prices. It may also be necessary to have sales material couriered out or back, particularly if a sales trip is lengthy and to several different countries. An academic publisher may have less need to contact home base during a trip.

Cultural mores

This book is not intended to serve as either a travel guide or a handbook on business etiquette. Suffice to say that rights staff may have to deal with a wide variety of customers from a range of cultural and political back-grounds, and that different cultural sensitivities may have to be taken into account, particularly when travelling abroad. This may affect dress code, particularly for women (e.g. in some countries in the Middle East, where an uncovered head, arms and a short skirt would be considered unacceptable). It would be prudent to undertake some research on business decorum when visiting a country for the first time – for example the need for extreme punctuality in countries such as Japan and China, and the tendency to start and end evening entertainment early in the latter country. On the other hand, it would be wise to expect extreme tardiness and radical last-minute changes of plan in countries such as Russia. Those travelling in countries which tend towards more exotic cuisine should perhaps not seek to enquire too closely into what they are eating at banquets in, say, Korea or China. For those wishing to develop good business relations with Russian publishers, thick strips of pork fat and large quantities of vodka (regardless of the hour) may be *de rigueur*.

Whilst relations with customers in Europe and Latin America may progress fairly rapidly to greetings with a hug and kisses on the cheek (the number may vary from country to country) and the use of given names, it is important to remember that other nationalities may be less tactile in business situations and it is unwise to greet Asian customers with such familiarity. The Japanese still employ at least a half-bow as well as a handshake.

In Asia the business card has a particular significance in the way it represents the status of its owner. There are formalities for presenting, accepting and studying the cards (for example, cards are presented and received with two hands in China, and studied carefully). It is definitely unacceptable to scribble notes on a customer's card or to staple it into a notebook, at least in the presence of the customer. However, especially in China it may be wise to annotate the card immediately afterwards as names are not immediately indicative of gender. In some countries it is helpful to have your own card translated into the local language, although it is advisable to try to ensure that the western name is translated in an auspicious way.

A supply of small gifts may be useful to give to people who have been particularly helpful or to customers with whom a warm relationship has developed. Whilst a bottle of Scotch or perfume may be welcomed in some countries, such items may be considered too personal in others. A supply of pocket dictionaries or nicely boxed pen sets would be more diplomatic in such cases. Some typically 'English' items such as tea, nicely packaged biscuits or chocolate may also be acceptable.

In-house reporting

An in-house rights report on each book fair or sales trip can provide not only information to colleagues in the editorial, marketing and direct sales areas, but also an invaluable summary for rights staff themselves. The exact style and coverage may vary; some companies may prefer an informal account, giving the flavour of the event or the market visited and perhaps highlighting only general trends and interest in key titles. In larger publishing groups, with different imprints or editorial divisions, it may be useful to produce a more detailed report for each sector, with a list of customers seen and a title-by-title report of interest expressed and deals finalized.

It must also be said that it is no bad thing to produce reports of this kind as a form of public relations for rights activities: to stress the importance of rights business conducted at a major fair such as Frankfurt, or perhaps to report back on the results of attendance at a newly established fair or a fair not hitherto visited. If a member of the rights staff is trailblazing in a new market, an assessment of political, economic and trading conditions may prove invaluable for export sales colleagues.

Chapter 9

English-language territorial rights

These are the sale of rights to key English-language markets for a British publisher; these may include the United States, Canada, Australasia and South Africa, while for an American publisher there may be a need to place rights for the United Kingdom and Commonwealth markets. The categories of books most eligible for licensing may range from highly illustrated books on topics such as gardening, cookery, handicrafts, art and photography; illustrated and non-illustrated children's books; fiction; biographies and autobiographies; popular reference topics; self-help, health and lifestyle books, through to business books (professional and popular) and specialized academic and professional books.

The trend in recent years in the publishing industry has been towards continuing consolidation within large multinational groups. Publishers operating in this way may have no need to make licensing arrangements in key English-language markets; they may have the facilities to distribute a single English-language edition worldwide through subsidiary or associate companies within their own group. An alternative policy may be to negotiate internal licence arrangements within the group; this may be a prerequisite for a multinational to acquire the rights, although such arrangements are not always the best deal for the author, who will then receive payment in the form of an agreed share of the licence revenue.

On the other hand, it may be that the subsidiary or associate company in one market is not the most appropriate channel for all types of publication produced, and in such cases it may still be appropriate to seek an external rights partner. Many smaller publishing houses do not have their own operations in the major English-language markets overseas, and hence they may seek a distribution arrangement for stock of their own edition, or some type of rights deal.

The most significant business in this area of licensing is undoubtedly between British and American publishers, but licensing separately to other important English-language markets may be worth considering for books with a local potential. Canada, Australasia and South Africa have long been regarded as part of the British Commonwealth territory, which traditionally formed part of the British publisher's exclusive market. However, local publishing industries in these countries have now developed to such an extent that it can no longer be assumed that the markets can always be best serviced by a distribution arrangement.

Territorial rights and parallel importation

The debate on the maintenance of territorial rights is of key importance to publishing in world languages such as English, and it has continued with renewed vigour in the columns of the trade press and at industry con-ferences over the last fifteen years, with a major survey in *The Bookseller* trade magazine in September 2005. Whilst some elements in the trade argue that the days of exclusive territorial rights are over and that globalization will prevail, particularly since the advent of bookselling on the internet through companies such as Amazon, others maintain that the protection of such rights remains essential, particularly now that many publishers have embarked on their own e-book publishing programmes. This has led to the escalation of 'turf wars' between UK and US publishers over the last five years (see *The trade in rights between the UK and the USA* later in this chapter, pp. 121–4).

Territorial rights are the exclusive right to exploit a copyright work in a given geographical market. Without exclusivity in a market, the local publisher or distributor has little incentive to invest time and money in stockholding and promotion if they may be undercut by the availability of rival editions of the same book entering the market at a lower price. Exclusive territorial rights are generally considered beneficial by literary agents and authors, in that the royalties paid are usually consistent with appropriate pricing of the book in the market concerned. A breakdown in territorial restrictions could mean that low-priced editions (e.g. those legiti-mately licensed to markets such as India) could enter more affluent markets and undercut sales of an edition legitimately on sale there from the original publisher or from an authorized licensee.

The doctrine of international exhaustion of rights holds that once a book is first sold in its country of origin, it can then freely move into other markets without restriction. This would allow for parallel importation, i.e. the importation of any legitimately published edition of the same book, regardless of the contractual rights held by the publisher of that edition and of who holds the national territorial rights in the country into which the edition is imported. This doctrine flies in the face of national copyright legislation; the Publishers Association in Britain has advised that where there is a UK rightsholder, imported copies of other editions of the same work would be considered infringing copies if making those copies in the United Kingdom would constitute a breach of an exclusive licence to that work. Internet retailers such as Amazon have stated that they will observe territorial restrictions for titles available from UK publishers if the necessary information is available to them via bibliographical services such as Nielsen BookData.

A further issue of territorial rights arose in October 2009 when Amazon launched its Kindle e-reader (see Chapter 24) in the United Kingdom but with books initially purchasable only from the US site, Amazon.com. As Amazon gradually rolls out the wifi device in Europe and elsewhere, it has stated its intention that e-books should be purchasable from national Amazon sites.

The issue of leakage of physical copies has arisen regularly when potential bestsellers are released earlier on one side of the Atlantic than the other – for example J.K. Rowling's *Harry Potter and the Chamber of Secrets*, where early copies leaked onto the US market. Since that time, the trend has been to aim for worldwide simultaneous publication of new titles by bestselling authors; subsequent *Harry Potter* titles have been launched at midnight in the UK with simultaneous publication throughout all time zones. However, this in itself can pose major logistical problems: the author cannot be in two places at once!

Canada

For some books, it is worth considering making separate licensing arrangements with a Canadian publisher. Trade books have been most successfully handled in this way, and there are many examples where the print run sold by a Canadian publisher far exceeds the number of copies of the British or American edition which might have been distributed by a Canadian subsidiary or distribution agent. The Canadian market has long resented being 'thrown in' with either the British or the American market. There would also be an excellent case for licensing Canadian rights in a book that required particular adaptation for the market, for example a school textbook adapted for the Canadian curriculum.

Australia

The Australian Copyright Amendment Act 1991, which became law on 23 December 1991, followed a long-running debate on whether Australia (as part of the Commonwealth) should be primarily dependent on British publishers for the supply of overseas English-language books to that market. The Act was intended to ensure speedier supply of books from abroad, but the effect was to open the Australian market to parallel importation of competing editions unless specific procedures are followed by British publishers and their Australian associates. The 1991 Act permitted importation of any edition of a book that had not been made available in Australia within thirty days of first publication by the publisher contractually controlling the Australian market. The result was that unless the British edition was made available in Australia within thirty days of publication in the UK, or an Australian publisher produced a local edition, a competing edition from the USA or some other source could be imported, despite the fact that the British publisher was likely to have exclusive contractual rights for the Australian market. This posed particular problems for British publishers seeking to acquire rights for the UK and Commonwealth market from a US publisher or agent, since the US edition was likely to be available earlier than the UK edition, and often at a cheaper price.

For existing UK backlist titles, competing editions could be imported into Australia if the UK publisher could not supply the market within ninety days of receiving an order, or did not inform the Australian bookseller within seven days of receiving an order that it could be supplied within ninety days. Market exclusivity could be restored once the UK publisher made the UK edition available again to the Australian market.

This legislation placed considerable financial and administrative pressures on UK publishers to supply the Australian market within the required deadline; one solution was to print copies in Australia for sale through a local subsidiary or agent if the market justified an independent printing; alternatives included air-freighting copies from another print location or making licence arrangements with a local Australian publisher, perhaps on the basis of a coedition. All of these avenues were explored by UK publishers.

Another result was that in some cases authors' agents preferred to sell Australian rights separately rather than to assume that the market would be serviced by a British or American edition. The advantage to the author would then be a full royalty on sales to this market, rather than a royalty based on the export price of bulk sales of a British or American edition to the market.

In August 1996, the Australian Industry Commission released a draft report which included a recommendation to abolish the thirty- and ninety-day requirements with a view to establishing a full open market situation; in May 2000 a Federal Government Committee also recommended completely lifting restrictions on parallel importation. Both recommendations were strongly contested by the Australian Publishers Association (APA) and in April 2003 the Copyright Amendment (Parallel Importation) Bill 2002 was passed with significant amendments; competing editions can only be imported if the original British edition or a local Australian edition has not been published in Australia within thirty days of initial publication or if such editions cannot be supplied within ninety days of the original import request. In March 2009 the issue resurfaced with a draft report from the Australian Productivity Commission which recommended allowing competing editions into the market twelve months after first publication in

Australia and abolishing both the thirty-day and ninety-day regulations; the final report, issued in June 2009, recommended that all restrictions should be lifted, making Australia a completely open market. The report was strongly opposed by the APA, the Australian Society of Authors (ASA), the UK Publishers Association and many UK literary agents, on the grounds that the resulting uncertainty on market exclusivity would restrict the ability of Australian publishers (both locally owned and subsidiaries of multinationals) to invest in the market, and hence impact on Australian as well as overseas authors. The report was eventually rejected by the Australian government in November 2009.

New Zealand

In May 1998, the New Zealand government announced an amendment to the 1994 Copyright Act to remove restrictions on parallel importing. As the change made no provisions similar to the thirty- and ninety-day rules in Australian legislation, this allows UK publishers no exclusivity in the market, even if New Zealand forms part of their exclusive contractual territory. Protests were submitted by the British and American Publishers Associations. A government discussion paper in December 2000 was followed by further amending legislation in 2003 which precluded the parallel importation of films; technically parallel importation of books is still possible, but has not posed a major problem to date.

The United States

The American market is undoubtedly the single most significant overseas English-language market for British publishers for both trade and academic titles. The larger UK houses may have their own subsidiary companies in the United States, or may themselves be part of US-owned conglomerates; in such cases the sale of US rights may not be necessary, as stock of the original edition may be exported for distribution in the US market; alternatively, the US publishing operation may manufacture its own edition, perhaps with a different jacket design and typeface. Regardless of the preferred *modus operandi*, UK publishers should continue to be aware of the discrepancies between UK and US copyright legislation, and should check the status of copyright protection for their works in the US market. The Sonny Bono Copyright Term Extension Act, which came into force on 27 October 1998, extended the term of protection for works created on or after 1 January 1978 from fifty years *post mortem auctoris* to seventy years, in line with legislation in the UK and other EU countries. This legislation also extended by twenty years the term of certain earlier works. For details of the very complex provisions for copyright in earlier works, see *Copyright legislation in the United States* in Chapter 1.

The trade in rights between the UK and the USA

For many years, it was common trade practice for British publishers to retain as their exclusive market the United Kingdom and the countries of the Commonwealth as it was constituted in 1947, and the Publishers Association issued a recommendation to its members that they should seek to retain these markets when selling to an American house, or to acquire these markets when purchasing rights from an American publisher. This was known as the British Publishers Market Agreement. American houses retained as their exclusive market the huge domestic market of the United States itself, its dependencies and the Philippines, the latter included because of the extensive American presence there since the end of the nineteenth century. The rest of the world was termed the 'open market', in which the British and American editions of the same book could compete.

This practical and usually amicable division of the world market (more relevant to trade than to academic publishers, who were more likely to distribute their own books worldwide) existed until 1976, when the Anti-Trust Division of the US Department of Justice took legal action against twenty-one major American houses, charging that 'the defendants and certain co-conspirators engaged in an unlawful combination and conspiracy to restrain foreign and interstate trade and commerce in the distribution and sale of books in violation of Section 1 of the Sherman Act'. Cited as co-conspirators were the Publishers Association, the British trade organization whose membership included virtually all significant United Kingdom publishing houses, and named individual member companies of the Association. Thus American and British publishers were held to have conspired in a monopoly arrangement that was considered to be detrimental to the interests of trade and the end consumer.

The result of the legal proceedings was a Consent Decree, which restricted the defendants from entering into arrangements 'which constitute an overall pre-determination for the allocation of countries and markets between American and British publishers'. The Publishers Association revoked the British Publishers Market Agreement from 11 July 1976. Since that date, it has been necessary for British and American publishers to agree exclusive territories on a title-by-title basis, and the territories traditionally held by British publishers on an exclusive basis can no longer be assumed to be British as of right.

The question of the territories in which British and American publishers compete is a vexed and complex issue, which has come to the fore periodically over the years. It arose particularly prior to the launching of the single European market on 1 January 1993 and the introduction of the Maastricht Treaty on 1 November 1993, which brought in the then six EFTA states (Norway, Sweden, Finland, Austria, Iceland and Liechtenstein) to create the European Economic Area (EEA). Since then membership of the European Union has been expanded to include a number of states from central and eastern Europe (see Chapter 1) and the Maastricht Treaty has been updated via the 1997 Treaty of Amsterdam which came into force on 1 May 1999.

At the heart of the European open market issue is the fact that there are major discrepancies between the exclusive nature of contracts in copyright and two sections of the Treaty of Rome affecting trade within the European Union and the EEA: Articles 30–35, which require member states to permit the free movement of goods across community borders, and Articles 85–86, which prohibit private arrangements to restrict markets. These regulations may make perfect sense for goods such as clothing, shoes, cutlery or ballpoint pens, but they cause major problems for a product where language is a key factor and where a major competitor operating in that language exists outside the Union, i.e. the United States.

The British Publishers Association has long sought to convince the European Commission to exclude contracts in copyright from these provisions, since such arrangements are normally based on territorial exclusivity and are generally held to be beneficial to consumers in the countries concerned. Their efforts have been unsuccessful to date, and contracts dividing the single market (which would include contracts between UK and US publishers where the UK market is isolated contractually from other European territories) are technically in breach of the Treaty of Rome.

Although this situation has existed since the United Kingdom joined the European Economic Community in 1973, there has long been concern amongst British trade publishers that parallel importation would increase; American editions entering the European open market may travel thence into the UK publisher's exclusive home market. The establishment of European and UK representation by American jobbers such as Baker & Taylor reinforced those fears. There has been particular concern about paperback editions, where the American edition will almost certainly undercut the UK edition on price.

The debate has become more heated in the last fifteen years with the advent of internet retailers such as Amazon, offering books to buyers at substantial discounts. This increased the possibility that the US edition of a book could be ordered by UK customers direct from such websites when an authorized UK edition was on the market or imminent. The online booksellers have stated that they will observe market restrictions if appropriate data are made available to them (see *Territorial rights and parallel importation* earlier in this chapter, pp. 117–8).

A number of major UK trade houses now seek to acquire world rights or, if this is not possible, to retain all the countries of the European Union as part of their exclusive market. This move has been resisted by a number of the major American trade houses, which feel that they should be free to compete with the UK editions in Europe. In some cases, the suggestion has been made that if the British publisher is to retain exclusively the countries of the European Union, then Australia or Canada should form part of the American publisher's exclusive market, and more recently some American publishers have been keen to retain rights for India (traditionally part of the British publisher's market) when selling rights and to acquire them when buying rights from a UK publisher, or to see India as part of the open market. The US view on Europe has generally been backed by the Association of American Publishers, which has felt that in practice parallel importation is unlikely to prove a major problem. The British Publishers Association and UK literary agents remain concerned both by problems arising from internet bookselling and by the fact that EU legislation deprives British publishers of protection against parallel importation of US editions into their home territory via continental Europe, a possibility that is not precluded under the UK Copyright Act of 1988. It was unfortunate that this possibility of parallel importation appeared to be reinforced by the wording of Regulation 9 of the Copyright and Related Rights Regulations 1996 (see *Copyright legislation in the United Kingdom* in Chapter 1).

The 'turf wars' escalated during a high-level and heated panel discussion at BookExpo America in May 2006, at which British publishers and literary agents raised again the implications of internet bookselling, the exchange rate with the US dollar and the danger of erosion of rights in the UK home market via an open European market. US participants defended their position strongly, questioning whether the exclusive grant of English-language rights in 'non-English territories' would benefit the interests of authors; they argued for increased competition and open markets and referred to the British requirement for exclusivity as a 'land grab'. UK literary agents have called for US publishers to increase their export royalties to match UK levels if they require European rights. European booksellers then entered the fray with an open letter to the US and UK book trades, supporting an open market for competing editions. The debate was taken up again at the 2006 Frankfurt Rights Directors Meeting and continues, with multinationals arguing that the grant of world rights might be the only solution. A further dimension emerged in 2008, with some US multinationals seeking to retain global electronic publishing rights; this has met with strong resistance from many UK trade houses who see e-book publishing as key to their publishing plans.

When negotiating sales territories as part of a licence arrangement, the main consideration should be the ability of the licensee to service the markets required, and to assess the relative benefit of licensing markets that might be considered negotiable (for example Canada) versus retaining them. If an American publisher has an established subsidiary or other regular outlet in Canada and the British publisher has not, it may be preferable to grant Canada as part of the American publisher's exclusive territory. However, the terms of the deal should reflect this, either in an increased coedition order or by a larger advance against royalties in the case of a reprint licence deal.

What kind of books travel?

For two countries using the same language (or, perhaps, divided by the same language – a sentiment variously attributed to Oscar Wilde and George Bernard Shaw) it is interesting that comparatively few titles appear on the bestseller lists on both sides of the Atlantic. There are of course exceptions to this – popular novels by US writers such as John Grisham, Stephen King, Tom Clancy, Michael Crichton, Danielle Steele, Sidney Sheldon, Patricia Cornwell and more recently James Patterson, Dan Brown and Stephenie Meyer regularly appear on the UK bestseller lists, whilst the books of Maeve Binchy, Jack Higgins, Wilbur Smith, Helen Fielding (of *Bridget Jones* fame), Nick Hornby, as well as more 'literary' authors such as Salman Rushdie, Martin Amis and Arundhati Roy, have all made their mark on the US market. There have also been 'surprise' bestsellers such as Lynne Truss's *Eats, Shoots and Leaves*.

The children's fiction market has often proved more difficult; although writers such as J.K. Rowling, of *Harry Potter* fame, and Geraldine McCaughrean have succeeded, major British writers such as Jacqueline Wilson have not yet captured the market on a large scale, possibly because young readers in the United States tend to be more cushioned against controversial themes in children's literature.

There has long been a successful market for illustrated books on topics such as art, craftwork, cookery, interior design and gardening. Areas such as self-help, personal improvement, diet and to some extent popular business books tend to be dominated by US writers; popular science writers such as Stephen Hawking and Richard Dawkins have proved successful. On the academic side, it is usually more common for British publishers to distribute their own editions through subsidiaries or affiliates, although titles on economics, politics, social science and literature may sometimes be sold to academic presses.

Methods of dealing

There are two main ways of selling rights to the United States or other major English-language markets: through undertaking a coedition or by granting a reprint licence. The method selected will depend on a variety of factors, including the type of book in question, the quantity involved, relative printing costs in each country and fluctuations in exchange rates, and also whether the book requires adaptation in any way to make it more suitable for the licensee's market. For a coedition, the originating publisher prints copies for his licensee in addition to his own print run, making appropriate changes; these may be limited to a simple change of imprint and ISBN (International Standard Book Number), but could also involve a change of cover design, addition or substitution of a preface, or complete Americanization of British text. For a reprint licence, the licensee is authorized to print its own edition, either by reproducing the typographical setting directly from the original publisher's edition or by resetting the book completely.

In either case it is vital to ensure that any necessary copyright permissions from external sources (for example other publishers, picture agencies, art galleries or museums) have been cleared in such a way that the material can be included if the book is licensed for publication under another imprint. It will not be sufficient to clear permission and pay for text and illustration rights for world English-language rights if such permission is restricted to a single edition, a specified print quantity or to publication under the imprint of the British publisher only. Some sources, such as museums and picture agencies, may specify in the small print of their contracts that if permission has been cleared for use restricted to the original applicant, that applicant would be in breach of contract with the copyright owner if reproduction material was then passed on to a third party. This could affect the supply of duplicate production material to an American licensee.

For heavily illustrated books, it should be borne in mind that the cost of clearing permissions from a variety of sources for world rights in all languages, including the granting of rights to licensees (vital if the project is being planned as an international coedition), can be extremely expensive and thus a major factor in the economic viability of the project. It will be necessary to include a proportion of these costs when quoting for manufacturing on behalf of overseas partners.

Coeditions

This method is often preferred when the book has a high colour content, since there can be considerable economy in combining print runs and hence reducing the unit cost. It may be that in many cases the only change required is that of the imprint where it appears on the spine, cover, jacket (if applicable), title page and verso. A separate ISBN will need to be provided by the licensee for inclusion on the title verso, cover and jacket, while American publishers will wish to include LC/CIP data (Library of Congress/ Cataloging in Publication data) on the title verso.

While the majority of coedition deals are for bound books, there may be occasions where a book could be supplied in the form of flat sheets or folded and gathered sheets ('f and g's'), which will then be bound up by the licensee; this may be appropriate if the licensee requires a different binding style from that of the licensor's edition or if it does not wish to publish until some time after the UK edition.

For American coeditions of certain categories of book, Americanization of text may be required. Some British publishers whose coedition business justifies the investment have specialized departments for this purpose. Key areas here are children's books, some areas of handicrafts, and cookery and gardening books, where such items as weights and measures, ingredients or planting and flowering seasons, as well as some terminology, may have to be changed to suit the market. Some publishers cope with the problem by printing both sets of terminology in a common text, for example ounces/cups, courgettes/zucchini. Illustrations may have to be replaced to show appropriate alternative items, but substantial changes of this kind may reduce the profitability of the coedition deal.

If the originating publisher does not have the facilities to make the changes required by the licensee, it may be appropriate to undertake the deal on the basis of a reprint licence arrangement, with independent manufacture by the licensee. This is often the case with children's books, where spelling and terminology (e.g. pavement/sidewalk, lift/elevator) may have to be adapted for the licensee's market.

It is possible to undertake English-language coeditions for other types of book. These include high-priced academic works, often unillustrated, where the individual print run for each market could be comparatively small, perhaps less than 1,000 copies. Here a combined print run could be vital to make the project viable at a price the market can afford. For such books, the modifications involved are usually a simple change of imprint and ISBN, although it may also be possible to consider some modification to the binding style. A joint imprint can present a saving if it is acceptable to both licensor and licensee.

Negotiating a coedition

Timing is crucial if a coedition is to be undertaken on the initial print run. The decision to seek an overseas partner must be made at a very early stage, to allow for approaches to be made to possible publishers to tie up a deal without delaying the production schedule. For this reason, it is wise to start approaching potential overseas partners as soon as the project is conceived, using appropriate initial material. For an academic book, a brief synopsis together with information on the author, bibliographical details and the intended schedule and price for the home market should be sufficient to identify possible interest. For a book where illustrations are a major feature, more elaborate sales material will be required. If sales material can be ready in time for use during a sales trip, or at a key event such as Bologna, Frankfurt or BookExpo America, it will usually be possible to canvass reactions quickly, although material can now of course be sent electronically at any time.

Sales material

For an illustrated book where a coedition deal is sought for the initial print run, a contents list and sample spreads (now often provided electronically on disk or, for smaller books, as a PDF e-mail attachment), a dummy (particularly important still for novelty books) or a 'blad' (brief layout and design – an eight- or sixteen-page sample section originated in advance of the book itself), and details of schedule and price will be needed. Although advance material can now be scanned to be shown on a laptop, most purchasers still seem to prefer to see physical material, and printing out from electronic files on to a standard paper size often fails to do justice to the project.

The aim of the licensor is to obtain a firm order from the licensee and to coordinate all the coedition requirements in time to catch the first print run. The amount of additional material that will be required in order to enable the licensee to reach a decision will vary according to the type of book in question. For an academic book, the potential buyer is likely to want to see a copy of the complete manuscript (these can now be supplied as PDFs) or initial proofs. To wait for a decision at proof stage can be dangerous, for if the project is turned down at this late stage of production it may prove impossible to find an alternative buyer in time without jeopardizing the publication schedule for the licensor's edition, which is likely to be time sensitive in a highly competitive market. For this reason, it may be preferable to make the initial submission to several potential purchasers simultaneously, provided that it is made clear to each that this is the method to be employed.

For an illustrated book, much will depend on the nature and content of the book and the reputation of the originating publisher. At both ends of the illustrated market – mass-market books at low prices on topics such as cookery and handicrafts, and higher-priced coffee-table books on topics such as art, interior design and natural history – there are publishers who have built their reputations on a particular genre of book, and in the case of the mass-market titles the books are often produced to a standard style and format. If a relationship is established with a coedition partner and a number of deals are successfully negotiated, it may well be that new deals can be done on the basis of a contents list, bibliographical details, a jacket design and a dummy containing several spreads. If more material is required, this can now be provided in the form of electronic files rather than the more traditional set of Ozalid proofs (familiarly known in the United States as blues).

If a coedition is being negotiated after publication of the original edition, to be coordinated with a reprint, the sales material will consist of the finished book, perhaps combined with details of sales of the original edition and a selection of favourable reviews.

Costing

The costing of coeditions is a complex process, and methods vary from company to company and indeed from book to book, making it difficult to provide a typical example. Some publishers work to a set profit margin, while others may be prepared to take a very low return per copy in order to increase the print run on the first printing of a particular project in order to make it viable. Some houses work with a pro rata spread of the origination costs across the UK edition and those of the American and any other coedition partners; others may be prepared to supply copies to partners virtually at run-on cost (the cost of printing materials and manufacturing only, without including a contribution towards the cost of creating production material from the manuscript and illustrations and a set profit margin).

The fixed costs involved in a coedition are editorial, design and artwork fees, permissions fees for external material, origination costs, typesetting and proofing for the interior and the cover. These costs may be fully or partially amortized over an entire coedition printing, which could consist of various English-language editions (e.g. the original publisher's edition, a book club order and a US edition) and foreign-language editions. The variable costs include paper and materials for the cover and jacket; the cost of an imprint change or any other changes involved in a US edition; printing and binding costs; and any additional costs such as lamination, shrink-wrapping and shipping expenses.

In an ideal situation, the price quoted for coeditions should include the actual cost of materials, printing and binding, a realistic contribution towards the origination costs (which can be high in the case of a full-colour book) and an additional profit margin. A range of prices can be quoted for varying quantities, with larger orders justifying a lower price per copy. The price may also include elements such as the cost of reclearing textual and illustration permissions for the licensee's market.

The price quoted must take into account any variations between the product which is to be supplied to the coedition partner and that of the original publisher. These may be limited to a simple change of imprint and ISBN, or could include a complete Americanization of the text if the licensor has the facilities to undertake this work. There is also the question of whether the type of paper and binding materials will be identical to those used for the UK edition, and whether a different jacket or cover design or specification will be required for the licensee's edition and, if so, whether this will be designed by the licensee and provided in the form of film or an electronic file.

It is also essential to establish whether the licensee requires the book to be shrink-wrapped or slip-cased if this packaging would not normally be allowed for in the price quoted. American publishers often require up to 10% additional jackets to be supplied for promotional purposes and for re-jacketing in case of damage.

It is wise to include a provision in the coedition contract that the licensee will accept up to an agreed over- or under-supply with payment adjusted accordingly – a common figure here is 5%. If sheets are being supplied rather than bound books, an additional 'free' allowance is usually 10% to allow for spoilage during the binding process. When arriving at a coedition price, a major consideration is whether it should be quoted royalty inclusive or royalty exclusive. The advantage of a royalty-inclusive deal is that the licensee will pay the full amount regardless of how many copies are eventually sold in his market. To be set against the advantage of receiving full payment in advance of actual sales is the fact that, when costing in the royalty element, one may have to make an educated guess not only at the eventual price at which the book will be sold in the licensee's market, but also at the mark-up factor the licensee employs to arrive at that price. It may be that a regular coedition partner simply specifies the maximum price that it can pay in order to arrive at its optimum retail price for the market, which makes the costing process much simpler. To quote royalty exclusive will mean that a full royalty is paid on the local price but that (after any initial advance on signature of the contract) payment will only be received as and when copies are sold by the licensee and accounted for once or twice annually according to the contract.

When deciding whether to quote royalty inclusive or exclusive, one must also take into account the relative benefits to the author. Many head contracts specifically provide for the author to be paid an agreed percentage of the publisher's net receipts in the case of bulk sales made at a high discount; this may make an American coedition viable if the costings are tight. Some authors may require that for bulk sales to an American publisher they still receive a full royalty based on the British publisher's recommended retail price, and this may make coedition costing difficult. Other authors may provide in their contract that they should receive a full royalty based on the American publisher's recommended retail price. In such cases it will be necessary to negotiate a royalty-exclusive deal, and the British publisher will seek to make its margin on the manufacturing price quoted to the American publisher. In the case of academic books, where relatively small print runs are involved, prices quoted to American publishers are usually royalty inclusive.

The question of how the shipment should be packed should be carefully considered since this may affect the price quoted. For example, flat sheets are best transported in custom-made wooden crates rather than on standard pallets for container shipment, in order to avoid damage in transit.

For books, a licensee may require a special pallet size that will be con-venient for storage in its own warehouse, but which may not be a standard pallet size for the licensor. If the licensee requires copies to be individually cartoned, this may be an additional charge. There may be special require-ments to comply with US anti-pest regulations. A decision must also be taken on what transport costs will be included in the unit price quoted. The possibilities here are:

1 Ex-works: the licensee pays for all transport and insurance costs from the licensor's printing location onwards.
2 FOB (free on board): the licensor will be responsible for transport of the consignment to the docks in the country of manufacture, but the licensor's responsibility will end halfway over the rail of the ship when the consignment is loaded.
3 CIF (cost, insurance and freight): the licensor pays for transport and insurance up to a destination port in the country of the licensee. The licensee is then responsible for all costs in connection with unloading, customs clearance and onward transport to its own warehouse.
4 Delivered into the licensee's warehouse: the licensor is responsible for all transport and attendant costs to the end destination.

The method selected depends on factors such as the printing location and whether the licensee regularly consolidates shipments from that location, in which case FOB to a port in the country of manufacture may be preferred.

When quoting a coedition price to a potential buyer, it is essential to make it quite clear how long the price will be valid for and exactly what it includes. Prices should be specified as holding provided that a firm coedition order is received by the licensor by a specified date; it is also wise to specify the minimum viable quantity. If it is intended that the coedition will involve two or more partners (for example if foreign-language coedi-tions are to be printed together with the British and American editions), it is wise to specify that the price will hold only if a total specified minimum coedition quantity is achieved. This allows for new prices to be quoted if the total falls short of the quantity required to achieve the initial prices quoted. Late delivery of material for imprint and jacket changes or Americanized text can delay the entire coedition and affect prices; publish-ers may wish to consider including a penalty clause in the contract that would require the US publisher to pay a higher unit price in such cases. If other partners are involved, it may also be wise to include a clause that would require the late partner to compensate other coedition participants for any additional costs caused by the delay.

The question of the safest currency to use when quoting for a coedition is a difficult one. A coedition deal agreed in February for supply in

September could result in income that does not cover the cost of manufacture if a major fluctuation has occurred between key currencies during that period. Technically, the safest currency to employ when quoting is that of the country in which the books or sheets are being printed, since the licensor is then assured of receiving sufficient currency to pay the printer. However, an American publisher joining a coedition organized by a British publisher may be reluctant to commit to a price quoted in Euros or Hong Kong dollars. In practice, most coedition business undertaken between British and American publishers is quoted in sterling or in US dollars; ideally, the production department of the originating publisher should supply prices based on 'buying forward' for a sufficient period of time to avoid problems of this kind. If one is to quote in a currency other than one's own, one must then take a calculated risk on whether there will be any gain or loss if there is an alteration in the exchange rate. When the pound is high, American coedition business may prove difficult, and proved particularly so during the period 2005–7 when the exchange rate approached US$2/£1 sterling. A compromise may be to agree to a price in sterling at a fixed exchange rate on a particular date; the contract can then provide that any fluctuation of more than 5% against that exchange rate will be borne equally by the coedition partners. Apart from the problem of exchange rates and generally lower pricing of books in the US market, coedition sales have proved generally difficult for high-priced illustrated books in recent years, partly due to the recession but also because of the prevalence of promotional editions in the US market (see Chapter 12); also, in the area of children's books US publishers are now producing more home-grown product and are less dependent on importing British and European projects.

The question of when and how payment will be made by the licensee is very important. Some coedition publishers may be prepared to accept full payment for books or sheets at an agreed point after delivery (say sixty or ninety days from invoice date or thirty days from arrival in the licensee's warehouse), but many publishers require part payment to be made well in advance of that point. This is justifiable, since the publisher organizing a coedition will have made a considerable investment in developing the project, and will be buying additional paper and incurring additional printing costs on behalf of its partners. It may be reasonable to require that 50% of the total payment is made on receipt of a confirmed order and the balance on shipment or at an agreed time after the date of the bill of lading or the invoice. Some publishers may require payment to be made at stages linked to the manufacture of the book, for example 25% on receipt of a firm order, 25% when production starts, 25% on delivery and the balance at an agreed date after the bill of lading. This method is usually employed where coeditions are for large quantities of full-colour books.

The investment by the originating publisher on behalf of a coedition partner may be substantial; trade and bank references should always be sought when dealing with a licensee for the first time and periodically rechecked. One method for ensuring safe receipt of payment is for this to be guaranteed against an irrevocable letter of credit drawn on a London bank. To require this arrangement from a customer will involve them in additional expense and may be deemed unacceptable, especially if the US publisher is part of a major publishing conglomerate, but it can be a useful safeguard when dealing for the first time with a less well-known partner. Some publishers require payment against a letter of credit for the first deal and dispense with the requirement once a satisfactory working relationship has been established. Others include a penalty clause with interest charged monthly on late payment at 2% above the base rate in the country of the licensor.

Technical details and schedules

Once a coedition order is finalized, there will be a number of technical details to be covered.

The licensee must provide in good time full details of its required imprint changes, including material for any logo, and specifications for the placing of the logo and imprint details. It will also need to provide its own International Standard Book Number (ISBN) and Library of Congress/ Cataloging in Publication (LC/CIP) data.

The easiest way to deal with these requirements is usually to send the licensee the copy and design for the relevant parts of the UK edition: for a jacket, the front cover design, spine design, front flap copy, back cover design and back flap copy plus details of the intended placement of the UK imprint, logo and ISBN on the case of the book itself. In addition to this, copy should be supplied for the full prelims of the UK edition. Such material can now be sent far more speedily electronically, but US publishers may still wish to mark up hard copy to show the exact placement of the required changes. Proofs of jacket, cover and prelim changes should be supplied to the licensee with a requirement for approval by a specified deadline; these are usually now supplied electronically as low-resolution pages showing the text in place.

In a small number of cases, the licensee may require a title change for its edition, perhaps to avoid confusion with another book of the same title within its market. The implications of this will need to be carefully thought through. The changes to jacket, cover and prelims may be simple, but if the licensor's jacket design has the original title reversed out in light lettering from a darker background, the cost of reoriginating new film for the jacket will have to be taken into account. A change of this nature may also cause problems if the title appears on the running heads (at the top of the page) throughout.

If the licensee has requested a complete change of jacket design and this has been agreed from the point of view of cost, the licensee must be instructed on the required form in which material should be provided. In practice, the simplest option will be in the form of film or electronic files to specifications provided by the licensor.

Some American publishers have detailed standard packing instructions involving the use of a particular pallet size and carton size. There may also be standard requirements concerning maximum weight per pallet and per carton, maximum number of books per carton, individual packing requirements, and so on. It is vital to obtain details of these at the earliest possible stage, as they may not correspond with the standard packing specifications employed by the printer.

From the licensor's point of view, it is essential to tie the licensee to specific deadlines for the provision of items such as imprint changes and documentation requirements, but to allow oneself leeway for possible unavoidable delays in the manufacturing and delivery schedule. A coedition order might thus read that the licensee must supply materials 'no later than … ', but that the licensor will supply proofs or finished copies 'on or about … '.

The licensee must provide to the licensor by an agreed deadline full details of the required port of entry for the consignment, the licensee's handling agent and the final destination address for the consignment. The method of transport is likely to be sea freight, although if a book is being printed in the Far East and the American publisher's warehouse is in the Midwest, it may be necessary to arrange for onward transport from a west-coast port by Amtrak or by truck. Air freight may be employed for a small quantity of advance copies if the schedule is tight, but the additional cost of this must be agreed.

The fact that a licensee's offices are located on the American east coast does not necessarily mean that their books will be shipped to New Jersey or Boston; they may require them to be shipped to Seattle. Thus, when dealing with a coedition partner for the first time, it is wise to discuss the question of shipping requirements during the earliest stages of the negotiation, since these could well affect the coedition price quoted.

The licensee must provide the licensor with full details of the invoicing and any other documentation required to enable the consignment to be imported without encountering customs problems. This may include a certificate of origin and a requirement that the commercial invoice carry a declaration on the nationality and domicile of the author. Exact details may have to be provided of the country of manufacture, the country of first publication, the country of domicile of the author and the author's nationality. Alternatively, this could read:

This title bears an imprint claim of copyright under the provisions of the Universal Copyright Convention and was first published in a country signatory to the convention. The author was a citizen of or was domiciled at the time of first publication in a country signatory to the convention other than the United States.

This latter requirement harks back to the days of the now defunct 'manufacturing clause' which restricted the importation of books by American authors from non-US sources, initially to 1,500 copies and latterly to 2,000 copies, before the provision was abolished from 30 June 1986. This was intended as a protectionist measure for the US printing industry.

Reorders

As with all coeditions, care should be taken to ensure that the US publisher is alerted in good time to reprint schedules for the book, either when the UK publisher is reprinting for the home market or perhaps to supply a book club order or the requirements of foreign-language licensees. Reorders can then be coordinated for the maximum number of partners, with a beneficial effect on the unit cost for all participants. If the US licensee requires copies at a time when reprinting is not practical, or if no compromise can be reached on timing or price, duplicate production material could be supplied to enable the US edition to be printed independently. However, this should be viewed as a last resort, since it will remove a major participant from any subsequent coedition reprints.

The question sometimes arises of what should be done if the originating publisher requires a deal on the basis of a coedition but the potential purchaser prefers to manufacture independently. This may be less likely to occur in the case of books illustrated throughout in colour, where the economy of scale derived from coprinting is normally apparent unless the exchange rate is prohibitive. It is more likely to be raised in the case of high-priced academic books, where the issue may be less one of reaching agreement on price than of who has direct control of the printing. In such cases a decision may have to be taken on whether to refuse rights unless a coedition is undertaken; this rather presumes that an alternative buyer is available. If no such buyer exists, it may be preferable to agree to a reprint licence than to forgo a deal for the market in question altogether.

Reprint licences

Many transatlantic rights deals are negotiated on the basis of reprint licences, with each publishing house manufacturing its edition independently; this is particularly prevalent in the area of fiction. A coedition may provide an economy of scale for certain types of book, but there are a number of factors which may mean that separate editions are preferable.

If both print runs are to be substantial, there will be no particular saving in combining them, and this is particularly so in the case of books containing no colour illustrations. The licensee may feel that it can obtain better printing prices locally, and there is an additional advantage of direct control over the timing of printing and delivery of stock, as well as over the quantity printed. Independent manufacture is also preferable if there are to be significant alterations to the text (Americanization of spelling or terminology), if material is to be removed or added, if the format, binding or jacket design is to be altered, or if the book is to be reset in a typeface considered to be more suitable for the market; British and American editions of the same book often 'look' quite different stylistically

Sales material here may consist of proofs or electronic files if the book is still in preparation, or a finished copy, sales details and favourable reviews if publication has already taken place.

Terms

The arrangements for a reprint licence will normally be based on an advance payment against a royalty on each copy sold. The exact terms will depend on factors such as the status of the author, the nature of the book, the topicality of the subject material, the size of the print run, the binding and the proposed local selling price. It is perhaps dangerous to attempt to give sample royalty rates, but an initial royalty rate of 10% on the recommended retail price of a hardback edition is not uncommon, perhaps rising to 12% and 15% after an agreed number of copies have been sold. Rates for a book first published in paperback binding (as opposed to a mass-market paperback edition sublicensed through the local hardback publisher) tend to be lower, ranging from 7% to 8% and rising to 10% and 12%. However, royalty rates on sales at high discount may be based on net receipts rather than the recommended retail price (see *The contract* later in this chapter, pp. 137–40).

The timing of royalty payments varies from once annually (common for some academic publishers) to twice annually for trade titles, where the income is likely to be more substantial. The size of the advance payment will vary enormously according to the importance of the author and the project. For a modest print run of, say, 3,000 copies of an academic book, the advance might represent one-third to one-half of the total royalty payable on the first printing, while a new novel by an author with a major international reputation could well generate a six-figure advance. Large advances may be paid in several instalments. The author will receive a share of the proceeds in accordance with the terms agreed in the original head contract; this could range from 50% up to 80%.

As mentioned earlier, permission may have to be recleared for any textual or illustrative material controlled by third parties if this has not already been covered. If the onus for undertaking this clearance plus the payment of any necessary fees is transferred to the licensee, the licensor will need to provide a list of the relevant names and addresses. It should be remembered that in some cases the holders of rights for the American market may differ from those in the United Kingdom. If the licensor agrees to undertake clearance work, the fees should be recharged to the licensee, with the addition of a handling charge of at least 15% of the total.

Licensing older works

Reprint requests may sometimes be received for UK titles that were published many years ago and that may well be long out of print with the original publishers.

The first step is to establish whether rights are still controlled by the UK publisher, both in an overall sense and in the market of the would-be licensee. The original head contract must be checked, but under UK copyright law there is an important point that must be borne in mind for books published before the implementation of the 1956 Copyright Act on 1 July 1957. Such titles are covered by the provisions of the 1911 Copyright Act, which, while it provided for copyright protection for the lifetime of the author plus fifty years, also specified that no assignment of copyright could endure beyond the first twenty-five years of the period *post mortem auctoris*. Thus, even if the author had assigned copyright and hence control of sublicensing rights to the publisher in the head contract, if the author of a book published before 1 July 1957 has been dead for more than twenty-five years but less than seventy years (after which the book would now fall into the public domain under UK legislation anyway) the copyright will have reverted without written formalities to the author's heirs. In such cases it will be necessary to locate the heirs or their representatives, and to ask whether they wish to handle licence arrangements direct, or if they are prepared to allow the UK publisher to handle the deal in return for an agreed share of the proceeds.

As outlined in Chapter 1 (under *Copyright legislation in the United States*), changes introduced into US domestic legislation from 1 January 1998 may mean that some older UK titles that had fallen into the public domain in the United States have had copyright protection restored for the remaining portion of the term of protection to which they would have been entitled had they not entered the public domain. As a result of the 1998 Sonny Bono Copyright Term Extension Act, the period of copyright protection for titles published on or after 1 January 1978, when the 1976 US Copyright Act came into force, is now seventy years *post mortem auctoris*, in line with legislation in the United Kingdom and other EU countries.

The contract

The contract should summarize all the terms agreed, whether the arrangement is being made on the basis of a coedition or a reprint licence. It is, however, important to note that many of the large American trade houses are not prepared to sign any form of contract other than those produced by their own in-house legal departments. This diverges from the unwritten rule that it is the seller who normally provides the licence contract.

American contracts can be extremely long and complex; the legal departments of major US trade houses can be very inflexible about any changes to boilerplate wording, even if the particular circumstances of a licence require these to be made. A recent contract supplied by a US trade house insisted in including 'theme park rights' for a professional book on business strategy. In some cases, American contracts appear to be modified versions of original author/publisher contracts rather than documents designed for the acquisition of licences from other publishers; this can lead to considerable confusion. If the licensee cannot be persuaded to accept a contract prepared by the original publisher, the contract submitted must be carefully checked and any necessary changes highlighted and explained, although it may be necessary to expend considerable time and effort to negotiate these.

The duration of the licence should always be carefully considered when territorial rights are being granted. In the case of a coedition, the contract may be limited by the number of printed copies that are being supplied, although in some cases the agreement may include a provision for the licensee to manufacture locally if at some future point the parties are unable to reach agreement on the timing or price of a reorder.

If the contract is to be limited by time, there is a choice between granting a licence for the full term of copyright or for a shorter period. Many American houses still seek a licence for the full term of copyright. The UK publisher will need to check whether its own head contract with the author allows for this; if the book has been acquired from an agent, the UK publisher may have received a limited-term licence, which may preclude granting rights for a longer period to a sublicensee.

If full term of copyright can be granted, and the licensor is prepared to do so, the contract must contain adequate provision for the recovery of rights if the licensed edition goes out of print, although there may have to be separate provision for any sublicences properly granted by the US publisher within that territory to run their allotted course. Even if the licence is granted for a shorter term, provision should be made for the recovery of rights if the US edition goes out of print, particularly in the case of a coedition deal if no reorder has been placed for stock or if no agreement has been reached to reprint the book locally. The question arises of what now constitutes 'out of print', particularly if the US publisher has been granted e-book publishing rights; provision for the recovery of rights might better be linked to revenue falling below an agreed amount in an agreed accounting period.

In recent years, the tendency has been to seek to grant shorter-term licences for trade titles, perhaps for eight to ten years, with provision to renew if the parties agree. This provides an opportunity for the renegotiation of terms, including a new advance payment. The ideal scenario would be for the term to run from the fixed date of the licence contract, but US publishers are more likely to require the term to run from their date of first publication, which could of course be later than originally estimated. It is probably impractical to seek to grant licences for less than eight years for titles with local sublicensing potential, as this will restrict possibilities for such exploitation (e.g. to book clubs, and perhaps paperback sublicensees if the US licensee has not acquired the right to publish both hardback and paperback editions 'vertically'). The expiry dates for American licences must be carefully monitored; here a computerized record system proves invaluable.

The question of the territory to be granted to an American publisher was discussed earlier in this chapter (pp. 121–4); it is now necessary for this to be negotiated on a title-by-title basis. While many academic publishers may be content to accept the United States, its dependencies and the Philippines alone, others with a strong presence through subsidiary companies in Canada, Latin America, Japan and now Australasia may seek exclusive rights for those territories also. Much will depend on the way in which the UK licensor covers those markets. American trade publishers are likely to seek open market rights in addition to their exclusive territories; the implications of granting these will need careful consideration but they may well be regarded by the US publisher as a deal-breaker.

Royalty provisions should be carefully monitored. While some American houses provide for royalties to be calculated on the recommended retail price, others specify that royalties should be calculated on net receipts rather than on the recommended retail price in the case of sales made at higher than normal trade discount, or for copies sold through special channels such as premium sales and mail order. This may have a major effect on the licence revenue generated. US publishers sometimes provide for base rate royalties under small reprint clauses for quantities as low as 2,500 copies; they may also require a set proportion of the royalties due to be held in reserve against stock returned unsold (returns).

The question of whether to grant e-book and other digital publishing rights to a US publisher, either for direct exploitation or via licensing to third parties, requires careful thought. Many US publishers now expect these rights as a matter of course, but they should not be granted automatically and it would be wise to ask for details of the US publisher's current plans in this area and whether they can reassure the UK publisher that market restrictions can be enforced, e.g. via the purchaser's credit card location. Some major US trade houses now offer a royalty rate of 25% of net receipts on their e-book sales.

The timing of publication of an American edition should be carefully considered, particularly with regard to the implications for the open market, where the US edition can compete directly with the UK edition and can even enter the British market (see *Territorial rights and parallel importation* earlier in this chapter, pp. 117–8). The contract should provide for publication 'not earlier than … ' and 'not later than … ' for both the home and the open markets.

When licensing rights it is common practice to include a clause in the contract that prevents assignment of the rights granted to a third party without the prior approval of the licensor. Some American publishers seek to be able to assign rights elsewhere, particularly in the case of selling off part of a publishing operation. A British publisher may wish to resist agreeing to this if the book in question is not to end up on the list of a completely different publishing house from the original licensee.

American publishers who insist on using their own form of contract when acquiring rights often make very stringent requirements in the clauses covering warranties and indemnities, particularly in areas such as libel, obscenity and the requirements for statements purporting to be facts to be true. Before agreeing to such requirements, it will be necessary to check that they are covered by the warranties and indemnities provided by the author in the head contract; if they are not, the relevant clause must be adjusted in the American contract. In the case of coedition copies, US publishers may also require stringent safety warranties on the materials used in the physical copies – this can include requirements for non-toxic glue, regulations for staples in wire-sewn books, plastic materials in items such as bath books for babies, and so forth.

Contracts drawn up by American publishers may include a provision for an option on the next book by the author if rights are controlled by the same licensor. Here the decision may depend on the status of the author and the degree of commitment to the US house; if the next work is likely to be auctioned, the American publisher of the previous work might be offered first sight of the work and/or 'topping' rights (see Chapter 6).

Most major American trade houses are not prepared to agree to a contract that is operable under the law of the country of the licensor; they insist on the contract being operable under the law of the American state in which they themselves are incorporated. No licensor favours a contract being operable outside home territory, but in some cases negotiation on this aspect of an American deal may prove difficult. American academic presses are usually more prepared to accept contracts provided by the licensor that provide for the contract to be operable under English law.

A coedition contract is likely to be more complex than a reprint licence contract. There are two schools of thought, one favouring inclusion of details of the quantity, specifications and dates for material to be supplied in the main body of the contract. The other prefers to list such details in the form of a purchase order attached to the main contract, which gives details of the quantity, price, shipping instructions, invoicing and payment terms, etc.

Subsidiary rights

Some licences involve granting only publication rights for the book in hardback and/or paperback volume form for the designated market, but licences for trade titles could well involve the inclusion of certain subsidiary rights for that market. Thus a deal with a hardback trade publisher might also include the right to sublicense mass-market paperback rights to another publisher as an alternative to publishing 'vertically' themselves; the right to license hardback rights to another publisher (this usually covers cheap promotional editions appearing some time after publication of the main US hardback edition); the right to license to book clubs – this may involve a supply of copies of the American publisher's edition or the book club manufacturing separately and paying a royalty; large print, digest, quotation and anthology rights; quotation rights; serial rights to newspapers and magazines; micrographic and reproduction rights; and so on. As for electronic rights, such rights should never be granted automatically but should be discussed at the same time as the main deal is being negotiated, with an appropriate proportion of the income generated from any such sublicences to be payable to the original UK publisher. Rights such as film and television rights should not be included in a territorial licence.

If first serial rights are to be included as part of the deal, the question of timing must be carefully discussed, as early publication of prepublication extracts in the US market could result in 'spoilers' in the UK market (see *First serial rights* in Chapter 14).

One area which requires special care is that of mass-market paperback rights, where some US trade houses seek to pass on only 50% of the proceeds from paperback imprints within their own publishing group. A split that might be acceptable for a licence granted to an independent mass-market paperback house hardly seems appropriate for a vertical publishing deal of this kind. For volume and serial rights it would be wise to require prior consultation or approval of any deals, such approval not to be unreasonably withheld. It is particularly important to have control over the timing of a sublicensed mass-market paperback edition if this will be released into the open market, since this would then compete there with the licensor's own paperback edition or with any UK sublicensed paperback edition (Chapter 11) and there is a danger that it could enter the

UK market, particularly via online booksellers (see *Territorial rights and parallel importation* earlier in this chapter, pp. 117–8).

The division of proceeds from subsidiary rights could range from 50/50 to 90/10 in favour of the UK publisher. The timing of payment arrangements for subsidiary rights income may vary, from accounting at the same time as payment of royalties is made on the main edition, to a requirement that such income be remitted immediately on receipt or within a short period of time (perhaps thirty days) from receipt of payment from the sublicensee. The latter may be preferable in the case of a book that will generate substantial income from local sublicences.

Offset fees

The licensee may wish to reproduce the typographical setting directly from the UK edition. This may produce satisfactory results for books consisting entirely of text, or perhaps with black and white line illustrations, but it is often unsatisfactory for books containing black and white halftone photographs. It is rarely employed for books illustrated in colour.

In such cases, it is customary to charge an 'offset' fee in recognition of the saving in typesetting costs for the licensee and as a contribution towards the typesetting costs incurred by the UK publisher. Offset fees are normally charged on a per-page basis and may vary according to the complexity of the setting; the saving on complex typesetting such as mathematical formulae can be considerable. An average rate at the time of writing is £3 per page. Offset fees are normally paid on publication rather than on signature of the licence contract, but the question of timing can be negotiable.

Under UK copyright law, copyright in typographical arrangement (the so-called 'publisher's right') was first accorded protection under the 1956 Copyright Act and runs for a period of twenty-five years from the end of the year in which the work was first published. However, it is a feature of relatively few other national copyright legislations and does not exist in US copyright law. For this reason, British publishers cannot demand offset fees from American publishers as of legal right, but rather in recognition of the saving in typesetting costs.

As an alternative, a US licensee may wish to purchase duplicate production material, usually in the form of electronic files (see Chapter 25).

Licensing to pharmaceutical companies

The licensing of medical information to pharmaceutical companies can be a lucrative source of extra income for medical publishers. In some cases, business of this kind may be handled by a special sales department rather than a rights department, and may involve the creation of material especially for a pharmaceutical client – perhaps the proceedings of a conference on treatment of a particular disease, or the trial results of a particular pharmaceutical product. In other cases, the arrangement may involve the sale of copies of an existing medical title, which the drug company will then distribute free of charge to general practitioners or medical specialists; the book is usually accompanied by general promotional material from the drug company or advertising for a specific product.

In some cases, however, the deal may involve a special printing of an existing book, an individual chapter from a book or a specific journal article in English; again, the name of the drug company or specific advertising material may be included. Deals of this kind may well fall to rights staff to handle if no special sales department exists.

If the deal involves printing copies for the drug company, a quotation will have to be provided in the usual way as for an English-language coedition, taking into account any change of imprint or the inclusion of advertising material, usually in the prelims or on an inside cover. The prime concern of the drug company will be to negotiate a low unit price, as the copies will be distributed free of charge; quantities can sometimes be substantial, varying from 2,000 up to as high as 50,000 copies. Payment will normally be quoted royalty inclusive; payment to the author will depend on the terms of their contract but will probably be calculated as a royalty based on the price paid by the drug company. It is normally wise to consult the author prior to finalizing any deal of this kind, particularly if the drug company wishes to include advertising for a specific product; any such advertising should be clearly separated from the text of the book or journal article itself to avoid the impression that the author is endorsing a particular product which may not be mentioned in the original text. Such deals can be very lucrative, but it is certainly not worth antagonizing the author if they do not wish their work to be used in this way. The timing of payment from the drug company is negotiable, but it is advisable to obtain a proportion of the payment on signature of the contract, and the balance within an agreed number of days of delivery of copies to the drug company.

In some cases, deals of this kind are made via a pharmaceutical packaging company, which may purchase copies for onward sale to a drug company. Again, the deal is likely to be negotiated on the basis of a royalty-inclusive price if the original publisher is manufacturing copies; care should be taken to obtain some payment in advance, and the balance within an agreed number of days of the packager receiving payment from the drug company or by an agreed latest calendar date.

Chapter 10

Book club rights

This area of activity has changed significantly over the last ten years and nowadays the term 'book club' is more commonly used to describe a group of friends meeting regularly to discuss books they have read. Despite the changes, sales to commercial book clubs are still of some importance to British, American, European and Latin American publishers and have become a significant factor in publishing in the markets of central and Eastern Europe. However, in the United Kingdom the impact of competing channels of supply is now very apparent: the ability of the retail trade (booksellers and also supermarkets such as Tesco and Asda) to offer discounts following the demise of the Net Book Agreement in 1997, sales to direct marketing companies such as The Book People (TBP) who sell to companies and individuals without a membership requirement, and in particular the rise in popularity of online booksellers such as Amazon offering books at a discount.

The main demand from the clubs is still for popular fiction and non-fiction, as well as for reference books such as dictionaries and encyclopaedias; in the late 1990s UK clubs launched more specialist and upmarket clubs, but this trend has now been reversed. The United States has long had clubs providing professional reading in areas such as architecture, engineering, nursing and psychiatry; the equivalents have never existed in the United Kingdom.

Book clubs were established primarily as mail order operations; they still recruit the majority of their members through advertisements in the daily, weekly and monthly press, although the clubs run in a number of countries by the German publishing giant Bertelsmann traditionally recruited through door-to-door sales representatives.

In 2000, it was estimated that the mail order book market (including the clubs, special sales operations such as The Book People and Reader's Digest) held 22.6% of the UK book market by value, of which the book clubs represented approximately half; by 2008 the figure had fallen to 12.5% as a result of the competing channels of supply, with book club sales representing slightly under half that percentage.

For many years Bertelsmann dominated the book club market; it was reputed to have 25 million members worldwide, of whom 4.5 million were in Germany, and had launched book club operations as far afield as China. However, in 2008 it closed down the club in China and sold its US clubs, operating under the umbrella of Direct Group North America, to Najafi Companies, a Phoenix-based private investment company. Rumours have circulated that it may sell its European club operations; in September 2009 it embarked on a pilot exercise to allow non-members to buy books from its German club retail outlets. Membership of the German club operation is reputed to have fallen from six million in the mid-1990s to three million in 2008. In February 2010, it withdrew from its Italian operation.

Its operation in the United Kingdom was for many years Book Club Associates (BCA – www.bca.co.uk). Established in 1966, it was originally jointly owned by the bookselling chain W.H. Smith and American publishers Doubleday. In 1988 ownership moved to a partnership of Reed and Bertelsmann, with Bertelsmann acquiring Reed's share in June 1998 when that company withdrew from the trade publishing sector. At its height, BCA had more than two million members; until late 2005 it operated twenty-two clubs in the United Kingdom, one in Eire, ten English-language book clubs in Europe (Austria, the Netherlands, Belgium, Denmark, France, Finland, Germany, Norway, Sweden and Switzerland) and one in South Africa. In early 2000, it acquired Books for Children, The Softback Preview (TSP) and the New Spirit club from Time Warner. In 2001, Bertelsmann's bol.com operation was combined with BCA's club services to enable new members to join via club websites and existing members to order online. During the course of 2004, BCA reported a doubling of online purchasers; however, despite optimistic forecasts it encountered difficulties with distribution backlogs and in late 2005 it announced significant job losses and reduced the number of its clubs to eight by combining many of its specialist clubs. In 2008 Bertelsmann entered into negotiations to sell the company and since 1 January 2009 it has been owned by Aurelius, a Munich-based industrial holding. BCA remains the largest UK book club operation and runs clubs under the banners of Books Direct, The History Guild, Fantasy and Science Fiction, Railway, Military and Aviation, Books for Children and TSP.

Other UK book club operations included Readers Union, founded in 1937, acquired in 1997 from Reader's Digest and operating clubs in various leisure and hobby areas such as craft work, angling, climbing and natural history (www.readersunion.co.uk). However, in September 2009, owners David & Charles announced that they had been gradually winding down the book club operation as it was felt to be 'no longer sustainable'. Continuing book club businesses include The Folio Society (www.foliosoc.co.uk), which produces special lavishly bound and illustrated editions of classic titles, and the Cygnus book club, based in Llandeilo, Wales, and offering titles in the area of mind, body and spirit.

For children, the main club for trade titles was Red House, founded in 1979 by David Teale, acquired by Scholastic UK and from 2002 run jointly by Scholastic and the direct marketing company TBP. In June 2009 the joint venture was disbanded; Red House was taken over by TBP and Scholastic continue to run their School Link bookclub (www.scholastic.co.uk). In July 2009 David Teale announced plans to launch an online venture, My School Book Club (www.myschoolbookclub.co.uk); parents and pupils can order from the site and participating schools will be credited with 20% of order values for school library purchases.

Recruitment and conditions of membership

The normal method of recruitment of new club members has been through press advertising. The initial offer is a book or a selection of books at a nominal price; such offers are called premiums and are loss leaders for the book clubs. An attractive premium offer such as a boxed set of a famous children's series, three lavish art books or a set of desk reference books traditionally generated a significant number of new members. A club may be general in nature (for example BCA's Books Direct) or specialist (for example the Gardeners Book Society operated by Readers Union).

The usual membership requirement is that once a new member has joined by accepting the initial premium offer, they must agree to purchase a minimum number of additional books during the course of the initial membership period; a requirement to purchase four books in the first year is common.

It is inevitable that some people sign up to obtain the initial premium offers, buy the minimum number of additional titles required and then leave membership, perhaps rejoining later as a result of an attractive new premium offer. The clubs are concerned about what they term the 'churn' rate and are able to monitor such tactics if they occur frequently. Some people remain loyal book club members for many years; there is, however, increasing evidence that they may also buy discounted titles from other sources such as TBP and Amazon, a development over the last ten years.

Members normally receive a book club magazine, monthly or quarterly, from which they can make a further selection of titles; alternatively, they can order from the equivalent magazine on the club website. These books are offered to members at a discount off the original publisher's recommended retail price that normally ranges from 25 to 35%. However, the key titles may be offered at a larger discount – perhaps up to 50%. Some clubs offer the choice of one major title (the main or editor's choice, which may be offered at a slightly higher than normal discount) plus a range of other titles (alternative choices). Some clubs operate a negative option on the main choice; the member must complete a form indicating that this book is not required, or cancel the selection by phone or online, otherwise it will be sent out automatically to all members of that club; in November 2009 BCA announced that it would be abandoning this practice. Members normally pay for the cost of postage and packing of the books they select, but some clubs may offer delivery free of charge for orders over a designated value.

The demise of book club regulations

Regulations for the operation of book clubs in the United Kingdom were introduced in the mid-1970s; all major book clubs agreed to be bound by the regulations, which were issued by the Publishers Association and approved by the Office of Fair Trading (OFT). The intention was to ensure that the clubs could offer a wide variety of books to their members, but on specified terms which would take into account the interests of the UK retail book trade.

The Publishers Association maintained a register of book clubs which agreed to comply with the regulations. Clubs were required to keep a register of members; there were regulations on the minimum period of membership and the minimum number of purchases required after the initial premium offer. The regulations also required clubs to advise the Publishers Association of all titles to be offered to club members at least four months in advance of first advertising the titles concerned; these were published in the form of lists in *The Bookseller* to give prior warning to the retail trade.

The final demise of the Net Book Agreement on 13 March 1997 (when it was declared illegal by the Restrictive Practices Court) ended the book club regulations, since they applied only to net books. However, a number of elements of the regulations remain important, and publishers may wish to consider including those points in their contractual arrangements with book clubs (see *Contracts for purchase of printed copies* and *Contracts for reprint editions* later in this chapter, pp. 151–3 and 153–4).

Book clubs and the retail trade

There has long been a divergence of opinion between publishers and booksellers on the effect of books being offered through the clubs. Booksellers in particular have protested at the offering of bestselling titles at nominal premium prices; even the larger chains cannot compete with such prices, though they can now offer significant discounts themselves. Publishers have often maintained that many book club members are not dedicated bookshop customers, but people who prefer to choose from preselected titles in the privacy of their own home, often because they do not have ready access to a good local bookshop, or possibly because they are intimidated by the range of choice in a bookshop. BCA's plans in 1993 – to expand, with a range of retail outlets where new members could join and existing members could collect their selections – met with much resistance from the UK trade and were subsequently abandoned.

Such is the continuing concern from the book trade that the wholesalers Bertrams insisted that publishers must alert them to impending book club deals when selling new titles. The issue was a key topic for discussion at the annual Booksellers Association conference in 2003 and this was followed in early 2004 by a similar requirement for early warning of book club deals from W.H. Smith and a number of independent booksellers. The topic continues to resurface in the columns of the trade press.

When advertising their offers, the clubs continue to indicate their club price against the recommended retail price of the trade edition; the usual formula is 'RRP £a, club price £b'; some club advertisements also give the name of the publisher in the text of the advertisement. The identity of the publisher may also be apparent from the title of the book, e.g. *The Oxford Dictionary of Quotations*. Since the demise of the Net Book Agreement, publishers cannot, of course, guarantee a fixed retail price for comparison with the club price, and this should be clearly specified in the book club contract or other paperwork.

Book club editions were originally required to be clearly distinguished from the trade edition by carrying the imprint of the club; in practice, the situation now is that the clubs either purchase copies of the publisher's own stock or acquire a licence to manufacture copies themselves, which will then carry their own brand (see *Reprint licences* later in this chapter, pp. 153–4).

Paperback book clubs

During the course of 1990, two book clubs were established offering paperback editions to their members: BCA's Quality Paperbacks Direct (QPD) and The Softback Preview (TSP), then owned by Time-Life, subsequently Time Warner, and later acquired by BCA; both aimed to offer upmarket fiction and non-fiction to their members.

TSP still exists under the umbrella of BCA and can obtain its copies either by purchasing copies of a special paperback edition produced by the hardback publisher, by purchasing standard paperback copies if the original publisher also produces an edition in that binding, or by purchasing copies from the sublicensed paperback publisher. Prices may be negotiated royalty inclusive or exclusive, although TSP tends to favour the latter arrangement.

There was initially some resistance from paperback publishers, who felt that sales of their own editions would be affected, even though a special paperback edition issued by the book club would be at a higher price than a mass-market paperback edition. Any hardback publisher wishing to license paperback rights direct to a paperback book club when a sub-licensed paperback edition is in existence or in preparation would be wise (and indeed may be contractually obliged) to obtain prior clearance from the paperback licensee in order to avoid conflict (Chapter 11). Most paperback houses would now expect the inclusion of paperback book club rights in their own licences.

Acquisition of books

Book clubs acquire their product in two ways: by purchasing copies from the original publisher or by acquiring a reprint licence to manufacture copies themselves.

Purchase of copies

If copies are purchased from the original publisher, they are usually bought in by the club at a substantial discount off the publisher's recommended retail price, to enable the club to offer the book at a good discount to its members but also to make a reasonable level of profit on the sale. Premium choices are offered at nominal prices and are hence loss leaders, which are offset by the fact that they attract new members to the clubs. The attraction for the original publisher of supplying copies to a book club is the chance to reach an additional readership and to increase the print run by adding the book club order to its own requirements, and hence to reduce the unit cost; however, lower book club orders mean that today there is less benefit in this area. There is some continuing evidence that there can be a spin-off benefit for sales of the trade edition if book club advertising is extensive and if the identity of the publisher is clear, perhaps from its inclusion in the title of the book. In the past, copies supplied under an exclusive licence arrangement carried the club imprint, but nowadays the books supplied to the club will be identical to the publisher's own stock.

Even for copies printed under licence by the club, BCA now uses a club imprint on the title page and verso only. If there is any substantial variation between the book club edition and the trade edition apart from the imprint (different paper or binding quality, a reduction of format, removal of some illustrations, etc.) the book club must clearly indicate this in its advertisements by specifying that it is offering a special book club edition. Unless it does this, it would be making a false statement if it compared the price of the book club edition with that of the trade edition.

The level of discount accorded to the club may range from 60% for a small quantity supplied to a children's book club to over 80% for most purchases by the larger clubs. The level of discount will depend on the number of copies required, the price at which the club wishes to offer a particular book to its members, and whether a simultaneous paperback edition is available from the original publisher or a sublicensed paperback edition is imminent. Book clubs are often looking to fill slots in their programmes for up to a year ahead, and it is therefore essential to keep the relevant club editor informed of a new project at outline stage, followed up by a copy of the manuscript or, at the very latest, page proofs. For an illustrated book a dummy or sample spreads and a jacket rough will be essential. In the area of children's books, some individual titles may be priced too low to appeal to the clubs; however, several books in the same series offered either as a pack or as a single compendium volume can sometimes be attractive.

Striking jacket or cover designs are particularly important for book clubs, since they rely on attracting new members, and orders from existing members, by depicting the books in their recruitment advertisements and the regular catalogues sent to members as well as using thumbnail images on their website advertisements. Books may sometimes be specially packaged for book clubs, or existing titles may be combined for a special book club edition (for example a dictionary and a thesaurus in a single volume).

To achieve maximum economy of scale, the publisher must aim to interest the book club buyer at a sufficiently early stage to allow for printing of the book club requirements in addition to the publisher's own initial print run. Much of the negotiating with book clubs is conducted by telephone or e-mail, with the club requiring prices for buying quantities urgently, and the publisher anxious to tie up the deal in time to catch its own print run. Once prices have been supplied, taking into account quantity and other factors, such as the royalty commitment to the author on such copies, there may be further negotiations until a suitable deal is agreed.

In some cases, the discount required may be too high for a deal to be reached; in others, the publisher may be prepared to accept a very low profit margin, or even a small loss on the initial book club quantity, in order to achieve an increased print run and in the hope that subsequent reorders from the club will achieve a better margin. It should be remembered that a reorder from a club at a later date may have to take into account higher production costs and a different quantity, and it may not have the benefit of riding on the back of a publisher's own print run, which might also include copies for an American coedition partner. It should also be borne in mind that, in the fortunate case of a large book club order, the club may require that delivery be staggered over a number of months, and then the cost of storage in the printer's or the publisher's own warehouse may be significant, particularly if large quantities of books are being held for a long period.

Since the demise of the Net Book Agreement, there has been a tendency for the clubs to place far lower initial orders in order to control inventory costs. They may then return for a series of reorders, which may have to be taken from the publisher's existing stock rather than added to the publisher's print quantity. This can make costing difficult and affect publishers' own stock levels.

For most sales, the price quotation provided by the publisher to the club includes the royalty element to the author. As the discount must often be very high in order to achieve a book club sale, provision may be made in the head contract with the author for the royalty to be paid on such sales to be based on net receipts rather than on the recommended retail price of the trade edition. Since the ending of the Net Book Agreement, many publishers now provide for all authors' royalties to be calculated on net receipts, but if the contract still provides for the author to receive royalties on the recommended retail price, it would be advisable to make some separate provision for royalties on sales at high discount to be paid on net receipts. It can easily be seen that if a full author royalty of, say, 10% is to be paid on a recommended retail price of £19.99 and a book club requires to buy copies at 80% discount off that price, this leaves very little leeway to cover the actual cost of manufacturing the book and for the publisher to make even a very modest margin on the sale. However, the practice of paying book club royalties on net receipts has led to some protest from authors; the historian Antony Beevor eventually vetoed the inclusion of book club rights in his contracts on the grounds that he felt normal trade sales of his books would be cannibalized; 35,000 copies of *Stalingrad* had been sold through book club channels.

Some literary agents representing major authors have required that prices are quoted to book clubs with the royalty specified separately, and with an advance against the royalty element. This is usually paid half on signature of the book club contract and half on first publication of the book club edition. In such cases, the advance and royalties will be divided between author and publisher in the proportion specified for book club sales of this kind in the head contract (usually at least 50% in favour of the author), while the price quoted to the club for the actual printed copies will be retained entirely by the publisher. In some cases, publishers have been asked to provide details of their manufacturing costs to agents when quoting to book clubs, with a view to negotiating a share-profit deal, although with the clubs seeking ever-higher discounts, margins have been slim.

Because of the *modus operandi* of book clubs, the date of publication of the trade edition and delivery date to the club are crucial, and it is essential that if there is any variation to either date the club is informed immediately, since it may involve rescheduling the offer of the book to members or, if it has already been advertised, writing to members to warn them that delivery will be delayed.

Contracts for purchase of printed copies

Readers Union traditionally operated on the basis of an overall contract with each publisher plus purchase orders to cover individual titles. Red House and Scholastic operate on the basis of purchase orders alone. BCA long operated on the basis of a separate contract and purchase order for each title purchased, but it now has a single master contract with each publisher, plus individual purchase orders.

As the old book club regulations can no longer be enforced, it may be wise for publishers to seek to cover some elements of the regulations in contracts with the clubs. In the past it was possible to impose an embargo on premium use by a club until several months after the trade publication date, but nowadays timing is by negotiation and the clubs may be permitted to advertise the book in advance of the publication date but not to supply copies to members before that date.

Contracts may be for an exclusive or a non-exclusive licence; BCA specifies slightly differing markets for each. An exclusive licence normally runs for a period of three years from first publication of the book by the club, with a four-year period for non-exclusive licences. All book club contracts should contain a provision that rights will revert if the book club exhausts its stock and does not place a reorder or seek a reprint licence to manufacture its own copies.

If the book club has a single master contract with the publisher, details of the recommended retail price and publication date of the trade edition will normally be contained in the individual purchase order relating to that title. Any variation to either must be notified to the club immediately, as it may affect their marketing plans for the book. As mentioned earlier, it is now harder to negotiate a restriction on premium use so that there is a time lag following publication of the trade edition.

If the book is being supplied in hardback to the club, the licensor will normally be required to guarantee that they will not publish themselves or license for publication a lower-cost hardback edition or a paperback edition (large-print and educational editions are usually excluded from this restriction) within the first twelve months following publication of the trade edition, without obtaining prior clearance from the book club. In practice, most sublicensed paperback editions will be restricted from appearing (at least in the UK market) for at least one year after publication of the hardback edition, but they may be published earlier in overseas markets as early export editions (Chapter 11), and BCA still supplies club members in some European markets. The terms of any paperback sublicence arrangement therefore need to be checked, and it is always wise to tell the book club at negotiation stage if a paperback edition is in the pipeline. If the hardback publisher is itself publishing a simultaneous paperback edition (quite common amongst academic publishers), this should also be notified to the book club at negotiation stage, since it may affect the club's decision on whether to purchase the hardback; it is also likely to affect the price at which it offers the book to its members if it does decide to go ahead, and hence the price it is prepared to pay for copies. BCA's specialist clubs, such as The History Guild, are prepared to buy paperback stock. The purchase order must specify clearly which edition is being purchased; BCA's order forms will carry details of the publisher's own paperback price even if it is purchasing hardback copies.

The licensor is also restricted from allowing the book to be offered as a premium in connection with other products (e.g. as a free gift for new subscribers to a magazine) without obtaining prior clearance from the book club. The clubs may also be reluctant to take on a title which is also being offered by a direct marketing operation such as The Book People (see Chapter 13).

The licensor must normally agree to a warranty and indemnity clause guaranteeing that the book is original and that there will be no infringement of any copyright. There may also be a requirement to warrant that the book is not obscene, indecent, libellous or defamatory. It is thus essential for the licensor to check whether any reclearance of copyright permissions is necessary if the book is to be published under the imprint of the club rather than that of the original publisher and to ensure that permission has been obtained for the use of any extracts or illustrations which belong to third party copyright holders (including the cover image) on the book club website. It is also vital to check whether the warranties and indemnities provided by the author under the head contract cover the warranties and indemnities required by the book club. If they are not covered, the book club will have to be informed that the warranty and indemnity clause relating to that particular title will have to be modified accordingly.

The licensor must provide the book club with specified advance material such as proofs, electronic files, final copies and jackets by agreed deadlines, as these are vital if the book club is to prepare its advertising material in good time. The licensor must then deliver the book club stock on a specified date or dates; delivery on a designated day is essential if the club is to fulfil its obligations to its members. BCA in particular has very specific requirements regarding delivery days and times and standard pallet requirements which must be observed. The clubs generally are now far less prepared to pay for over-supply, even on limited numbers of copies.

If there is any slippage in the delivery date, the club must be informed immediately, as it may have to reschedule the book in its programme or write to its members to warn them of late delivery. The publisher may be liable for reimbursing the club for doing this if delivery is more than ten days late; and if delivery is delayed by more than three months, the club may no longer be obliged to purchase the stock. This could be disastrous in the case of a large order; careful monitoring of the production and delivery arrangements for book club orders is therefore vital.

Both parties are normally restricted from remaindering their stock within a given period of publication of their editions without prior consent from the other party and without first offering their stock to the other party. Recent club contracts have reduced the period from two years to one year. Book clubs are inventive in disposing of overstocks, often by including books in 'mystery parcel' offers to their members.

Given that some of the UK clubs do operate in some overseas markets, it is important to ensure that a book is not offered as a premium in a particular market just as the trade edition is being launched there by the subsidiary of the UK publisher or by a local licensee.

Reprint licences

For titles that are likely to be used in large quantities as main selections, as regular premium offers over a long period of time, or produced in a special binding, e.g. for The Folio Society, the clubs may seek an exclusive licence with a provision to print their own copies. This gives them direct control over the manufacturing cost and the date of delivery of their own stock. It does not, of course, have the benefit of increasing the original publisher's print run and reducing the unit cost, but it does remove the administration from supervising a book club coedition deal.

Contracts for reprint editions

Reprint licences normally run for an exclusive period of three years from the date of first publication by the club, and for a further non-exclusive period of four years, with provision for termination if the stock is exhausted and no new printing is in hand. The royalty rates paid are usually modest (5% is common) and are based on the price at which the book is offered to members; in the case of a premium offer, the price could be nominal. However, this may be compensated for by the large number of copies printed and the fact that the book may be used regularly over a period of years. If the publisher's own edition goes out of print in the meantime, the book club should be required to specify in its advertising that theirs is an exclusive club edition, as it will not be possible to make a valid comparison with the recommended retail price of the trade edition. Royalties are normally paid twice a year. The advance payment against royalties will vary according to the importance of the book and the size of the print run. It is normally paid half on signature of the contract and half on first publication of the book club edition.

Book clubs usually expect to be able to reproduce their editions from the typographical arrangement of the trade edition, and will therefore require electronic files, for which they will pay a 'production compensation fee'. A price will need to be negotiated for the material, or an offset fee could be charged on a per-page basis if the book club edition is repro-duced directly from the original. Again, it is important to check if any third party permissions for text or illustrations include use by a third party licensee.

The markets granted to book clubs in the case of either purchase of printed copies or reprint licences will vary according to the size of the operation. While very small clubs may be content with the UK alone, the larger clubs will seek a much broader range of markets, depending on their activities outside the UK; these will certainly include the Commonwealth countries and western European countries, but will exclude the United States, its territories and possessions, Canada and the Philippines. When dealing with this aspect of book club contracts, the licensor must be careful to check that it has control of the markets requested, and also that the granting of book club rights to those markets will not be perceived as undermining distribution arrangements for the trade edition or English-language licences granted in the countries concerned.

Book clubs normally require a first option on the next book by the same author, provided that rights are controlled by the same licensor.

The future of book clubs

Since the last edition of this book, the effect of competing supply channels has undoubtedly had a major and negative effect on the clubs, as evidenced by the fact that the major player, Bertelsmann, has divested itself of much of its business in this area and Readers Union are winding down their operation. If the clubs are to survive, it is likely to be in more streamlined form. They continue to promote their services on the grounds that they offer good prices on books, convenience of supply with online ordering facilities, and in particular a wide but carefully chosen selection of titles for their members; and in the case of The Folio Society, editions in special bindings for collectors.

From the point of view of some publishers, they are now regarded as simply another sales channel rather than a rights opportunity, and in some cases book club arrangements are handled by direct sales staff rather than by rights staff. If the business is handled in this way, it is important that sales staff are alerted to the fact that clubs with contractual arrangements with their publisher suppliers will need assurance that the purchase by the club of each individual title complies with the contractual requirements in terms of warranties and indemnities, geographical market granted and the duration of the arrangement, and that there is no potential conflict with other arrangements such as supplying to direct marketing operations (e.g. The Book People), the publication of or granting of rights for a paperback edition, which would be perceived to conflict with the book club offer of a hardback edition, or remaindering of the publisher's own edition within the restricted term.

Chapter 11

Paperback rights

It was once the case that the sale of mass-market paperback rights attracted attention both in the trade and the general media, since it was in this area of publishing that licensing revenue rose spectacularly. The trend started in the United States in the 1970s and led to advances such as the $3,208,875 paid by Bantam in 1979 for Judith Krantz's *Princess Daisy*, still the all-time record for fiction. By the 1990s, advances tended to be more modest (although Pocket Books reportedly paid $2,600,000 for Terry McMillan's *Waiting to Exhale*). There has been a substantial shift in the overall strategy for hardback/paperback editions in the last twenty-five years.

In the past, the sale of paperback rights involved the original hardback publisher licensing the rights to an independently owned, mass-market paperback publisher. Almost all such imprints are now part of large publishing groups, many of them multinationals. This consolidation of publishing houses has had a major impact on paperback rights; many of the groups embarked on a systematic programme of recovering paperback rights from external licensees and publishing the books under their own paperback imprints. Publishing a trade title in hardback alone is rarely profitable in the present climate. For new titles, a more comprehensive package of rights is now sought from agents and authors, with many titles now being published by a hardback imprint and a paperback imprint under the umbrella of the same group: a 'vertical' publishing deal. Thus, if a major property is being auctioned by the author's agent, the hardback and paperback imprints from the same group may well bid together to secure rights. A purchase of this kind may be more beneficial for the author, who would then normally receive a full royalty on both hardback and paperback editions rather than receiving a contractual share of the royalty from a sublicensed paperback edition. In the United States, in particular, the impact of chains such as Costco discounting the original hardback book at 50–70% has had a significant impact on the size of paperback sales.

If a vertical publishing deal is not involved, a hardback house may still seek to team up with an outside paperback house in order to bid for rights. In such cases, the hardback publisher may then issue a sublicence to the paperback house, and an agreed share of the proceeds (at least 50% but sometimes as high as 90%) is passed on to the author; alternatively, both publishers will contribute to the advance payment and the author will be paid royalties separately on each edition. It may also be the case that a title first published by a small independent publisher which has limited access to the major retail outlets is of interest to a mass-market paperback imprint, and licensing may then be a sensible route to make the book more widely available.

Although publication of a sublicensed paperback edition normally takes place some time after the appearance of the hardback edition, if a licensing policy is to be pursued it is important to keep the appropriate editors at the paperback houses informed of possible titles at the earliest stage. An outline followed by a copy of the manuscript is the usual sales material; at the very latest, page proofs or electronic files. If the book or the author is unknown, it may still be possible to generate interest from a paperback house after publication if the hardback edition is unexpectedly successful; a reading copy can be supplied with copies of favourable reviews and details of initial hardback sales figures.

When promoting to paperback publishers, it is essential to become familiar with the profile of each house by studying its catalogues and website, its output in bookshops and at book fairs, and by scanning the trade press for features on forthcoming paperbacks, advertisements and news of acquisitions (and, if possible, the amounts paid!). It is also vital to find out the likely tastes of individual editors.

If a project is submitted to a paperback house, it is important to make it clear on what basis this is being done – whether it is an individual submission, a multiple submission to several houses or a full-scale auction (see Chapter 6). While the money involved in paperback licences can still be significant, it is almost certainly a mistake to oversell a property if one is to maintain good relations with the buyer in the future. A licence negotiated on the basis of a more modest advance payment may earn well over a period of years if the property has been placed with a publisher prepared to put the weight of its marketing and sales forces behind the book.

Once a deal has been agreed, the paperback house will usually submit its own form of contract rather than follow the tradition of the licensor providing the contract. However, there is usually some flexibility for alterations, depending on the circumstances of the licence and the importance of the title.

Paperback houses often seek to acquire rights in 'all paperback editions' in the English language; there is no automatic definition of the format in which the paperback edition will be produced, although educational editions containing critical apparatus (see Chapter 13) may specifically be excluded. For many years, all UK paperback editions were published in the traditional pocketbook format of 175 × 111 mm. This size is referred to as 'A format'; for some titles a larger 'B format' of 198 × 129 mm has been introduced. Large-format trade paperbacks – sometimes referred to as 'C format' for marketing purposes to distinguish them from pocketbook editions – may be published in royal format (250 × 150 mm) or demy octavo (222 × 143 mm) by some houses, often following the format of the original hardback edition. By leaving the format unspecified in the contract, the paperback publisher has the choice of which to use, and if there is a perceived market for both editions the same book could be published first as a larger-format, more expensive trade paperback and then as a cheaper pocketbook edition. The licensor should bear in mind that by granting rights for all paperback editions, they themselves are giving up the right to produce a trade paperback edition even if the licensee subsequently produces only in the traditional pocketbook format.

The term of licence granted to a paperback publisher could be for the full term of copyright, with provision for termination if the paperback edition goes out of print or in the case of breach by the licensee. For a reference work such as a dictionary, the contract should be limited to the current edition, so that a new contract would have to be negotiated if the hardback publisher produced a revised edition. In recent years (as for author contracts), the trend has been towards granting limited-term licences. A UK paperback house will usually be prepared to accept a minimum period of eight years from first publication of the paperback edition, with a possibility of renewing for a further period (perhaps for five years) on terms to be agreed at the time; a refresher advance would be common. It is therefore important that any hardback publisher granting a paperback licence ensure that they themselves have control of the rights in the property for a sufficient period to cover the period between signature of the paperback licence and publication of the paperback edition, plus the term of the licence granted. Some paperback houses now require that if the licence expires, the hardback publisher may not offer paperback rights elsewhere at the same or lower terms than those negotiated for the original licence without returning to consult them. If the licence is to terminate, the paperback publisher will require a period of time (usually twelve months) in which to sell off any remaining stock; they should not be permitted to reprint within that period.

It is usual to require that the paperback edition shall first appear in the exclusive market granted at least one year after publication of the hardback edition, to give the publisher a reasonable period of time to achieve sales of the hardback edition. Thus, if a licence is being granted for a new hardback publication, it is advisable for the contract to specify that the paperback edition is to be published 'no earlier than … and no later than … ' Some publishers may wish to qualify that they will meet the publication date unless prevented from doing so by circumstances outside their control.

It should be remembered that late publication may affect payment of one instalment of the advance.

The market granted to the paperback publisher depends on a number of factors: the market under the exclusive control of the licensor; the market required by the paperback publisher and their ability to service that market; and whether arrangements have already been made or are planned for an alternative paperback edition in another part of the world market. A paperback publisher could seek exclusive rights in the United Kingdom and countries of the Commonwealth, plus designated European markets; if anything less than world rights are to be granted, a full schedule of territories should be attached to the contract.

A paperback house with its own American operation might seek world paperback rights. However, if the licensor has already made arrangements for a US edition with an American house, it is likely that the right to produce or to sublicense an American paperback edition will have been included in that licence, and in this case the rights available to license to a UK paperback house will be restricted. Even if an American hardback deal has not yet been finalized, to offer such rights minus US paperback rights may lessen the chances of placing the book in the American market. The timing of deals with American houses (Chapter 9) and UK paperback houses therefore requires careful thought.

If US paperback rights are unavailable, the UK paperback publisher may accept exclusive rights in the United Kingdom and Commonwealth, but if there are to be two paperback editions the question of the open market will arise. The European market in particular remains the subject of controversy, and paperback editions are a sensitive area; some paperback houses may seek at least the original fifteen member countries of the European Union (see Chapter 1) as part of their exclusive market.

If Europe is an open market, many British publishers remain concerned that American paperback editions, often priced lower than their UK counterparts, may enter the UK market under the provisions for free movement of goods across the borders of EU countries, and that parallel importation of this kind has increased as US publishers, wholesalers, jobbers and internet booksellers on both sides of the Atlantic have all become more active (see Chapter 9). It is important that such suppliers are provided with clear information on territorial restrictions so that buyers are referred to the correct source.

If the open market is included in contracts with paperback publishers on both sides of the Atlantic, the UK paperback publisher may seek to restrict the hardback publisher from issuing any English-language licence within the open market (other than to a contracted US publisher) without their agreement. They may also seek a provision to publish an early export edition in the open market territories in order to compete with the US edition. This export edition could therefore appear in advance of the earliest publication date specified in the contract. Some thought should be given to whether the appearance of a cheap English-language edition earlier than was originally planned in some overseas markets with a high ability to speak English (say the Netherlands and the Scandinavian countries) could have an adverse effect on publication plans for licensed translations in those markets, even if there has been no contractual requirement for the English-language edition to be barred from those markets. Dutch publishers in particular have been known to lobby against early export editions of potential bestsellers.

Another reason for early release of the paperback edition would be if the book is considered to be a likely candidate for exploitation on the stage, as a cinema film or on television. In such cases, the paperback house may include a provision for early release in order to maximize sales generated by such exposure; it will then seek to publish its edition with a tie-in cover. Some paperback houses may include in their contract a requirement for the hardback publisher to use its best endeavours to secure for them the right to use the title of the film or television version if this differs from that of the original book.

Paperback publishers now commonly require the right to publish 'reasonable extracts' from the book free of charge in print or online for marketing purposes.

Payment for paperback rights is made on the basis of an advance payment against a royalty for each copy sold; the advance payment is usually made in instalments. Advances can range from a modest four-figure sum (usually payable half on signature of the licence contract and half on publication of the paperback edition) to the high six-figure advances commanded by a major author. Then, the advance might be paid one-third on signature of the contract, one-third on publication and one-third an agreed number of months after publication. The trend in recent years has been to push up advances to very high levels, particularly if paperback rights are auctioned. However, subsequent sales of the paperback have sometimes not justified the initial outlay, and this can make the same buyer more cautious of future offers from the same source.

Royalty rates for paperback licences also vary according to the nature of the book and the status of the author. An initial modest royalty rate could be $7\frac{1}{2}\%$ of the UK recommended retail price for sales made in the home market, rising to 10% after an agreed number of copies have been sold. If the licence has been granted for the full term of copyright and the paperback edition is expected to have a long life, further royalty escalation points can be introduced. For an exceptional property the initial royalty rates may be higher and could rise to as high as 15%.

Royalty payments for export sales are now usually calculated on the sum received by the paperback publisher and could start at 10%. With the major book chains pressing for high discounts, there will almost certainly be special arrangements for copies sold at high discount (some paperback houses currently specify $52\frac{1}{2}$% or over, others 55% or over) and for copies sold outside normal trade channels, e.g. as mail order sales or as a premium in connection with other goods or services (often paid for at 5% of sum received). Royalties on high discount sales may be calculated on the sum received by the paperback publisher or the contract may specify that royalties on such sales will move to a proportion of the full royalty (e.g. $\frac{4}{5}$ of the full royalty rate for sales made at a discount of 55% or more and $\frac{3}{5}$ of the full rate for sales made at 60% or $62\frac{1}{2}$% or more discount).

Paperback publishers may want to be able to make arrangements with book clubs, and will usually share the royalties on royalty-exclusive book club deals with the hardback publisher (often on a 50/50 basis), or pay the hardback publisher a designated royalty (often equivalent to the base rate on normal home sales) on the price received from the book club for a royalty-inclusive deal (see Chapter 10).

The question of whether a paperback licensee would also seek e-book rights is an interesting one. They are unlikely to be granted by the licensor while the original edition is still in print, but some paperback houses are now seeking to add e-book rights to older licences where the original hardback edition is long out of print. Some paperback houses are currently offering the original publisher e-book royalties of either 15% or 25% of net receipts where the e-book version is offered from the paperback publisher's own website or through online retailers such as Amazon, both methods of supply which will be categorized by the paperback publisher as a sale rather than as a sublicence and where the sum received will be the e-book price less VAT and any discount granted. Some paperback houses are offering 10% of net receipts for different e-book arrangements which they view as sublicences, where their licensee is either paying on a flat-fee basis or a royalty basis. For more on e-books in general, see Chapter 24.

Traditionally many paperback houses sought to include in their contracts a small reprint clause which permitted them to undertake small top-up printings that would not accrue to cumulative sales and hence towards a rising royalty rate. The justification was that such reprints are only under-taken when a larger printing is uneconomic, but some paperback publishers have now abandoned this requirement on the grounds that improved technology and print-on-demand makes small printings far more viable. If the clause is to be included it would be advisable to restrict it by speci-fying that no more than one such printing should be undertaken in any twelve-month period.

Paperback royalties are usually accounted for twice yearly, but because of the high incidence of copies returned unsold from retailers (often over 50%) most paperback contracts will specify that there should be a reserve against returns, so that some part of the royalties will be held back until accounting can be adjusted to allow for the unsold copies, often after the third royalty statement. Some paperback publishers specify the percentage holdback, which could be as high as 25–30%.

The paperback publisher will make certain requirements of the hardback publisher in the contract. If India is regarded as a major export market for the paperback edition, a provision may be included whereby the hardback publisher cannot license a low-price edition of the book to that market (see Chapter 12) without first obtaining permission from the paperback publisher, since the price of the Indian edition could well compete with that of the paperback. While the hardback publisher can make arrangements for a hardback book club edition of the book, there is usually a restriction on issuing or licensing any low-price hardback edition at a price of less than one-third of that of the original hardback without obtaining the prior consent of the paperback licensee. The question of book club deals, special sales arrangements (e.g. with The Book People, see Chapter 13), or premium deals for the same book requires careful thought, especially if they are not all handled within the rights department; a book club contract normally specifies that no paperback edition or low-price hardback edition shall appear within one year of first publication of the original hardback edition. There is also the possibility of a paperback book club seeking to issue a special paperback edition that has not been acquired from the paperback licensee (e.g. The Softback Preview, see Chapter 10).

The paperback publisher may require that the hardback publisher does not remainder the original edition before or within six months after publication of the paperback edition. Paperback publishers were restricted from remaindering within an agreed period of time after first publication, but most now seek to be able to remainder at any time and pay a reduced royalty rate (often 5% on sums received from such sales, unless copies are sold at or below cost). The paperback publisher must not knowingly sell copies of that edition to be bound up in hardback; this is intended to protect sales of the hardback edition to the library market and is usually reinforced by a notice on the title verso of the paperback edition precluding any form of rebinding.

The licensor is normally required to provide stringent warranties and indemnities to the paperback publisher to guarantee that the work is original, that it will not infringe any copyright, that it is not obscene, indecent, defamatory or libellous and that any statements in the book purporting to be facts are true. Some may require that the content does not contravene the requirements of the Official Secrets Act (this in view of the publication of memoirs of former employees of the security services). The licensor will thus need to check whether such warranties and indemnities have been guaranteed by the author in the head contract; if some elements have not been covered, the text of the warranty and indemnity clause may need to be modified. Paperback publishers may require the text to be amended if it is deemed actionable, and if agreement on this cannot be reached with the hardback publisher the contract may have to be cancelled and any advance paid returned. Paperback publishers will normally expect their licence to include the right to reproduce any third party copyright material contained in the book without further charge. The hardback publisher will therefore need to check whether the original permissions secured for the use of text or illustrations extend to English-language publication generally or may perhaps have been restricted to a specific print run, edition or imprint.

Paperback publishers often reproduce the typographical setting of the original hardback edition; they may require as many as ten working copies of the hardback edition. Alternatively, the paperback publisher may wish to have access to electronic files; these can be particularly useful if the work is to be abridged or edited, e.g. a dictionary, and should be charged for. If they wish to reproduce directly from copies of the hardback edition, an offset fee can be charged; at the time of writing, a rate of £3 per page is not uncommon. In cases where hardback and paperback publishers are involved in bidding jointly for a property, they may agree to share the origination costs.

A paperback publisher will usually seek an option on the next book by the same author (or the next edition of a reference book) if control of the rights will lie with the same licensor, on financial terms to be agreed at the time. An option clause will normally specify the period of time from receipt of adequate material for the new title, with specification that if no agreement can be reached on terms, the rights may be offered elsewhere provided that the licensor will not accept another offer equal to or lower than the original offer from the option holder. The decision on whether to agree to an option clause of this kind may depend on the status of the author, and hence on whether the rights in the next work are likely to be offered on the basis of a single submission of this kind or by auction. If an auction is planned for the next book, it could perhaps be agreed that the paperback publisher of the current title could have first sight of the book and/or 'topping' rights (see Chapter 6).

The current trend towards granting shorter terms for paperback licences may mean that when the licence expires the paperback publisher has to re-contract for substantially higher terms or compete at auction for a renewal of the licence, or finds that the paperback rights are placed elsewhere. There have been many instances of this, particularly where the original hardback publisher has since acquired or set up its own paperback imprint within the same publishing group. The long-term effect of removing a title from a licensee must be balanced against the benefit that would be derived from placing the rights elsewhere or recovering them for publication 'in the family'. If a licence is terminated, the paperback publisher must be allowed a period of grace in which to dispose of existing stock (usually twelve months).

It is essential for those handling paperback rights to monitor carefully when licences are scheduled to expire in order to formulate a suitable strategy in good time. A computerized database greatly facilitates this exercise. It should be capable of producing a report of all licences due to expire within a given future period of time so that appropriate action can be taken in advance of the expiry date. It is of course also vital to check whether there has been, or is likely to be, any change in the overall control of rights in the title in question. If the hardback publisher's own publication arrangement with the author is about to expire and may not be renewed, this will affect the possibility of renewing sublicences. If a contract is terminated, provision should normally be made for any sublicences properly negotiated during the term of the contract to be allowed to run for their allotted term.

Chapter 12

Low-price reprint rights

An area of licensing that is perhaps of more relevance to educational and academic publishers than to trade publishers is the licensing of low-price English-language reprint rights to publishers in countries where the original publisher's edition is perceived as being too expensive for the market. The prime candidates for such licences are university textbooks, although there may also be requirements for books at primary and secondary school level in those overseas countries where the education curriculum has been modelled on that of the United Kingdom. As English has increasingly become the *lingua franca*, there is also a growing need for low-price editions of English-language teaching materials and dictionaries.

The main markets where low-price editions are required are the developing and newly industrialized countries, particularly those of the Indian subcontinent, Asia and some African countries. There may also sometimes be reasons for licensing certain categories of books to local publishers in central and eastern Europe, Russia and other former Republics of the Soviet Union (see later in this chapter, pp. 171–3).

Developing and newly industrialized countries

The question of whether to grant low-price English-language reprint rights to these countries has a long history. The key targets are usually well-established university textbooks, although school textbooks, dictionaries and English-language teaching material may also be requested.

Reprint licensing to these markets is normally undertaken on a reactive basis in that rights are not actively promoted to publishers there. This is because, copy for copy, the original publisher will always make more from sales of its own edition than from a royalty on a licensed reprint, and British academic publishers have long depended on many of these countries as significant export markets. For this reason, they are unlikely to wish to volunteer licences, but they may nevertheless be required to grant them because of legal or market circumstances in the countries concerned. It is easy to see that if separate local reprint licences were granted for the same medical textbook to publishers in India, Pakistan, the Philippines, Malaysia, Taiwan, China and Indonesia, the original publisher's own print run would be reduced and this would eventually start to affect pricing and sales to other markets and the ability of the publisher to invest in developing new books.

The countries in question fall into two broad categories: those that have acceded to the international copyright conventions and those that have not. The majority of countries in the world now belong to one or more of the major international copyright conventions. The main absentees at the time of writing are Taiwan, Myanmar (Burma), Iran, Iraq, Somalia and some African countries (Angola, Burundi, Eritrea, Ethiopia, Mozambique, Sierra Leone and Uganda). The question of licensing reprint rights to non-copyright countries is covered later in this chapter (see p. 173).

It is essential to be aware of the copyright background of a country when considering licensing to publishers there, for both English-language reprint rights and translation rights. It is particularly important in the case of developing countries, many of which continue to pose copyright problems even when they are members of one or more of the conventions. Membership of a convention requires the country concerned to provide for the works of other member states the same standard of protection that they accord to works of their own nationals (national treatment). However, it is important to remember that this standard of protection may be less than that which is enjoyed in the country where the work originates. While international conventions seek to impose minimum standards of protection on member countries, it must be emphasized that there is no such thing as international copyright law; the regulations on copyright in each country are governed by domestic legislation, and in many of these countries the situation is far from satisfactory. Piracy is still a major problem in some countries, despite membership of one or more conventions.

Compulsory licensing

In 1971, following years of pressure from the developing countries, revisions were made to the text of both the Berne Convention and the Universal Copyright Convention (UCC); these were designed to give the developing countries easier access to books required for educational and academic purposes. They were termed the Paris Revisions; not all countries have agreed to ratify the text of these revisions. The United Kingdom ratified the Paris text of the Universal Copyright Convention on 10 July 1974 and that of the Berne Convention on 2 January 1990.

In essence, the Paris Revisions provide the opportunity for a country to claim status as a developing country, and hence to take advantage of procedures for the acquisition of compulsory local reprint or translation licences in the works it requires, if voluntary licences cannot be negotiated from the copyright holders. The country concerned must be officially recognized as eligible for developing country status by the United Nations (such status to be reviewed by the United Nations every ten years) and must submit a declaration of its intention to take advantage of compulsory licensing with the bodies responsible for administering the appropriate international convention. An excellent account of the practical procedures laid down for the acquisition of compulsory licences was given in *The Copyright System: Practice and Problems in Developing Countries*, by Denis de Freitas (Commonwealth Secretariat, 1983, but now out of print).

In summary, the applicant for a local reprint licence must demonstrate that the book is required for educational or academic purposes and that the book is not available in the country concerned at a price appropriate to that market. The applicant must also demonstrate that they have made every effort to locate the copyright owner and either have failed (despite having copied the application to the publishing house and any designated clearing house in the country of origin – in the case of the United Kingdom, the Publishers Association) or have located the rightsholder but been refused a licence without adequate reason.

Application can then be made for a compulsory reprint licence, provided that a specified period of time has elapsed since first publication of the original edition; this depends on the category of book. In the case of works of fiction, poetry, drama, music and art, the period is seven years; in the case of works in the natural and physical sciences, including mathematics, and technical works, three years; and in the case of all other categories, five years. The regulations for compulsory translation licences are different (see Chapter 16).

Once these periods have expired, application can be made to the local organization responsible for administering the licence system (often the Ministry of Education). A period of grace ranging from three to nine months is allowed for negotiations with the rightsholder, after which a compulsory licence may be granted if agreement has not been reached. The administrative organization will decide on the level of payment to be made to the copyright owner or their representative once located. There is a responsibility to ensure that payment is made promptly and in a transferable currency, and the Paris Revisions to the Berne Convention (Appendix I, Article IV (5) (i)) state that there should be 'just compensation' to the rights owner and that the level of payment must be consistent with terms freely negotiated for a voluntary licence.

Due acknowledgement must be made to the author, title and source. A compulsory licence is non-exclusive, and copies of the edition must not be exported outside the country concerned.

In practice, the provisions of the Paris Revisions have been much misunderstood, with some applicants assuming that licences can be granted free of charge (a misinterpretation of the words 'freely negotiated') or at preferential rates. It is in the area of English-language reprint licences that UK academic publishers have been most affected, since they are very dependent on export markets for their books. The fact that time limits are imposed on the licence application process means that negotiations may have to be conducted under the threat of a compulsory licence. In fact, relatively few true compulsory licences have been awarded, but many more 'voluntary' licences have been granted in the knowledge that refusal may lead to a compulsory licence.

A number of countries have introduced a form of compulsory licensing into their domestic legislation, and operate by their own rules rather than by the regulations specified by the Paris Revisions. While some legislation is roughly in line with Paris (e.g. the provisions of the Indian Copyright [Amendment] Act 1983), other countries have introduced legislation that in no way corresponds with Paris. The two most obvious examples have been the Philippines and Pakistan, both of which are signatories to the Berne Convention; the Philippines has also ratified the WIPO Treaty.

For many years the Philippines operated the infamous Marcos Decree (PD1203), which permitted any book required for educational purposes and priced in the Philippines at more than 250 pesos to be reprinted under compulsory licence on the basis of a royalty of 8% of the local published price or 3% of the original publisher's price. Many of the applications for British books were for titles already available in low-price editions via the Educational Low-Priced Books Scheme (ELBS – see later in this chapter, p. 174) or publishers' own low-price editions. In mid-1997, enactment of the Intellectual Property Code repealed the provisions of PD1203. In practice, an amnesty for the 'sell-off' of books supposedly printed under the terms of PD1203 has enabled some Philippine publishers to continue to act as if PD1203 were still in force, and the February 2009 report of the International Intellectual Property Alliance (IIPA) highlighted this as a continuing problem. On 18 June 1997, the Philippines stated its intention to avail itself of the compulsory licensing provisions under Berne.

Pakistan is a member of both Berne and UCC, but in neither case has it ratified the Paris text. Subsection 2A of Section 10 of the 1962 Copyright Ordinance specified that 'Copyright shall not subsist in any work referred to in subsection (2) as respect its reprint, translation, adaptation or publication, by or under authority of the Federal Government as textbook for the purpose of teaching, study or research in educational institutions' – hence no requirement to seek permission from the original publisher or the copyright holder, or to make payment.

New legislation in 2000 has given further cause for concern. Section 36 (3) of the 1986 amendment to the Copyright Ordinance was revised to include provision for royalty-free compulsory licences. This enables the Pakistan government to grant any institution, including the National Book Foundation (NBF, a part of the Ministry of Education), reprint or translation rights without permission from or payment to the rights owners. This provision is blatantly in violation of the requirements of TRIPS, and in 2010 the IIPA continued to lobby the Pakistan government to have it withdrawn.

Since the early 1970s, the NBF has conducted a major English-language reprint programme of both British and American university textbooks, many already available in Pakistan as low-price editions. In most cases, permission was not sought and no payment was made. The NBF has tended to lie dormant for some time, but periodically a batch of reprints appears and NBF staff intermittently appear at international book fairs. In mid-2000, two British publishers took legal action against the NBF for infringement of rights and one obtained an injunction, but in practice the NBF has continued to produce the books concerned; the publisher reacted by granting adaptation rights for the same works to a local agent to be published at a lower price.

Although long the most conspicuous absentee from the international copyright conventions and a major unauthorized user of western intellectual property, the People's Republic of China finally acceded to the Berne Convention on 15 October 1992 and to the Universal Copyright Convention on 30 October 1992, so there is now a legal obligation for Chinese publishers to seek permission for and make payment for rights in works from other member states. Although there is no real evidence to date of applications for compulsory licences from China, on accession that country stated its intent to take advantage of the Paris Revisions, and Article 23 of the revised domestic copyright law of 2001 allows for the use of extracts or short works in anthologies for use in elementary and high schools and in 'state plan' textbooks – as yet, it is unclear whether this can apply to university textbooks and to foreign copyright material.

Since early 1994, Chinese publishers have normally been able to remit hard currency licence payments abroad provided that they have a valid licence contract registered with their local copyright bureau. Some western licensors may still favour expressing the licence payment in the form of a lump sum to cover a designated print quantity, perhaps payable half on signature of the licence contract and half on publication of the licensed edition or by an agreed calendar date to ensure payment if publication runs behind schedule.

There is a particular demand in China for local English-language reprint licences in English-language teaching materials, dictionaries, business books (used in courses at major universities taught by visiting overseas faculty) as well as high-level scientific books and journals where prices of the original editions are prohibitively high for importing on a large scale; unauthorized reprinting of more than 2,500 foreign academic journals by Guanghua, a state-owned body, continued well after China acceded to the conventions but was suddenly terminated in November 2001 following government-level protests by the UK and US publishing industries; however, large-scale internet piracy of journals and photocopying of textbooks still occurs on university campuses. The UK Publishers Association and the Association of America Publishers have worked together with the National Copyright Administration of China to clamp down on such activities and a number of major Chinese universities have been subject to substantial fines.

The general question of licensing reprint rights to China has required careful thought since Hong Kong (a market well able to import full-price original editions) was returned to China as a Special Administrative Region on 1 July 1997, followed by Macao on 20 December 1999. It is strongly advisable to restrict such licences contractually to 'the mainland territory of the People's Republic of China excluding Hong Kong and Macao', although some Chinese publishers are reluctant to print this market restriction notice on reprint editions for political reasons, especially on the outside cover. There have been cases of leakage of low-price editions, particularly into Hong Kong, so licensors should insist on a clear market restriction notice; some in addition require licensees to purchase holograms to affix to the licensed editions.

If an applicant mentions the possibility of compulsory licensing, it is always wise to check whether the country concerned has introduced such provisions. South Africa, a signatory to the Berne Convention, introduced compulsory licensing provisions in its 1978 Copyright Act.

Financial terms

In addition to familiarity with local copyright circumstances, it is also vital to be aware of any local financial conditions such as banking restrictions. For example, Indian publishers are not permitted to remit an advance payment of more than $500 or royalties of more than 15% of the retail price without special clearance from the Reserve Bank of India. Chinese publishers have occasionally stated that it is not permitted to agree to royalty rates of more than 10%, but no government regulation has been quoted to support this claim. The availability of hard currency may also pose problems for publishers in some countries.

It is significant that reprint applications from the developing countries are never for new books that have not yet been established in the market. They are always for major textbooks and dictionaries that have been long established through the sale of successive editions in the markets concerned by the original publisher (often via aid-funded editions such as ELBS or the publisher's own international student editions) or because the books are well known from earlier unauthorized editions or piracies. It is also important to realize that the true saving in printing a local edition does not lie in making a reduced rate of payment to the original publisher, but rather in the lower costs of local manufacture and the fact that there is little need to spend money on extensive promotion, since the book in question will already be well known in the market through the original edition. There is therefore no valid argument for the licensee to pay a lower percentage royalty; no editorial work is involved as the book will simply be reproduced from the original edition. Reasonable royalty rates should therefore be in the region of 10–20% based on the local selling price, with a modest advance payment, perhaps equivalent to one-third to one-half of the total royalty from the first print run. Since the local price is low, the total income is likely to be modest. Indeed, in some cases it will barely cover the cost of the paperwork involved in the licence, a point not always appreciated by an applicant requesting concessionary royalty rates. Most publishers in such countries are unwilling to incur the additional cost of purchasing duplicate production material or paying offset fees.

Many multinational academic publishers have sought to minimize the risk of piracy, unauthorized editions or leakage of authorized licensed editions by licensing reprint rights to their own subsidiary companies in markets such as India and the Philippines, especially since the demise of the ELBS programme (see later in this chapter, p. 174). Even so, such editions can end up being offered for sale by middle men on websites in affluent markets such as the United States, and publishers must monitor such sites vigilantly.

The contract

When drawing up a reprint licence contract, it is wise to limit the licence as tightly as possible to the current edition of the book, with a specified initial print run, with provision for renewal of the agreement if the arrangement proves satisfactory. It is also wise to limit such licences by time, perhaps to a period as short as two or three years from the date of the contract. The territory granted should be defined, with a specification of the exact wording and placement required for a clearly visible market restriction notice on copies of the licensed edition. Depending on the level of payment involved, royalties could be accounted for twice yearly or subsumed into a lump sum, perhaps payable half on signature of the contract and half on publication or by an agreed calendar date. It is an annoying fact that many licences to such countries involve additional paperwork such as stamped and signed invoices or even notarized documents to certify the true identity of the copyright holder. Much depends on the regulations in the countries concerned.

Central and eastern Europe, Russia and the former Soviet Republics

Many of these markets are now more stable and operating more in line with western practice. However, it takes only events such as the collapse of the Russian rouble in August 1998. political upheavals in Ukraine and

Georgia and the particular impact of the 2008–9 economic recession in the region to demonstrate that these markets can be volatile, and this has an effect on export sales and licensing policy.

In the past, there was a substantial gap in price levels between western and local books, but paper and manufacturing costs have risen throughout the region and this has reduced the incentive to grant reprint licences; western publishers have been able to market their own editions of English-language teaching materials and dictionaries via distributors or their own local companies, pricing to market where appropriate. However, piracy and unauthorized photocopying remain major problems, a situation which rarely occurred in communist times when the printing industries in these countries were controlled by the state, and photocopying machines were either non-existent or kept under lock and key to prevent their use for *samizdat* publishing.

Under communist rule, the requirements for textbooks of all levels were met by state-controlled publishers publishing in the relevant language of instruction.

Most school publishers in the region have remained under state control and relatively few of the many private publishers established since the political changes in the 1990s have chosen to specialize in educational publishing, choosing instead to concentrate on mass-market titles with a faster financial return.

There may still be valid reasons for considering granting reprint licences for selected titles in areas such as English-language teaching (ELT) course materials and dictionaries if working with a local publisher would facilitate validation of a course by the Ministry of Education, and in countries where large-scale distribution is difficult for western publishers to achieve (e.g. in Russia and other republics of the former Soviet Union). There may also be a need to adapt the material for the local curriculum.

If a reprint licence is granted, the licensed editions should carry a clear market restriction notice limiting the sales to the agreed territory. However, one of the less welcome results of political freedom in the region is that of leakage, with goods travelling across borders far more freely. This may be a major consideration when deciding whether to license. A dictionary licensed to a publisher in Moscow or Kiev may well turn up in quantities on market stalls in Poland or the Baltic Republics, where the original publisher may be marketing their own edition direct.

Another problem in the region may stem from the sale of duplicate production material to licensees; there have been cases of substantial under-reporting of print quantities (see Chapter 25).

The political and economic situation remains volatile in some parts of the region; rights staff should monitor the situation and liaise closely with direct sales colleagues and local representatives. It is still important to assess on a regular basis the merits of licensing versus direct sales, and any licences should be carefully defined and made on a short-term basis so that they can be replaced by direct sales if policy should change.

Licensing to non-copyright countries

Still remaining outside membership of the international copyright conventions at the time of writing are Taiwan (which is prevented from joining by its unique political status), Iran, Myanmar (Burma), Iraq, Somalia and the African countries of Angola, Burundi, Eritrea, Ethiopia, Mozambique, Sierra Leone and Uganda. North Korea and Vietnam, long significant absentees, finally ratified the Berne Convention on 28 April 2003 and 26 October 2004, respectively.

Following the political changes in central and eastern Europe and the former Soviet Union, many newly independent countries had to take steps to join the conventions, most recently Uzbekistan, which joined the Berne Convention on 19 April 2005. One former Soviet Republic – Turkmenistan – remains outside membership.

As far as copyright holders are concerned, if a publisher in a country that does not belong to either of the international conventions makes use of a foreign book by reprinting or translating it, there are no legal grounds for taking action against the perpetrator provided that the edition remains inside the country concerned. Editions produced in this way are unauthorized editions rather than piracies; however, such copies are often exported to countries which are members of international copyright conventions; unauthorized editions of ELT course materials and dictionaries produced in Iran can be found in Armenia, Georgia and many Arab world countries. In such cases, action can be taken against importers and retailers in the countries concerned. In some cases, bilateral treaties provide some protection, or at least some basis for legal action in cases of infringement; Taiwan has signed such treaties with both the United States and the United Kingdom, and Vietnam had signed a treaty with the United States in April 1997 prior to its accession to Berne.

Although the number of countries absent from the international copyright community is growing smaller, it is the hope of all those with a theoretical and practical interest in copyright that eventually all countries will come into the copyright fold. In the meantime, it is vital for anyone handling licences to these markets to be aware of the copyright situation country by country, and to keep up to date with developments which may affect licensing procedures.

Is licensing the best solution?

Few would deny the need for books at reasonable prices in the poorer countries of the world, particularly when such books are required for educational, academic and professional purposes. But it should be borne in mind that licensing may not always be the best way of meeting this requirement. The resulting editions are frequently of poor production quality; the financial terms offered are low and sometimes limited by local legislation or banking restrictions; the remittance of payment is slow, heavily taxed at source and sometimes may not be made at all. Worse still, licensed editions may leak out into other markets, further damaging sales of the original publisher's edition or those of another licensee.

There may be alternative ways of providing low-price editions of the required books which do not require licensing, and these should certainly be investigated first on a case-by-case basis. For many years, British academic textbook publishers benefited from ELBS, the Educational Low-Priced Books Scheme funded by the Overseas Development Agency (ODA) of the British government, now the Department for International Development (DFID).

The scheme entitled publishers to produce special low-price English-language editions of books accepted for the scheme in a special livery for sale to designated developing countries, at a price of about one-third of the original edition. Availability of an ELBS edition was normally a valid reason for refusing a licence application from a country included in the scheme, and for fighting off the possibility of a compulsory licence. Unfortunately, a change in policy resulted in the termination of the scheme in 1997, and an attempt to establish a similar scheme for sub-Saharan Africa under the name of Access Books did not secure government approval.

The Low-Priced British Books Scheme (LPBB), initiated by the British government Know-How Fund in 1992 as a means of enabling publishers to supply selected titles in the areas of economics, management and business English to the countries of central and eastern Europe, terminated in 1998.

There are, however, some other possibilities:

1 British academic textbook publishers set up a trust in the form of a registered charity in December 1996, initially under the name of Educational Low-Priced Sponsored Texts (ELST). This was succeeded by BookPower (120 Pentonville Road, London N1 9JN; tel. 0207 843 1938; www.BookPower.org). Intended as a partial replacement for ELBS to supply textbooks in key subjects to university and vocational students in Africa, the Indian subcontinent and the Caribbean, it is dependent on adequate funding and to date only a small range of titles have been offered.

2 International Student Editions (ISEs). These are low-price editions produced by the publisher without the benefit of an outside subsidy. Again, they are often produced in a recognizable livery. They are priced at approximately half the price of the original edition, and are sold in

developing and newly emerging countries. They may be printed on slightly lower-grade paper and in a different binding from that of the original edition. Both author and publisher take a lower return on such copies.

3 The use of India as a print location by a number of western publishers led to the possibility of supplying low-cost editions to that market by printing in the export processing zone (EPZ). The western publisher can print a designated quantity and either deliver the whole run to an approved Indian wholesaler for sale at a low price to service that market (usually using a separate ISBN from the original edition) or supply an agreed quantity to the wholesaler as part of a larger run undertaken in the EPZ.

4 Sheet or book block deals. A further alternative would be the sale of sheets or book blocks printed by the original publisher to a local associate company or distributor in the country concerned, for local binding. This can be suitable for a title where the quality of illustration is crucial.

These possibilities have the advantage of keeping the printing of the book under the control of the original publisher rather than a licensee, thus maintaining a reasonable standard of production. The return per copy will also be higher than a royalty paid on a licensed edition. It should also be remembered that granting a local reprint licence may affect the interests not only of the original publisher by immediately terminating sales of the original edition to the market; it may also affect the interests of other licensees. Some paperback publishers specify that the original publisher should not grant a low-price reprint licence to India without first obtaining clearance from the paperback publisher.

It is vital to recognize that when dealing with these countries no licence should simply be granted automatically, because of the possible consequences. These are markets where it is extremely inadvisable for rights staff in a publishing house to operate in isolation.

Whenever licence applications are received from such sources, it is vital to consult export sales colleagues handling the markets concerned, and also to check if there are already low-price editions available under a scheme such as BookPower, or if an ISE is available or planned. Equally, staff responsible for submitting books for inclusion in such schemes (usually export sales staff) should consult rights staff beforehand to check if any licences have been granted or are under negotiation that might affect inclusion of a title in the scheme. There should be further liaison if titles are withdrawn from the schemes or if new editions are submitted.

In markets where there are subsidiary companies or local distributors, these representatives may be able to assist, perhaps by importing copies of the original edition to sell at a special low price in the market, or by themselves acquiring local reprint rights. Certainly, it would be disastrous to license rights to a third party without consulting them, as their sales will be affected.

If it can be shown that a low-price edition is already available in the market or that one is planned, a compulsory licence application can usually be forestalled. However, if there is no alternative but to license, care must be exercised in choosing a suitable licensee, who may well be someone other than the applicant seeking the licence. A number of considerations should be taken into account: the ability of the licensee to produce the book to as high a standard as local circumstances will permit (the purchase of duplicate production material is often too expensive for these markets; if electronic files can be supplied at a low cost, it is essential that the licensee is reliable); the ability to promote and distribute the book effectively; reliability in remitting payment; and the ability to control the edition within the designated market (a clear market restriction notice should be required both on the cover and inside the book, for example 'Licensed for sale in India only. Not for export'). Despite this, local editions may leak outside the licensed market: editions from the Indian subcontinent frequently appear in East Africa, the Middle East, Malaysia and Russia, as well as some western markets, but at least if they carry a restriction notice, they can be recognized and action taken against the importer and the exporter, if they can be identified.

Trade or bank references should always be sought when dealing with new applicants. If there is a good reason to believe that the original applicant cannot fulfil the required conditions, it is preferable to seek an alternative licensee, perhaps a subsidiary or associate company or a regular distributor of the original publisher. Publication under a joint imprint should only be permitted with a reliable licensee.

Chapter 13

Other reprint rights

Other types of reprint rights, in addition to major territorial rights, book club rights, paperback rights and low-price reprints for developing countries, may include categories such as promotional editions, cover mounts, educational editions, reprint editions of long out-of-print titles, and large-print editions.

Promotional editions

This concept originated in the United States, where promotional editions ('cheaps'), remainders and returns ('hurts') form an important part of retail sales. They are usually hardback editions of previously published titles with mass-market appeal, often in large format and heavily illustrated in colour. Favourite topics include cookery, gardening, DIY, craftwork and illustrated general reference books for children and adults. There is also a significant market for low-cost compendium collections of novels or short stories by a single or several well-known authors. The publishers seeking to acquire licences of this kind are often the special promotional imprints of large publishing groups, e.g. the Bounty Books imprint of Octopus and the Greenwich Editions imprint of Chrysalis Books.

Major players in the US market are Book Sales, World Publications, Book Club of America, the Main Street imprint of Sterling, the Fall River Press and Metro Books imprints of Barnes & Noble, and imprints of trade houses such as Random House Value Publishing and the Abradale imprint of art publisher Harry N. Abrams. The US market is highly competitive and has its own trade fair, CIROBE (Chicago International Remainders and Overstocks Book Exposition) every November. In the United Kingdom, CIANA operates two Remainder and Promotional Book Fairs at London venues each year, in January and September. Remainder and promotional houses also exhibit at the London International Book Fair.

A book first acquired as an overstock may subsequently be reprinted as a promotional edition if there is a continuing demand. In the United States, such a deal is familiarly known as a 'put', where the promotional house guarantees to pick up overstocks of the more expensive trade edition and may then go on to print further copies for sale at a low price. The lining up of a 'put' in advance can sometimes be useful when first seeking a US coedition order for a heavily illustrated title.

Promotional editions are usually published several years after first publication of the original hardback edition, when sales of this have dwindled or ceased altogether. The reappearance of the book at a low price (perhaps £7.99 compared with the original price of £19.99) can give it a new lease of life; print runs are often large and books are sold on the 'pile 'em high and sell 'em cheap' principle. Payment is usually made on the basis of an advance against royalties. Advances can run to several thousand pounds and may be paid in several instalments. Royalties may range from 5% to 10% and are usually calculated on the licensee's net receipts rather than on the recommended retail price, which may vary during the life of the promotional edition. The promotional publisher may wish to have access to production material for the book.

If the hardback edition is out of print or if sales are low, a promotional licence may be well worth considering as a continuing source of revenue. However, careful checks must be made in case the granting of such a licence could conflict with the terms of other licences still running, in particular those to paperback houses and to book clubs, who will feel that a promotional edition will compete on price with their editions of the same book. Both these licensees may have specified in their contracts that the original publisher cannot remainder or license a low-price hardback edition without prior clearance, and may veto such arrangements. It is certainly not worthwhile antagonizing major licensees, if their interests might be affected.

It is also vital to define tightly the sales territory granted in a promotional licence contract, and to act swiftly in the case of any copies exported outside the designated market. There have been cases of 'dumping' promotional editions into unauthorized territories.

Special direct sales

It is worth mentioning here the successful company run in the United Kingdom by The Book People (TBP), a direct-selling operation whose representatives visit offices and workplaces. Catalogues and samples are left and orders collated from company staff; catalogues are also sent to individual customers by mail. TBP often places orders with publishers to be added to their normal print runs, similar to the arrangements made with book clubs. Since special sales of this kind may be handled by UK sales staff rather than rights staff, early liaison is vital, as the same book may already be under licence to a book club which would regard such sales as competition. TBP also have book club interests through the

Puffin Book Club and in 2002 they set up a joint venture with Scholastic to run the Red House children's book club and the School Link book club. That venture was ended in June 2009 but TBP still run the Red House club (see Chapter 10).

Cover mounts

Perhaps also worth listing here are cover mounts, where a book is given away with a newspaper or magazine or available to readers at a special price. The arrangement may be handled as a rights deal if the licensee is permitted to manufacture a special edition for such use, e.g. a special hardback series of classic modern fiction at £4.99 per volume to be collected by readers of the newspaper concerned. Such arrangements are made on an advance and royalty basis, with the author receiving a designated share of the licence revenue.

If, however, the book or books concerned are supplied from the original publisher's stock or printed by the publisher for the magazine or newspaper, this would normally be handled as a special sale by the relevant sales department. The author would receive a royalty on high discount sales as per the terms of the original head contract.

There are also some cases where the publisher's marketing department may reach an arrangement with a women's magazine to supply copies to be given away with the magazine; this is viewed as a purely promotional activity, with the publisher covering the cost of the books. The author receives no royalty, but (one hopes) benefits from better sales for future books as a result of the publicity.

Educational editions

These rights are not normally actively promoted but may be licensed in response to applications from educational publishers seeking to republish the full text of a novel, or perhaps an existing collection of short stories, for the school market. The titles for which licences are sought thus depend on the requirements of the curriculum.

An educational edition cannot consist of original text alone; at least 20% of the book must consist of additional study aid material, which may include a biographical/critical preface, a glossary of terms, notes on the content and literary style of the work and questions or exercises. This additional material may often be subject to the approval of the original publisher or the author's agent as licensor.

Payment for an educational edition is normally made on the basis of an advance against royalties for each copy sold; royalty rates may range from 6% to 10% of the licensee publisher's net receipts. Licensors may be reluctant to accept royalties on the licensee's net receipts. The licensee will also be paying a small royalty to the author of the additional study material, and perhaps also to a series editor.

When dealing with an application for educational rights, the licensor must consider any potential effect on sales of the original edition and also on sales of any sublicensed paperback edition, since the educational edition is likely to appear at a lower price than that of the paperback. There have been cases where the mass-market paperback publisher objected strongly to the granting of an educational licence on the grounds that its own edition was selling to the school market; in such cases the agent or hardback publisher may be reluctant to grant an educational licence. In other cases, both hardback and paperback rights are controlled within the same publishing group, which may feel that the granting of such a licence is detrimental to its interests.

In the past, a mass-market paperback edition and an educational edition looked very different, the latter having little visual appeal. Today, cover designs are far more attractive, but an educational edition is still usually published in the established livery of a school series. Inside, it will include the critical apparatus mentioned above. Such editions are sold at low discount and do not appear in large quantities in bookshops; they usually reach schools either through educational suppliers or direct from the publisher.

Another type of application that may be received from educational publishers is for the right to produce an abridged and simplified text of a novel, a collection of short stories or a play. Such editions are normally intended for the English-language teaching market, for non-native speakers who may not be able to cope with the full text of a novel by George Orwell, or by a more modern writer such as Patricia Highsmith or Peter Benchley. Some requests may also be received for the right to produce a simplified text as a remedial reader for native speakers. In both cases, publication is usually in the context of a recognized educational series; in the first case, the majority of sales are made outside the United Kingdom.

The simplification work is undertaken so that the resulting text is carefully controlled in terms of vocabulary level and grammatical complexity. The licensor may require the right to approve the abridged and simplified text. Sales of such editions can be considerable over the years, although they are normally sold at a low price; they should not affect sales of the full text. Payment is normally made on the basis of an advance payment against a royalty on either the retail price or net receipts for each copy sold. The publisher acquiring such rights will also have to pay a royalty or fee to the author undertaking the simplification work, as well as to a series editor. The simplified text will by definition have a new copyright, so publishers seeking to acquire simplification rights may wish to consider whether their licence should include the right to sublicense rights in their simplified version elsewhere, although this may need to be subject to the approval of the original full-text publisher.

Out-of-print titles

In the mid-1960s, there was a major industry in the production of short-run, high-priced reprints of academic and specialist titles that had been unavailable for many years. The boom started in the United States and was designed to service the requirements of libraries for the many new universities and colleges established during that period. Key players were reprint houses such as Archon, Greenwood Press, Kraus Reprint and Shoestring Press. In addition to those titles for which applications were made, many British titles were reprinted without permission, since they had fallen into the public domain in the American market through failure to renew copyright registration in that country (see Chapter 9). Publishers such as Dover continue to reprint titles in areas such as art and architecture.

A number of specialist publishers were also established in the United Kingdom, reprinting classics in such areas as anthropology, archaeology, industrial history and travel; David & Charles also undertook reprints as part of their programme. Since print runs were often limited to a few hundred copies, the terms were usually modest but the books had a renewed lease of life.

The boom has now long subsided and not all the reprint houses still exist, although publishers such as Wordsworth Editions and Collector's Library entered the field reprinting classics of literature, and publishers such as Amberley Press, the new company founded in 2008 by Alan Sutton, revive titles in the area of history, as does the Phoenix imprint of Orion. Publishers with long-standing backlists may therefore still be approached to grant reprint rights to other publishers who feel that a book could be profitably revived.

Such licences are often dealt with on a passive basis, since the applicants make it their business to undertake market research in their particular fields of interest. However, if there is access to good historical records within a publishing house and an archive of publications, it may be worthwhile combing the backlist with a view to offering reprint rights actively to appropriate houses. Without ready access to copies of the books, active promotion becomes a problem, since it is hardly a strong selling point to alert a reprinter to a gem on the backlist and then ask them to locate a copy themselves.

If a publisher receives an application for reprint rights in a title long out of print, the first step is to establish whether it is still in copyright in the required market or markets and who controls the rights. Under the present UK copyright legislation, if the author has been dead for more than seventy years the work will have passed into the public domain in the United Kingdom and may be reprinted without permission or payment, although reprinters may offer some finished copies of the work as a matter of courtesy.

If a reprint application is received for a British title either from a reprint house located in the United States or from a reprinter located elsewhere but seeking to include the United States in its sales territory, it is vital to check the copyright status of the work in the United States. In previous years, many British titles had fallen into the public domain in the United States through failure of the British publisher or an authorized American sublicensee to reregister the work for protection with the Library of Congress. Since 1 January 1996, many such works have had copyright protection restored following changes to US domestic copyright legislation to comply with the Uruguay Round of the GATT. As a general principle, some works that originated in Berne member countries after about 1925 and that have hitherto been in the public domain in the United States are eligible for a further period of US copyright protection, provided that their authors were citizens of, or domiciled in, a Berne member state and provided that the work in question was still in copyright in its country of origin as at 1 January 1996. It should also be remembered that the US has now extended its own period of copyright protection to the life of the author plus seventy years, in line with the period in the United Kingdom and other EU countries. For further details, see *Copyright legislation in the United States* in Chapter 1 and *The United States* in Chapter 9.

In the case of a British book covered by the 1911 Copyright Act but published before 1 July 1957, when the 1956 UK Copyright Act came into force, and where the author has been dead for less than seventy years, rights originally assigned to the publisher may have reverted to the heirs of the author twenty-five years after his or her death; this anomaly has already been described in Chapter 9 since it may also affect dealings with US publishers. It may nevertheless be possible to offer to negotiate for reprint rights on behalf of the heirs if they wish this, subject to receiving an agreed share of the proceeds. Locating the heirs of deceased authors can prove problematic if there has been no contact for many years since the book went out of print. If the author was employed by an academic institution or large commercial company, its personnel department may be able to assist; other sources of information may be the Society of Authors (more relevant for literary authors), the Authors Licensing and Collecting Society (ALCS – see Chapter 23) or the WATCH website, run by the Harry Ransom Research Center at the University of Texas in association with the University of Reading in the United Kingdom (http://tyler.hrc.utexas.edu). If the date of death of a British author is known, a will search may reveal some information.

Research could also reveal that although a work is still in copyright, rights may have been returned to the author or their representatives if the original edition went out of print. Some older contracts with authors provided for automatic reversion of rights in such cases, but this has long been regarded as unrealistic since legitimately sublicensed editions may still be in print and selling well even after the original edition has ceased to sell. Most head contracts now require that the publisher must inform the author when the main edition goes out of print or that the author must provide written notice of his or her intention to reclaim the rights; there may nevertheless be provisions for existing sublicences to run for their full term. Many head contracts for trade titles are no longer granted for the full term of copyright, but for a specified period of years with or without a provision to renew for a further period.

If after avenues of research have been exhausted the author or the author's heirs still cannot be located, the work is in effect an *orphan work*. Some publishers may nevertheless choose either to reissue the work themselves or to license reprint rights to a third party, perhaps including a notice in the book to state that they have been unable to locate the copyright owner and that they would welcome any information enabling them to do so. Such actions constitute a calculated risk and, if followed, the publisher would be well advised to set aside payments to be made if the copyright holder is eventually located.

The question of how orphan works can be made more readily available is currently the topic of much debate at both national and international level (see Chapter 1) and also in the context of the Google Settlement (see Chapter 23). One suggestion is that orphan works might be handled through a trusted intermediary such as a reproduction rights organization which might seek assurances that the would-be user of the orphan work has first made every effort to locate the rightsholder, and then act as a depository for payments in case the rightsholder is eventually located. In the United Kingdom this route is being considered by the Copyright Licensing Agency (CLA – see Chapter 23).

If a licence is granted, payment is normally made on the basis of an advance against a royalty on the recommended retail price in the main market, although some applicants may seek to pay royalties on their net receipts for bulk export sales or sales at high discount. If world rights are requested, it should be established how the reprint edition will be marketed outside the home market. Licences can often be limited to a period as short as three years, with provision for renewal if there is a continuing demand for the book at that point.

Reprint houses frequently ask to borrow a copy of the book from which to originate their editions as the original publisher is unlikely to hold film or electronic files for older books which have been out of print for some time. For books published before 30 June 1957, there is no legal justification for requiring an offset fee, since copyright protection for typographical setting was first established when the 1956 UK Copyright Act came into force on 1 July 1957, and is limited to twenty-five years from first publication. If the book requested for such use is a first edition and the only copy owned by the original publishing house, it may have some intrinsic value. Some reprint houses have been known to slice the spine off the book for easier scanning access and may replace the binding incompetently or use a different binding altogether. It is thus inadvisable to lend an only copy or a copy borrowed from a source such as the London Library, even if assurances are given that the book will be well treated. If the licensees can be persuaded to locate their own production copy, such risks can be avoided.

If a reprint application is received indicating that a book could have a new lease of life after a dormant period, there may be a good case for alerting in-house editorial colleagues in case they feel that the book could be revived by the original publishing house rather than through the medium of a licence. Authors and topics may come back into fashion as trends change, and the applicant for a reprint licence will undoubtedly have undertaken research to assess this. On the other hand, if the original publishing house has changed its profile since the work was first published, it may be more sensible to grant a licence to a publisher who has developed a specialized list in the field and may be better able to reach the target market.

Large-print editions

Large-print rights have not been included in the category of rights for the reading impaired (Chapter 18) since large-print books are produced on a commercial basis for such readers by publishers in the United Kingdom such as the Ulverscroft Group (which includes the Magna Large Print and Isis Publishing imprints) and BBC Audio Books (which includes the Chivers and Galaxy imprints). In the United States, the Thorndike Press Group is a major player which also includes the Wheeler Publishing and Christian Large Print imprints, although publishers such as Random House, Simon & Schuster, HarperCollins, Doubleday and Walker & Co. also have their own large-print programmes.

Books are normally produced in hardback to a larger format than that of the original edition; they are usually blown up from the original typesetting arrangement. Although there are some sales of large-print editions through bookshops, they are promoted through catalogues and sold largely to public libraries, hospital libraries, homes for the elderly and schools for the partially sighted. Enquiries received from individual partially sighted readers through libraries are, however, passed on to the large-print publishers, who then add the names and addresses of individuals to their catalogue mailing list. Individuals can also obtain books by mail order direct from the large-print publishers. The year 2006 saw the launch of an online bookshop for large-print titles and audiobooks (www.largeprintbookshop.co.uk).

The bulk of rights requested for large-print editions are for popular fiction and non-fiction, but some reference books such as dictionaries are also included in the programmes. Regular advance information on relevant titles should be sent to the specialist companies. Although most of the rights acquired are for books already published, large-print editions may be published soon after publication of the trade edition of a new book by a well-established author, and in such cases the assessment will be made on the basis of page proofs or electronic files rather than on a finished copy. Advances can be substantial for a new title by a bestselling author, and in the United States have sometimes reached six figures.

When granting a large-print licence, it is important to specify that the designated market is persons with impaired vision; the minimum type size should also be specified (usually 14 point). The market should also be carefully defined: the key large-print players may require world rights, since they now have the facilities to cover the major English-speaking markets. If the book is illustrated, the licensee may wish to omit the illustrations if they cannot be reproduced satisfactorily in the larger format. Payment is usually made on the basis of an advance against royalties calculated on the recommended retail price for UK sales and on net receipts for export sales. In some cases, payment may be made on the basis of a lump sum to cover a designated print run, payable half on signature of the contract and half on publication. Licences may be limited to an agreed number of years from the date of publication of the large-print edition; five is usually considered acceptable.

A point that may occasionally have to be taken into account is that the increase in format to accommodate the large type size may necessitate a change of title. *Pocket English Dictionary* is no longer a suitable title for a book that has been enlarged to a format of 250 × 170 mm.

In response to a campaign in the United Kingdom for a wider choice of material for the reading impaired, April 2009 saw the launch of the FOCUS programme of large-print books. Initiated and funded by the Royal National Institute for the Blind (RNIB – see also Chapter 18) and the Publishers Licensing Society (PLS – see also Chapter 23), over fifty bestselling titles are available on demand for sale through high street bookshops, priced at £12.99 for trade paperback format and £16.99 for hardback, with the RNIB responsible for administration of the printing arrangements. At the time of writing participating publishers include HarperCollins, Random House, Pan Macmillan, Penguin, Hachette Livre UK and the BBC Chivers imprint; featured authors include Barbara Vine, Bernard Cornwell, Barbara Taylor Bradford and Nigel Slater. The FOCUS campaign is being supported by the major bookselling chains as well as independent booksellers.

Chapter 14

Serial rights and one-shot periodical rights

Serial rights normally involve the sale of extracts from a work to a magazine or newspaper; they are divided into first and second serial rights. One-shot periodical rights involve granting a licence for a whole work to appear in a single issue of a newspaper or magazine.

In all cases, promotion will involve regular liaison with the relevant feature or literary editors of the newspapers and magazines that acquire such rights. Listings of national newspapers and magazines can be found in the annual publications *Writers' and Artists' Yearbook* (A. & C. Black) and *The Writer's Handbook* (Macmillan).

An approach on a likely title must be made well in advance of publication of the book itself, since these publications will be buying many months in advance of the issues in which the material will appear and publishers compete to place key spring and autumn titles. The various supplements and feature sections of the Sunday broadsheets are filling slots up to one year in advance, while many monthly magazines work at least six months in advance of publication. Editors therefore need information and material together with reliable details of the date of publication of the book. In previous years, the importance of this area for rights sales was highlighted when the London Book Fair first provided opportunities for 'speed-dating' between publishers and the literary editors of *The Times* and the *Daily Mail* at the 2005 fair. However, at the time of writing, the market for serial rights has been seriously affected by the economic recession – factors include slimmer newspapers, falling circulation, a reduction in book coverage in some newspapers, reduced advertising revenue and the fact that newspapers are investing substantial sums in websites and four-colour printing presses; they have also sought to attract more readers by giveaways of CDs, DVDs, books and posters.

Decisions on the purchase of serial rights may be made on the basis of a copy of the typescript or proofs; if illustrations are to be a major feature, early visual material will also have to be provided. Material on a potential bestseller may have to be supplied in conditions of some secrecy, often under a confidentiality agreement, particularly if there is a danger of a 'spoiler' from a rival paper.

For anyone responsible for selling such rights it is vital to study a wide range of daily, weekly and monthly publications in detail in order to gain in-depth knowledge of the type of material featured and the tastes of editors and the readership, and also to gauge general trends that may affect the purchasing policy of the publication.

First serial rights

These are defined as the right to publish an extract or series of extracts from a book, beginning in advance of publication of the book itself. Some forty years ago, serial rights were bought mainly by the *Sunday Times* and the *Observer* – when editor of the former paper Harold Evans paid substantial sums to serialize major political memoirs – but since then the daily papers – the tabloids and the broadsheets or former broadsheets – have entered the market and over the years there have been regular battles between Express Newspapers and Associated Press (the *Mail* newspapers), with celebrity magazines such as *OK!* and *Hello!* also entering the fray.

Payment for first serial rights can range from a few hundred pounds and in good times have reached high six-figure sums; in 1993 Mrs Thatcher was reputedly paid £1 million for the sale of first serial rights in *The Downing Street Years* to the *Sunday Times*. They can still be very valuable, depending on the title in question, and may be auctioned; even if payment is more modest, they can provide invaluable advance publicity for the title in question. The key attraction for the buyers is access to material which would not otherwise be available to the newspaper or magazine concerned. Biography and autobiography (particularly if sensational) are both favourite candidates for serialization, with subjects such as politicians, showbusiness stars and sports personalities. There is a feeling that unauthorized biographies are less attractive, with litigation a potential hazard. The royal family remain perennial favourites, with serializations of books about Princess Diana continuing long after her death in 1997; the *Sunday Times* is reputed to have paid £250,000 for Andrew Morton's *Diana: Her True Story* and to have gained 210,000 additional readers for the issue containing the first extract; the same newspaper reportedly paid £400,000 for *Shadow of a Princess* by Patrick Jephson, Diana's former private secretary. The *Daily Telegraph* serialized Trevor Rees-Jones's *The Bodyguard's Story* in 2000 and the *Sunday Times* took on Ken Wharfe's *Diana: Closely Guarded Secret* in 2002 for a reputed £50,000.

Other topics with a more limited lifespan have included the SAS, books connected with the war in Iraq and Afghanistan (e.g. *Soldier: The Autobiography* by General Sir Michael Jackson, serialized in the *Daily Telegraph*), and there is an ongoing demand for human interest stories, as when *The Times* serialized Sheila Hancock's *The Two of Us: My Life with John Thaw* and John Brett's *Stolen Innocence: The Sally Clark Story: A Mother's Fight for Justice*. In recent years 'misery memoirs' have also proved popular.

The perceived benefit to a newspaper or magazine acquiring first serial rights in a major property will be the opportunity to start publishing in advance of the appearance of the book itself, to boost sales for those issues carrying the extracts and perhaps to maintain some of those additional readers after publication of the extracts has ceased. Cases have been quoted of readership of newspapers increasing by between 50,000 and 250,000 during a major serialization; Edwina Currie's *Diaries 1987–1992* (for which *The Times* is reputed to have paid £150,000) generated 130,000 extra readers over the serialization period, whilst in 2003 Princess Diana's ex-butler Paul Burrell's *A Royal Duty* (serialized in the *Daily Mirror* for a reputed £500,000) drew one million extra readers over the six-day serialization, but this figure was not retained. Some serializations have proved disappointing in terms of attracting additional readers, as with the *Daily Mail*'s serialization of Paul Gascoigne's *Gazza: My Story* and the serialization of *The Blunkett Tapes* by the *Guardian* and the *Daily Mail*.

National newspapers may trail extracts on the front page and may take advertising time on radio or television to publicize the appearance of the extracts; a major commitment to publicity of this kind may be a deciding factor in the auction of serial rights.

A development in the last few years has been the introduction of book ordering services 'off the page' by many daily and Sunday newspapers; these enable readers to order the book itself at a discount off the publisher's recommended retail price after reading reviews or serial extracts. *Telegraph* newspapers and *You* magazine, published by the *Mail on Sunday*, have both claimed impressive sales following the publication of serializations; the *Daily Mail* has reported sales as high as 6,000 copies in a day, although this is exceptional. Some newspapers that do not offer this service may, however, be prepared to add details of the publisher's own warehouse telephone number to facilitate sales.

The advantage to author and publisher from the sale of first serial rights may be not only income from the sale itself, but also the large-scale advance publicity for the book provided by the extracts and any attendant advertising. An ideal scenario would be the appearance of prepublication extracts of, say, 5,000 words each on the front page of the review section of a major Sunday newspaper for the three issues immediately preceding publication of the book itself. At the time of writing, it is harder to place multiple extracts with a Sunday newspaper, although daily papers may be prepared to run several extracts from a major title on successive days. Ideally, it should be a requirement that the extracts chosen and any editing undertaken by the newspaper are subject to prior approval by the licensor, but this is not always achievable. It should be a requirement that each extract is accompanied by the name of the author, the title of the book, the name of the publisher, the recommended retail price, the date of publication and a copyright line.

The timing of publication for first serial rights is crucial, and publishers would normally prefer to have such rights under their own control in order to maximize publicity value for the book. In the last twenty-five years, it has been common for literary agents representing major authors to retain such rights, while including the less valuable second serial rights as part of the package granted to the publisher. This can be problematic for the publisher in the case of a book that is sensational, as they may have to embargo their own advance publicity in order to allow the newspaper arrangement made by the agent exclusivity. Some major trade publishers now press for control of such rights; if secured, publishers will almost certainly have to pay a substantial premium, which places additional pressure on rights staff to make a realistic assessment of the value of those rights when the publishing decision is being taken on the project. If first serial rights are retained by the author's agent, it is vital to liaise closely with them to ensure appropriate timing and maximum publicity value.

The proportion of income paid to the author is often as high as 90%. From the author's point of view, much will depend on whether the head contract with the publisher specifies that income from rights sales will be set against the main advance or whether the author's share will be paid out immediately on receipt.

It is important when placing first serial rights that the amount and nature of the material should be carefully monitored. If too much is allowed to appear, or if too many key elements are revealed from a sensational biography, readers of the newspaper or magazine may feel that there is no need to buy the book. But there have been notable exceptions to this rule. In 1984, Jeffrey Archer broke with tradition by allowing the whole of *First Among Equals* to be serialized in four successive editions of the *Mail on Sunday* for a substantial sum (reputed to be between £750,000 and £1,000,000). There were apparently no adverse effects when the book subsequently appeared, although this was a case where hardback and paperback rights were controlled within the same publishing group. A similar arrangement for Frederick Forsyth's *The Fourth Protocol* was aborted following adverse reaction from his paperback publishers, who felt that sales of their edition would be affected.

As noted above, the price paid for first serial rights varies enormously, depending on the status of the author, the subject and topicality of the book, access to material not normally available to the newspaper, the expected effect on sales of the publication in which the extracts will appear and hence the budget of the buyer. Figures may vary from several hundred pounds for a short extract in the colour magazine or a special supplement of a Sunday broadsheet, and in the boom years of the 1980s and early 1990s reached high six figures or even over £1 million for substantial extracts from a controversial biography serialized in a daily or Sunday tabloid, with newspapers spending between £10 million and £15 million annually on the purchase of serial rights. Political memoirs continued to command large sums, with the *Mail on Sunday* paying £250,000 for Alan Clark's *Diaries* and the *Sunday Times* paying £400,000 for Robin Cook's memoirs, *The Point of Departure*. Falling circulations and a slump in newspaper advertising revenue in the mid-1990s and again in the last three years have led to a significant drop in the money available to purchase serial rights. From 2008 onwards, a modest deal might fetch £25,000 but mid-market deals of £60,000–£80,000 have been harder to secure. In 2009 prominent deals were for Freddie Flintoff's *Ashes to Ashes*, Keith Floyd's *Stirred but Not Shaken* and Antonia Fraser's *Must You Go?* (all to the *Daily Mail*), Ozzy Osbourne's *I am Ozzy* (to *The Times*), with more modest deals for Paddy Ashdown's *A Fortunate Life*, Shirley Williams's *Climbing the Bookshelves: The Autobiography* and US politician Sarah Palin's *Going Rogue: An American Life* (all to the *Sunday Times*), Lynn Barber's *An Education* and Andrew Rawnsley's *The End of the Party: The Rise and Fall of New Labour* (to the *Observer*).

In today's tougher market, newspapers may be more inclined to bid for rights if the offer includes additional material not appearing in the book itself – for example, illustrations, or an exclusive interview with the author or the subject of the book either as a podcast for downloading by readers or to appear on the newspaper's website for a limited period of time.

Magazines generally tend to pay less for serial rights, with the exception of the major 'celebrity' magazines. Circulation wars and some changes of literary editor amongst both the tabloids and the broadsheets mean that substantial sums can still be paid for some properties, in particular for controversial biographies and autobiographies. The *Daily Mail* and the *Mail on Sunday* have traditionally had the largest budgets and are still estimated to account for about half of the total amount spent on serial rights in the UK. The year 2005 saw *The Times* paying £180,000 for *Talk to the Hand*, the book on bad manners by Lynne Truss, and the *Daily Telegraph* paying £250,000 for *Margrave of the Marshes*, the autobiography of the late BBC DJ John Peel completed by his widow, Sheila Ravenscroft.

There can also still be fierce competition between a small number of newspapers with larger budgets, with other buyers falling into a more modest category. Prices can be driven up if several papers are fighting for the same property; this may include competition between daily and Sunday newspapers in the same group. However, such newspapers may also bid together to secure rights, as when the *Daily Mail* and the *Mail on Sunday* joined forces to pay a reputed £700,000 for Ulrike Jonsson's autobiography *Honest* following a bidding war with Express Newspapers.

There are also cases of newspapers with diverse readerships teaming up to secure joint first serial rights, as for Sir Alex Ferguson's *Managing My Life* (for which *The Times* and the *Sun* reputedly paid £450,000), Greg Dyke's *Inside Story* following his departure from the BBC (for which the *Mail on Sunday* and the *Observer* are thought to have paid £300,000) and the *Sun* and *The Times* combining forces to publish extracts from Cherie Blair's *Speaking for Myself*. Associated Press, owners of the *Mail* newspapers, teamed up with *Hello!* magazine to pay a total of £750,000 for Victoria Beckham's *Learning to Fly*, with the newspapers paying £450,000 of the total. There was much controversy over the publication and the joint serialization of *DC Confidential*, the memoirs of Sir Christopher Meyer, the former British ambassador to Washington, in the *Daily Mail* and the *Guardian* for £250,000, a sum which Sir Christopher stated was being donated to charity.

In previous years, the sale of serial rights in fiction was difficult, with many magazines preferring to publish short, specially commissioned work. There were some serializations in the *Mail on Sunday*, the *Daily Telegraph* and the *Independent*, including more literary fiction such as *Longitude* by Dava Sobel, *The Information* by Martin Amis and *Captain Corelli's Mandolin* by Louis de Bernières. However, in the last few years there has been something of a revival in this field, with the *Daily Telegraph* taking Zadie Smith's *On Beauty*, *The Times* taking Salman Rushdie's *Shalimar the Clown* and Sebastian Faulks's *Human Traces*, the *Guardian* buying *Stories We Could Tell* by Tony Parsons and the *Independent on Sunday* taking Geraldine McCaughrean's *The White Darkness*. On a more populist note, the *Independent* published extracts from Helen Fielding's *Bridget Jones: The Edge of Reason*. In July 2009 it was announced that *Playboy* magazine had acquired first serial rights in Vladimir Nabokov's unpublished novel *The Original of Laura* for an undisclosed but substantial sum.

Generally, serial rights for fiction consist of a single extract and are felt to have less impact on newspaper sales than non-fiction; however, their publication reinforces the identity of the paper. Serial sales of fiction to magazines remain somewhat difficult, as there is no equivalent of the *New Yorker* magazine, which has long trailed important new literary fiction. Serialization of poetry remains rare, although *The Times* published extracts from *Birthday Letters* by Ted Hughes, with the added human interest factor of his marriage to Sylvia Plath, and serialization of literature-related titles remains popular: the *Sunday Times* has serialized *The Blue Hour: A Portrait of Jean Rhys*; *Mad: Evelyn Waugh and the Secrets of Brideshead*, Paula Byrne's account of the house and family on which Waugh's *Brideshead Revisited* was allegedly based; and extracts from the second volume of *The Letters of T.S. Eliot*.

The amount paid may be the main consideration in deciding who will acquire first serial rights in a major property if an auction is being conducted, but on occasion there could be good reason to take slightly less than the top offer if an alternative offer is backed with a better guarantee of expenditure on press and/or television advertising. The choice of vehicle for serial publication is also an important factor, particularly if the author has views on where extracts may appear. The profile of a newspaper's readers is crucial in selecting the most appropriate buyer. For titles not in the major league, the size of payment may be a secondary consideration when compared with the publicity provided and hence the effect on sales of the book. It is important to make this clear to potential buyers from the start, particularly if the author has the final word on the choice of publication.

There may be reasons why books which might have seemed ideal candidates for serialization despite current economic constraints are not in fact exploited in that way. In 2007, Alastair Campbell and his agent decided against serialization of *The Blair Years*, choosing instead to create publicity for the book through Campbell's own website. In 2009, restrictions from Buckingham Palace meant that William Shawcross's *Queen Elizabeth the Queen Mother: The Official Biography* was not serialized, although there were interviews with the author and extensive review coverage.

It is usually not possible to sell first serial rights in a major property to more than one buyer; a major selling feature will be the exclusivity. However, as mentioned earlier, it is sometimes possible to split first serial rights within a single newspaper group or, in special circumstances, between newspapers from different groups, if they have chosen to work together, as in the *DC Confidential* case. The tabloid paper may carry a shorter, more sensational piece based on a particular episode, while the broadsheet publishes a more in-depth extract. It is also sometimes possible to make more than one deal for a book with a potentially diverse market, say in a national newspaper and in a specialist magazine. In such cases, the extracts chosen would have to be different, and each potential buyer should be told of the other negotiations to ensure that there is no conflict of interest.

Several problems can arise that particularly affect the sale of serial rights in major properties. The first is that of 'spoilers' – features on the subject of the book or interviews with the author, published by a rival newspaper just in advance of publication of the first instalment of a major serialization. Spoilers can now be far more immediate via a rival paper's website. The resulting need for secrecy has reduced the number of first serial rights sold by open auction and has led to the need for caution in the timing of the release of review copies and author interviews. A spoiler run by the *Sun* led to the *Daily Mirror* refusing to pay the whole fee for James Whitaker's *Diana v. Charles*. The *Sunday Times* reclaimed £150,000 of a payment made for extracts from Andrew Morton's *Diana: Her New Life* when a number of other newspapers ran extracts following the publication of extracts in *People* magazine, which held US serial rights. There is also a danger of spoilers if the US edition of the book is made available via the UK website of Amazon.

The second problem has been one of early selling, where booksellers have put a book on sale in advance of the publication date set by the publisher, and in some cases anticipating the first instalment of a major series of prepublication extracts. For newsworthy or sensational projects, the newspaper purchasing first serial rights will insist on secrecy and require that no books are released until after they publish. This involves the publisher in strict secrecy in the warehouse, as well as tight security at the printers and even in despatching proofs to and from the author and the copyeditor. No review copies can be sent out until the deadline has passed, or the newspaper will cancel the deal. This can prove problematic if the book is appearing separately in a market such as the United States, as leakage may occur. All this reinforces the view of many publishers that in order to sell first serial rights effectively they need to control those rights worldwide. This must be remembered if one is including serial rights as part of a licence to American or foreign-language publishers; liaison on timing is vital if deals in the home market are not to be jeopardized.

Another development was the insistence of most major newspapers on the inclusion of a clause in the contract for first serial rights enabling them to reduce the price paid if the final product did not live up to the buyer's expectations. In today's market, most newspapers are reluctant to bid for serial rights sight unseen.

A further problem in recent years has been 'overbuying' by some newspapers (often to preclude deals by rival papers) resulting in an overcrowded schedule and failure to publish. This reinforces the need for the rights seller to insist that payment should be made on publication or by a specified calendar date, so that there is at least some financial compensation if publication does not take place. However, it will hardly be adequate compensation for the publisher if a major serialization has been a key feature in the advance publicity campaign.

Second serial rights

These are extract rights for publication in a newspaper or magazine, starting after publication of the book itself. They are thus less valuable to the purchaser, although they still provide excellent publicity for the book. Here it is possible to make different arrangements with a range of different publications, provided that each purchaser is aware of the other arrangements and that the extracts featured do not conflict. It might, for example, be possible to have extracts from the same interior design book in an upmarket women's magazine and in a specialist monthly magazine such as

House and Garden. A popular autobiography could well justify the sale of first and second serial rights, as with Sharon Osbourne's *Extreme*, with first serial rights being sold to the *Sun* for a reputed £200,000 and second serial rights to the *Daily Mail*.

The contract

Serial rights are frequently conducted by telephone, and auctions may also be conducted through this medium, with a floor for the bids and a deadline for offers; auctions may go through several rounds before a deal is concluded. Once a price is agreed, a contract is signed to confirm the arrangements; most major newspapers supply their own contract. This should specify the name of the author and the title of the work, the name of the newspaper or magazine acquiring the rights, whether first or second serial rights are being granted, the language and the market granted (usually defined as exclusive for the United Kingdom and Eire, but with non-exclusive rights to cover the sale of the newspaper outside its home territory). Most UK newspapers now require the right to use the material electronically on their websites; it is important to check that any third party permissions secured for text and/or illustrations extend to such use. The contract should confirm that website publication should not take place before the official release date for the serialization in the newspaper itself, but the material can then be retained on the website, which offers access to the newspaper's back issue archives. The newspaper may require the work to be supplied in the form of electronic files to facilitate the selection of material.

The contract should also specify the number of words to be used, the number of extracts to be published (and illustrations, if relevant) and the date of publication of each extract, since timing in relation to the date of publication of the book is crucial in the case of first serial rights. The sum to be paid should be specified, together with the date or dates of payment (all on signature of the contract, half on signature and half on the date of publication of the first extract, etc.). As mentioned earlier, it would be desirable to specify calendar dates for payment in case for some reason one or all of the extracts fail to appear. The newspaper will require VAT invoices to remit payment.

The use should be limited to single serial use; syndication rights to other newspapers or magazines should not be included, unless financial terms and other requirements such as prior approval by the licensor have been agreed.

The contract should also specify that prominent acknowledgement to the author, title and publisher accompanies every extract, and that the date of publication and price of the book are clearly shown together with the appropriate copyright notice.

The question of approval of the choice of extracts, any editing and any accompanying material added by the newspaper is a sensitive one, particularly in view of the moral rights now covered by the 1988 UK Copyright Act; these allow the author to object to changes he or she considers detrimental to the work, unless moral rights have been formally waived; this can be particularly important in the case of books containing sensitive material. If the author has the right of approval, perhaps in the head contract between the author and the publisher, it may be necessary to check the extracts very quickly (perhaps within twenty-four hours) in order to avoid delaying the newspaper publication schedule. However, it is not always possible to secure right of approval; much depends on the status of the author and the incentive for the newspaper to secure the serial rights, perhaps in the face of strong competition from rival publications. If approval is not possible, it is wise to require the right for the person handling the serial rights sale to have prior sight of the extracts for checking of accuracy. There have been a number of recent cases of authors objecting to the way in which serializations were undertaken, in particular Janet Street-Porter over extracts from *Baggage: My Childhood* and John Coldstream over the serialization of his biography of actor Dirk Bogarde; Coldstream tried to stop publication in the *Daily Mail* and subsequently wrote an article for *The Bookseller* in which he referred to the resulting extracts as a 'hatchet job' on his subject; he gave the proceeds from the serialization to charity. Extracts from Michael Mann's controversial biography of actor David Niven, *The Man behind the Balloon*, in the *Sunday Times* drew criticism from family and colleagues.

The newspaper will require that the licensor provides warranties and indemnities; these will have to match those provided by the author in the head contract, and the issue of libel will be a sensitive one in the area of serializations. If the deal includes the right of approval by the author or the publisher, it might be assumed that the warranties and indemnities extend to any changes made and/or additional material added by the newspaper, so it is important to clarify in the contract that this is not the case. It is also important to ensure that any third party permissions secured for text and illustrations extend to use in the serialization.

The sale of serial rights is usually associated with major properties, but it is sometimes possible to place such rights in more specialized titles if there are appropriate newspapers, journals or magazines that are prepared to pay for them. Their placement may require time and creativity. Examples in the past have included a series of extracts from the edited journals of Captain Cook, run daily for several months in two Australian newspapers on dates corresponding to the journal entries, and extracts from the text of the *New English Bible* accompanied by appropriate modern-day photographs of the Holy Land in the *Observer* colour supplements. Serial rights are also bought for the cookery and children's sections, whilst extracts from topical business or economics titles can be sold to the business pages of the broadsheets; the *Sunday Times* has published extracts from *iCon: Steve Jobs, the Greatest Second Act in the History of Business* by Jeffrey S. Young and William L. Simon, *End of the Road: The True Story of the Downfall of Rover* by Chris Brady and Andrew Lorenz and *The Accidental Billionaires: Sex, Money, Betrayal and the Founding of Facebook* by Ben Mezrich.

Sometimes an approach to a newspaper or magazine with the intention of placing serial rights may eventually result in an extended review or a feature on the author, rather than in direct extracts from the book itself. Unless this precludes the possibility of placing lucrative serial rights elsewhere, such a feature provides excellent advance publicity and should not be lightly dismissed. For this reason, there can sometimes be a blurred line between promotion and serial rights, which may lead to serial rights being handled in some publishing houses by the promotion department rather than by rights staff.

Online serial rights

In 1998, there were a number of early experiments in the United States in offering extracts from forthcoming titles online; Douglas Cooper's novel *Delirium* was offered in instalments – but minus the final chapter – by Warner Electronic Publishing; there were subsequent experiments by Hotwired, the electronic counterpart of *Wired* magazine. The financial models for such use have varied from an outright fee to the author and free downloading for users, to the 'pay-per-view' model, where the author shares the revenue stream with the web publisher. The most famous case occurred in March 2000, when Stephen King made the complete text of his sixty-five page novella *Riding the Bullet* available via the Simon & Schuster website at a price of $2.50 per 'hit'; 400,000 people accessed the site in the first two days, before the material was pirated and distributed freely. In July, King followed this by offering instalments of his novella *The Plant* from his own website at a charge of $1 per download, with the proviso that the next instalment would only appear if 75% of those accessing the site paid the charge via the amazon.com payment service or agreed to do so in future. Approximately 150,000 'hits' were received in the first week. The author announced plans for fees for the fourth instalment onwards to rise to $2.50, with instalments lengthening from 5,000 to 25,000 words and seven or eight instalments planned. In December 2000, King announced he would suspend publication after the sixth instalment as payment for downloads had fallen to less than 50%: an interesting experiment by an author with status as a brand name.

In a variation on this theme, MP3lit.com commenced serialization on the web of the complete audiobook version of Armistead Maupin's novel *The Night Listener*, read by the author, one month before publication of the print version, with a new instalment added every weekday; listeners were able to access the material free of charge as an incentive to visit the site.

Now that all major newspapers have their own websites, online serialization is likely to become more common if it is not felt to impact negatively on print sales of the book. Little, Brown recently licensed Patricia Cornwell's *The Front* to *The Times*, with chapters appearing daily in the print version of the newspaper over a two-week period and the previous day's chapter appearing online, so that eventually the whole book had appeared on the newspaper's website – the material was then removed from the website a few days before publication of the book itself. In September 2009 Alexander McCall Smith's *The Dog Who Came in from the Cold* was serialized online by the *Daily Telegraph* on weekdays, with print extracts appearing in the Saturday *Weekend* supplement.

One-shot periodical rights

These rights involve publication of the full text of a complete book in a single issue of a newspaper or magazine. Fees for such usage will vary according to the status of the author and the topicality of the book.

This type of licence proved controversial, and in the early 1980s the establishment of a magazine entitled *Complete Bestsellers* led to a considerable backlash from paperback publishers, who held that their rights would be infringed if titles licensed to them were also licensed in this form, albeit a transient one. A case between Jonathan Cape and Consolidated Press established that one-shot rights constituted part of volume rights rather than a form of serial rights, and in recent years there have been few cases of this type of licensing.

Chapter 15

Digest and condensation rights

Both these rights involve the condensation of the text of a literary work. Digest rights are the right to publish a condensed version of whole or part of a work in a single issue of a newspaper or magazine. Digest book condensation rights cover the right to publish a condensed version of the complete text in volume form, often accompanied by the condensed texts of other works. In each case, the major player in the field is Reader's Digest, with its magazine of the same title and its compendium volumes. The Reader's Digest Association was founded in the USA in 1922 and has grown into a worldwide brand. Its readership is recruited almost entirely through direct mail shots rather than through press advertising. It also has websites advertising its products. In August 2009 the US company announced that it was filing for voluntary Chapter 11 bankruptcy protection with a view to reducing substantial debts and addressing a deficit in the pension fund. On 17 February 2010, the UK company filed for administration; five days later the US company emerged from Chapter 11 with the aid of exit financing and a new board of directors. In April 2010, the UK company was subject to a management buyout backed by Better Capital, a private equity company, although it is as yet unclear whether all the company's operations will continue.

Most of the rights acquired for both forms of publication are for the work of well-established authors with popular appeal. Book condensation rights are acquired for works of fiction and non-fiction; the majority of magazine digest rights are for works of non-fiction.

Reader's Digest editors need to maintain close contact with both literary agents and rights staff from the major trade houses, both through regular meetings and through a flow of information and material on likely titles, provided well in advance of publication. Assessment of key titles will be made on the basis of the manuscript or page proofs, although the editors also monitor the trade press for possible candidates from smaller publishers with whom they may not have regular contact.

The proceeds from digest book condensation rights acquired through the trade publisher are normally shared with the author on a 50/50 basis.

Digest rights

First established in the United States, *Reader's Digest* magazine is published in fifty editions in twenty-one languages. It is issued in the UK twelve times per year and distributed by mail to subscribers, although it is also sold on newsstands. The British magazine often looks for suitable non-fiction extracts, and also features short highlights from key books in their end-of-article 'fillers'. Payment is by negotiation and payment is normally made to the licensor on publication.

Book condensation rights

Since 1954, Reader's Digest in the UK has been publishing its series of condensed books. Its hardback series has recently been renamed *Select Editions* in line with the series published by Reader's Digest in the USA; six of these volumes are published per year, with each volume containing four condensed works by different authors, providing a range of different writing aimed to appeal to a family readership; this series now contains an increasing number of narrative non-fiction titles. The price per volume is currently around £18.99, excluding postage and handling. Specially commissioned title pages are added to each title included in the compendium.

At the beginning of the decade, Reader's Digest introduced a paperback series entitled *Of Love and Life*; five volumes are published a year, currently priced at around £14.99 excluding postage and handling; each contains three condensations of contemporary books chosen to appeal to women of all ages. This series may come to an end in July 2010, but it is hoped that there may be a future for it amongst the Reader's Digest Anglophone editions.

The work of condensation is commissioned by in-house editors and undertaken by a highly skilled team of freelance editors, who are often former full-time employees of the organization. The standard of work is regarded as extremely high. Rights are normally negotiated on the basis of a set rate per copy for each of the titles included in the compendium; the exact rate depends on the length of the condensation, the importance of the title to the volume and, to some extent, the status of the author. The rate per copy is currently not less than 4p, with major titles commanding a higher rate per copy.

A standard contract is issued by Reader's Digest for each work included; for *Select Editions*, this normally provides for an advance payment equivalent to a guaranteed sale of 125,000 copies. Print runs for the *Of Love and Life* volumes tend to be lower, with correspondingly lower advances (currently based on 60,000 copies). Payment is made half on signature of a contract and half on publication. Payment for copies in excess of the quantity guaranteed for the advance is then accounted for on a twice-yearly basis. Licences normally run for five years from the date of first publication. Stock of a particular volume is not always sold out in the first mailing, but may be used in subsequent follow-up mailings. A certain proportion of the books printed are offered free, through bi-annual promotional mailings to attract new customers to the series, and royalties are paid at half the normal rate on these copies.

The market requested for book condensation rights may vary, but the London office of Reader's Digest negotiates for world English-language rights excluding the United States and its dependencies, the Philippines and Canada. Because the Australian *Select Editions* almost always contains the same selection of four books as the United Kingdom, the UK office seeks to include Australia under the terms of its UK-originated contract for World English-Language condensation rights, at the same royalty rate as the UK. There is a separate advance for the Australian deal, currently based on 50,000 copies, payable on signature of contract. The Australian edition of *Select Editions* is further sold in small quantities in a handful of tertiary territories (e.g. Hong Kong, Singapore, South Africa, India) and rights for these territories are sought under the same single World English-Language contract.

Once a title is included in the Reader's Digest programme, interest may be generated from other Anglophone parts of the organization, for example in the United States and Canada, and further rights may then be negotiated. In addition, the foreign-language operations of Reader's Digest (in markets such as France, Germany, Portugal, the Netherlands, Finland, Sweden, Brazil, Russia and central and eastern Europe) may seek to acquire translation rights in the condensation; in this case, rights would also have to be cleared with any foreign-language licensee of the full text of the work. The American Reader's Digest operation maintains a 'pool' of condensed titles from which the foreign-language companies can select; appropriate rights would then need to be cleared. Rates paid per copy can differ considerably from country to country.

In the past, condensed editions have not been considered to affect trade sales, but the situation may perhaps be changing. They can undoubtedly generate substantial extra revenue and may generate extra sales of trade editions when readers of a condensed edition become familiar with the work of a particular author. The compendium volumes contain full credit to the authors, titles and the publishers of the full trade editions in the market concerned; they also include photographs of the covers of the trade editions. If a book is being offered by an agent, strong interest from Reader's Digest in condensation rights can often be helpful in placing the trade rights, if these have not already been sold.

Chapter 16

Translation rights

The sale of translation rights often forms a large part of the work of a publisher's rights department; with reductions and fluctuations in licensing income from areas such as paperback rights, book club rights and serial rights they have taken on greater importance and may be sought as part of the publisher's overall package of rights, particularly if a large advance is being required by the author or the author's agent. However, translation rights may not always be granted, particularly if the agency has a specialist department for handling such rights. Literary agents often work through a network of subagents in individual overseas markets; in such cases, their agreements with authors may provide for the deduction of 20% commission, to allow for the additional commission for the local subagent.

Translations of English-language books tend to dominate the market, perhaps hardly surprising when it was confirmed in a Bowker survey in 2004 that 40% of all new titles produced were English-language original titles; at the time of writing there has been no updated survey, but the figure is thought to remain accurate. The accessibility of the English language makes English books easier to assess than those in many other languages and translators tend to be easier to find. In addition to this, Anglophone publishers have the advantage of long experience in placing their rights abroad, and have a stable of well-known authors of literary and popular fiction as well as non-fiction and academic writers.

While the aim of placing translation rights is certainly to generate welcome additional revenue, there is also the motivation of bringing the book to a wider readership. Here there may be some difference in the method of operation between academic and trade publishers.

Some academic authors are keen that their books should be licensed for translation less for financial reasons than to 'spread the word', particularly if they are writing in a field where they feel that information is badly needed in the poorer countries of the world. Examples here might include books on medicine, economic development, new business techniques and aspects of technology. A rights department in an academic publishing house may therefore be prepared to invest time in arranging a licence for a nursing book to Nepal, a logistics book to Mongolia or a book on rural development to Malaysia, often following up contacts provided by the author. Such arrangements may be on the basis of a token fee and may not cover the cost of administering the licence, although the exercise usually generates considerable goodwill from the author and should contribute to the general process of maintaining a long-term relationship with such writers.

Academic publishers may also spend considerable time dealing with licence applications from countries that have limited resources for payment, or from developing and newly industrialized countries which may have introduced forms of compulsory licensing. They may also be dealing with publishers in countries that do not belong to any of the international copyright conventions or which have a poor record of copyright compliance. In such cases, licensing should be regarded as 'defensive' rather than as a voluntary activity, as a means of combating piracy, compulsory licences and unauthorized editions.

The importance of copyright knowledge when dealing with a wide range of countries cannot be overemphasized. There is a tendency to assume that the major developed countries of the world operate against a similar background of copyright protection, but there may still be anomalies in both the duration and the standards of protection. For example, at the time of writing, Japan still has a copyright term of fifty years *post mortem auctoris*, although there are plans to extend this to seventy or even seventy-five years. The EU duration directive removed discrepancies in the periods of protection in member states, which are now harmonized to seventy years *post mortem auctoris* (see Chapter 1 for further details). However, many other countries have shorter terms of protection, which may mean that a British work still protected in its country of origin and elsewhere within the European Union may have entered the public domain in other countries. China, now a major buyer of rights, also has a copyright protection period of fifty years *post mortem auctoris*. EU legislation can also affect the territorial aspects of licence arrangements; for example, the granting of German translation rights for the territory of Germany alone would be viewed as impeding free trade within the area, whereas the granting of world German-language rights to a publisher in Germany would be acceptable.

The provisions of foreign copyright legislation elsewhere can prove problematic for British works; for example, the copyright law introduced in Japan from 1 January 1971 provided that foreign titles published before that date are considered to be in the public domain as far as translation rights are concerned, if no authorized Japanese translation has appeared within ten years of first publication of the original edition. Egypt, Sri Lanka and Yugoslavia (whose legislation is still in force in Serbia and Montenegro) also have compulsory translation legislation. Russia, a member of the Berne Convention since 1995, joined with the proviso that foreign works first published in their country of origin before 27 May 1973 (the date of the accession of the then Soviet Union to the Universal Copyright Convention) remain in the public domain and can be freely used in Russia.

Promoting translation rights to foreign-language publishers normally involves a variety of techniques: general mailing of catalogues and perhaps selective rights guides for key new titles, provision of information and material on specific projects, attendance at the relevant international book fairs, and, if rights potential is high, separate sales trips to visit customers in individual countries. Rights can now be promoted via company or dedicated rights department websites (see *Specific promotion: advance information and promotional material* in Chapter 7) and via e-mail alerts linking to the URL of a particular book description on such websites.

In most cases, business correspondence is conducted from the British side in English, but it could well be that a proportion of incoming correspondence is in languages other than English. It is here that linguistic expertise will prove valuable, as well as in face-to-face contact with customers.

Some foreign-language publishers employ scouts in Europe, the United Kingdom and the United States who will comb catalogues and the trade press for suitable titles on their behalf. Some western publishers and literary agents will choose to employ subagents in markets such as Japan, Korea, Taiwan, mainland China and central and eastern Europe if they feel that this is preferable to visiting or promoting directly to such markets (see *The use of subagents* in Chapter 7).

It is inevitable that titles with excellent potential for translation in some markets are non-starters in others. This is only natural when one is dealing with a wide range of licensees whose cultural, social, political and economic perspectives may differ greatly from country to country. Until the 1990s, many western books in the fields of modern history, politics, economics and business were completely unacceptable in countries ruled by a communist regime, and these restrictions also extended to fiction which touched on sensitive ideological areas. Ironically, one of the first western cinema films to be shot in Russia in the throes of the country's political and economic changes was *The Russia House*, released in 1990 and based on the novel by John Le Carré – long a banned author in the former Soviet Union.

In recent years, restrictions have been lifted, and there is now a keen demand for books that would previously have been confiscated at a book fair or 'gone astray' in the post. However, some problems may still be encountered in mainland China; in the run-up to the 2008 Beijing Olympics, copies of Lonely Planet's *China Tourist Guide* were confiscated by customs authorities from a number of tourists on the grounds that the book contained incorrect information about Taiwan.

A book such as *Wild Swans* by Jung Chang and the biography of Mao by the same author and Jon Halliday cannot yet be published in China.

There are regular examples of censorship if books refer to topics such as the status of Taiwan, the treatment of ethnic minorities such as Tibetans, and the Tiananmen incident of 1989. High-profile cases of complaints about censorship during the translation process have included Hillary Clinton's autobiography *Living History*.

The official publishing industry in China remains state controlled, and in 2008 there were moves by the Chinese authorities to encourage state publishers to acquire ownership of the so-called 'second channel' private publishers (sometimes referred to as 'cultural studios'). They are unauthorized by the state authorities and have to acquire SBNs by 'purchasing' them from state publishers.

Some political issues also remain sensitive in Vietnam, a relatively recent member of the Berne Convention whose publishers are now actively buying rights from abroad.

In March 2001, Turkish domestic copyright law was amended to specify that publishers were obliged to purchase 'banderoles' or holograms from the Ministry of Culture; this was used as a means of censorship and the International Publishers Association lobbied for the provision to be withdrawn. The system became redundant in 2005 owing to piracy and the theft of two million genuine banderoles.

Other factors may affect the attractiveness of titles for translation. In the educational sector, it is difficult to sell a full-scale course which has been designed for the National Curriculum in the United Kingdom, although supplementary material may have better prospects. In general, foreign-language publishers prefer to commission course material from teachers in their own country who are familiar with the requirements of the local curriculum. There are, however, translation possibilities within the United Kingdom, for Welsh and Gaelic rights. At tertiary level, titles may have a better chance of transferring to another country, although scientific books are usually easier to adapt than books in the humanities and the social sciences, which may be more geared to circumstances in the United Kingdom, or at least to the English-speaking world. Some subject areas have specific problems, for example technical titles that include regulations (e.g. construction engineering) or normative standards (e.g. for the manufacture of concrete) that may prove too laboursome and hence too expensive to adapt to local circumstances.

It should be borne in mind that many British and American university textbooks are adopted in considerable quantities for use abroad – in Europe in areas such as the Benelux countries and Scandinavia, but also further afield in South-East Asia and the Indian subcontinent. It would therefore be unwise to undertake extensive promotion of translation rights in key textbooks to publishers in those countries. Copy for copy, the revenue will always be greater from the sale of the English-language edition than from the royalty derived from a translation. The loss of sales of the

English edition in such markets will rarely be compensated for by higher unit sales of the translation. For this type of book in these markets, there should be regular liaison between rights and export sales staff. But it is important that the relative merits of licensing versus direct sales are assessed book by book and market by market. There can sometimes be an element of territoriality between rights and export sales departments, and there is also a danger that sales turnover is compared (incorrectly) with rights revenue (see Chapter 4).

In countries where textbooks can be licensed without a conflict of interest, it should be remembered that licensees are often nervous of the risk inherent in taking on a translation of a book still in its first English edition. It is much more likely that they will wait to assess the performance of the first English edition, and good sales figures may thus form part of the sales package when promoting rights in subsequent editions. High-level monographs normally have a relatively limited market in English worldwide. In the countries of western Europe they are likely to be read in the original English edition. However, where the ability to read English is not so high, there may well be opportunities for licensing translation rights, albeit with small print runs.

Children's books often provide a good market for translation rights, both for unillustrated fiction and for picture books. Some classic children's books have been widely translated: Beatrix Potter's *The Tale of Peter Rabbit* is available in more than thirty languages. Some works transcend cultural borders, as with J.K. Rowling's *Harry Potter* books, which caused as much excitement in Japan and Thailand as they have in Europe and the United States; at the time of writing they have been published in sixty-seven languages, including Latin and classical Greek. They have also had the added benefit of film exploitation.

In this field, much depends on the status of the author (and the illustrator if appropriate). For illustrated books, however, there may be a considerable difference in style between countries. For example, France and Belgium favour the comic-strip storybook (*bandes dessinées*); books from central and eastern Europe and China often reflect the local folk-art style; Japan has picture books with delicate watercolour illustrations, but also the *manga* tradition of comic books, popular with both children and adults.

The actual content of the illustrations may also affect their saleability; for example, the ethnic mix of people shown in a British children's book may be quite inappropriate for a publisher in Denmark or Latin America. In some countries, there is even a gender requirement for children's books; in Sweden, illustrations must show an equal number of male and female characters and they should not be performing gender-stereotyped activities. Street scenes showing double-decker buses and traffic on the left-hand side of the road may reduce the chance for foreign licences.

In the area of adult fiction, the status of the author and the quality of the writing within the genre are key elements. The works of authors such as John Grisham, Robert Ludlum, Danielle Steele, Stephen King and John Le Carré are translated extensively, including in the former socialist countries, and Agatha Christie remains a firm favourite there. With the lifting of censorship laws, the early 1990s saw an explosion in translations of more sensational foreign fiction in the region; by the mid-1990s it was estimated that 90% of all legitimately published books in Russia were translations of foreign titles; the initial wave of translations of pulp fiction was followed by translations of popular non-fiction for both adults and children, much of it illustrated information books and coffee-table books on topics such as cookery, gardening and interior design, reflecting a more affluent readership. The period also saw massive piracy of western titles, often in multiple editions.

There has since been a noticeable reduction in the number of rights acquired from the west, and the size of print runs has also dropped significantly. This has been influenced by a number of factors – the initial novelty wore off, there was something of a backlash against western domination of the market, and there have also been economic difficulties in some markets, in particular Russia, where the market for luxury books plummeted after the currency crash in 1998 and has been affected again by the current economic recession. Children's publishers in the region now produce high-quality illustrated books of their own (doubtless influenced by western titles) and are keen to license rights in their home-grown product.

As a general rule, a first novel by an unknown writer usually proves difficult to license. Until a writer has become established in the home market through two or three books, or is perhaps shortlisted for or wins a literary prize, foreign publishers may remain uninterested. Once a reputation has been gained, earlier books may well be picked up. On the literary fiction front, Chinua Achebe's 1958 novel *Things Fall Apart* has been translated into fifty languages, making him the most translated African writer of all time. And there can be exceptions to the 'unknown author' rule; Vikas Swarup's 2003 novel *Q & A* – admittedly with the benefit of an Oscar-winning film version, *Slumdog Millionaire* (see Chapter 21) – has been translated into thirty-seven languages to date, and at the 2009 Frankfurt Book Fair the debut novel from Australian writer Rebecca James, *Beautiful Malice*, was set for translation into over thirty languages.

The areas of autobiography and biography may also prove difficult if the author or the subject is not well known internationally. However, a book by a key international figure may have excellent potential, as with Nelson Mandela's *Conversations with Myself*, another key title at the 2009 Frankfurt fair.

As with children's books, prospects improve greatly for books adapted for television or the cinema; Michael Ondaatje's *The English Patient* was licensed into over thirty languages. Tolkien's *Lord of the Rings* trilogy is available in more than forty languages. Dan Brown's *The Da Vinci Code* had also been translated into over forty languages before the film version appeared in May 2006 and his later bestsellers, *Angels and Demons* and *The Lost Symbol*, have also been extensively licensed. However, books can often surprise, as when Irvine Welsh's *Trainspotting* was translated into Japanese at a time when the author was not well known and before the book had been made into a film; its success in translation was all the more surprising given its controversial themes and its use of Edinburgh dialect. Zadie Smith's *White Teeth* and Monica Ali's *Brick Lane*, with their multicultural view of British society, have also proved successful in translation, as have the gritty novels of Martina Cole, which have been translated into twenty-eight languages. Books which might be regarded as peculiarly British in their humour can succeed: Douglas Adams's *The Hitchhiker's Guide to the Galaxy* has been translated into twenty-five languages.

Poetry poses its own self-evident problems. It is difficult to capture the style and quality of the original in translation, which may limit licensing to the work of only the best-known writers.

Size may prove a very real problem in placing translation rights. Translation is an expensive (and often troublesome) way of acquiring a new product; while a blockbusting novel by Danielle Steele or Maeve Binchy may pose no obstacles since length is expected and sales success is guaranteed, an academic book of 750 pages may be a very different matter unless it is on a major topic or by an author who has crossed the border to reach the general reader (Ian Kershaw's two-volume biography of Hitler is an example here). For many non-fiction titles, the attraction is very often the information rather than the writer; in many cases there may be strong competition, both from local publishers in the licensee's market and from other foreign sources. *Gray's Anatomy*, currently in its fortieth edition and probably the best-known medical book in the world, weighs in at 1,576 pages but its reputation is such that there are few problems in placing translation rights, except in markets where there is strong competition from a long-established local medical publishing industry. Similar 'bibles' in key topics can be licensed, even if they run to 3,000 pages in a multi-volume set.

The trade in translation rights can of course be affected by a change in circumstances in the markets concerned. Countries opening up to foreign contact may see a boom in purchasing, followed by a plateauing out when the novelty factor has worn off – this happened in the late 1990s in central and eastern Europe. An economic recession will see a downturn in business, as was evident in the Far East from the mid-1990s and again in 2008–9 in some markets in the current economic recession.

Methods of dealing

As with same-language territorial rights, there are two ways of handling translation rights: a coedition where the originating publisher develops the project, pre-sells it to a range of foreign partners and prints for them; and a straightforward licence arrangement, where the foreign licensee manufactures its own edition. In both cases, the responsibility for finding suitable translators and the cost of the translation work will normally lie with the licensee.

Also as with same-language territorial rights, it is essential for the licensor to check that permission has been cleared for the reuse of textual or illustrative material belonging to external copyright holders in any foreign-language edition published under the imprint of sublicensees. For projects planned from the start as international coeditions, this will involve the clearance of world rights in all languages, including the right to sublicense for publication under other imprints. For titles with less obvious potential, the cost of such clearance may be prohibitively high; in such cases it may be necessary to reclear permission only as individual languages are licensed, which can be time consuming and more expensive.

It may be possible to transfer the onus of the clearance work and the payment of fees to the licensee, in which case it will be necessary to provide an up-to-date list of the relevant names and addresses, preferably with contact e-mail addresses; it is also wise to require evidence that clearance has been completed satisfactorily. If the licensor is to undertake the clearance work on behalf of the licensee, the cost should be charged on to the licensee with the addition of a handling charge of no less than 15% of the total fees. If the licensee is from a less affluent country, it may be possible to negotiate preferential rates far lower than those charged to the original publisher for a substantially larger market; however, not all external copyright owners will agree to this. Alternative solutions (for licences rather than coedition deals, where illustrations are crucial) would be to include only a selection of the external illustrations in the licensed edition, to allow the licensee to substitute illustrations of their own finding or to omit the illustrations altogether; in all cases the author should be consulted for approval.

Again, it should be remembered that to supply duplicate production material to a licensee could result in a breach of contract with an external picture supplier, if permission for reuse by a licensee has not been cleared for the market in question.

Coeditions

Foreign-language coeditions form a significant part of licensing business for many publishers, and indeed some British publishers such as Dorling

Kindersley and Mitchell Beazley built their business on the production of books with a high colour content for the coedition market; packagers (initially a British phenomenon) have also specialized in this area.

The real economic advantage of a coedition lies in extending the print run and hence in lowering the unit cost for books with a high origination cost; in practice, this means books illustrated in colour. There would be little real advantage in printing coeditions of books illustrated solely in black and white. The most obvious books with coedition potential are children's picture books and books on topics such as art, architecture, collectibles, craftwork, cookery, gardening, do-it-yourself, interior design, and general information books for adults and children where illustrations are a key feature. Books linked to television series which have also been licensed abroad may have a real advantage (for example, at the time of writing, the cookery books of Jamie Oliver have been translated into over thirty languages), although the timing of foreign-language coeditions to tie in with overseas broadcasts may be very complex.

In recent years, novelty books have also become popular – for example pop-up books, board books for babies with spiral plastic cords to attach them to cots and prams, bath books, books with an audio dimension (either by pressing a point in the book or with the use of an audio pen which 'reads' the book); and books with tarot cards, runestones or aromatherapy oils included as part of a pack with the book.

In many cases, the cost of developing projects of this kind can only be sustained by coordinating large coedition printings. Because of the complexity of coedition deals, it is unwise to involve subagents; one-to-one communication between seller and buyer is vital.

Coedition sales can sometimes suffer in times of economic recession, particularly if they are affected by fluctuating exchange rates, which may make printing their own edition cheaper for the licensee (see *Coeditions* in Chapter 9). However, they can sometimes benefit in difficult times if they are perceived as an economical way to acquire complex books with high origination investment by sharing in the costs of a combined printing. The year 2008 saw substantial business in markets such as Korea and Brazil, although there was some decline in markets in central and eastern Europe.

Negotiating a coedition

The licensor will normally approach potential buyers at a very early stage of development with an outline for the project, some sample text and visual material. This could include artwork, transparencies, photographs or colour prints, colour scans, mocked-up spreads of the book, proofs, a jacket mock-up, a dummy with sample pages pasted into place, or a 'blad' (brief layout and design – an eight- or sixteen-page section of the book originated in advance to show content and quality). Even though it is possible to scan material for display on a laptop and to send potential buyers electronic files, most potential purchasers still seem to prefer to see some form of physical material before making a final decision.

A number of potential buyers may be approached simultaneously in each country, or the material may be taken straight to a regular partner if such a relationship exists. If the originating publisher produces books that are standard in format and style and known for their reliable quality, a regular partner may not require to see full material; for a new buyer, or for an expensive project, a decision may not be taken until a large proportion of the text and illustrations has been studied.

The aim of the licensor is to gauge the level of interest at a very early stage in order to assess whether the project will be viable; if several publishers in the same market are interested, the book may go to the publisher who places the largest order, or alternatively to the publisher on whose list the book will receive the maximum attention (not necessarily identical). The licensor aims to obtain as many orders as possible from overseas partners, which will be coordinated into a coedition printing; this may be combined with the initial English-language printing for the licensor themselves and any other English-language partners such as a book club and an American publisher. Alternatively, publishers with long experience and substantial business in coeditions may choose to print the English-language editions first and then undertake a separate coedition for the foreign-language editions. Most publishers specializing in coeditions set a minimum print run on the basis of which the project will be viable; any additional quantities are then a bonus.

Coedition prices must take into account the cost of replacing the English-language text with the translated text by means of a black (printing) plate change; this means that a coedition project must be planned from the start to allow for a second black plate carrying the English text but not the black element of the illustrations. When the English edition has been printed, this plate will be removed and a black plate carrying the text of a foreign edition substituted; successive plate changes will allow for a sequence of different-language editions to be printed. It is therefore vital to remember that any English-language words or single letters within the context of the illustrations (for example street names, speech balloons, labelling or single letters in scientific illustrations) must be provided from the start on an overlay and hence on a separate black plate. Single-letter labels may correspond with the first letter of a word that will be explained in the caption to the illustration; however, in translation, the word may not begin with the same letter or even be in the same script. This particular problem can sometimes be avoided by the use of numerals for labelling instead of letters. Some books feature decorative letters in colour at the start of each chapter. This problem was neatly solved by Ralph Steadman for his illustrated edition of *Treasure Island* by the provision of a separately drawn alphabet; film was then provided to foreign-language licensees, who could select an alternative letter when this was needed.

If possible, books developed for coedition sale should avoid jackets or covers where the title and other wording are reversed out in pale lettering against a dark background, as this will be far more expensive to alter for foreign-language editions than a straight black plate change.

What about coeditions with countries where books are in effect read 'from the back to the front' such as Arabic or Hebrew? This problem can normally be overcome by binding the book block on the right-hand side instead of on the left.

Mention should perhaps be made here of bilingual or multilingual editions. These are sometimes undertaken for books such as medical atlases where the key feature is the colour illustrations; text and captions may be printed in, say, English, French and German and the book may carry the imprints of all three publishers involved. This has the attraction of economy of scale since only one edition is produced for sale by all three partners; however, such titles are often less attractive to the buyer than a dedicated single-language edition.

Responsibility for commissioning a translation of the text lies with the licensee, and normal procedure is for the licensee to supply imposed film or electronic files of the translated text to the exact specifications required by the licensor so that it will fit round the existing layout of the illustrations. It is essential to take into account that when the English text is translated its length may increase, in some cases by as much as 30%. This should be allowed for in the overall design of the book; the alternative is for the licensee to cope with the space problem by setting the translated text in a smaller type size than that of the original, but this may not always make for legibility and is inadvisable in the case of books for young children.

Costing

Most foreign-language coeditions are for bound books, ready for sale by the foreign licensee. When quoting coedition costs, methods differ between publishers and from book to book (see also Chapter 9). Some publishers may amortize the origination costs against all coeditions in addition to the manufacturing costs and a fixed profit margin; others may be prepared to supply partners virtually at run-on cost in order to gain the economy of scale of a larger print run on an expensive project. The cost of reclearance of external permissions for each edition must also be included if such clearance is being undertaken by the licensor.

The fixed costs involved in a coedition are editorial, design and artwork fees, permissions fees for external material, origination costs, and typesetting and proofing for the interior and the cover. These costs may be fully or partially amortized over the entire coedition printing.

The variable costs include paper and materials for the cover and jacket; a plate change for each foreign edition; printing and binding costs; the author's royalty if this is to be costed into the price; and any additional costs such as lamination, shrink-wrapping and shipping.

Ideally, when the unit cost has been calculated to include a proportion of the fixed costs and the variable costs relating to the foreign deal, an acceptable profit element should be added; this will have to take into account the maximum price a publisher in a particular market may be prepared to pay in order to achieve a suitable retail price in their own market.

When quoting for foreign-language editions, it is wise to be armed with prices for a range of quantities; larger orders justify a lower unit price. It is also essential to specify that the prices given depend on a stated minimum total coedition quantity being achieved; this then allows for the prices quoted to be increased if the ideal minimum run cannot be achieved. The price must also take into account any special packing requirements such as cartoning if these are not standard. A variance of up to 5% on over- or under-supply should be agreed.

As with English-language coeditions, it will be necessary to decide whether to quote prices royalty inclusive or exclusive. An inclusive price will ensure that full payment is received in advance regardless of how many copies of the foreign edition are sold; it will be necessary to estimate each customer's local selling price and required mark-up in order to arrive at a price that is likely to be acceptable. The mark-up factor may vary from four to six times the unit price quoted by the originating publisher. Local market circumstances could mean that the end selling price for the same book in translation varies greatly from market to market; for example, a Swedish edition could carry a much higher price than a Portuguese edition. A royalty-exclusive arrangement should aim to ensure that the royalty is paid on the full local price, but payment will then be made only as copies are sold by the licensee. Advance payments on royalty-exclusive deals may be paid in instalments, e.g. one-third on signature of the contract, one-third on commencement of manufacture of the coedition and one-third thirty days after publication of the licensed edition.

The question of the currency in which the quotation will be made should also be considered, particularly if the coedition copies are being printed outside the country of the licensor (e.g. in Hong Kong, China, Colombia, Spain or Italy). An experienced production department should brief the printers to allow for possible currency fluctuations during the life of the quotation. Customers in some countries (e.g. central and eastern Europe and China) may find it easier to remit payment in US dollars, and this should be discussed at negotiation stage if dollars would not be the normal currency for quotation. More coedition business is now being conducted in euros; this works best when the buyer and the printing location are both within the euro zone.

Payment to the author for foreign-language coeditions will depend on the terms of the original head contract; there may be provision for the author to receive a royalty on net receipts in the case of a royalty-inclusive deal, whereas for a royalty-exclusive deal the author's share will be covered by the provision for division of proceeds on translation rights – this could range from 50% to 80% of the advance and royalties negotiated.

It is also necessary to take into account packing requirements and responsibility for shipment and insurance costs; prices can be quoted ex-works, FOB a port in the country of the printer, CIF a port in the country of the licensee, or delivered to the licensee's warehouse. Shipping and documentation requirements must be obtained from each licensee; the question of timing and method of payment will also have to be agreed, together with any penalties, such as interest on late payment – this is often set at 2–3% above the base rate in the country of the licensor.

Publishers specializing in coeditions are likely to require a substantial proportion of the total amount due to be paid in advance; payment may be made in several stages corresponding to production stages of the coedition. This is because they are incurring real costs such as paper purchase and print costs on behalf of their licensees. For this reason, it is particularly advisable when dealing with a new contact to request references, both from the licensee's bank and from other publishers with whom they have dealt. It may also be advisable to require payment to be made against an irrevocable letter of credit drawn on a London bank.

Technical details and schedules

The technical aspects of a foreign-language coedition are more complex than those of an English-language coedition, where the only change may be that of imprint.

Provision of material

Once a sale has been agreed, the licensor must finalize schedules for the provision of material to each licensee. In the past, publishers experienced in coeditions provided each partner with a layout grid to indicate the design of each spread and the space available for the insertion of the licensee's translated text; the foreign publishers were then provided with a set of imposed proofs of the English text to enable them to undertake the translation work. Today, coedition partners can receive this material as a PDF, with low-resolution images embedded to show the layout, or on disk, as files can be very large; a physical printout will also be supplied. The licensee can then supply the translated text by the same methods, imposed with the text fitted around the illustrations; they will also need to supply any material necessary for the cover or jacket. Whilst electronic supply may seem convenient, it has the disadvantage that the incoming material is less easy to check by rights staff and will normally be passed straight to the production department.

Timing

The licensor must ensure that each translation, whether in film or electronic form, is received by an agreed deadline; if one participating publisher is late, the schedule for the whole coedition will be jeopardized. Some licensors make the provision that if this occurs, textless sheets will be run on for the offending publisher to meet the minimum coedition quantity required in order to hold to the prices quoted to the other partners. The latecomer can then arrange to have those sheets overprinted with their text after the coedition is completed, although this will prove much more expensive for them. One way to try to prevent delays would be to include a contractual provision that the offending publisher must pay a higher unit price and also compensate the other coedition partners for any additional costs caused by the delay.

The licensor will normally supply electronic files of each foreign publisher's edition for checking, together with cover proofs and colour proofs of the complete book printed off on paper, as checking for colour accuracy cannot be done effectively onscreen or by printing off locally. Approval will be required from each participant by a tight deadline so that the final printing can go ahead. Final copies will then be shipped off to each coedition partner.

Coedition publishers occasionally run on flat textless sheets on spec in order to achieve some economy of scale in a printing. These can either be supplied to a foreign publisher for local overprinting and binding, or they can be overprinted with English text and sold to an American partner or used for the licensor's own edition. This is, however, an expensive way to obtain additional copies.

Coeditions can also be undertaken in more specialist areas of publishing; an obvious area is that of cartographic publishing. Here publishers must ensure that atlas maps are designed from the start with all labelling on a black plate, rather than the traditional use of blue lettering for seas, lakes and rivers.

Another area is that of scientific 'atlases' – books illustrated throughout in colour with the text mainly in the form of short captions. Key topics here can be medicine, biology and geology; such books are expensive to originate and may be planned from the start with coeditions in mind. The same considerations will need to be taken into account: ensuring that labels or lettering are on a separate black plate, and allowing space for the possible expansion of text in translation.

In this area of publishing, it is common for coeditions to be undertaken on the basis of supplying flat textless sheets rather than bound foreign-language editions. The main justification is that many books of this kind are designed for the undergraduate market and it is therefore crucial that the English edition be available in good time for the beginning of the new academic year. To risk delay if a coedition partner were to be late in providing film or electronic files of translated text would be disastrous for the originating publisher, who might lose the market for the original edition of the book not only for that academic year but permanently if a competing title were available on time. Another consideration is that in some areas of publishing, particularly medical, some of the partners may require binding to be undertaken in their standard company livery, which could mean different binding specifications for each coedition partner.

When quoting prices for deals of this kind, it is important to remember that a licensee purchasing flat textless sheets will incur considerable expenditure in overprinting and binding their edition, and this will affect the mark-up they will require in order to achieve their optimum local retail price. The mark-up factor on sheets could be from 6.5 to 8, compared with a mark-up factor of 4 to 6 for bound books ready for sale. It is advisable to provide potential licensees with details of the sheet dimensions at the earliest stages of negotiations, to ensure that they have access to suitable machinery for overprinting. Frequently, 10% additional sheets are supplied as 'free overs' to allow for spoilage in the overprinting process.

As for English-language coeditions, the licensee must provide the licensor with full shipping and documentation instructions for the consignment, including the required port of entry, the licensee's handling agent and the eventual destination of the consignment. The method of delivery is likely to be sea freight, perhaps with onward trucking across another country or countries if the country of the licensee is landlocked. Full details of the required documentation must be provided; this may include a certificate of origin as well as the commercial invoice and packing list. It should be remembered that some countries may have import restrictions designed to protect local printing industries, which may make the importing of coeditions into some countries difficult; the countries of Latin America are a particular problem here.

Coedition deals can prove problematic when dealing with publishers in the developing countries, as local book prices are usually too low to allow for importing from more expensive print locations. The situation is complicated in China, where book prices are still very low but where there is growing interest in coedition projects. Despite rising prices in the last two years, China is still a favoured printing location for many western publishers for their own editions, but print orders placed by western firms for export are charged for at higher prices than local publishers would be quoted for domestic publications, making viable coedition costings for

Chinese licensees difficult. Some western publishers have found a solution by working through regular Chinese partners with a designated printing house which has state approval for this type of business.

When political and economic circumstances changed in central and eastern Europe, there was an explosion of interest in illustrated non-fiction titles and hence in coeditions. In the early 1990s, this boom in selling coedition copies (often by western publishers new to the markets, working with newly established private publishing houses) led to very successful business for some publishers. In other cases, overenthusiasm on both sides resulted in a massive over-purchase of copies, often with inadequate guarantees for payment; in some cases this led to substantial debts, the collapse of the purchasing companies and more caution from western publishers in their subsequent dealings in the region. Although translations of western titles have flooded most countries in the region, these can still be volatile markets where all possible precautions should still be taken: references from other western publishers where possible; prepayment of a significant proportion of the total amount prior to printing and shipment; and bank references and letters of credit. Even then, circumstances can be unpredictable; the collapse of the Russian rouble in August 1998 (a shift from 8 to 28 roubles to the dollar in a week) left some western coedition publishers with substantial debts, even with well-established customers.

One positive aspect for publishers in the region of coprinting by the originating publisher is that control of the print run is secure; there have been many cases of massive unreported over-printing by licensees or by printers themselves when duplicate film or electronic files were supplied for a licence arrangement. However, there are still some countries in the region (e.g. Albania and some republics of the former Soviet Union) where potential sales and the level of book prices remain too low to allow for the importation of books printed abroad.

Coordination of reprints

As with English-language coeditions, coordination of subsequent printing orders for foreign publishers is vital to maintaining the economic benefits of larger print runs. The originating publisher should alert each partner of an impending reprint in good time to establish if further copies are required. It is not always necessary to time such supply with a reprint of the English-language edition; coordination of several foreign-language orders may result in a sufficient quantity to produce an attractive price. Foreign partners (particularly those inexperienced in participating in coeditions) should be urged to monitor their stock to enable them to reorder in good time.

If a particular foreign publisher requires copies at a time when no printing is imminent, there are several possible alternatives. A single printing in their own language is likely to prove too expensive; either they will have to wait until the next printing can be coordinated or, if textless sheets are available, they might be prepared to purchase these for overprinting and binding locally. The offer of duplicate production material to enable them to print their own copies may not solve the problem unless the licensee is located in a country where printing costs are substantially lower than in the licensor's print location. In any case, production material should be offered only as a last resort, since possession of this will remove the licensee permanently from the coprinting partnership, affecting the potential size of future print runs.

Licence deals

A large proportion of translation deals are undertaken on the basis of straightforward licence arrangements, with the licensees manufacturing their own editions. This is appropriate for unillustrated books, books with very few illustrations or books illustrated in black and white, where there will be little economy of scale in undertaking a coedition. In such cases, the licensor may supply the licensee with duplicate production material (see Chapter 25). Alternatively, the licensee may wish to reproduce the illustrations directly from the English edition; this may be satisfactory for black and white line drawings or diagrams, but may not produce good results for halftones. In such cases, the licensor should require to see samples of illustrations from the book reproduced in this way, and should select in advance some examples where definition is less sharp to test the performance of the licensee's printer. If the quality is inadequate, the licensor may refuse to allow the licensee to proceed unless duplicate production material is purchased; however, it must be accepted that publishers in some markets may not be able to afford to buy this, and that local production techniques may not be comparable to those in developed countries.

The option technique is commonly employed when offering translation rights, although for major titles rights may be offered simultaneously to competing publishers or auctioned (see *Option, multiple submission or auction?* in Chapter 6). Sales material could include an outline, a sample chapter, a full manuscript, proofs, electronic files or a bound copy, depending on the topicality of the book. If the book has already been published and has received favourable reviews, these can be a powerful additional sales tool.

When licensing translation rights in some languages, thought should be given to whether to grant world rights in that language to one publisher or whether there may be an argument for making separate licence arrangements in different markets where the same language is spoken. The obvious examples here are Portugal and Brazil, and mainland Spain and the Spanish-speaking countries of Latin America. For an academic title, it is unlikely that a publisher on either side of the Atlantic would be prepared to accept limited rights in this way, since for such books print runs are relatively small and publishers depend on an export market. However, for fiction or general non-fiction, there could well be adequate independent markets. Potential licensees requesting world rights should be asked how they intend to service the transatlantic market, and rights should be restricted if no adequate distribution arrangement or tie-up with another publisher is in place. It should also be remembered that there may be a very real linguistic distinction on each side of the Atlantic; it is generally considered that a Castilian Spanish edition published in mainland Spain is more acceptable in the Mexican and Argentinian markets than a Latin American edition would be in mainland Spain; the same would apply to Portuguese and Brazilian editions. It should also be remembered that Castilian is not the only language spoken in Spain; rights could be licensed quite separately for Catalan, Galician, Valencian and Basque editions.

A particular problem that has arisen since the break-up of the Soviet Union is the market to be granted for Russian-language rights. A Moscow-based publisher may well request world Russian-language rights or rights for Russia plus designated republics of the former Soviet Union. In reality, the collapse of the Soviet state distribution system may mean that the translated edition is available only in Moscow and St Petersburg. On the other hand, it must be remembered that there are still substantial Russian populations in all the former republics, and publishers in republics such as Belarus and Ukraine may well apply for Russian rights rather than rights in their own languages with a view to maximizing sales in their own state, Russia and other republics with a significant Russian-speaking population. A potential licensee should be asked for a realistic assessment of its distribution facilities.

It is also important to remember that the break-up of some countries, often in acrimonious circumstances, means that extreme tact should be employed when dealing with publishers there. One should no longer refer to Serbo-Croat rights, but make a clear distinction between the languages spoken in the countries that once formed Yugoslavia – Serbian (which uses the Cyrillic alphabet), Croatian (Roman alphabet) and Bosnian (can use either Cyrillic or Roman). Macedonian still utilizes Cyrillic script.

On one famous occasion, the same John Fowles novel was licensed separately for world Romanian and Moldovan rights, despite the fact that the language spoken in both countries is identical (Moldova has now abandoned the use of Cyrillic script in favour of Roman). In this case, the publisher in Moldova published first and sent copies to Romania, radically affecting the market for the licensee there.

The question of Chinese-language rights is particularly complex. Many dialects are spoken that may be incomprehensible to speakers of other dialects (e.g. Mandarin and Cantonese). A system of traditional (complex) characters is used in Taiwan and also in Hong Kong and Macao, both now

Special Administrative Regions of the People's Republic of China but with much higher purchasing power than China itself. Simplified characters are used in the People's Republic of China (PRC), Malaysia and Singapore. Potential licensees both inside and outside mainland China may sometimes apply for 'world Chinese rights', but it is important to establish exactly which markets each licensee can realistically cover, and how. At the time of writing, mainland publishers still do not have good facilities to export their editions outside the PRC, so it would be wise to specify that any licence for that market is for the Chinese language in simplified characters for sale in the mainland territory of the People's Republic of China only, excluding Hong Kong and Macao; Taiwan (an island) is, of course, regarded by Beijing as a renegade province of the PRC. This specification will allow for separate licensing to territories using traditional Chinese characters, and would also allow for separate licensing of simplified character editions to Malaysia and Singapore.

It remains to be seen whether simplified characters will be introduced into Hong Kong and/or Macao in future. Some Chinese publishers have been prepared to accept the territorial restriction outlined above in the licence contract, but have been reluctant to print a notice to such effect on licensed editions, at least on the outside cover. Political sensitivities remain very much in force in the Chinese publishing industry (see also Chapter 12).

Publishers and agents in Taiwan have often requested that rights for mainland China should be included in their licence, and in the past some western rightsholders have agreed to this if they did not have direct contacts with mainland publishers; sublicences of simplified Chinese rights were then granted from Taiwan. However, it should be remembered that political sensitivities make mainland publishers averse to acquiring rights via Taiwan, and there are now much better contacts with mainland publishers as they travel more extensively to overseas book fairs and more western rights owners visit China. Subagents are active in the market; the Big Apple Tuttle-Mori agency, originally set up in Taiwan, opened offices in China in late 1997; the Taiwan-based Bardon agency is also active there and British agent Andrew Nurnberg now has a Beijing office in addition to his operation in Taiwan (see *The use of subagents* in Chapter 7).

Terms

The method of payment for licences falls into two categories: an advance against royalties deal or a lump sum deal. The majority of licences tend to be based on an advance against royalties, with payment usually calculated on the retail or recommended retail price of the translated edition; most countries in western Europe, with the exception of Belgium, Finland and Sweden (and of course the United Kingdom), have a fixed-price system for books. Royalties should be calculated on the price less VAT if this is applicable to books in the country of the licensee. If payment is to be calculated on net receipts rather than on the retail or recommended retail price, a higher royalty rate should be negotiated to allow for the discrepancy between the two prices. This may be necessary in countries without a fixed retail price system, and is still a feature of licensing to many publishers in central and eastern Europe, where the price of a book may vary radically from outlet to outlet. Publishers in the region often refer to the price that they themselves receive from their distributors as the 'publisher's price', which can be misleading as this price can be anything from 25% to 50% lower than the average retail price. It is therefore advisable to press the potential licensee for an exact definition of any price quoted.

It is difficult to give specific information on levels of royalty; much depends on the type of book, the status of the author and the topicality of the subject matter, the financial resources of the licensee and the market circumstances. As a general guideline, initial royalty rates for children's books could range from as low as 4% to 7% of the retail or recommended retail price, in each case escalating after an agreed number of copies have been sold. While 4% is a low rate, it could be well worth accepting if it is the standard royalty paid for a well-established series where the book may have a long life over many years.

For academic books, initial royalty rates could be $7–7\frac{1}{2}$% of the retail or recommended retail price, again escalating after an agreed number of copies have been sold. If the book in question is to be published in a pocketbook series, where print runs may be larger than average, it may be worth agreeing to accept a lower initial royalty rate of $6–6\frac{1}{2}$% with a rising rate after an agreed number of copies have been sold. Royalties should be set higher if they are to be based on net receipts, to allow for the discount granted to retailers and wholesalers – perhaps an initial rate of 10%. Inter-company licences may be agreed at preferential rates.

The number of escalation steps in a royalty-based deal may vary; on the whole, the longer the expected life of the book, the more escalation steps. For non-fiction titles, where any revised edition would be the subject of a new licence, one or two escalation steps may be appropriate.

For fiction or popular non-fiction, the crucial consideration will be the status of the author and the expected sales in the market concerned. A new novel by a bestselling author already established in the market could command a much higher starting royalty and a large advance payment.

It is perhaps worth mentioning here the market which has developed in a number of countries in continental Europe for special low-priced editions sold either with newspapers such as *La Repubblica* in Italy or *Süddeutsche Zeitung*, *Weltbild* and *Bild* in Germany, or in the Netherlands via supermarkets and petrol stations. To some extent, this has been a reaction against the fixed price system; prices may be as low as 4–5 euros and print runs can be substantial (in Italy, from 500,000 to one million copies). The offer usually consists of a series of books to be collected by newspaper or magazine readers.

The share of licence revenue paid to the author for translation rights will depend on the provisions in the head contract; the share can range from 50% to as high as 75% or 80% for major authors.

When licensing translation rights, it must be remembered that the licensee may be incurring considerable costs in undertaking the translation work. Many translators are paid an outright fee linked to the length of the work, but an established translator may be paid an ongoing royalty, particularly if they have experience in translating the work of a popular foreign author on a regular basis. As a general rule of thumb, many foreign licensees may be working to a budget of up to 10% of the retail or recommended retail price as the initial royalty rate, to cover payment to both licensor and translator. If an established literary translator holds out for a higher royalty, the foreign publisher may seek to pay a lower initial royalty rate to the licensor. Japanese and Korean publishers frequently offer low initial royalty rates for this reason. If a specialist academic translator is employed, they may require a royalty as high as 6–7%, and no other suitable translator may be available to undertake the work. In most cases, concessions of this kind (which affect the author and the original publisher) should not be made; however, there are sometimes cases where it may be appropriate to agree to a low initial royalty rate, provided that the rate rises sharply after an agreed number of copies have been sold.

Advance payments may also vary greatly according to individual circumstances. As a general rule, for an academic book an advance equivalent to between 25% and 50% of the total royalty income from the first printing would be realistic, although the translation of a bestselling science or economics textbook would certainly justify more. Some western rights-holders now tend to specify that advances for mainland China represent the entire royalty on the first printing, on the grounds that there are often difficulties in obtaining regular royalty statements from Chinese publishers.

The first question asked of the would-be buyer should therefore be their proposed initial print run and estimated local selling price; terms can then be calculated. If the royalty is best calculated on the distribution price (net receipts), this should be made clear and a higher royalty rate negotiated.

Potential trade bestsellers can command very high advances, such as the $1,000,000 advance paid by Belfond for the French rights in Alexandra Ripley's *Scarlett* (the commissioned sequel to *Gone with the Wind*), the $450,000 paid by Plon for the French rights in Salman Rushdie's *The Moor's Last Sigh*, the DM 1.2 million paid by German publishers Beck for *Primary Colors*, the US political *roman à clef*, and (large in Chinese terms) the $50,000 paid by Peking University Press for *The Road Ahead* by Bill Gates. Rowohlt recently paid an advance of €252,000 for German rights in Australian author Rebecca James's debut novel, *Beautiful Malice*.

Advances may be paid entirely on signature of the contract, or staggered in two or more instalments, perhaps half on signature of the contract and half on publication, or one-third on signature of the contract, one-third on publication and one-third six months after publication. If it is thought that publication may slip, payment dates could be specified as 'on publication or by ... (date) ... , whichever is the earlier'.

Information on print run and price will also be needed to calculate terms on a lump sum basis. This method can be useful for licences involving small print runs, where accounting on an annual basis would be inappropriate. It may also be the preferred method when dealing with publishers in countries where there are procedural delays in remitting payment, or where monitoring sales precisely is difficult.

In such cases, the calculation can be undertaken on the basis of a royalty percentage based on the retail, recommended retail or wholesale price of the translation, but then expressed as a lump sum to cover an agreed print run, with payment for any printings beyond that quantity to be negotiated. Payment could be made entirely on signature of the contract, or half on signature and half on publication, or in a larger number of instalments by specified dates. Licensees sometimes pose the argument for accepting a lump sum equivalent to a slightly lower royalty rate than would have been negotiated for a traditional advance and royalty arrangement, on the grounds that the licensor receives full payment earlier.

When licensing on a lump sum basis, one should take into account that a calculation undertaken today is based on an estimate of the eventual retail, recommended retail or distribution price of the book. In practice, the final price may be much higher, particularly if publication is slow. This would not matter in the case of an advance and royalty deal, but it will greatly reduce the value of a lump sum payment. It is therefore essential to include in the contract an inflation-proof clause that will require payment to be increased *pro rata*, in line with the increase in the final published price of the book, with the top-up payment to be made on publication when this factor is known.

There may be some doubt as to whether a licensee granted a licence for a limited print run will adhere to that figure; however, the same situation could occur with a royalty-based deal. On the whole, one trusts the majority of one's licensees until there is reason not to do so. Some licensors may wish to write into the contract that they receive a copy of the licensee's invoice from the printer, which should indicate the exact run.

The question of what currency to employ for translation licences may arise; many translation licences for British books are expressed in sterling, but there may be good reason to specify payment in another currency, for example in euros for European countries which have adopted that currency. Some countries (those in Latin America, for example) think more naturally in US dollars and may find remittance easier if the contract specifies payment in that currency; publishers in Japan, Korea, China, Taiwan and central and eastern Europe may also favour payment in dollars. When a currency other than sterling is chosen, there is a risk of fluctuation of that currency against sterling; gains can be made or losses incurred, and it may be necessary to decide whether one is in business to license rights or to indulge in currency speculation.

If the licensee will need to order duplicate production material in order to reproduce illustrations in the book, it is strongly recommended that the likely cost and availability of appropriate material be discussed before the contract is finalized, even if a firm order is not placed until after the contract is signed.

Tailoring terms to special circumstances

It is in the area of translation rights that one is perhaps most likely to encounter unorthodox licence requests, whether because of special circumstances in the markets concerned or perhaps because of inexperience in commercial publishing practice on the part of the applicant.

A common request may be for translation rights to be granted completely free of charge, either because of economic circumstances or because the translation is to be distributed free of charge (perhaps to students in a particular university faculty, to employees of an industrial concern or as a promotional gift to the applicant's customers).

There may also be cases where authors volunteer to give up their share of licence income (and urge their publishers to do the same) if they feel that a translation of their book is particularly needed in a market (a typical example was a request for a Serbian translation of a history of the Balkans). It is of course the prerogative of any author to forgo payment, and of any licensor to decide on their licensing policy on a case-by-case basis, but as a general principle one might hold that to grant rights for any copyright work completely free of charge sets a precedent for future arrangements and tends to devalue recognition of the expertise, effort and indeed expense that was involved in publication of the original work. These are principles which it is important to reinforce, particularly in countries with a less than satisfactory record of copyright compliance. A purely nominal fee may represent an appropriate compromise.

In the case of copies of a translation that are genuinely to be distributed free of charge, a solution may be to set a nominal price commensurate with the economic circumstances in the country concerned, and to calculate a fee for an agreed print run on that basis. Free distribution normally has some promotional value to the licensee organization and this should be recognized.

Previous editions of this book have highlighted the need for flexibility when licensing to countries undergoing radical political and economic change. Whilst the countries of central and eastern Europe and the former Soviet Union, some of which are now EU members, are still in varying stages of development, relationships with the publishing industries there are now far better established, although caution is still advisable when dealing with completely new contacts and it is still the case that publishers there may suddenly withdraw from a particular area of publishing, resulting in cancelled contracts. This has been particularly apparent during the recent economic recession.

Few countries in the region now have major obstacles to remitting hard currency abroad to licensors, provided that the licensee has a valid contract and adequate local funding. It is usually advisable to supply a stamped and signed invoice for all payments. Some publishers in the region continue to favour making payment on the basis of a lump sum to cover a specified print run, the system prevalent in communist times when stock sold quickly and paper shortages meant that reprints were uncertain. Many publishers, particularly in the mass-market sector, still aim to sell their entire stock to distributors within months of publication for reasons of cash flow; fear of inflation and devaluation of the local currency may also prove an incentive to pay quickly.

However, many publishers in the region have moved towards western-style advance and royalty arrangements, although this does presume that they are able to track actual sales of their books in countries where distribution remains problematic after the collapse of the state networks, and some western licensors seek to make the initial advance payment equivalent to the total royalty income on the first print run. A compromise arrangement would be to continue to work on the basis of a lump sum for an agreed number of copies, but to stagger the payment in several instalments: perhaps 25% of the total on signature of the contract, 25% on publication, 25% six months after publication and 25% twelve months after publication, with the three later payments tied to precise calendar dates in case publication slips.

Some publishers in central and eastern Europe and the former Soviet Union may seek sponsorship for a translation – for example from a pharmaceutical or medical equipment company for a medical book, from investment companies or banks for a business book, or from hotels for a book on travel or tourism. It is important that the licensor is aware of this in advance, and also what would be involved in any sponsorship arrangement – a logo of the sponsor on the cover and title page, or advertising for the sponsoring company or for particular products or services. If the latter is suggested, it would be wise to check the details with the author, especially in the area of pharmaceutical advertisements, where the book may then appear to endorse particular products.

Book clubs, once unknown in central and eastern Europe, have now established a strong presence there, particularly in Poland, where the Bertelsmann-owned Swiat Ksiazki now supplies over 45% of mass-market sales. Care should be taken not to enter into potentially conflicting arrangements; there have been instances of separate translation licences to a trade publisher and to a book club (rather than to the club via the trade publisher); the club sales undercut the trade publisher's sales, with resulting complaints.

Licensing to publishers in the People's Republic of China is now far less problematic than in the early 1990s. The official publishing industry is still completely state controlled, but it is no longer a problem for Chinese publishers to remit hard currency abroad for licences, provided that they have a valid licence contract, a stamped and signed invoice for the amount due and adequate local funds. Ironically, western publishers may find that, despite the inclusion of warranties and indemnities in their licence contract, Chinese publishers require evidence of the publisher's authority to handle licences in cases where the copyright ownership remains in the name of the author; this would normally require the provision of a copy of the head contract, or at least relevant sections of that document. The transfer of payments can be slow, partly because Chinese publishers have to register every licence contract with their local copyright authority in order to acquire a registration number; only when this procedure is complete can they deal with bank transfers and tax deductions, which can mean that there is a lapse of several months between the date of the contract and receipt of the advance payment. Despite this, licence business saw a boom in the late 1990s and early years of this century, with Chinese publishers purchasing over 10,000 licences a year from foreign rights owners in the period 2005–9. Since the acquisition of rights has exceeded rights sold in Chinese titles by a factor of ten to one, the Chinese publishing authorities are seeking to redress the balance and in 2005 they established a programme, Going Abroad, which offers subsidies to foreign publishers acquiring rights in Chinese titles and incentives to Chinese publishers to promote the sale of rights in their publications.

Some western publishers remain concerned that although blatant book piracy is less apparent in China in print form than in previous years, there is evidence that unreported additional copies are being printed. Some western licensors require Chinese publishers to purchase a contracted quantity of holograms to affix to legitimate copies, although there have been reported cases of piracy of the holograms themselves. There has also been a substantial increase in online piracy, which the UK Publishers Association is addressing with the Chinese publishing authorities.

Some western publishers and literary agents have chosen to license rights initially to a publisher, or to delegate control to a subagent, in Taiwan, with a provision for onward sublicensing to a publisher in mainland China, and a number of agents in Taiwan specialize in deals of this kind. But it is important to be aware that many Chinese publishers continue to express resentment at having to acquire rights via Taiwan, particularly given the differences in the written language (simplified characters used in mainland China, traditional or complex characters in Taiwan), the population and purchasing power of the two markets, and the continuing political tensions between the mainland and Taiwan.

Educational and academic publishers (including ELT publishers who may wish to license bilingual editions of their books) are more likely to wish to separate the markets completely. Some may not wish to license translation rights to Taiwan, preferring to market their original editions direct through agents or local subsidiary companies. Large-scale direct sales of original editions into mainland China remain problematic, both in terms of book prices and access to distribution channels, so licensing may well be desirable and some ELT publishers have close working relationships with Chinese partners to tailor courses to the needs of the market. Licences are likely to be granted to specialist state publishing houses.

It is strongly recommended that permission is never granted totally free of charge, even if applications come from specialist academic institutions requesting permission for limited print quantities of a licensed edition. This simply reinforces the old concept that prevailed prior to China's accession to the conventions, that foreign works were there for the taking. It is perhaps significant that the academic community was a powerful force in opposing China's accession to the conventions; it saw this move as closing the door to foreign publications after many years of unauthorized translations and reprints of books and journals. There is still a continuing reluctance on the part of some smaller Chinese publishers and academic institutions to pay for translation rights in specialized works where print runs may be modest and which they claim are 'unprofitable'.

Applications from translators

Rights staff may from time to time receive applications for translation rights from individuals rather than from established publishing houses or academic institutions with publishing facilities. Such applications come particularly from Chinese academics but may also be received from other countries, especially from individuals working in the same field as the original author.

It is usually inadvisable to enter into detailed negotiation directly with an individual translator, who will rarely have the facilities to print, promote and distribute the translation. It is preferable to explain that a licence arrangement can only be concluded with an organization that has those facilities. Unfortunately, the fact that a translator is available does not necessarily mean that a suitable publisher can be found for the book, or that (if found) the publisher will necessarily wish to employ the same translator; foreign publishers frequently have their own stable of specialist translators with whom they work regularly. This can pose particular problems if an approach comes from a potential translator who is known to the original author as a colleague or an ex-student; the author often feels a commitment to the translator.

It may be that the existence of a translator familiar to the author could tip the scales when a foreign publisher is making a decision; if publisher and translator can be married up, so much the better. However, it is unwise to promise anything more than to pass on details of the translator to potential publishers.

Some approaches come from translators who are quite unfamiliar with publishing practice; a common expectation is that the original publisher will pay them for their work and publish the translation. In such cases, one can only explain that translation arrangements are normally made on the basis of a licence between the original publisher (if the publisher controls translation rights) and an appropriate publisher in the country concerned.

Particular problems can arise if a translator has already commenced (or even completed) the translation work before applying for the rights. This can result in major disappointment, as the rights may already have been sold elsewhere. On occasion, translators in mainland China have spent years translating a long out-of-date edition of an academic title, only to be told that a much more recent edition exists. China poses further problems in that the translator may already have made contact with a local publisher and may indeed have paid the publisher towards the cost of publishing the translation before attempting to contact the copyright owner. When payment is then requested for the rights, the translator has no means of paying and the Chinese publisher usually seeks to withdraw from the arrangement with the translator rather than pay for the rights. Despite more than fifteen years of membership of the conventions, copyright education in China still has a long way to go. It is vital to reinforce the concept that a work worth translating is worth some payment, albeit tailored to local circumstances.

Developing and newly industrialized countries

Publishers in these countries often seek translation rights in educational and academic textbooks. Here payment will almost certainly be based on a very low local price; in some cases the entire income from the licence may barely cover the cost of dealing with the paperwork. Academic publishers do not usually undertake active promotion of such licences, although they are usually prepared to grant them if the applicant can be shown to be reliable, simply to make their books more widely available.

It should be emphasized that there is no valid reason for accepting low royalty percentages for such deals, as the royalties will be based on a local price substantially lower than that of the original edition.

In the past, titles that had received a subsidy for production in English in a low-price ELBS edition (see Chapter 12) could not be licensed for translation into the local language of any country covered by the scheme. The ELBS scheme was terminated during the spring of 1997, but rights staff should remember that if their publishing house has since decided to produce the book in a low-price International Student Edition (ISE), the sale of local translation rights in some of the markets concerned could affect sales of that edition (e.g. the sale of Hindi rights in India).

Subsidy schemes

Although countries such as the United States, France, Germany, Italy, Sweden and Finland have long had national subsidy schemes to assist with the translation of their publications, and a number of countries of central and eastern Europe have now introduced similar schemes, the United Kingdom has never had such a scheme, although the Arts Council does administer a scheme to assist with the translation of certain types of foreign literature into English.

In the last twenty years there have been various small-scale schemes to assist with the translation of British books in certain categories in countries deemed worthy of financial assistance. The British Council administered two short-term schemes for the translation of a limited number of educational and academic books and some literary fiction in both Russia and China; mass-market publications were not eligible. Funding for both schemes has now ceased.

The British Books for Managers Translation Scheme, established in 1998 by the British government Know-How Fund and subsequently funded by the Department for International Development (DFID), allowed selected books (in areas such as accounting, banking and finance, management, environmental and energy management, EU-related topics, information technology in business, law and legislation for market-based economies, social welfare management and public administration) to be translated in Albania, Armenia, Belarus, Bosnia-Herzogovina, Bulgaria, Croatia, Georgia, Latvia, Lithuania, Macedonia, Moldova, Romania, Slovakia, Ukraine and Yugoslavia (Serbia and Montenegro). The scheme ran until 30 September 2001 and was very successful, making a significant number of titles available to these markets, which might not otherwise have been possible.

There have been a number of other schemes which have sometimes assisted with translations. In particular, the Centre for Publishing

Development in the Budapest office of the Open Society Institute of the Soros Foundation (www.soros.org) ran schemes through its local operations in most of the countries of central Europe to enable selected titles concerned with democracy, economic development and good governance to be translated – Books for an Open Society. The schemes moved from designated lists of titles compiled by Soros advisors to a system where would-be licensees could propose their own suggestions. Since 2001, this initiative has become part of the Information Program.

The Fund for Central and East European Book Projects (CEEBP) is located at Jan van Goyenkade 5, 1075 Amsterdam, Netherlands (www. ceebp.org); it supports the translation and dissemination of high-quality literary and scholarly books in the languages of the region. Some recent schemes to assist with translation in the Middle East have included the programme from Kalima (www.kalima.ae) under the aegis of the Abu Dhabi Authority for Culture and Heritage (ADACH), which offers subsidies for the translation of classic and modern literature (fiction and non-fiction) into Arabic, and Spotlight on Rights, a three-year scheme established in 2009 by KITAB (the partnership between the Frankfurt Book Fair and ADACH, which administers the Abu Dhabi Book Fair) to offer subsidies for the translation of books into and from the Arabic language, linked to negotiations where buyer and seller are present at the Abu Dhabi Book Fair.

Compulsory licensing

In some countries, it may be necessary to act promptly in order to forestall the granting of a compulsory translation licence, either under legislation in line with the Paris Revisions to the Berne Convention and the Universal Copyright Convention, or as a result of national legislation, e.g. in countries such as Japan and Egypt. (Further background to the compulsory licensing provisions of the Paris Revisions is provided in Chapter 12.) In the case of translation rights, a compulsory licence can be granted for a book required for educational or academic purposes if no authorized translation has already been made available in the relevant language in the country concerned. In the case of a language not in use in one or more developed countries, such a licence can be applied for one year after first publication of the book in the original language, regardless of the subject area, provided that the applicant follows the designated procedures.

In the case of a translation licence for a language in use in one or more developed countries (for example French or Spanish, both spoken in developing countries such as those of Francophone Africa or Latin America), a licence may be applied for three years after first publication in the original language. The local body administering such licences is usually the Ministry of Education.

The conditions governing the mechanics of applying for a licence are similar to those governing English-language licences (see Chapter 12). In practice, few true compulsory licences have been granted, but many more 'voluntary' licences have been issued as a result of the provisions. While translations do not have the direct impact of local low-price English-language reprints, which will terminate completely sales of the original publisher's edition (Chapter 12), the appearance of a major British textbook in a local language in a country used to importing such titles in English will certainly affect sales of the English-language edition.

Licensing to non-copyright countries

As far as non-copyright countries are concerned, the problem of unauthorized editions continues (see Chapter 1 for more details on countries which do not belong to any convention). There is no legal basis for taking action against such editions unless copies are exported to countries protected by copyright, a more likely occurrence for English-language reprints than for translations. Some publishers may nevertheless be prepared to negotiate for the purchase of rights in return for a modest payment.

Unauthorized Arabic translations are undertaken on a large scale despite the fact that the majority of countries now belong to one or more of the conventions (only Iraq is now an absentee), and the same book may be targeted for translation separately in different countries in the region. Because of its diplomatic status, Taiwan is unable to join the copyright conventions but has signed bilateral copyright treaties with both the United Kingdom and the United States. Unauthorized translations have not been completely eliminated but have been much reduced in recent years following diplomatic pressure and strong legal action, in particular by the United States. Of the former republics of the Soviet Union, only Turkmenistan remains outside the conventions.

National publishers' associations, the International Publishers Association and the International Intellectual Property Alliance continue to apply pressure to persuade all remaining countries to join the international copyright community.

The contract

Whether the deal is a coedition or a straightforward translation licence, it is always advisable to request references when dealing with a publisher for the first time, unless their reputation is already well established. These can be obtained from other publishers with whom they have dealt, or from their bank. Only if references prove satisfactory should a contract be finalized.

The contract should set out all the aspects of the arrangements. As for US coeditions, a coedition contract may include the schedule and specifications for the supply of materials by both parties within the body of the contract or in the form of a purchase order attached to the contract. Many of the other provisions in both types of contract will be the same.

When contracting for translation rights, it is likely that the licensor will provide the contract, although some elements may have to be tailored to deal with local circumstances.

For non-fiction titles, it is wise to limit the licence to the current edition; it will then be necessary to renegotiate terms if the licensee wishes to translate the next edition at a later stage. Although it is usually preferable to keep such titles with the same house through successive editions if the arrangements are satisfactory, limiting the contract in this way does allow the licensor to make alternative arrangements if there have been problems with the quality of the translated text, production quality or remittance of payments. Some licensees may ask for inclusion of an option clause for the next edition, particularly if the book in question is a major textbook. If this is agreed, the option period should be tightly defined. It should be remembered that if rights in the next edition are placed elsewhere, it may be necessary to clear permission with the previous licensee for the reuse of translated material common to both editions (see *Copyright in the translated text* later in this chapter, p. 241).

For a trade title, some foreign publishers may request the inclusion of an option clause on the next work by the same author.

A translation licence may also be limited by time, and here there is the choice of full term of copyright or a shorter period. As with any licence contract, the full term of copyright can be granted only if the licensor itself controls rights for that period, and provision should be made for the recovery of rights if the translated edition goes out of print. However, provision may also have to be made for any properly granted sublicences in the language concerned to run their course. If the period granted is shorter than full term, the length is negotiable, but, in view of the high cost of translating a book, a period of less than five years may be unacceptable to the licensee. Provision for renewal for a further term may be included on terms to be agreed.

A translation contract should specify the language rights that are being granted and the geographical territory – world rights in the designated language or a more limited territory if separate licences are being granted. When licensing to EU countries, it should be remembered that to grant only part of the market (e.g. a German licence for Germany only) is technically in breach of the provisions of the Treaty of Rome permitting free movement of goods across borders within the region.

A licensee may sometimes request that their home market be barred to the English edition; this may occur particularly with highly illustrated books, or sometimes in the area of mass-market fiction. The decision on whether to agree to this will depend on how valuable the relationship is between licensor and licensee. If a large proportion of a British publisher's list is licensed to a single partner in the country concerned, the relationship may be such that the concession is worth making. If the relationship is less close, the main consideration will be whether revenue from the translation deal outweighs the lost revenue from sales of the English-language edition. Again, it should be remembered that to bar one country of the EU is in breach of the Treaty of Rome, and this may be a good reason to refuse to agree to a market bar.

In the majority of cases, the requirement should be for publication of the translation to be under the imprint of the licensee. However, there may be cases where the licensee wishes to publish under a joint imprint with the licensor – this is often the case with bilingual editions of dictionaries, and also computing titles and some business books where the brand name of the licensor would be a valuable additional selling point in the licensee's market. The use of the licensor's name and/or logo must always be agreed in advance, and some companies with particularly valuable brands charge an additional royalty or fee for the use of their name.

The contract should set out the financial arrangements that have been agreed, including the price and timing of payment for a coedition if this is relevant. Arrangements for the purchase of duplicate production material may be included in the contract if details are finalized at that stage; alternatively, they may be covered by an addendum or by separate correspondence. The latter is perhaps preferable so that it is clear that any income received for such material is not subject to division with the author. There can also sometimes be contractual complications if, for example, the advance and royalties have been specified in US dollars at the request of the licensee but the charge for production material is a sterling charge.

The contract should specify that the text will be translated accurately (some licensors may wish to have details of the translator and their qualifications) and that no changes should be made without prior permission from the licensor. This would include adding, omitting or altering text or illustrations. There may often be good reason for a licensee to wish to undertake changes in order to make the book more suitable for the local market (for example substituting a list of local suppliers in the case of a book on interior design, or the removal of references to the National Health Service and the substitution of details concerning local health facilities) but there have been instances in academic publishing where unwelcome changes have been suggested. The translator, often an academic in the same field as the author, may seek to include theories of their own and even seek to be named as a co-author. Since this material may not meet with the author's approval, all proposed changes should be submitted to the licensor (in English if required) so that consultation may take place. Any changes should be clearly identified as such, either by reference to them in a special preface or perhaps by including them as footnotes or appendices to the translated text.

Other types of changes proposed have included the addition of comic illustrations to a nursing text, the addition of a preface criticizing the theory behind the book, and the omission of illustrations or textual passages considered unacceptable in the country of the licensee; coverage of recent political history and items such as border demarcation lines on maps can be sensitive areas. Such instances were particularly common in central and eastern Europe and the Soviet Union, and can still arise in China. If such changes are made without consultation (and can be identified – often difficult in a translation), the licensee could be held to be in breach of contract and the licensor could demand that copies be withdrawn, although in practice this would be difficult in countries where books sell out soon after publication. If a book offered for translation is known to include sensitive material, it would be better to deal with this issue in advance of finalizing any negotiations to avoid disputes after the contract is signed. Some publishers may wish to include wording in the licence contract that the licensee is liable for any problems which may arise from changes made in translation or from any inaccuracy introduced into the translation.

The contract should include a standard provision that the licensor reserves the right to approve the translated text before production commences. In practice, this facility may be taken up only in a small number of cases, for example if the author or a colleague speaks the language concerned; there have been problems over the translation of management terms in transitional countries new to western business practice which may not yet have developed accurate equivalent terminology in their own languages. There may be valid reasons to have a translation checked if there is a suspicion that the licensee may make unauthorized alterations, particularly in a book where some content may be politically sensitive in the country concerned. There is also the question of liability in the case of any legal action resulting from inaccurate translation of the original work (this could be significant in the case of medical books). The normal method of protection would be via the contractual requirement for accurate translation and the licensor's own insurance, since it is obviously impractical to expect to check the accuracy of every translated edition.

If relevant, the contract should specify which party will be responsible for reclearing and paying for the reuse of any copyright material controlled by third parties.

It is important that the contract specifies that the original author's name be prominently displayed on the translation. There have been many cases where the name of the local translator appeared in larger letters or perhaps as a co-author, particularly if the translator was a well-known academic. A case in Brazil had only the translator's name on the spine, and the names of the two British authors in tiny type under that of the translator on the front cover and title page. Again, the licensor would be entitled to have such copies withdrawn and the offending parts of the book corrected and reprinted. If the book is being translated into a language that uses a non-Roman script (e.g. Russian, Japanese or Chinese), it may be advisable to require that the author's name appears in English as well as in the local language, and to provide the licensee with a phonetic transcription of the author's name to facilitate a translation that is as accurate as possible. Even in some languages that use Roman script, an author's name may appear to have been changed when perhaps it has been transmogrified to its female form if the author is a woman (Latvian is a case in point). A recent oddity has been the news that it is a Chinese government requirement that the nationality of the foreign author appears on the cover of the licensed edition.

The text of the copyright line relating to the original English-language text should be specified for inclusion on the title verso. Some licensees have been known to deliberately omit the date from this copyright line in their edition, particularly if they have been slow to publish, thus concealing the age of the book; this practice should be resisted. There should of course be a separate copyright line covering the copyright in the translated text; this will probably be in the name of the licensee, but could be in the name of the translator in countries that require this under local copyright legislation.

The publication time limit specified for translations will vary according to the book in question and the overall publication programme of the licensee. For a coedition involving the supply of finished copies, the period could be relatively short. A highly topical book where the translation work is undertaken from the English manuscript or proofs could also appear shortly after the English edition, although the licensor may wish to consider the effect of early publication on export sales of their own edition to the market concerned. Publishers in countries such as the Netherlands and Denmark (and, more recently, France) have often complained about the publication of early export editions of bestsellers by British and American publishers, which they claim have an adverse effect on the market for their translations, and they may seek to publish their editions within a short timescale to secure the market.

An academic book could take from twelve months to five years to appear, depending on the pace of the translation work, the size of the book and market circumstances. In principle, it is better to grant a modest period – say, eighteen months – and be prepared to extend the deadline if genuine difficulties occur. If publication is continually delayed, there may be a valid reason to charge a top-up advance as a condition for a short extension of the deadline.

Academic publishers who regularly revise their books may face a dilemma if a translation schedule is delayed and the new edition is imminent. Much depends on the nature and extent of the revisions; if the foreign licensee is already far advanced with the old edition, it may not be possible to switch to the new edition. To avoid such problems, early warning of new editions should be given by the relevant editorial departments. The question of revised terms for a new edition should be subject to negotiation. Regular revisions may deter academic publishers from granting timed licences, even for five years.

While it could be inappropriate to grant a foreign publisher a full range of subsidiary rights in an academic title, a foreign licensee might well wish to acquire subsidiary rights in their own language for a novel or a popular non-fiction work, including the right to sublicense paperback rights, book club rights, serial rights to newspapers and magazines, single-voice reading rights for radio, anthology and quotation rights, etc. Since the licensee is usually better placed to do this, such rights might be granted subject to an agreed division of the revenue, which could range from 50% to 90% to the licensor. A distinction should be made between the sublicensing of mass-market paperback rights of the translation to an independent paperback publisher, and publication of such an edition by a paperback imprint within the same group as the main licensee of the translation rights; ideally the latter situation should be covered as part of the main translation licence, with a full royalty payable on paperback sales. It is wise to stipulate that all sublicensing deals should be subject to the prior approval of the licensor.

One area of increasing importance is the question whether e-book rights or other forms of electronic publishing rights should be included in the grant of translation rights. Here, much will depend on the plans and capabilities of the chosen licensee, and licensors should ask for information on their plans rather than simply include such rights as a matter of course. Will the licensee develop e-books for direct sale from their own website or via aggregators, or do they intend to enter into sublicensing agreements with third parties within the market granted? Where the licensee is developing the e-book version themselves or selling via a chosen aggregator, payment should be on a royalty basis based on the e-book price less any VAT and trade discount; for a true arm's length sublicence, an agreed share of the licence revenue is more appropriate. In either case, the licensor should ask for detailed information on the financial model or models, the reliability of any proposed sublicensees, what end-users are permitted to do with the content and whether technical protection measures (TPM – see Chapter 23) will be put in place to prevent unauthorized use.

Royalty accounting for translations may be required once or twice a year; the latter is more common for trade titles. While the licensor may specify accounting dates, it may sometimes be necessary to alter these if the licensee has computerized accounting dates that differ. Three months is normally regarded as a sufficient period of time in which to remit payments after the due date; however, Scandinavian publishers sometimes ask for up to nine months in which to make payment, which seems excessive. It is advisable to specify that any income from sublicences be remitted within an agreed number of weeks of receipt by the licensee, rather than allow such income to be held back for inclusion in an annual or twice-annual accounting.

Contracts for coedition deals where the price for books has been quoted royalty inclusive sometimes do not require the licensee to submit regular statements as no separate royalties are due. But it is useful to specify that the coedition licensee should submit regular statements of sales and remaining stock levels, since this enables the licensor as coordinator of future reprints of the same book to judge how soon a reorder might be required.

The currency in which payment is to be made should be specified in the contract. There should also be a requirement that if local regulations require that the licensee deduct tax other than VAT at source, full documentation is provided to the licensor, who may be able to reclaim the deductions against corporation tax (UK companies such as the university presses of Oxford and Cambridge are established as charities and are therefore not able to reclaim tax in this way). Tax requirements will depend on the country of the licensee and whether a double taxation exemption treaty is in force with the United Kingdom (see *Monitoring the payments* in Chapter 6).

The question of whether VAT should be charged on royalty payments is a complex one and varies from country to country; this is not VAT applied to the price of the licensed edition, but a tax applied in some countries to royalties remitted abroad. Russia introduced a provision for the deduction of 18% VAT in 2004 and there has been considerable variance in the way this has been handled by Russian licensees, with some paying the tax separately from the contracted payments expected by the foreign licensor, and others attempting to deduct it from the contracted payments. It would be wiser to specify that the payments expected – any initial advance or advances and subsequent royalties – are the sums to be paid to the licensor after VAT has been deducted from a VAT-inclusive figure; in other words, the licensee should gross up the sums concerned so that the licensor receives the correct amount. This may mean that the licensor has to supply invoices showing the grossed-up amount for each payment and a deduction of 18% to then arrive at the contracted amount.

If the contract has been negotiated through a local subagent (e.g. in Japan, Korea or Taiwan) this should be specified in the contract, as all payments will be transferred through the agent. If agency commission is payable, this too should be specified; the author will receive his or her share of the sum received less agency commission. However, if a British publisher promotes a book directly to a foreign publisher and the publisher chooses to respond through an agent, agreement can be reached that the agent takes commission only from the local publisher rather than from the licensor.

Provision should be made to recover the rights if the translation goes out of print or if there is any breach of the contract by the licensee that is not remedied. The contract should require that the benefits of the licence are not transferred to any third parties, other than through properly granted sublicence arrangements if these have been permitted by the licensor.

A contract usually specifies that the agreement is operable under English law, but certain countries may not agree to accept this. Socialist and former socialist countries have historically been nervous of accepting the legislation of capitalist countries, and a possible compromise was to agree to arbitration in a neutral location such as Stockholm or to operation of the contract under the law of the summoned party in case of dispute. In recent years, publishers in central and eastern Europe and the former Soviet Union have been prepared to accept operation of the contract under the legislation of the country of the licensor. In some countries (mainland China is one example) the agreement must be operable under the law of the country of the licensee for the contract to be validated and hence for payment to be made.

In the case of a lump sum agreement, the number of copies to be printed should be specified, with a requirement for the licensee to inform the licensor as soon as stock is exhausted. The contract will then terminate, although terms for a further quantity can be negotiated and covered by a later addendum. A contract of this kind should also include the estimated retail or wholesale price of the translation and a requirement that if the final price exceeds this the terms of payment should be increased *pro rata* at the point of publication. Publishers in some countries will require an invoice in addition to the contract to remit payment; for some markets (e.g. central and eastern Europe) it may be necessary for each invoice to be stamped and signed on behalf of the licensor. There may also be specific requirements from some licensees imposed on them by local regulations – at one time Poland required contracts to be prepared in both English and Polish (mainly because of banking requirements), but this does not seem to have been applied consistently.

Some Russian publishers now require bilingual contracts and may also require foreign licensors to provide an extra document called a 'Statement of Services Rendered' – a document which in effect specifies that a separate contract has been issued granting the rights concerned. Ukraine requires that publishers there obtain signed certificates confirming that the licensors have received all payments due.

Once the contract has been signed and any payment due on signature received, no further action may be required from the licensor on a straightforward translation licence until publication of the translation. In some cases, however, the licensee may wish to order duplicate production material for the illustrations (see Chapter 25). The author may wish to have corrections included in the translated text, or may have been asked to write a special preface or additional material for the translation. Authors should be discouraged, however, from undertaking substantial rewriting of the book for a foreign edition.

In the case of a coedition deal, rights staff will have many further tasks to perform after signature of the contract and before finished copies finally reach the licensee (see *Technical details and schedules* earlier in this chapter, pp. 213–7).

Conditions for the sale of translation rights vary enormously from country to country, both in terms of titles that may be suitable and the revenue that may be generated. Licensors should be aware of the copyright and licensing background against which they are operating in each territory, and take adequate precautions to ensure that they deal only with reliable partners.

Again, licence expiry dates should be carefully monitored, and a computerized database will prove invaluable here.

Licensing to pharmaceutical companies

The area of licensing to pharmaceutical companies remains important to medical publishers. In the last thirty years, this has developed into significant business and can involve either packaging material specifically for a pharmaceutical client or printing copies in English for them (see Chapter 13), or producing or licensing material in translation for promotional use by overseas drug companies. Some UK medical publishers have overseas subsidiaries that specialize in producing foreign-language material for this market.

If existing material is to be licensed for translation, the approach may come directly from a drug company, but more commonly the deal may be handled via a pharmaceutical packager or an overseas publisher specializing in supplying material to the local pharmaceutical industry. Packagers of this kind are particularly active in Italy, Spain, Latin America and Japan. These companies negotiate for the rights, undertake the translation and production work, and sell copies on to a pharmaceutical client. In the case of a heavily illustrated work such as a medical atlas, they may request coedition prices for flat textless sheets or for finished copies of the translated edition. The licensed edition may carry only the name of the packager/publisher, or the name of the packager plus the name of the drug company, or the name of the drug company alone. There may also be a request to include general advertising for the pharmaceutical client or specific advertising for a product or products manufactured by the client.

The most suitable candidates for deals of this kind are likely to be small pocket-sized books (colour atlases or ready-reference titles are particularly popular), larger books that can be produced as a series of fascicles or individual journal articles which can be produced as small booklets.

In some cases, a packager/publisher will produce a substantial quantity for onward sale to the pharmaceutical client, plus a small quantity for sale through traditional book trade channels. It should be remembered that if copies or fascicles are produced for the pharmaceutical market, it is unlikely that a separate trade edition can then be licensed to a traditional book publisher, since most of the market will have been supplied through free promotional distribution.

It is sometimes possible to arrange for a pharmaceutical deal after publication of the standard trade edition, either via the trade licensee or by referring a packager to the trade publisher for reuse of the translated text.

A pharmaceutical client will always wish to buy copies at a very low price, as they will be given away free to the medical profession in the country concerned as a form of promotion. The price will be very much lower than the selling price of a trade edition through normal channels, and for this reason the royalty rate on pharmaceutical deals (whether included in a coedition price or specified separately) should be correspondingly higher: perhaps 10–12% of the price per copy paid to the packager by the drug company. Since the sale is likely to be a single order, payment could be expressed in the form of a lump sum equivalent to the agreed royalty on a specified print quantity, with a proportion to be paid on signature of the contract and the full balance within an agreed number of days of the packager receiving payment from the client or by an agreed latest calendar date. Payment for any copies sold by the packager through trade channels can be calculated as a lump sum based on a more usual royalty rate (e.g. $7\frac{1}{2}\%$) of the retail price. If a translation deal is negotiated directly with the drug company, with manufacture arranged by the company itself, which is common with journal articles, there will be no selling price as such and payment will have to be calculated on a notional price.

It is important to establish from the start the exact nature of the promotional endorsement by the drug company, whether this will consist of a simple imprint or logo, or perhaps a statement to the effect that the book is being presented free of charge as a service to the medical profession. Alternatives may be specific product advertising in the form of loose inserts or material printed within the book itself (often on the inside covers or on the outside back cover). As with any sponsorship arrangements, if specific advertising is to be included, it is strongly recommended that the authors are consulted prior to finalizing the deal in case they do not want their work to be associated with advertising of this kind. On no account should permission be given to make mention of a specific pharmaceutical product within the text of the book if it does not already appear there, since this would give the impression that the authors are actively endorsing the product; any agreed advertising material should be clearly distinct from the text. It will save time if the packager provides clear information, such as a data sheet for any product to be advertised, to enable the author to make an informed judgement; not all products have been granted government approval in all markets. Pharmaceutical deals can be extremely lucrative, but it is not worth antagonizing an author who is unhappy for the book to be used in this way. Pharmaceutical deals could range from 2,000 to 50,000 copies, and print runs for translated journal articles can also be very large.

Acknowledgements should be made to the author and the original publisher as for a normal translated edition, together with the usual copyright details. In the case of individual journal articles, reference should be made to the year, volume and issue number of the journal in which the material first appeared.

Journal licensing

Mention has been made of licensing individual journal articles to drug companies, but arrangements can also be made for licensing translation rights in scientific and technical journals on a larger scale. This could mean a straightforward licence to a foreign journal publisher to produce an entire journal in translation issue by issue, possibly with the addition of some local material, or perhaps to publish selected translated articles in an existing foreign-language journal. The most obvious market is for medical journals, which may be funded by subscriptions only or by partial or total sponsorship through advertising for pharmaceutical or medical equipment companies.

The first consideration should be whether licensing rights for a whole journal will adversely affect the level of subscriptions for the original journal in the market concerned. Another important point will be whether the foreign licensee should be permitted to use the original name of the journal, either in English or in translation, or both; this should only be permitted if all or a substantial proportion of the material in the original journal is to be translated, and the editorial board of the original journal may wish to approve the insertion of any additional local material; if permitted, this material should be clearly identified. Acknowledgement should be made to the original journal, the editorial board and the original publisher in each issue of the licensed edition. Any variances, such as the reorganization of articles between issues or the number of issues per year, should be subject to approval.

A particularly important aspect of journal licensing is that of speed, since material can date quickly. When licensing an entire journal, it will probably be necessary to set up an arrangement to ensure that the licensee receives material for new issues in manuscript or proof form, to narrow the gap between publication in the original language and publication in translation.

Copyright in the translated text

As mentioned earlier in this chapter (p. 234), there is a completely separate copyright in the translated text, and the ownership of this will depend on the terms of the contractual arrangement between the licensee and the translator or translators. In Anglo-Saxon countries, it is common for a publisher commissioning a translation to require that the copyright in the translated text be assigned to the publisher and this may also be possible in some other countries. This would mean that if a title such as a novel were to be licensed for translation to a particular publisher and the same title were to be relicensed to another publisher at a later date, the new licensee would have to apply to the original licensee to negotiate an arrangement for the reuse of the translated text.

It should, however, be remembered that the continental *droit d'auteur* concept of intellectual property accords much stronger rights to the translator as creator, and in the countries of continental Europe and other countries following that model copyright in the translated text may well be retained by the translator, regardless of the text of the copyright line that appears in the translated edition. Although this may be an academic point in most cases, it can have some bearing if translation rights in a book are licensed to one publisher and then subsequently relicensed to another publisher in the same language; the second publisher may then need to obtain permission for the reuse of the translated text from the translator rather than from the earlier licensee.

It should also be remembered that if an educational or academic title is revised in the original language and the new edition is licensed to a foreign publisher other than the licensee of the previous edition, there may well be substantial passages of common text between the editions, and the new licensee may need to seek permission from the previous licensee for the reuse of the translated text of such passages. This can be a sensitive area, particularly if the change of licensing arrangements was not accepted amicably by the previous licensee. It is often difficult for a new licensee to demonstrate that the common passages have been freshly translated without reference to the earlier translation.

One feature which sometimes occurs in translation licences issued by academic publishers is a requirement for the licensee to assign the copyright in the translated text back to them. This may well be resisted by foreign licensees, particularly if they envisage a situation where an overseas subsidiary of the licensor may subsequently wish to take over translation of the book in the market concerned.

Chapter 17

Anthology and quotation rights

These rights cover the reproduction of passages of original copyright text or illustrations from one source in another, for example in another book, magazine or journal. They are normally handled on a passive basis in that they are not actively promoted but must be dealt with when requests come in. The right to grant permissions – to allow a licensee to quote material from a work – is normally included as a part of the rights granted to the original publisher of that work; the proportion of any fees passed on to the author is usually 50%.

Publishers may themselves control the rights in photographs or illustrations if that material has been specially commissioned for a book rather than created by an author, photographer or illustrator who has a royalty contract with the publisher. In many cases, however, the author (or the publisher on behalf of the author) has obtained permission to include photographs and illustrations from an external source such as a picture agency, art gallery or museum. An application for permission to reproduce such an illustration in another publication would then have to be referred back to the original source. It is, however, important to remember that a publisher may wish to sublicense the whole book in which such third party copyright material appears (for example for translation into another language), in which case it will be necessary to reclear permission for the reuse of any text or illustrations if the proposed sublicence is for publication in a form, language or market that was not included in the original permissions clearance.

Fair dealing

Not all usage of copyright material requires official clearance. In the United Kingdom, the concept of 'fair dealing' was embodied briefly in the 1911 Copyright Act and then spelled out more fully in the 1956 Copyright Act. This specified that copyright work could be drawn on without infringement for the purposes of research and private study, for the reporting of current events or for the purposes of criticism and review, provided that due acknowledgement was made to the source. There was also some provision for the use of short extracts from literary and dramatic works in anthologies clearly intended for school use, provided that the original works from which the material was drawn were not intended for schools, that due acknowledgement was made to the sources of the material and that the majority of the material to be included in such a collection was in the public domain. A further requirement for such use was that no more than a total of two extracts from works by the same author still protected by copyright could be included in collections by that publisher, either in the context of the same collection or in any other collection published in the previous five years.

The 1988 UK Copyright Act reinforces these aspects of fair dealing in Sections 29, 30 and 33, and also adds that the rights in the typographical arrangement (defined in the 1988 Act as the publisher's right) are not infringed provided that the purpose of the usage is in keeping with the definition of fair dealing. The restrictions on the number of extracts from works by the same author that can be included in anthologies for educational purposes have been simplified, to read that no more than two extracts from copyright works by the same author can be included in collections published by any one publisher under the provisions of fair dealing in any five-year period. The amendments made to the 1988 UK Copyright Act as a result of implementation of the EU Directive on the Harmonization of Certain Aspects of Copyright and Related Rights (see *Copyright legislation in the United Kingdom* in Chapter 1) state clearly that fair dealing does not apply to commercial use; this would include the right to reuse copyright material in another published work. Thus, publishers may have to allow a substantial budget to cover the cost of clearing permission for the use of third party material in, say, a history of art, the biography of a writer whose work is still in copyright, or a school or university textbook.

The 1976 US Copyright Act and the subsequent Digital Millennium Copyright Act of 1998 tackled this issue when dealing with the question of 'fair use' in Section 107; US law allows for similar categories of usage of copyright material, but also states:

> In determining whether the use made of a work in any particular case is a fair use the factors to be considered shall include:
>
> 1   The purpose and character of the use, including whether such use is of a commercial nature or is for non-profit educational purposes;
> 2   The nature of the copyrighted work;
> 3   The amount and substantiality of the portion used in relation to the copyrighted work as a whole; and
> 4   The effect of the use upon the potential market for or value of the copyrighted work.

The American view is thus that the length of the extract is not necessarily the most significant factor in assessing fair use; the quotation of the most salient sections of a short magazine article could be considered detrimental. The question is rather one of economic, artistic or even personal harm to the interests of the copyright owner of the original work. Thus the reclusive American novelist J.D. Salinger was able to secure extensive rewriting of an unauthorized critical biography of him through the medium of copyright, by refusing permission to allow extensive quotation from his work, rather than by attempting to restrain publication of the book on the grounds of libel or invasion of privacy. Other extreme cases have included that of Howard Hughes, who sought to acquire rights in articles in *Look* magazine in order to hinder publication of an unauthorized biography, and the blocking of access to the papers of the Duke and Duchess of Windsor for many years by their legal representative.

In the United Kingdom, legislation has not sought to regulate the amounts of material which it is permitted to use under fair dealing; this was traditionally addressed by trade practice rather than by legislation. In 1958, the Society of Authors and the Publishers Association of Great Britain laid down guidelines for their members. It was generally accepted that no formal permission need be sought or fees paid for such usage (listed below), although full acknowledgement to author, title and source should be made.

1 Single extract (prose): up to 400 words.
2 Series of extracts from the same work (prose): up to a total of 800 words, of which no one extract shall exceed 300 words.
3 Poetry: a single extract of forty lines or a series of extracts totalling forty lines, provided that these do not constitute more than 25% of the total poem.

However, these guidelines are not officially recognized by the Office of Fair Trading (OFT).

Illustrations have never been included in the provisions for fair dealing, and those controlling rights in the works of major literary authors (particularly of poetry) may still seek to charge substantial fees for the use of short extracts.

The question of whether there can be a concept of fair dealing in the electronic environment has been controversial and is still the subject of discussion, particularly between academic publishers and the university community. In 1998, a joint UK working party of representatives from the Publishers Association and JISC (the Joint Information Systems Committee) produced *Guidelines for Fair Dealing in an Electronic Environment*, which outlines a number of uses which are considered to be fair dealing, including the printing onto paper of a single copy of part of an electronic document for the purpose of research or private study, and transmission to enable printing of part of an electronic publication for the purpose of printing a single copy. There is no concept of fair dealing for print material reproduced electronically for the purposes of commercial publication (e.g. as part of a database), and the decision on whether or not to charge for such use lies in the hands of the copyright owner or their authorized representative.

Publication of certain types of UK material that fall into the category of Crown copyright (Acts of Parliament, Statutory Instruments, Statutory Rules and Orders or press releases from Crown bodies) or parliamentary copyright (Hansard reports, parliamentary bills, etc.) is normally allowed without permission or payment, provided that they are accurately reproduced for the purpose of analysis or commentary and that the source is fully acknowledged. For use of such material in the context of commercial publications, Her Majesty's Stationery Office (HMSO) introduced in September 2001 two convenient 'click-use' licences for Crown copyright material (the Core Licence and the Value Added Licence) and one for parliamentary material (details are available on www.hmso.gov.uk).

For the use of copyright material outside the very defined uses permitted under fair dealing, permission should be sought and a fee may be charged. The level of fee will vary considerably according to the status of the author, artist or photographer; the amount of material to be used and its importance as part of the source publication; the context of the use; the extent of the use (the print run of the work in which the material is to be quoted); and the geographical and language markets required. If permission is granted, it will always be on a non-exclusive basis. If a passage of text is to be condensed, abridged or altered in any way, permission should be sought to quote it in its new form. While there is no copyright in ideas, paraphrasing copyright work can be actionable, whether this is done through the rewriting of text or the redrawing of illustrations.

Dealing with permissions tends to be a high-volume, low-value business; the administrative cost of dealing with permissions requests can be high, and some publishers may set minimum permissions rates to reflect this.

To enable permissions requests to be processed with maximum efficiency, the applicant should supply full details of the source work, including the name of the author, the title of the publication, the journal issue or book edition number where appropriate (quoting the ISSN (International Standard Serial Number) or ISBN (International Standard Book Number) is also helpful), year of publication and exact details of the textual and/or illustrative material for which permission is being sought (quoting chapter, page or illustration references from the source work). The applicant should also provide full details of the work in which the material is to be quoted: author, title, type of work, publisher, expected publication date, estimated number of pages, hardback, paperback or other format, and expected price; as well as details of the language, territorial and any other media rights required. Some copyright holders require that a standard form is completed to provide these details and may include this in a Permissions section on their company website. If the request is for reuse of the same material in a new printing, new edition or sublicensed edition of a work (e.g. a translation), it will be helpful for the applicant to supply copies of the previous correspondence granting the original permission.

When permission is sought for inclusion in an electronic product (whether an offline product such as a CD-ROM or a dedicated hand-held device, or as part of an online product) of material from a print-on-paper product, it is helpful to provide some indication of the proportion of the overall work which will be formed by the material in question. For online use it is particularly important to obtain details of the potential scale and nature of the user base, the method of access and security of the material, and the proposed payment models, both the charges to users of the material (subscription, pay-per-view?) and the payments to be made to the owners of the material quoted.

All this should enable the person handling the permissions request to check whether the work is still in copyright in the required market (for example, at the time of writing a work still in copyright in the United Kingdom may be out of copyright in Japan or China, which have shorter terms of copyright protection than the United Kingdom); whether the necessary rights in the specific material requested are controlled by the publisher of the source material, have been transferred elsewhere or perhaps have always belonged to an outside copyright holder; if rights are held, whether permission should be granted and whether any special conditions should apply (e.g. one-time use for a designated edition and print run in a designated language; permission granted for an agreed number of years; whether the original author or their representative may require to see the overall context of the quotation). Payment may be required immediately on receipt of an invoice from the licensor, within one year of the date of granting of permission, or on publication of the applicant's publication. If permission is granted, the exact conditions should be confirmed by letter or e-mail, together with the required wording for copyright acknowledgement and a requirement for a voucher copy of the applicant's final publication if appropriate.

As the number of applications has increased for the right to use material in electronic form (either instead of, or as well as, in print form), publishers have been developing their own practice, and the tendency initially was to charge between one and three times the rates recommended for print-on-paper publication; however, academic publishers John Wiley led the way in automatically including electronic permission together with print permission. Permission may be restricted to a limited licence term of between one and four years. But arrangements may vary considerably, depending on the identity of the applicant and on the proposed use of the material: for example, the use of key material from a business book by a major financial or management consultancy firm on its intranet for the purpose of staff training could command a substantial five-figure sum.

The licensor may, of course, decide not to grant permission at all (for example if the use is considered too extensive or detrimental to the original author); alternatively, they may decide not to grant the full range of rights requested (for example, rights may not be extended to the applicant's sublicensees without further reclearance).

Anthology and quotation rights

Permission for the inclusion of copyright material in anthologies may need to be treated with special care, especially if lengthy or numerous extracts from the work of a single author are requested. If such extracts form a substantial part of the anthology, it may be preferable to require payment on the basis of a small but ongoing royalty based on the published price of the anthology, rather than on the basis of permission fees related to the length of the individual extracts quoted. For example, if the extracts in question form 25% of the total anthology, it might be reasonable to request a 2% or $2\frac{1}{2}$% royalty on the retail price (3% or $3\frac{1}{2}$% if calculated on the licensee's net receipts), although lower percentages might be paid if the anthology is intended for the educational rather than for the general market.

The context in which the material is to be published is particularly important in the case of an anthology; significant use of a single writer's work in this way justifies careful consultation with the author or the author's agent. Many authors have strong views on the extensive use of their work in this way, and also on the company in which they may find themselves in an anthology.

Payment is often charged by the length of the extract, and in the early editions of this book I was able to quote from the guidelines on charging agreed between the Publishers Association and the Society of Authors, which were regularly reviewed and submitted to the Office of Fair Trading for registration. Since 2003 the OFT has not felt it could register the guidelines and, regrettably, for this reason it is not possible to provide guidelines in the context of this book. The Society of Authors does provide some information on the rates it charges for the use of works where the literary estates of the authors are handled by the Society (see www.societyofauthors.org). The UK Publishers Association also has a list of Permissions Guidelines (www.publishers.org.uk/en/copyright/copyright_guidelines) offering general advice on when it is necessary to seek permission for the use of copyright material; however, these stress that the question of permissions fees is a matter for negotiation between the parties.

Poetry is traditionally charged for at a fee for the first ten lines, then at a rate per line for the next twenty lines, and at a slightly lower rate per line thereafter for world English-language rights. The rates for established poets may be charged at a premium.

Prose is normally charged for at a rate per thousand words, taking into account whether permission is required for world English-language rights, a more restricted English-language market or if additional rights are also required; again the work of an established author could command high rates. Much may also depend on the context of the use requested; for example, the rate quoted for the use of extracts from the work of a major novelist might be higher if they are quoted in the context of a popular biography of the novelist than if they are quoted in a specialized work of literary criticism.

If world rights are required in all languages in addition to using the material in an English edition, the rate could be doubled, although granting permission of this kind requires care if there are extant translations of the material in question, since these will have intrinsic copyrights of their own which will probably belong to the publisher in the market in question.

For the UK and Commonwealth market only, or for the US market only, the rate charged is usually 50% of the rate for world English-language rights. The usual practice for the US and Canada, or for the United Kingdom and all European Union territories, is to charge two-thirds of the rates quoted for world English-language rights. The rate for a single English-language market such as Canada or Australia, or a single foreign-language territory such as Italy, is usually one-third of the rate for world English-language rights.

If the material to be used is complete in itself (say a chapter or a short story) an additional fee of half the agreed rate per thousand words may be added. For quotation in the context of a scholarly work, the rate per thousand words of prose is usually halved. The rate per poem or per line of poetry may be reduced by one-third if the material is to be reproduced in a literary or scholarly journal, in an anthology containing more than forty copyright poems or in a book with a print run of fewer than 1,500 copies. Permission may also be limited to a single, specified printing, and also to publication under the imprint of the applicant; it would then be necessary to reclear permission for any further usage such as new printings or revised editions published by the applicant.

It would also mean that if the work in which the material is to be quoted is subsequently licensed to an American or foreign-language publisher, permission would have to be recleared for the reuse of the material by the sublicensees.

In the United Kingdom, anthology and quotation fees charged on the basis of the length of material used will attract VAT at the rate prevailing at the time of charging. UK VAT should not be applied to overseas applications.

Applications for the partial use of copyright works in the context of publishing-on-demand or in coursepacks for universities are now commonly dealt with via the medium of central licensing agencies (see *Photocopying and scanning* in Chapter 23).

It is often the case that an author may request permission for the reuse of extracts of their own work in another context. In most cases it is customary to permit such use free of charge and subject to appropriate acknowledgement, unless, of course, substantial amounts of material are to be used in a work to be published by a competing publisher; this may raise the question of whether restrictions on competing works are included in the original head contract. Some publishers have also chosen to list in the head contract various uses which an author may make of his or her own work without permission or charge, e.g. the use of limited extracts on the author's own website, in the context of teaching activities or as the basis for a lecture.

Some publishers may set a minimum of 250 words, below which no fee is charged (it should be remembered that the figure of 400 words quoted earlier in this chapter for fair dealing refers only to specific contexts such as research and study, reporting of current events and criticism or review).

It is often uneconomic to charge purely nominal fees, since they may not themselves cover the cost of administering the correspondence involved. Thus, if the usage falls outside the context of fair dealing but nevertheless involves a small amount of material, permission may be granted free of charge provided that due acknowledgement is made to the author, title and the original publisher. Some permissions departments simply rubber-stamp applications of this kind, although they may need to specify the exact text of the acknowledgement they require.

Members of the International Association of Scientific, Technical and Medical (STM) Publishers have voluntary guidelines (www.stm-assoc.org/documents-statements-public) whereby they streamline the procedures for the use of each other's copyright material by agreeing not to charge permissions fees unless the amount of material requested is substantial and hence outside the bounds of fair dealing or fair use; for example, extensive use of articles, chapters or illustrations from a single journal or book would not meet fair dealing criteria. The Guidelines recommend that permission is granted for the use of up to three figures (including tables) from a journal article or book chapter, but that no more than five figures should be used from a whole book or journal issue, and not more than six figures from an annual journal volume. For text, the recommended amount is up to 400 words for a single extract from a journal article or book chapter, but no more than a total of 800 words from a whole book or journal issue. There is a requirement to maintain the integrity of the quoted material and to credit the source fully, and members need to check whether the STM member publisher from whose content they seek to quote has formally endorsed the Permissions Guidelines; a list of participating publishers is available on the STM website.

These guidelines originally applied to print-on-paper use only; however, in October 1998 they were amended to recommend that the use of limited amounts of copyright material should be permitted in electronic versions of similar types of work. That amendment carried the proviso that STM publishers were then in a period of transition from publishing in print-on-paper to providing content in a range of media on a variety of platforms; the situation would have to be reviewed in the light of future developments. The guidelines were then further amended in March 2003 with a recommendation that electronic use of similarly limited amounts of material should be included; also that permission should be extended to cover quotation in future editions of the same work and in translations of the work. They were last updated in October 2008 to recognize the fact that some participating members do not require formal requests for permission to quote material provided that the proposed usage falls within the permitted boundaries of the Guidelines, but that others still wish to receive formal applications and confirm whether or not permission is granted, even if no fee is charged. Again, it is advisable to check the STM website to see which publishers require formal applications to be submitted.

Illustrations

The fees charged for photographs, illustrations, diagrams or graphs vary enormously depending on their nature and their source. A publisher may not always control rights in any or all of the illustrations included in his books, since they may have had to be obtained from an outside source. In some cases these may be 'clipart' from a copyright-cleared collection available on CD, but in many cases permission will have been obtained from the original copyright owners or their representatives; these may be other publishers, museums, art galleries or commercial picture agencies.

Where rights are controlled, a number of factors have to be taken into account when assessing whether to grant permission, including the nature of the usage, the size at which the illustration will be reproduced, whether it will appear in colour or in black and white, and the geographical territory required. A typical illustration fee will contain elements relating to all these aspects. As a general rule, the fees for colour illustrations and photographs tend to be double those charged for black and white, and publishers granting rights tend to reflect the practice used by commercial picture agencies.

Thus an illustration that is to be reproduced inside a book to half-page size in an English-language edition for sale in the UK and Commonwealth market might be charged at a particular fee, while the fee for the same illustration to be used to the same size for sale in an English-language edition for the world market might be 50% higher. However, if the same photograph were to be used for the whole front jacket for the UK and Commonwealth market, the fee could run to a much higher rate. Some galleries and picture agencies charge supplementary rates for use in print runs of more than 10,000 copies. Lower rates can sometimes be negotiated for use in the context of an educational work or for the use of many illustrations from the same source.

As with textual permissions, permission will be non-exclusive and may be restricted to a single defined print run of the book in which the illustration is to appear under the imprint of the applicant, and permission would then have to be recleared for any reprints or sublicensed editions. All fees in the United Kingdom are liable to VAT. The text required for acknowledgement of the illustration, artist or photographer and the source of the material should be provided to the licensee. It is important to remember that any changes (e.g. cropping or the alteration of any elements of the picture) may constitute an infringement of the moral rights of the artist or photographer, and permission should always be sought for any proposed changes of this type.

Requests for permission to use illustrations in the context of an electronic product may require the provision of detailed information to the licensor. Rates will depend on the illustrations in question, the nature of the product in which they are to be used and the importance of the illustrations to the project. Copyright holders are also concerned about the possibility of further and unauthorized reproduction of valuable images for commercial purposes, and applicants would be well advised to provide information on the way in which the end user of their product can access and use such images if permission is granted.

The featuring of an illustration in the context of a completely different medium such as a commercial poster, birthday card or T-shirt begins to move into the area of merchandising; the terms of use would then have to be carefully defined and may be charged for on a different basis (see Chapter 22).

It is important to remember that where illustrations are concerned there may be another charge to be made in addition to the fee charged for the copyright aspect of the illustration. This is an access or facility fee for supplying the applicant with the material needed to reproduce the illustration; this could be a photographic print, a transparency or material in electronic form, and will apply whether the work is in or out of copyright. Fees are likely to be higher for access to a well-known painting than for a standard street-scene photograph. The material must be returned promptly and there will usually be a further holding fee per week if the material is held beyond the agreed period of time. There will also be a loss fee (often several hundred pounds) to cover any damage or loss while the material is in the care of the licensee.

Almost all commercial suppliers such as picture agencies, art galleries and museums now offer access to their catalogues in electronic form, either on CD-ROM or via their websites; this is for selection purposes only, with the images not of sufficient quality to allow for reproduction. The process of digitizing existing print holdings is extremely expensive in terms of equipment, time and labour required for scanning. Such suppliers can then provide the selected material in electronic form, either on CD or for downloading, once an account has been set up with the applicant. The largest multinational picture agencies, Getty Images and Corbis Images (owned by Bill Gates), now control about half the images supplied worldwide and operate entirely digitally.

Some suppliers may still forbid the scanning of their material by licensees for electronic storage unless this right is specifically negotiated. In view of this, publishers applying for permission should remind the licensor that developments in production technology mean that book projects are now held in electronic rather than in film form; it would also be advisable for publishers to alert the licensor if they intend to reproduce the illustration on their own website, even if it is in the context of reproducing the illustration appearing on a book cover or as part of a book spread shown in their 'electronic catalogue'.

For the use of works of art controlled by such sources which are still in copyright, an additional fee is also paid to the Design and Artists Copyright Society Ltd (DACS), which deducts a commission before passing the balance on to the artist or their heirs; DACS is also responsible for supplying to the licensee the correct text for the acknowledgement byline.

For pictures controlled by a publisher, a transparency, photographic print, piece of duplicate film or (more likely) an electronic file may be supplied in return for a copyright fee plus a fee for the cost of manufacturing the material; the exact basis of the arrangement (loan or purchase) should be clearly spelled out in the documentation provided.

It can be seen that when dealing with the granting of permissions for both text and illustrations, it is important to define the rights to be granted as precisely as possible to avoid wider usage of the material than was originally envisaged.

Chapter 18

Rights for the reading impaired

These include the right to license individuals or organizations to produce editions which are accessible to the blind or partially sighted (visually impaired persons, VIPs) or others with reading disabilities – these may include people with dyslexia or with disabilities which prevent them from holding or reading a book in the usual way. These rights are non-commercial in nature; they cover the production of books in Braille and Moon (another embossed tactile system, using large characters similar to the alphabet) and the recording of undramatized readings of books on cassettes, CDs or as digital downloads for use by the reading impaired (RIPs). Increasingly, those organizations producing material for this readership seek rights to supply material in other media, for example in disc format for computer-driven Braille display, magnified screen display or text-to-speech (TTS) versions.

These rights have traditionally been granted free of charge or in return for a purely nominal fee. Large-print rights for the partially sighted who can cope with such editions, including the new FOCUS programme, are excluded from this category as they are produced on a commercial basis (they are covered in Chapter 13).

Since the last edition of this book appeared, there have been even more developments on both the political and legislative fronts to facilitate the provision of accessibility and inclusivity in relation to the use of copyright material by visually impaired and disabled people, and the legal situation at the time of writing is described later in this chapter. The practical situation concerning the supply of material in accessible formats for RIPs is described below (on pp. 257–8).

Braille and Moon editions

In the United Kingdom, these are produced mainly by the Royal National Institute for the Blind (RNIB) (www.rnib.org.uk), which receives some government funding to assist with its work in this area; and the Scottish Braille Press (www.royalblind.org). The National Library for the Blind (NLB), originally a separate organization, was merged with the RNIB in January 2007 to form the RNIB Library service. Material is offered either on a loan basis to members, delivered to people's homes, or for sale at below cost price. A standard letter of application to the rightsholder (usually combined with a request for rights in the other forms outlined above) is received, and permission is usually granted free of charge, subject to appropriate reproduction of the copyright notice and acknowledgement to author, title and publisher on the title page of the tactile edition. The geographical market granted may vary; the RNIB may apply for world rights, British Commonwealth rights or the United States and Canada. There will normally be a restriction on the number of copies which can be made.

Recordings for VIPs and RIPs

In the United Kingdom, these are produced primarily by the RNIB, CALIBRE and the National Listening Library. The RNIB runs a library of academic and professional texts for visually disabled students and professionals. These are recorded in full by volunteer readers, and will include critical apparatus such as footnotes and appendices. The RNIB Talking Book Library also provides recordings of fiction and popular non-fiction for leisure purposes; the books are recorded full length by actors or professional broadcasters in the RNIB's own studios. Books are usually on a single CD. They are in DAISY (Digital Accessible Information System) format, which is easy to navigate. The RNIB charges an annual subscription to members of its service, which includes delivery, but the costs of its operations are heavily subsidized. At the time of writing, a books-only subscription is £50; a subscription of £79 includes the loan of a lightweight DAISY player.

The American Foundation for the Blind and Recordings for the Blind in Princeton, New Jersey, provide a similar service in the United States. A further scheme is run by Bookshare (www.bookshare.org). Based in the United States, it was originally founded to provide accessible versions of educational and academic publications and initially operated under a special educational exception in US copyright law and with funding from the US Department of Education; it has since expanded its programme to include trade titles and has reached commercial agreements with publishers. In 2009, Bookshare extended its service to people in the United Kingdom with a qualifying print disability, and their programme includes titles for which rights have been cleared for the UK market. Bookshare members can download the texts in DRM-protected files either in DAISY format for text-to-speech use or in Braille refreshable format; alternatively, they can order a book as an embossed Braille edition.

CALIBRE (www.calibre.org.uk) produces full-length recordings of fiction and popular non-fiction on standard cassettes, CDs and in some cases

MP3 format, recorded by volunteer readers, who often make the recordings in their own homes. It runs a postal lending library service, free to CALIBRE members.

The National Listening Library (www.listening-books.org.uk) runs an audiobook library service for anyone with an illness or disability which makes it difficult to hold a book, turn pages or read a book in the normal way. Recordings can be supplied to individuals or to schools, colleges, hospitals or residential care institutions either as MP3 CDs by post or streamed over the internet. At the time of writing, annual membership rates are £20 a year for individuals for the streaming service, £35 per year for MP3 CDs or £45 a year for both. For institutions, annual rates are from £20 a year for streaming, from £45 per year for MP3 CDs or £90 a year for both.

A distinction must clearly be made between the licensing of recording rights in a book for users of this kind and commercial recording rights (Chapter 20), since many titles could be licensed for both purposes. The letter of agreement provided by the RNIB states that the recording will be available only to blind and print-disabled people on a non-profit-making basis. A copyright statement will be made verbally at the beginning of the recording, confirming that the copyright owner has authorized the recording for this use. The production of copies is usually limited to 500; such licences should also be limited by time if the licensor's own contract with the author is for less than the full term of copyright. The copyright in the recordings remains the property of the RNIB.

The recordings may only be sold or loaned to the designated audience or to recognized agencies representing the blind and the reading disabled. The RNIB has arrangements whereby similar organizations in the Commonwealth countries (and in some cases the US Library of Congress) can produce non-commercial versions from its master recordings.

Customized large print

The RNIB and the National Library for the Blind also produce large-print versions. The material may have to be customized in the sense that simply blowing up the material to a larger size may distort graphics and tables; these may have to be redesigned. Most requests are for 18-, 24- and 32-point size.

Changes in legislation for VIPs and RIPs

Recent years have seen significant changes in international and UK legislation affecting these constituencies; the latter legislation resulted from lobbying by the visually impaired and the organizations representing them, such as the RNIB. The RNIB-backed Right to Read alliance campaigned for publishers and retailers to produce and stock more titles in accessible formats for the estimated three million people in the United Kingdom with sight problems. There was also a vigorous lobbying campaign to Parliament, despite an initiative already taken by authors and the publishing industry in 2001 in consultation with the RNIB; through the Publishers Licensing Society (PLS – see Chapter 23) they had issued joint industry guidelines for publishers and rights owners when dealing with permissions requests from VIPs or the organizations representing them. The guidelines recommended a prompt and sympathetic response to such requests and that the granting of such rights should be free of charge, although the cost of supplying digital files for conversion to accessible editions was regarded as a separate issue. The guidelines also referred rightsholders to the arrangements already run by the RNIB and to the CLA licensing scheme (see *Licences via the CLA* later in this chapter, pp. 258–9, and Chapter 23).

Whilst publishers would have preferred a voluntary rather than a legislative solution, the lobbying resulted in the Copyright (Visually Impaired Persons) Act 2002, which granted VIPs special copyright exceptions. Under the terms of the Act, VIPs are now entitled to make copies of copyright works in accessible formats for personal use without being obliged to seek permission from the copyright holder, provided that such copies are made from lawfully acquired originals, are not adapted unnecessarily and are not passed on to others. Approved bodies acting on behalf of VIPs are able to make multiple copies on behalf of their constituency unless a suitable licensing scheme exists to cover this.

On the international front, April 2008 saw the launch of the World Blind Union's (WBU) International Right to Read campaign. The International Right to Read Alliance is a partnership between the WBU and the Libraries for the Blind section of the International Federation of Library Associations (IFLA). The Alliance aims to work with publishers, booksellers and libraries to make a wider range of publications accessible to the reading impaired. At the time of writing, the International Publishers Association is working with the WBU to discuss accessibility issues, with a plan to trial the transfer of accessible files between countries via trusted intermediaries in 2010. In the meantime, in 2009 the World Intellectual Property Organization (WIPO) received a proposal from Brazil, Paraguay and Ecuador for an international treaty on copyright exceptions allowing access to copyright works by reading-impaired people; this is being considered. Some sixty countries (including, since 2002, the United Kingdom) already have such an exception as part of their national copyright legislation; however, over 100 countries do not.

What are publishers doing?

While publishers have generally been sympathetic to the needs of VIPs and RIPs and to the granting of permission without charging copyright fees, the increasing demands on them to provide digital files have proved to be something of a problem. Requests come primarily from visually impaired students or from university or college staff acting on their behalf; requests may run to hundreds or even thousands in the course of a year and may come by telephone or e-mail with a degree of urgency for a particular course, and may be for files in formats not held by the publisher. In such cases publisher reaction has been mixed, with some publishers prepared to supply copies of files in an existing format free of charge, whilst others make a charge for direct copies or for conversion to the required format. There have been considerable concerns over the supply of copyright material in electronic format, with the implicit ease of copying, and some publishers have required applicants to sign a simple form confirming their VIP status and that the file is required for personal use only; some publishers include the form on their website. In principle, publishers would prefer a system whereby electronic master files could be passed to a trusted intermediary such as the RNIB and all requests would then be referred to them.

Rightsholders also need to be aware of the 2007 UN Convention on the Rights of Persons with Disabilities and, in the United Kingdom, the provisions of the Disability Discrimination Act 1995 (parts of which only came into force in 2004) and of the Special Educational Needs Act 2001. Both pieces of legislation make it an offence to discriminate against the provision of material to disabled people, including VIPs and also dyslexics. Although the main thrust of the Disability Discrimination Act was aimed at libraries, schools, shops, restaurants and hotels, publishers also come under the category of 'service providers' and are under an obligation to make their publications accessible to those who need them. In September 2007 the Publishers Association issued practical guidelines on dealing with permissions requests; an updated version can be found at www.publishers.org.uk/en/home/accessibility.

Research in 2004 indicated that only 4.4% of titles are available in any format accessible to VIPs (audio, large print or Braille); 2.8% are available in audio format, 1.5% in large print and 1.9% in Braille. After a positive response from authors, publishers, booksellers and the reproduction rights organizations, and following discussions chaired by the then Department of Trade and Industry and involving the RNIB, the NLB, publishers and trade associations, a scoping project was launched in 2006 with the aim of increasing substantially the number of titles available in accessible formats, and preferably making such versions available simultaneously with first publication of the title concerned. The project is led by the RNIB as sponsor, with an independent project manager. The initial focus has been on investigating the extent to which publisher content can be made available in suitable digital form, which can then be converted and processed into large print, Braille and audio products, which can then be made available through mainstream bookshops as well as other distribution channels and online services. A pilot scheme for trade titles is being trialled, taking publishers' PDFs, converting them to XML and then producing multiple output versions from the XML file. A similar pilot is in hand for textbooks. In late 2009, the Universities' Joint Information Systems Committee (JISC) and the Publishers Licensing Society invited participation and they are funding a small-scale project to investigate accessibility issues with publications from selected publishers and e-book aggregators. The Publishers Association and the TechDis service of JISC have also set up a database of accessibility information; participating publishers from the education sector are listed on the Publisher Lookup UK site (www.PublisherLookup.org.uk). Library professionals, learner support staff and disability officers can use the site to find contact details of the appropriate publisher's department which will deal with requests for accessible versions of learning materials. Publishers can find more information on how to improve accessibility on the TechDis website (www.techdis.ac.uk).

A regular Publisher Accessibility newsletter is now produced by the Accessibility Action Group, which includes the Publishers Association (PA), the Periodical Publishers Association (PPA), the Independent Publishers Guild (IPG), the Association of Learned and Professional Society Publishers (ALPSP), the Copyright Licensing Agency (CLA), the Publishers Licensing Society (PLS), the Newspaper Society, the Newspaper Publishers Association and Book Industry Communication (BIC).

In a separate initiative, in late 2005 the print-on-demand specialist Lightning Source announced that it was entering the large-print market, working with publishers, and in 2007 it won an Innovation Award for the programme. A listing of available titles can be found on the Amazon site (www.amazon.co.uk) by accessing 'large print'.

The advent of various dedicated e-book readers in the last two years (see Chapter 24) raised various issues in connection with TTS technology. When Amazon's Kindle 2 offered that capability, Amazon was targeted by the American Authors Guild, who saw the facility as an unauthorized audio right; this was then contested by various groups representing VIPs as unfair to their members. Amazon initially stated that it would not remove the facility, but later said that it would respect the wishes of rightsholders on individual titles. A further issue arose with the large-screen Kindle DX, which also offers a TTS facility but where the menu for the device was not accessible for VIPs wishing to order titles from the Amazon website. In December 2009 Amazon announced that it would update its devices to provide an audible menu system and would also add a seventh font size, which will be double the size of the largest font currently on the devices. The Apple iPad may encounter problems from rightsholders with its VoiceOver screen reader.

Licences via the CLA

In 1999, the Copyright Licensing Agency requested mandates from authors and publishers via their licensing organizations, the Authors Licensing and

Collecting Society (ALCS) and the Publishers Licensing Society (PLS), to allow licensed charitable institutions to scan or retype works for the sole purpose of creating Braille or Moon editions. The licence is currently available and is designed for approved not-for-profit organizations representing VIPs, such as the RNIB; it permits them to make Braille, Moon and digital Braille versions, audio versions, including digital audio formats such as DAISY, large-print and digital copies. The licence runs for an initial period of one year and continues to run on a year-to-year basis subject to three months' notice of termination. The first-year licence is granted free of charge but CLA reserves the right to charge a fee for continuation of the licence, subject to issuing the organization concerned with six months' notice of its intention to do so. It is a condition of the licence that the organization supplies single copies of works from the mandated repertoire in the required accessible format to authorized users only, that copies are made from a legally acquired original, that if a charge is made it is at cost, and that a record is kept of copies made.

The CLA is also responsible for photocopying licences to the education, business and professional sectors (see *Photocopying and scanning* in Chapter 23). These licences allow for enlarged copying for visually disabled persons in a minimum type size of 16 point and allow not only for traditional photocopying but also for scanning or for copying from a digital original. Such copying is permitted free of charge provided that the copies are made from a legally acquired original work, that no commercial large-print edition is available and that such copies are not sold; the 5% limitation on material copied does not apply. The licences do not permit electronic storage or onward transmission.

Chapter 19

Single-voice readings

This covers the right to read from the text of a published work in undra-matized form through the medium of radio or television, or public performances in other media. The author's share of the income is usually 75%. Obvious examples of a single-voice reading of literary material would be the BBC Radio 4 programmes *A Book at Bedtime* and *Book of the Week*.

For use of copyright material by the BBC on radio or television, set rates are negotiated regularly between the BBC, the Publishers Association and the Society of Authors. Payment is calculated according to the length of time of the broadcast. The rates from 1 August 2009 are as follows:

1 *Television*
   Prose (per minute) £29.44
   Poetry (per half-minute) £35.32
2 *Radio*

   (a) Domestic service
       Prose (per minute) £17.10
       Poetry (per half-minute) £17.10
   (b) World Service (English) and BBC Digital Service originations
       Prose (per minute) £8.55
       Poetry (per half-minute) £8.55
   (c) Local radio
       Prose (per minute) £4.27
       Poetry (per half-minute) £4.27

Translations of prose and poetry are payable at two-thirds of the above rates payable to the translator and the licensor.

The agreements provide for initial broadcasts within three years of the date of signature, with repeat fees within designated time periods. Repeat fees for television broadcasts range from 100% of the appropriate initial fee for broadcasting at peak times to 25% of the initial fee for off-peak and night repeats. Repeat fees for radio use are payable at 100% of the appro-priate initial fee for repeats on domestic services, the World Service and local radio, and at 10% of the appropriate initial fee for rebroadcasting via the digital services or via what the BBC refers to as 'new public services', which include access on demand via the internet. The licence for such usage runs for five years from the date of first broadcast via the core services. Unless the licensor imposes territorial restrictions, the BBC also acquires the right to license the broadcast of the material worldwide. For the licensing of free-to-air television rights, payment is made at the rate of 100% of the initial fee for arrangements in the United States and at 50% of the initial fee for use in the rest of the world. For licences for pay television use, payment is made at 15% of the initial fee for use in the United States and at 10% for the rest of the world. For the licensing of radio rights, payment is made on the basis of a 5% royalty of the BBC's gross receipts from licensing undramatized straight readings or a $1\frac{1}{2}\%$ royalty on gross receipts from other types of exploitation. The BBC also has agreed rates for the inclusion of literary works in teachers' educational support materials to accompany their programmes at the following rates:

1 Prose: £35 for the first 300 words; £9 for each subsequent 130 words (or part thereof).
2 Poetry: £35 for the first 12 lines; £8 for each subsequent 8 lines (or part thereof).

The BBC now has a range of digital radio channels, of which BBC7 is a speech-based public service channel broadcasting programmes from the BBC Radio archive as well as programmes specially commissioned or acquired for the channel, featuring drama and readings, comedy and children's programmes.

While many applications for single-voice reading rights come to the publisher of appropriate books unannounced, it is obviously worthwhile to identify the producers of programmes which use material in this way, and to keep them informed of projects which might be suitable for such treatment. Full credit is given to author, title and publisher at the end of each reading.

The independent television companies periodically agree rates of payment with the Writers' Guild for the use of original teleplays and for adaptations and dramatizations; but these are the rates paid to screen-writers rather than rates paid for the use of the underlying copyright work. However, payment for the use of literary works can be negotiated on a similar basis to the rates quoted above in this chapter if the occasion arises. In recent years, independent radio stations have tended to use a substantially smaller proportion of spoken word output in their broadcasts. July 2000 saw the launch of Oneword, a digital radio station which included book and film reviews, author interviews and serializations of audiobooks (abridged and unabridged) for both adults and children. In January 2004,

Channel 4 television stepped in to buy a 51% shareholding in the station, with UBC Media retaining 49%; however, in December 2007 Channel 4 decided to withdraw its funding and Oneword ceased to broadcast in January 2008. The failure was blamed on a lower than expected take-up of DAB radios. Channel 4's subsequent plans to launch its own DAB stations were abandoned in October 2008.

If copyright material is to be used as the basis of a programme of single-voice readings at a public performance for which an admission charge is made, payment could be assessed on the basis of a royalty of the gross box-office receipts. If, however, the work is controlled by several different copyright holders, the proportion of the royalty paid to each would have to be calculated *pro rata* depending on the proportion of the total material belonging to each copyright holder.

Chapter 20

Audio recording and video recording rights

For many years, these rights were included under the overall heading of 'mechanical and reproduction rights'. Technology has been moving so fast that this catch-all heading is no longer an appropriate definition for the range of rights which can now be exploited. This chapter therefore deals only with audiobook recording rights and video recording rights; forms of reproduction of print content such as microform, photocopying and electronic copying and delivery are covered in Chapter 23, with electronic publishing and multimedia rights covered in Chapter 24.

Since the last edition of this book appeared, the growth of audiobook sales in a variety of formats has been a major area of expansion; the last official figures from the Audiobook Publishers Association valued the UK market in 2006 at £71.4 million per year; Bookscan updated this to £75 million in 2008. The US market was valued at just under $1 billion in 2008. There has also been an increasing move towards services which provide for the downloading of audiobooks to computers and a variety of portable devices and this development is covered later in this chapter (see *Download services for audiobooks*, pp. 267–9).

In the United States, in particular, audiobook sales can be substantial – at the time of writing, the audio version of Stephen R. Covey's *7 Habits of Highly Effective People* has sold over two million copies, whilst John Gray's *Men Are from Mars, Women Are from Venus* has sold over 1.5 million copies. Audiobooks of J.K. Rowling's *Harry Potter* books have each sold over one million copies to date. Financial terms for audio licences have risen accordingly and there are rumours that a $1 million advance was paid for at least one major bestselling title; high advances are likely to be loss leaders to attract major names to an audio list. In the United Kingdom, the profile of audiobooks has been raised by an annual trade initiative to promote the Top Forty Audiobooks of the Year, launched in 2008. In August 2009, a personal endorsement of the joys of listening to audiobooks by Stephen Fry (who also regularly appears as a reader on audiobook recordings) on the BBC *Top Gear* programme led to a surge of £220,000 in audiobook sales over the following four weeks.

In both the United States and the United Kingdom, there has been an increasing demand for unabridged over abridged versions; traditionally, the former were more popular in libraries, with abridged versions more popular for individual purchase through retail outlets. In the United States, unabridged recordings now represent about 85% of the market; they hold a 50% share in the United Kingdom.

The last five years have seen a clear shift in format from cassette to CD, despite the smaller capacity of discs – this reflects the general availability of CD players both in homes and as standard equipment in new cars. The rise in popularity of CDs also reflects a move away from the perception that the audio market is dominated by older buyers or is aimed at the visually impaired, and this is reinforced by the fact that audio products are now sold in discount stores, supermarkets and service stations as well as book and music outlets. In 2006, there were predictions that audiobooks in CD format would be completely superseded by digital downloads within three years. This has not yet happened, but the increasing move towards downloads also indicates a market amongst a younger audience on the move – the 'iPod generation', who have never used cassettes or discs in devices such as a Walkman or a portable CD player. In September 2001, Simon & Schuster Audio launched the first audiobook in MP3 CD format in addition to the more traditional cassette and CD formats – *The Talisman* by Stephen King and Peter Straub. MP3 CDs hold twelve hours of recorded material, provide navigation and bookmarking facilities and can take up as little as one disc by comparison with multiple cassettes or CDs (*Harry Potter and the Goblet of Fire* was originally available on twelve cassettes or seventeen CDs). At the time of writing, digital downloads account for approximately 21% of the total audiobook market in the United States and 15% in the United Kingdom, but these shares are gradually increasing. One reason for the survival of the CD format may be that the audio quality is generally higher than that of a download.

Single-voice audiobook rights

This covers the licensing of the right to issue an undramatized single-voice recording of the text of a book, abridged or non-abridged, on a commercial CD or (far more rarely now) an audio cassette, as opposed to dramatized recordings (Chapter 21) or non-profit recordings for the use of the visually impaired and the print disabled (Chapter 18).

In the United Kingdom, there has been some consolidation of audiobook producers in the last few years. In 2001, Isis was sold to Ulverscroft, an audio publisher of unabridged versions and also large-print books (see Chapter 13) which services the library market. Also in 2001, BBC Worldwide took over Cover to Cover, which had produced unabridged versions of classic adult fiction, and then Chivers. In 2002, the companies were integrated with BBC Word for Word (producing unabridged contemporary books for adults) and BBC Radio Collection (producing adaptations from the BBC radio and television archives) into BBC Audiobooks.

The BBC is estimated to hold about 34% of the UK audiobook market. However, in September 2009 it embarked on an exercise to sell a majority stake in BBC Audiobooks, perhaps to a major trade publisher, with a view to completing negotiations in 2010.

Other specialist audio publishers include W.F. Howes (Whole Story Audiobooks), the CSA Word Group and Naxos Audiobooks. In 2009 Naxos appeared at number five and CSA at number nine in the top ten listing of UK audio publishers. Naxos traditionally specialized in unabridged recordings of classic literature; however, more recently they have included more modern fiction writers such as Cormac McCarthy in their catalogue. Literary agents have shown an inclination to sell rights separately to specialist audio publishers if audio rights in a particular title do not seem to be high on the agenda of the print publisher.

A number of major UK trade publishers do have their own audio imprints, including Penguin, Random House, Hachette Livre UK, HarperCollins, Simon & Schuster, Macmillan, as well as smaller publishers such as Mills & Boon, Bloomsbury, Faber & Faber and Canongate. In the United States, major specialist producers include Brilliance Audio Inc.; another significant player, Audio Book Partners, was acquired by BBC Audiobooks in 2007. Time Warner, Simon & Schuster, Random House, HarperCollins and Macmillan all have audio divisions. HarperCollins in the USA acquired Caedmon, publisher of recordings of classic literature such as the poetry of Dylan Thomas, as far back as 1987; Caedmon was founded in 1952, initially issuing recordings of the spoken word in traditional gramophone disc format.

Titles most likely to be produced as audiobooks are the classics (many of them now out of copyright, although some major twentieth-century authors are now back in copyright following the extension of the copyright term in the UK); popular fiction; thrillers and mysteries; an increasing amount of literary fiction; some poetry; biography and autobiography of celebrities; diaries of prominent people such as politicians and writers (in 2009, Barack Obama reading his own *Dreams from My Father* was a bestseller); popular management titles; 'self-help' titles; 'spiritual' titles; and a large range of titles for children. Sales of bestselling titles find a ready audience in audio form, e.g. Orion's 2004 audiobook version of Dan Brown's *The Da Vinci Code* (unusual in that it was not produced by the print publishers Random House). A similar arrangement was made for the same author's 2009 bestseller *The Lost Symbol*, available in abridged form on six CDs from Orion and in unabridged form on fourteen CDs from Whole Story Audiobooks, who also offer the unabridged version as a download.

Books which have also appeared in film form see an increase in audio sales, as with the *Harry Potter* titles, Tolkien's *Lord of the Rings* trilogy and C.S. Lewis's *Chronicles of Narnia* titles.

A single-voice recording for the library market will normally be of the full text of the book, which will be issued as a set of four to twelve CDs, currently priced at between £16.99 and £25.99. Payment for such rights is normally made on the basis of a royalty of $7\frac{1}{2}$–8%, based on the full price of the set of CDs. With the advent of downloadable audiobooks (see *Download services for audiobooks* later in this chapter, pp. 267–9) and podcasts, licensors will need to check whether they themselves clearly control such rights under the terms of the head contract and whether such rights should also be included in an audiobook licence.

Recordings sold to the general market are more likely to consist of an abridged text, although as mentioned earlier unabridged texts are now becoming more popular. An abridged version is normally contained on a set of no more than two CDs (currently priced at £6.99 to £17.99), although the playing time may vary. Royalty rates here are usually 10% or more depending on the title in question, but they are based on the price received by the audio company rather than the price paid by the end purchaser. Advance payments could range from £1,000 to £5,000, although an advance for a bestseller could be considerably higher. The recordings may be undertaken by the authors themselves (e.g. Bill Clinton reading *My Life*, Michael Palin or Alan Whicker reading their travel books, Alan Bennett reading his own *Untold Stories*, Richard Dawkins and his wife Lalla Ward reading *The Greatest Show on Earth* or William Shawcross reading his *Queen Elizabeth the Queen Mother*) or by an actor or actress – these have included Brad Pitt, Joseph Fiennes, Juliet Stevenson, Tim Pigott-Smith, Jude Law and Stephen Fry, as well as actors renowned for their range of voices such as Martin Jarvis and Miriam Margolyes. In the case of children's books, a short tape may be packaged in with the book itself.

In both the United Kingdom and the United States, many titles have now been released in both abridged and unabridged editions, with unabridged editions the strongest growth area. British producers have tackled unabridged versions of substantial projects such as Anthony Trollope's *Barchester Chronicles*, Anthony Powell's *A Dance to the Music of Time* and James Joyce's *Ulysses*.

Most audio publishers now offer the majority of titles in CD format; cassette sales have dwindled away. In some ways, CDs are a less suitable medium for audiobooks since their capacity (about seventy-five minutes as opposed to ninety minutes for a cassette) results in a need for more discs. In addition, CDs do not 'bookmark' the point where the listener interrupted their listening to enable them to resume listening at that point later. MP3 CDs are growing in popularity.

Download services for audiobooks

By mid-2009, 18 million households in the United Kingdom and 211 million households in the United States had access to broadband internet services, with a resulting rise in users accessing radio and television via the internet. The last five years have also seen a significant rise in purchases of MP3 players, particularly for the purpose of downloading music for access 'on the move' so that users can listen whilst walking, jogging or commuting. The Apple iPod and similar devices have become the accessory of choice for the young (by the end of 2009 it was estimated that over 220 million iPods had been sold worldwide), as have smart phones such as the Apple iPhone and other models which have the capacity to download music, audio and other applications.

All these developments have led to a perceived market for downloadable audiobooks. The pioneer in this area was Audible (www.audible.com). Founded in the United States in 1997 by author and journalist Donald Katz, this company predated and outlasted the controversial peer-to-peer file sharing music operations (see Chapter 23), and the dot.com collapse of 2000–1 and outlived its rival Audio Highway, which is now defunct. In 2001, the company was still running at a loss; by 2004, it was profitable and in January 2008 it was acquired by Amazon for a reputed price of $300 million, thus removing the need for competition with Amazon's own reported plans for an audio download service. At the time of writing it has arrangements with over 600 content providers, has over 400,000 subscribers and offers over 30,000 spoken word titles for download, including classic and modern fiction, business books, children's books, as well as magazines, radio content and podcasts. The ideal scenario is for Audible to be able to offer downloads to time in with the publication date of major trade hardback titles.

Downloads are to computers and to hand-held devices such as MP3 players and mobile phones. Audible has a content deal to supply titles to the iTunes service for the Apple iPod. It has partnerships with XM Satellite Radio and Texas Instruments which allow for downloads to radio and to an increasing range of mobile phones.

By mid-2005, Audible had set up operations in France and Germany and, in June 2005, in the UK (www.audible.co.uk). Currently, a monthly subscription to the AudibleListener programme at £7.99 (in the United States, $14.95 per month or $149.50 per annum) allows access to one audiobook per month.

There are other players in the audio download market. July 2005 saw the launch of Audioville UK (www.audioville.co.uk), which offers downloads of audiobooks (including tourist guides) and comedy sketches via a partnership with BBC Worldwide, as well as content from periodicals such as the *Economist*. Mid-2005 also saw the launch of Spoken Network (www.spokennetwork.co.uk), which offers titles for downloading to computers, smart phones and MP3 players (or to an iPod by first burning the audiobook to a CD to import via iTunes). Payment is on a per title basis rather than a monthly subscription. Simply Audiobooks (www.simplyaudiobooks.com) offers rentals of audio CDs as well as a download service; GoSpoken (www.gospoken.com) offers downloads to mobiles and eMusic (www.emusic.com) offers audio downloads as well as music. Naxos launched its Download Shop in 2006 and Silksoundsbooks.co, launched in 2007, employs major actors such as Judy Dench and Bill Nighy to make unabridged recordings for downloading to a computer; the recording can then be transferred on to an MP3 player. Other significant players include Talking Issues (www.talkingissues.com). In July 2009, Spotify, the music streaming service (see Chapter 23) announced its first audiobook download, Chris Anderson's *Free: The Future of a Radical Price*.

Thus far, there have been two possible payment models for the licensing of audio content to a company supplying audio content in download form; first, a royalty of 10–15% on net receipts for each download (although this can be affected by 'bundling' or special offers, so securing a minimum royalty guarantee would be advisable); alternatively, when content is sourced from publishers who have themselves invested in producing the original audio recording, the purchase of digital downloads from the publisher at a discount off the retail price of the physical product. In this case the publisher would then pay a royalty to the author on the discounted price for the download as per the head contract, rather than dividing a licence royalty with the author.

The question of Digital Rights Management (DRM) on audio downloads remains controversial. Audible employs a DRM system which enables purchasers to download to a PC or Mac and then transfer the content to an MP3 player or smart phone, or to burn the recording to a CD; however, it is not possible to e-mail the file to a friend. There is also a facility to pay for the content to be delivered direct to a device such as an iPhone. Most publishers with their own audiobook programmes initially employed DRM, but in 2008 Random House abandoned the practice and a number of other publishers followed suit, although at the time of writing BBC Audiobooks still maintain DRM for their content. Naxos use open source MP3 technology; they supply a zipped file containing the audio download and a PDF of the 'sleeve notes'. Audible maintains its DRM system is 'benign and flexible'; however, there is a general feeling that lessons from the music industry (see also Chapter 23), where DRM is perceived as a barrier and a factor in encouraging piracy, will lead to it eventually being abandoned.

Downloadable audiobooks are now one of the fastest growing sectors, although it is estimated that they still represent around 15% of the total audiobook market in the United Kingdom and around 21% in the United States. There have inevitably been concerns about piracy and the philosophy of 'everything on the internet should be free' has now extended to many websites offering downloads of the texts of complete books free of charge, not all of them in the public domain – titles range from trade bestsellers to college texts. J.K. Rowling has not yet allowed downloadable versions of her books, but many unauthorized versions in both print and audio form can be obtained from illegal streaming sites. Legitimate sites can offer protection in the form of coded content, and territorial restrictions can be controlled to a great extent by allowing access only to credit cards registered in the appropriate region.

The increased sales of audiobooks of high-profile titles and the advent of downloading for audiobooks have led to a shift in attitude amongst authors' agents, who are no longer so inclined to include audiobook rights automatically in the publisher's package of rights. In late 2005, the Society of Authors advised against authors agreeing to a block percentage share of revenue from such rights since much depends on who is investing in producing the audiobook version. Publishers with specialist audio divisions and specialist audiobook publishers argue that the cost is high – usually a minimum of £5,000 before the costs of duplication, marketing and distribution. Downloading carries no costs of storage of inventory and shipping, but involves the cost of encoding, uploading, rights management systems and running a website; publishers also stress that the margins on audio download sales are slim. It has been recommended that authors should receive a 50% share of download income if the service is supplied directly from the publisher's own website, but that for income from content licensed to companies such as Audible the publisher should receive an initial revenue stream of at least 50%, with the publisher retaining 10–20% before passing on the balance to the author.

Most authors reading their own books for audio versions produced by audio publishers independently from the print publisher normally receive a modest reading fee of several hundred pounds, and then a royalty rate commencing at about $2\frac{1}{2}\%$ based on the sum received by the audio publisher. If they record audiobooks for the original print publisher, they will usually receive a rather higher flat fee for the reading and then a contractual royalty on audiobook sales, often starting at around $7\frac{1}{2}\%$ of the publishers' net receipts from such sales.

A particular issue for audiobooks in the United Kingdom is that they still carry the full rate of VAT. The Audiobook Publishers Association, the Publishers Association and the Royal National Institute for the Blind (RNIB – see also Chapter 18) are lobbying for a reduced rate.

Video recording rights

These rights cover the use of a book as the basis for a video recording. DVDs (digital versatile discs) now dominate the market over VHS videotapes; most UK households now have DVD players or can play discs via computers. With prices for new releases ranging from £12.99 to £19.99, DVDs are more expensive than videotapes, which are still available but on a much reduced scale. DVDs are sold through a variety of outlets, including UK bookstores and music stores such as HMV, but are also available in retail chains such as W.H. Smith, as well as in supermarkets and service stations.

In addition to videos based on dramatized versions of books via the media of film and TV (see Chapter 21), books that might be exploited in video form are likely to be in non-fiction areas where a video could add a useful dimension to the information contained in the book, such as cookery, make-up, physical exercise or craftwork. Payment would normally be made on the basis of a royalty calculated on the sum received by the producer of the recording, rather than on the full price of the DVD.

In practice, what is more likely to happen is that a television programme or series may be based on the book, in which case video rights are likely to be granted as part of the television rights (see Chapter 21). Alternatively, the video may be based on a television series and a book only produced as a result of the series and licensed to the publisher by the television company.

Video recording rights for a film, stage production, television film or television series based on a book would normally be included in the grant of those rights; the aim should be to ensure that separate payment is made if a video version is issued. Whether the publisher controls any of these rights will of course depend on the terms of the head contract with the author.

Rental rights

Regulation 10 of the Copyright and Related Rights Regulations 1996 introduced a rental and lending right for sound and video recordings, as well as for electronic products such as software and CD-ROMs, on 1 December 1996; this requires an equitable remuneration to be paid to rightsholders and performers. In February 2007 an initiative was launched by the online audio retailer Audiobooksonline (www.audiobooksonline.co.uk). They offer a range of monthly subscription packages whereby customers can borrow from one to four audiobooks a month, ordering online and receiving and returning the audiobooks by post – similar to some DVD rental systems described in Chapter 21. Some audio publishers were reluctant to support this service as they felt the scheme would impact on core sales of audiobooks.

In February 2009, BBC Audiobooks signed an agreement with distributors OverDrive to facilitate downloads of a collection of 1,500 audio titles to borrowers in libraries in the United Kingdom, Ireland, Australia, New Zealand and South Africa.

The question of the inclusion of video rental rights in film contracts is covered in more detail in Chapter 21.

Dramatization and documentary rights

Stage, radio, television and film rights

These rights cover the right to make a dramatized version of a literary work through a variety of media: the stage, radio, television and cinematograph film. In recent years, it has become far less likely for these rights (in particular stage, television and film rights) to be held by the publishing house; they are more likely to be retained by the author's agent. For older books, books with less obvious potential for exploitation in these media and books where the author is not represented by an agent, the rights may well lie with the publishing house. It is therefore vital that the head contract be checked carefully before entering into any negotiations; even if the publisher is contractually entitled to handle such rights, it may still be necessary for the author to approve a deal or to be the signatory to a contract for audiovisual rights if the author remains the copyright owner, because of the stringent warranties required in this area of licensing.

With the exception of radio broadcasting by the BBC, these are areas where it is extremely difficult to provide definitive guidelines for levels of payment, since much depends on the project in question and the negotiating powers of buyer and seller. This is particularly true of film and television rights. A book that has been established as a bestseller will understandably have a higher value where these rights are concerned.

Stage rights

These may include the performance on the stage of a work already written in the form of a play, or the right to convert a work written as, say, a novel or short story into a play for performance.

The method and level of payment for such rights will depend greatly on the status of the author and the work and the nature of the application. It would certainly be unwise to grant an exclusive licence for theatrical rights in a work if the application comes from a schoolteacher who wishes to use the work as an end-of-term play.

For professional productions of a dramatized work, the basis of payment is normally a percentage of the gross box-office receipts; the percentage varies according to the nature of the work and the reputation of the author, but could be anything from 5% to 12%. The agreement in force between the Theatre Managers Association (TMA) and the Writers' Guild regulates the commission of stage plays by producers in the TMA, and some of its terms relating to the duration of licence, the type of venue in which a play can be performed and options to take the production on tour, to the West End or abroad, might usefully be adopted in a contract for the underlying rights deal.

Determination of the fee by reference to box-office receipts is sometimes applied to performances of amateur musicals. For amateur production of plays, payment is usually calculated on the basis of a fee per performance, perhaps in the region of £40–50, payable in advance of the performance licence is then issued for an agreed number of performances. Due acknowledgement should be made to the author, the work and its source in the programme. Another approach is to base the fee on 10% of the potential maximum box-office receipts. There is no standard way of negotiating this.

A survey of the London theatre over the last two years reveals that a number of shows have been based on books; these include several musicals (including the long-running *Les Misérables*, based on a Victor Hugo novel), stage productions based on books but also known as films (Truman Capote's *Breakfast at Tiffany's*, Patrick Below's satirical version of John Buchan's *The Thirty-Nine Steps* and the ill-fated musical productions of Margaret Mitchell's *Gone with the Wind* and J.R.R. Tolkien's *Lord of the Rings*), stage productions based on films (*The Lion King* and *Billy Elliot: The Musical*), stage productions better known as films but which first had their origins in fiction (*Guys and Dolls*, based on the short stories of Damon Runyon, and *The Shawshank Redemption*, based on a novella by Stephen King), as well as theatrical performances based on Wilkie Collins's *The Woman in White* (a musical), Susan Hill's *The Woman in Black* and Michael Morpurgo's *War Horse*. Seasonal performances at Christmas have included a revival of *Scrooge*, the musical based on Charles Dickens's *A Christmas Carol*, and stage versions of Spike Milligan's *Adolf Hitler: My Part in His Downfall*, Raymond Briggs's *The Snowman*, Francesca Simon's *Horrid Henry* stories, Philippa Pearce's *Tom's Midnight Garden*, as well as summer and Christmas performances of J.M. Barrie's *Peter Pan* and a Christmas season production of Dr Seuss's *The Cat in the Hat*. September 2009 saw a live performance in London's O2 Arena of *Ben Hur*, best known from the 1959 film starring Charlton Heston and based on the book by Lew Wallace.

Radio

As with single-voice readings (see Chapter 19), published literary material used by the BBC is paid for at an agreed rate; scales of payment are regularly renegotiated between the BBC and the Publishers Association together with the Society of Authors. Revised rates have been agreed for payment from 1 August 2009. The rights granted to the BBC include simultaneous broadcasting throughout the domestic services for the British Isles or throughout the world services in English or in foreign languages, broadcasting via the BBC's digital radio services and also non-simultaneous broadcasting throughout the domestic radio services: access may be by traditional radio or via the internet.

1 Domestic service
    Plays (per minute) £17.10
    Prose for dramatization (per minute) £13.33
2 World Service (English language) and BBC Digital Services originations
    Plays (per minute) £8.55
    Prose for dramatization (per minute) £6.66
3 Local radio
    Plays (per minute) £4.27
    Prose for dramatization (per minute) £3.32
    provided that local radio broadcasts syndicated over five or more local radio broadcasts shall be deemed as a domestic broadcast and the domestic services rate in (1) above shall apply.
4 World Service (foreign language)
    Translations of plays and prose shall be payable at two-thirds of the above rates payable to each of the translator and the original author (or to the publisher to be divided with the author as per the head contract).

The BBC has a standard form of contract for dramatic use of literary work, under which a non-exclusive licence is granted for a three-year period to broadcast the work either live or by means of recording on its radio services. Repeat broadcasts must take place within five years of the initial broadcast. Listeners can also use the internet to access on demand material broadcast during the previous seven days via the BBC iPlayer service. The licence also permits the BBC to translate, abridge or adapt the work for broadcasting purposes and to broadcast short extracts for 'trailer' purposes.

The BBC is also permitted to make or to authorize the making of audio recordings of programmes that can be distributed throughout the world; the recordings can be played to non-paying audiences and used in educational institutions.

No officially negotiated rates exist for the independent broadcasting companies, and payment would thus be by negotiation with the individual broadcasting company. Since the 1990 Broadcasting Act came into force on 1 January 1993, most independent radio stations have tended to reduce their speech output in favour of music, and the digital station Oneword Radio ceased to broadcast in January 2008 (see Chapter 19).

Television

As mentioned earlier, television rights in the works of well-established authors may now be retained for handling by the author's agent. However, there may well be cases where publishers are authorized to handle television rights, and an active rights department should explore the possibilities for exploitation by monitoring the types of work that lend themselves to adaptation through this medium. Details of British television production companies are listed in the *Writers' and Artists' Yearbook* and on the website of PACT (the Producers' Alliance for Cinema and Television) – www.pact. co.uk – and contact should also be made with appropriate departments and broadcasting companies. Not all producers are members of PACT so additional research is advisable.

When a copyright work is used in the medium of television, not as a single-voice reading (see Chapter 19) but as the basis of a dramatized play, film, series or serial, whether dramatized, animated or partially animated, the rate of payment is negotiable. It is impossible to give precise guidelines for the level of payment, as this depends on the status of the author, the budget of the broadcasting company or independent production company, and how attractive the project is to them. Following the introduction of the 1990 Broadcasting Act, the BBC and ITV companies were required to purchase 25% of their programming from independent production companies and this figure has risen in recent years; it is more common to have a back-end profit share, which provides the independents with more development money. A low-budget film for television will command a lower fee than that for a mini-series, which in turn will command a lower fee than that for a high-budget feature film. Mini-series are now less common; single features or two-parters are prevalent from time to time but go in and out of favour. In December 2005, the BBC broadcast a made-for-television film based on Gerald Durrell's 1956 autobiographical work *My Family and Other Animals*; the earlier BBC version in 1987 was a ten-part series. Broadcasters are more reluctant to take risks and may commission a one-off programme to test the characters and story – a 'back-door pilot'. However, mid-2005 saw a BBC three-part dramatization of William Golding's sea trilogy *Rites of Passage, Close Quarters* and *Fire Down Below* under the title of *To the Ends of the Earth*, while in late 2005 the BBC's sixteen-part adaptation of Charles Dickens's *Bleak House* in association with WGBH Boston drew major viewing figures. In 2006, the BBC showed a televised version of Zadie Smith's *On Beauty* and in 2009 a production of Andrea Levy's *Small Island*; 2008 saw a joint BBC/HBO production of a series based on Alexander McCall Smith's *The No. 1 Ladies' Detective Agency* series. In 2006 BBC4 showed a ninety-minute adaptation of Jean Rhys's *Wide Sargasso Sea*, her prequel to *Jane Eyre*; in 2007 FilmFour produced an adaptation of Monica Ali's *Brick Lane*. Sky has started offering drama, usually based on bestselling novels by writers such as Terry Pratchett and Martina Cole; a series based on the latter's *The Take* was shown in June 2009. In 2009 Channel 4 showed David Pearce's powerful *Red Riding* quartet and in 2010 ITV will broadcast the US series based on L.J. Smith's *The Vampire Diaries*. BBC2 is planning dramatized versions of Sarah Waters's *The Night Watch* and *Money* by Martin Amis.

The BBC does not operate on the basis of a fixed formula such as a calculation of the fee as a percentage of the production budget; fees generally range from under £10,000 to over £30,000. Payment of the initial fee is made half on signature of the contract and half on first transmission of the programme. A deal with the BBC will entail a licence of rights rather than a grant of copyright.

The Writers' Guild has three sets of officially negotiated terms on behalf of scriptwriters; these are with BBC Television, the ITV companies and PACT (for independent producers, who initially produced mainly for Channel 4 but who now produce for the BBC and ITV as well). Julian Friedmann's *How to Make Money Scriptwriting* (second edition, Intellect Books, 2000) provides valuable information on this area and the scriptwriting website www.TwelvePoint.com has articles about the business aspects of the industry, including adaptation.

The BBC has a number of specific terms in its contract to option books, some of which are listed below:

1 The author (or publisher, if rights are being handled by the publisher) will be required to grant the BBC an exclusive option on the television rights in the work, and this will include format and character rights – see item (4) below.
2 The BBC will require the right of first refusal to option on terms to be agreed in good faith later any further work by the author based on the same character or characters which may come into existence.
3 The BBC requests a twenty-year exclusive licence, to be non-exclusive thereafter. This would then permit for the licensing of the work to another company, if that company is prepared to proceed given the existence of the BBC version.
4 In addition to the basic right to make a programme or series, the BBC requires foreign-language rights, video rights of the programme or series in all formats, merchandising and changed format rights. Unless they are specifically excluded from the contract, changed format rights permit the BBC to make or to license the making of the work in another format – this could, for example, include locating the work in a country other than that in which the original was set. The BBC also

requires the right to make BBC-originated sequels, as well as the right to acquire author-originated sequels.

5 The usual reserved rights may still be retained by the author or the publisher acting on the author's behalf (e.g. literary publication rights, radio rights, stage rights and possibly theatrical (film) rights).

6 In return for the rights granted, the BBC will also pay repeat fees and royalties – see items (7) and (8).

7 Repeat fees are usually around 75% for a peak-time repeat and 50% for an off-peak repeat or a narrative repeat (a broadcast made within seven days of the initial broadcast).

8 Royalties are paid on sales of the programme (e.g. to overseas broadcasting companies) and are usually 1.5% of the BBC's gross receipts. However, receipts from changed format rights are divided 50/50 with the rightsholder after the BBC has deducted a 10% commission and any direct costs or subagent's commission. In the case of merchandising rights, the rightsholder will receive 30% of net monies received, although the BBC definition of 'net monies' is not advantageous to rights owners.

Fees paid by independent production companies (one of which is now ITV Productions) may be calculated as a percentage of the production budget for the project; the percentage could be in the region of 1–3%, and fees generally range from under £10,000 to £100,000. The calculation of the budget figure may exclude financing charges, insurance and contingency, and money paid to the author for the script or to the book author for the rights. It would be wise to avoid having overheads, legal fees or any other items included in this list of what are known as 'the usual exclusions'. Payment was traditionally made on the basis of an option fee of 10% of the purchase price, although the percentage now is frequently lower, closer to 5% or less. The option period, which was traditionally twelve months, renewable for a further twelve months, is now sometimes eighteen months. A total of three periods of twelve months, in which case the third option payment should not be deducted from or set against the final purchase (or exercise) price, or two periods of eighteen months is not uncommon. The final balance is paid on commencement of production when the final budget – the 'certified' budget – is known. In the case of a series or a serial, the purchase price may be formulated as £x per hour, with rates ranging from less than £2,500 per hour to £15,000 per hour.

In contracts with independent producers (ITV is now a broadcaster which takes drama from independent companies), the purchaser is more likely to acquire television, video and sometimes film rights by means of a partial assignment of copyright. Turnaround clauses may provide for these rights to revert if they are not exploited within agreed time limits (usually on repayment of some or all of the money paid to purchase the rights in the first place; this is an area where skilled and experienced negotiation can make a significant difference to the deal).

On the whole, a deal done with an independent production company producing for the BBC or for ITV will be more lucrative than a deal done directly with the television company. However, if the production is dependent on the raising of finance by the independent producer, there could be a greater risk of the production not starting than if it were wholly owned by the television company. In most cases, the level of fee will be influenced by the status of the book that is being acquired for adaptation; for example, payments are lower for a first novel than for a new novel by a well-established author. Adaptation of a novel for television is likely to be undertaken by a professional scriptwriter rather than by the original author.

A contract with a broadcaster is likely to include rights to make simultaneous or non-simultaneous broadcasts of the work through any or all of its transmitters, usually within a three-year period of the signing of the contract. Repeat fees (usually between 50% and 100% of the original fee) must be paid each time the programme is rebroadcast. If the purchase price includes a 'buy-out', this replaces repeat fees; this type of arrangement is more common with independent producers under the PACT agreement, and is between 100% and 200% of the purchase price.

Television has often proved a major medium for the dramatization of novels written much earlier; many classics are of course now out of copyright and do not require a licence, and can draw substantial viewing figures, as for the 2005 BBC version of Charles Dickens's *Bleak House*; 2009 saw a dramatization of Jane Austen's *Emma*. Other novel-based television productions have included the hugely popular 1981 version of Evelyn Waugh's 1945 novel *Brideshead Revisited*, two versions of John Galsworthy's *The Forsyte Saga* in 1967 and 2002, the 1984 production of Paul Scott's *Raj Quartet* as *The Jewel in the Crown*, the production of Anthony Powell's twelve-volume work *A Dance to the Music of Time* (published between 1951 and 1975) and, more recently, several popular series of *Monarch of the Glen*, based on Compton Mackenzie's Highland novels. More controversial topics can now be tackled on television, as in the dramatized versions of *Tipping the Velvet* and *Fingersmith* by Sarah Walters and Alan Hollinghurst's *The Line of Beauty*.

After a rather disappointing version of C.S. Lewis's *The Lion, the Witch and the Wardrobe* on television in 1988, CGI (computer-generated imagery) and more sophisticated animation techniques have enabled children's books to be brought more successfully to the television screen, as in the 2004 three-part version of Raymond Briggs' *Fungus the Bogeyman*.

Terry Pratchett's *Discworld* novel *The Hogfather* was shown as two two-hour films on Sky 1 over Christmas 2006. In 2009 CITV broadcast a series based on Francesca Simon's *Horrid Henry* series; BBC1 broadcast

Horrible Histories, based on the books by Terry Deary and Martin Brown, as well as Aardman Animations' version of Julia Donaldson's bestselling *The Gruffalo.* The BBC also has options to film all Arthur Ransome's novels; *Swallows and Amazons* was last filmed in 1974.

A contract with the BBC usually provides for a dubbed foreign-language soundtrack to be added, or foreign-language subtitles. A successful mini-series for the BBC or commercial channels such as that based on Michael Dobbs's *House of Cards* can generate revenue from foreign sales that is several times higher than the original purchase price; the various series based on the crime novels of Ellis Peters (the *Brother Cadfael* series), John Mortimer's *Rumpole of the Bailey* titles, and works by Ruth Rendell, P.D. James, Ian Rankin, Reginald Hill (*Dalziel and Pascoe*), Elizabeth George (*Inspector Lynley*), Caroline Graham (*Midsomer Murders*) and Colin Dexter (*Inspector Morse*) also earn substantial sums from sales abroad and from video recordings (see *Video* later in this chapter, p. 279). The year 2008 saw the launch by the BBC of an occasional series based on Swedish author Henning Mankell's *Wallander* series; BBC4 has also shown episodes of the original Swedish television series.

The BBC currently acquires rights for a period of twenty years to transmit or to license the transmissions of telerecordings of the work throughout the world. Viewers can also see BBC programmes broadcast during the previous through the iPlayer service via the internet; this service was launched in December 2007. A BBC licence is of course required for normal terrestrial television viewing and for viewing ptogrammes over the internet at the same time as they are broadcast. Channel 4 and Channel Five both launched similar services in 2006 (4oD and Five Download). ITV Player offers a thirty-day catch-up service.

Video-on-demand (VoD) now has a significant user base. An experimental VoD service was first launched as early as 1994; this was the Cambridge Interactive TV trial which provided content from BBC and Anglia Television to 250 homes and schools connected to the Cambridge Cable Network, but the project closed in 1996. An integrated internet access and broadcast TV service via a set-top box was launched by Kingston Communications in 1998, followed by HomeChoice in the London area; the latter operation was bought by Tiscali in 2006. Cable providers Telewest and NTL (now Virgin Media) both launched VoD services in 2005; BskyB launched its SkyAnytime on PC service in January 2006. Plans for a collaborative venture between BBC Worldwide, ITV and Channel 4 for a broadband VoD service under the working name of Kangaroo failed when it was blocked by the Competition Commission in January 2009; the technology was subsequently acquired by Arqiva, the Winchester-based owner of six Freeview groups and of the UK's 1,100 television and radio masts; at the time of writing, it plans to relaunch a VoD service, offering the back catalogue of the three broadcasting organizations.

Commercial recordings

Video

Television companies may also wish to market physical copies of video recordings of popular programmes or series that they have broadcast. For some years, the dominant medium was videotape, but DVDs now dominate the market, with Sony's BluRay format having won the battle against the rival HD-DVD format originally favoured by Toshiba and Microsoft.

It is now likely that a BBC contract for the use of dramatized literary material on television will include the right to make and sell video recordings of the material. Payment for such rights is normally made on the basis of a royalty, the level of which varies. Royalties are calculated on the net invoice value of the video recording rather than on the full retail price. Arrangements are similar for material sold by the commercial television channels, although these may be packaged by an outside video firm. The Writers' Guild of Great Britain website has figures for writers (rather than books), but these are interesting as a yardstick.

Sound

These are commercial sound recordings based on material originally licensed for use on radio or television. The BBC publishes, through BBC Worldwide, sound recordings of popular radio and television programmes, some of which may have been based on previously published literary works; some cassettes are still available but the main medium is now that of the CD. A common package would be a set of two cassettes or CDs with a running time of three hours. A separate licence agreement is required if these rights are not included in the original broadcasting contract. Payment is made to the licensor on the basis of a royalty calculated on the price paid by the dealer; the reader or performers also receive an ongoing royalty.

Cinematographic film rights

The area of film rights is complex and it is therefore difficult to give definitive guidelines. Although some years ago rights might have been sought to make a film for showing only in cinemas, film studios today are also heavily involved in television production, and the range of rights sought is therefore much wider. It would be almost impossible for most European production companies to finance the cost of many of today's cinema films without involvement in and investment from television. Even the giant American studios will wish to exploit all audiovisual media in order to generate maximum revenue from the property.

Publishers and literary agents representing authors whose works are likely candidates for this form of adaptation are often in regular touch with scouts for the major studios and independent production companies. Details of British film production companies are listed in the *Writers' and Artists' Yearbook* and on PACT's website (www.pact.co.uk). The importance attached to the exploitation of literary works is evidenced by the facilities now provided for film and television producers to meet publishers and agents at the Frankfurt, London and Bologna book fairs (see Chapter 8). Nevertheless, it may be that the first intimation comes in the form of an unsolicited letter expressing interest in acquiring film rights in a project. Many publishers have no experience in this field and will need to take specialist outside advice. Applications could come from established film studios, independent production companies or individuals to whom the project appeals; these could include experienced producers, scriptwriters or actors – for example, film rights in Audrey Niffenegger's debut novel, *The Time Traveler's Wife*, were originally acquired by Brad Pitt and his then wife, Jennifer Aniston. Beware of 'shopping around', when producers who have not acquired the film rights to a book seek finance from the industry and broadcasters. Allowing free or very modest option fees can result in a property becoming 'shop soiled' if the producer is not credible; the industry may reject the proposal because of the producer who claims to hold the option, even if in principle the project is attractive.

Film rights in what is termed the 'underlying work' are normally acquired on an option basis (i.e. an option to purchase the relevant rights). An exclusive option for a period of time is granted, during which the would-be producer will investigate all the necessary aspects – finance, availability of a suitable director, screenwriter, location and actors – in order to establish whether a film would be viable. The knowledge that a major actor is interested in a lead role can be crucial in securing finance, distribution channels and so forth.

Tolstoy, after being shown a short film in the early years of cinema, wrote:

> You will see that this little clicking contraption with the revolving handle will make a revolution in our life – in the life of writers. It is a direct attack on the old methods of literary art. We shall have to adapt ourselves to the shadowy screen and the cold machine. A new form of writing will be necessary – but I rather like it.

It has been estimated that in any one year approximately one-third of all films produced in Hollywood are based on previously published literary works; over 40% of the Oscars awarded for best picture are based on novels, as opposed to about 28% based on original screenplays. The late 1990s saw something of a craze for 'Britlit' after the success of a number of films based on British literary works, including several costume dramas based on classics such as Jane Austen's *Sense and Sensibility*. Although many classic works are in the public domain, the extension of copyright duration within the EEA and the United States and the revival of copyright in some works from Berne member countries in the United States mean that the copyright status of underlying works must be very carefully checked. The proportion of films based on literary works should be seen in the context that between 5% and 10% of options are exercised and of those perhaps one in ten finally proceeds to production; television options have a higher success rate than film options. Since options should be paid for rather than granted free of charge, the income is nevertheless welcome.

Increasingly producers are attempting to get free or notional (£1) options. It is doubtful that a producer who cannot raise even £500 for a twelve-month option will be able to attract production finance. If possible hold out for 5% of the purchase price. Saying no to a poor offer sometimes results in a better one, so do some bluffing.

Nowadays it is unlikely that film rights in the work of a major author will be controlled by the publishing house. These rights are likely to be handled by the author's agent and may be the subject of an auction. The sale of film rights in some literary works has generated substantial sums.

It is so unlikely for an author to receive a share of the box-office receipts or gross profit that one should assume that it is not negotiable except in very special circumstances; J.K. Rowling is believed to receive 1% of the box-office receipts for the *Harry Potter* films. In 2009 the trust representing the estate of J.R.R. Tolkien and HarperCollins, publishers of the *Lord of the Rings* trilogy, reached a settlement with New Line Productions to enforce payment of a share of the gross receipts from the highly successful Warner Brothers films. Authors may be able to obtain a small percentage of the net profit that is paid to the producer after all other parties' shares of the profits have been allocated. The producer's share may be as low as 5–10% of the gross (i.e. 100% of the profits); 5% of the producer's share may therefore be the equivalent of $\frac{1}{4} - \frac{1}{2}$% of the gross. However, the producer's share may go up to 50% of the gross, in which case a share of the producer's profit could represent a significant amount of money.

In some cases the author may have an additional involvement as screenwriter for his or her own novel (as John Irving did for the 1999 film of *The Cider House Rules*), but this is rare as the skills required for each medium are very different.

The question of ownership of film rights is crucial as, if the project is to go ahead, substantial sums of money will be involved. If an expression of interest is received, the first step is to establish who controls the rights, and this will necessitate checking the head contract with the author. In the case of older works, it is necessary to establish whether the work is still in copyright in the relevant markets, especially if there is a discrepancy in the term of protection (see *Copyright legislation in the United Kingdom* and *Copyright legislation in the United States* in Chapter 1). In older contracts, the rights may not have been mentioned specifically, but a publisher may have been granted publishing rights 'and all other rights pertaining to the work', or 'all other rights in the work which exist or which may hereafter come into existence'; in both cases, film rights would be included. However, it is also important to check whether such rights are still controlled by the publisher, even if they were granted by full assignment in the head contract. This is because of the provision in the 1911 UK Copyright Act which may mean that although the work is still protected under UK copyright law, control of the rights has reverted to the author's estate twenty-five years after their death (see Chapter 9). The 1998 US Sonny Bono Copyright Term Extension Act also made amendments to the provisions for reversion of rights in US works (see Chapter 1).

Even if film rights are not controlled by the publisher and the application must be referred elsewhere, it is likely that the publisher will be asked to sign a quitclaim confirming that although they are the publisher of the underlying work, they have no direct financial interest in the film, television rights and allied rights (other than straight reading rights of the text). This quitclaim is required by the company acquiring the rights from the copyright owner or the copyright owner's agent. The publisher will also be required to confirm that they will raise no objection to the publication of short extracts from the book on which the film is based, provided that they are used for the purpose of publicizing the film and used only in the context of press notices, trade journals or fan magazines. A maximum number of words that can be used in this context should be specified in the quitclaim; this could be up to 10,000 words, although it might be reduced to 5,000 words in the case of a very short work or a children's book. Publishers should insist on a full credit for the title of the book, the author and the publishing company, especially if the film has a different title from that of the original book.

A company seeking film rights will place considerable importance on verifying the unencumbered chain of title to the rights because of the potential level of investment involved. All too often rights have been sought for an older work, only to find that they were encumbered by the existence of a document tying up film rights elsewhere, even if the film was never made.

If a publisher has control of film rights under anything less than a full assignment of copyright from the author (for example through an exclusive licence of rights that includes control of film and television rights), it is advisable to obtain a supplementary document from the author to obtain a full grant of those rights, and for the publisher to be designated in the film contract as the agent for the author. In practice, if the author has maintained the copyright in his or her own name, it will be the author who has to sign the contractual documents.

One aspect of film rights that can pose difficulties for publishers without experience is that the full price is negotiated from the start, even though there is no guarantee that production of the film will actually go ahead. This means that the worth of the rights must be assessed at the start, and there may be a fear of negotiating too low a price in relation to the budget of the film.

When film rights are acquired, an option is granted for which payment will be made at a percentage of the total price agreed for the rights; 10% is a desirable rate, but the figure can be lower. One possibility if the percentage figure is lower (e.g. 3–5%) would be to negotiate an additional payment to be made at a later stage, e.g. an additional £5,000 on the first day of principal photography. The general rule is that if a producer pays less than the going rate on the earlier option payments, they will usually agree to pay more at the 'back end', i.e. closer to the time of production of the film. There are so many small production companies with relatively little access to funding that it is preferable to deal with companies that have both a good reputation and also a regular track record in producing films for the cinema or programmes for television.

The total price paid for the rights in the underlying work (the purchase price) may be set as a percentage of the total budget or production costs envisaged for the film – perhaps in the region of $1\frac{1}{2}$–$2\frac{1}{2}$%. A similar percentage will normally be allowed for the script. The total budget or production costs will in turn depend on the reputation of the author, the financial clout of the organization acquiring the rights (a major Hollywood studio or a small independent production company), the status of the director, the availability of key actors and other factors.

For the grantor of the film rights, the first step should therefore be to establish the likely level of those figures. Thus the budget for a film could be agreed to be (say) £1 million; the fee could then be agreed as 2% of that figure or of the certified budget (only available at the point when production – the first day of principal photography – actually starts). The certified budget figure will be provided by the accountants of the production company and is used when dealing with financiers, co-producers and insurance companies. There are three stages of payment: the option fee, the exercise price (also known as the minimum guaranteed purchase price) and the principal photography fee (the full or maximum purchase price), which tops up the exercise price to the negotiated percentage of the budget when the final budget for the film is known at the actual start of production. In this way, the cost of rights rises with the cost of the film, but it is usually subject to a floor (the exercise price – as much as can be negotiated) and a ceiling (also as much as can be negotiated – it can be two or three times the floor or higher).

A deal is often put together in the following way: an option of £x, an exercise price of £y, or 2% (or whatever percentage is negotiated) of the budget, whichever is higher, less finance costs, completion bond, contingency and money paid to the author (these are known as the usual exclusions). The £y figure will normally be less than the principal photography (or full) purchase price, although in theory it could be the same if the budget of the film is actually less than was anticipated.

It is common for film producers to offer additional payment based on the net profits of the film; this may sound attractive, but it should be borne in mind that most films do not make a profit and for those that do it may be difficult to establish exactly what profits are made. If payment is to be made on this basis, it is crucial to have expert advice on the definition of net profits. In practice they are the gross receipts derived from exploitation of the film in all relevant media granted, less the cost of production (including the cost of financing), the cost of distribution (including fees, commission and expenses) and deferments (payments usually deferred to what would normally be first profits, and dependent on the success of the film). Expenses include prints and advertising, known as 'P&A'. These tend to be the main costs of distribution and marketing and can be higher than the production budget of the film. The overall definition of net profits should, however, be spelled out as fully as possible in the contract, and should always use the same definition as is used for everyone else involved; if there are variations, they should be the same as in the most favourable definition of profits.

The option fee should be a non-returnable advance to be set against the full purchase price of the rights, and is normally granted initially for a period of one year to eighteen months. Contractual provision may be made for the option period to be extended (after giving due notice) for a further period of a year or eighteen months. In this case, a further option payment must be made *pro rata*, although this may not be set against the final purchase price but regarded as additional fees as compensation for delaying the decision on whether to go ahead with the project. In no case should an option be granted free of charge; if necessary, insist on an additional 'back-end' payment. It is advisable to secure agreement that the second option payment is not set against (deducted from) the purchase price. A third option – if there is one – definitely should not be deducted from the purchase price. It is also preferable for each successive option price to increase, e.g. if the first option payment is £1,000, the second could be £1,500 and the third £2,000. This can be justified by arguing that the longer the property is off the market, the less attractive the situation is for the copyright owner as they are earning very little and the project runs the risk of becoming 'shop soiled'.

If a nominal option fee of £1 is offered, seek instead a reasonable option fee of, say, from £1,000 to £5,000 for twelve or eighteen months, but agree to defer all but £1 until such time as the producer signs a coproduction or finance deal with a third party on the project, or receives subsidy funding from a body such as the UK Film Council or any of the regional film bodies. Agreeing to a deferred option imposes on the producer the task of securing the deferred amount for the licensor, since they will have to show the contract to a third party in order to secure a deal.

The document covering the granting of film rights is normally in two parts: the option agreement and the assignment; such a document with a major studio could be fifty pages long, in which all terms are agreed at the time the option is negotiated and signed. The latter document will not be signed unless the option is taken up, although each page is sometimes initialled at the time the option document is signed. The option agreement specifies the sum that is to be paid for the option, the period of time that this covers and what rights are being optioned exclusively. During that time, the company has the exclusive right to make any adaptations to the work that may be necessary, for example preparation of a screenplay. No filming can go ahead, however, until the option has been actually exercised.

While the option document spells out the main rights on which the option is being taken, it may also cross-reference a more detailed list of rights contained in the assignment document. The film company will seek the widest possible grant of film, television and allied rights; it may, however, be crucial to establish from the start what type of production is envisaged, particularly in the case of a children's book, which might be produced in animated, partly animated or in traditional dramatic form.

The grantor will be required to give stringent warranties confirming ownership of the rights and that the work does not infringe any copyright and is not obscene, indecent, defamatory or libellous. Indemnities against action arising from such aspects will have to be given to the film company, and it will therefore be necessary to check carefully the warranties provided by the author in the original head contract. This aspect of the deal is vital, since the production company may be unable to secure finance and, more particularly, insurance (without which production cannot commence) without such warranties. This can prove problematic in cases where the production company requires a full warranty that all facts contained in a book are true; the author may only be able to warrant that they are true to the best of his or her knowledge or belief. Deals can be lost on this basis.

If a deal is to go ahead, the publisher or agent acting on behalf of the author should insist on a reverse warranty – a guarantee that if the production company changes any aspect of the book in the film and that change results in any form of legal action, the production company will indemnify the publisher and/or the author against such action.

Film contracts normally provide a clause allowing the purchaser to assign their option or exercise rights to a third party, and this may be necessary to secure financial backing. Were such an assignment to take place without undertakings from the third party to perform the assignor's obligations to the grantor, the grantor would have no contractual nexus with the assignee. In the event that the assignee went bankrupt, the grantor would not be able to claim payment from the assignor even if the film subsequently went into production. Thus it is essential to provide that no assignment of rights can be made without the assignee directly covenanting to the grantor that it will discharge all the assignor's obligations or (preferably) that it will enter into a new contract with the grantor (a novation) embodying the terms of the contract with the original producer.

Assignment to a bona fide bank as surety for being lent money will have to take place without a direct covenant or novation. Banks will not enter into such arrangements. However, where producers assign to other producers or distributors, it is essential to insist on some form of undertaking from the assignee. Do not believe them when they say that this will hinder the assignment; it is extremely unlikely to be true, even if the assignee believes it to be so. In the case of a deal with a major studio, a direct covenant is desirable but not as necessary.

The assignment document is attached to the option agreement. This spells out in detail the rights to be acquired, which will almost certainly be for the full term of copyright. The rights will include not only the right to adapt and produce the work in the form of a feature cinematograph film for initial theatrical exhibition, but also the right to broadcast the film on television, including broadcasting on pay TV, through a cable service, a satellite broadcasting service or via the internet, and the production and sale of video recordings of the film on DVD – these rights are now all infinitely more valuable than they were some years ago, and the copyright holder will receive their share through their profit participation arrangement. The question of a broader range of electronic rights now arises; companies may seek rights for any recording in interactive format and the right to present the film publicly 'by all means now known or hereinafter to be invented'. With the advent of video-on-demand, cable and satellite transmission and the internet may all be used to enable subscribers to dial up and view a film at a time of their own choosing on a variety of platforms – via a television set, a computer, a portable media player or a mobile phone.

To date, the movie studios have not chosen to supply download services directly from their own websites, partly to avoid alienating major DVD retailers such as Walmart and also because of concerns about piracy; the Motion Picture Association of America currently estimates that illegal downloads and streaming of films account for approximately 40% lost revenue annually, and 2008 saw DVD film sales fall to the lowest level in five years. A host of legitimate intermediate services have been established to supply legitimate VoD, with a significant and negative effect on traditional video rental companies like Blockbuster; the latter has undertaken a number of initiatives to enter the VoD market and is likely to close nearly 1,000 'bricks and mortar' rental stores in 2010. In the United States, there are a number of different models: Time Warner provides a film-on-demand service via its own television channel, Disney's MovieBeam service allows users to access Disney and Warner Brothers movies via their set-top box, and Movielink and 4Flix.Net offer downloads of films and television programmes. Netflix also offers a streaming service to computers or televisions in the United States. It also offers a rental service which enables customers to order a movie online; a DVD is supplied and then returned by mail. Amazon launched a service in 2006 in the United States as Amazon Unbox (now Amazon Video on Demand), which enables customers to view video content via the Unbox video player, via Windows Media Player, on the Xbox 360 or via mobile devices, with a subscription model or pay-per-view. BitTorrent, best known as a peer-to-peer operation, offers a legal download service for video and music content on a pay-per-item basis, allowing customers to store the content for up to thirty days. There are a number of services for film and television content in the United Kingdom (see *Television* earlier in this chapter, p. 278). Sky Box Office provides a service for viewing films via a set-top box, with orders placed over the telephone. BT Vision offers a range of packages to BT broadband subscribers, including a monthly subscription service for films and television programmes or a pay-per-view arrangement for individual items. LoveFilm offers an online service as well as a rental service for DVDs supplied and returned by mail. In November 2008 supermarket chain Tesco launched its Tesco Digital Download service for film and television programmes.

The studios are, however, considering more direct supply of content online in view of falling DVD sales; in late 2009, Disney announced that it had developed Keychest, a system to track digital ownership. The main challenge is how to allow legitimate customers to play video recordings on a range of devices whilst preventing them from transmitting them to unauthorized users. There is speculation that Disney may partner with Apple to facilitate delivery to computers, mobile phones and via cable VoD services. A consortium of the other studios is working with companies including Comcast and Intel to reach a common set of standards and formats, in an initiative named the Digital Entertainment Content Ecosystem (DECE).

The European Directive on Rental and Lending Rights of 19 November 1992 came into force in the United Kingdom from 1 December 1996 via Regulation 10 of the Copyright and Related Rights Regulations (see *Copyright legislation in the United Kingdom* in Chapter 1). The intention is to provide authors and performers with a fair and continuing remuneration from later exploitation of their work; an obvious area here is that of video rentals and video-on-demand services. This right was strongly opposed by the film industries on both sides of the Atlantic. Payment is required for rental arrangements entered into after 12 January 1997 and applies to film agreements entered into before 1 April 1994, provided that the owner of the rental right (be it the author or an agent or publisher acting on behalf of the author) had notified the film production company prior to 1 January 1997 that they intended to exercise the new rental right in the work. In the absence of anything to the contrary, it will be assumed that rental rights were included in the grant of film rights, but any new film contracts entered into should clearly specify loan or rental rights in the rights granted. The source of payment to the copyright owner will be the film company, rather than the rental outlets themselves.

The assignment document should also make provision for payment for prequels, sequels and remakes; these could be payable at 50–100% of the rate for the initial film. A clear distinction must be drawn between prequels and sequels based on original literary works by the author as opposed to spin-off films generated entirely by the film company, where money should still be paid as if it were an author-generated prequel or sequel. The usual offer is $33\frac{1}{3}$% of what was paid the first time for a remake and 50% for a sequel. For many reasons this is not an attractive deal – the film company would hardly wish to undertake the exercise if the initial and more risky film had been a flop. Inflation makes the finite sum even less since remakes and sequels are normally made some years later; the industry norm is $2–2\frac{1}{2}$% for underlying rights, so why should such a drop be justified? If possible, aim for a compromise of $1\frac{2}{3}$% of the budget of the new film – specify that it could be a deal-breaker; with strong negotiating skills, success may be possible.

The film company will also expect ancillary rights, including merchandising rights (see Chapter 22) and the right to exploit music connected with the film in soundtrack recordings. In some cases, it may wish to publish 'the book of the film', illustrated with stills, although if the underlying work is a novel this would have to be confined to a book on how the film was made. In the case of original film scripts, there may be a possibility of exploiting 'novelization' rights, but novelization of a film loosely based on an original work of fiction must be refused.

Merchandising rights are an increasingly important element of the negotiation, especially in the case of a highly visual children's book; merchandising rights allied to films such as those of A.A. Milne's *Winnie the Pooh*, J.K. Rowling's *Harry Potter* novels and J.R.R. Tolkien's *Lord of the Rings* trilogy have proved extremely valuable (see Chapter 22). Merchandising revenue from films based on characters from comics such as Batman and Spider-Man can exceed takings at the box office. Ideally, income from this source should be accounted for as a separate stream, but in practice this may prove difficult to achieve. Income may be set against production costs and other items listed earlier, and hence become part of the overall deal, with the original rightsholder receiving their share by means of their profit participation.

The assignment agreement will spell out the full payment for the property against which the initial option payment will be set. The full balance (the 'consideration') may fall due when the option is exercised; this can take place at any time during the option period, but no production is permitted prior to exercise. It is, however, more likely that the payment will be made in instalments, with payment dates usually expressed both in terms of a calendar period and a stage of production, e.g. '£x on exercise or on the first day of principal photography, whichever is sooner'. This aims to ensure payment if principal photography is delayed or does not take place at all.

It should be noted that principal photography without exercise of the option is a breach of copyright because the right to commence production of the film should only pass (if that is what the agreement achieved) to the producer on exercise of the option, i.e. the actual purchase of the rights under option. There is usually a clause in the agreement to the effect that non-payment does not normally entitle the rightsholder to injunct the production. It is therefore very advisable to include wording to the effect that copyright does not pass and exercise does not take place (and thus the rights granted on exercise do not pass to the purchaser) until the purchase price has been received.

If the option is exercised, the grantor will be required to deliver an executed engrossment of the assignment document. A counterpart will then be executed by the film company and returned to the grantor. Assignment documents should contain provision that the rights acquired on exercise will revert to the grantor if the film has not gone into production within, say, five years of the date of exercise. This is sometimes expressed as reversion or the right of buy-back. Ideally, nothing should be paid on reversion. Frequently, the deal is that the rights can be bought back at any time after the reversion date for the exercise price or a percentage thereof; this figure is negotiable. Argue against paying back any more than was paid and dig your heels in.

It is rare for any but authors of the highest international standing to be able to secure the right of creative approval for a film, although it may be possible in some cases; Douglas Gresham, one of the stepsons of C.S. Lewis, was heavily involved in advising on the making of the films in the *Narnia* sequence. The medium of film is very different from that of the novel, and major rewriting may be required in terms of telescoping, expanding or rearranging the time sequence of the story. Action may be slowed down or (more likely) speeded up; characters may be added, subtracted or combined for the purposes of the plot. The requirements of the medium are therefore unlikely to preserve the integrity aspect of an author's moral rights, and this must be recognized from the start. Most film contracts require what is in effect a waiver of the author's moral rights of integrity, a step permitted under UK copyright legislation (moral rights do not exist in US copyright legislation). However, it should be remembered that the legislation of the countries of continental Europe, with their *droit moral* tradition, do not permit the waiver of moral rights.

The final version of a film may bear little resemblance to the underlying work, and there have been a number of cases where authors were so distressed by the treatment of their work that they required that their name be removed from the credits. It is therefore vital to make provision for this possibility in the contract. It has been known for film companies to acquire rights in a book in order to use only the title, or to use the personality of one character from the story in the context of a very different plot, or even to keep the property off the market and prevent anyone else from basing a competing film on it.

There is a school of thought in the film industry that the best films are based on books that are not of the highest literary merit. The 1995 film based on Robert James Waller's novella *The Bridges of Madison County* (which starred Clint Eastwood and Meryl Streep) is generally thought to be far superior to the original book. A strong storyline by a popular writer often makes for a better film, as in the 1997 film of James Ellroy's *LA Confidential* and the 2006 film of the same author's *The Black Dahlia*. A book on an unusual theme by a less well-known writer may also appeal, as evidenced by the $3 million paid for film rights in Nicholas Evans's first novel, *The Horse Whisperer*. A standard of writing that could win its author a major literary prize may stand in the way of making a good film, although there have been a significant number of exceptions to this maxim in recent years. These include J.M. Ballard's *Empire of the Sun*, Thomas Keneally's *Schindler's Ark* (known in the US and on film as *Schindler's List*), Kazuo Ishiguro's *The Remains of the Day* and Michael Ondaatje's *The English Patient* (which won eight Oscars). The last few years have seen productions of Frank McCourt's autobiographical *Angela's Ashes*, John Irving's *The Cider House Rules*, David Guterson's Pulitzer prizewinning novel *Snow Falling on Cedars*, *Captain Corelli's Mandolin* by Louis de Bernières, Graham Swift's *Last Orders* (a Booker Prize winner), Sebastian Faulks's *Charlotte Gray*, Michael Cunningham's *The Hours*, William Trevor's *My House in Umbria*, Ian McEwan's *Enduring Love* and *Atonement*, Khaled Hosseini's *The Kite Runner*, Giles Foden's *The Last King of Scotland* (a Whitbread Prize winner) and John Le Carré's *The Constant Gardener* – Le Carré's works have been consistently produced in film or television form over the years. However, the record for adaptations is probably still held by W. Somerset Maugham, with over ninety versions of his works for film or television.

A survey of the last few years confirms that a substantial proportion of films successful at the box office have been based on published works. The year 2003 brought Peter Weir's *Master and Commander: The Far Side of the World*, based on the Aubrey Maturin novels by Patrick O'Brian, Clint Eastwood's version of *Mystic River* by Dennis Lehane, *I, Robot*, based on the work by Isaac Asimov, and films based on Tracy Chevalier's *Girl with a Pearl Earring* and Charles Frazier's *Cold Mountain*. The year 2004 saw Clint Eastwood's *Million Dollar Baby*, based on *Rope Burns*, a short story by F.X. O'Toole, and Martin Scorsese's *The Aviator*, whose screenplay was inspired by *Howard Hughes: The Untold Story* by Peter Henry Brown and Pat H. Broeske. Films in 2005 included a version of Frank Miller's graphic novel *Sin City*, John Le Carré's *The Constant Gardener*, Anthony Swofford's *Jarhead: A Marine's Chronicle of the Gulf War*, Arthur Golden's *Memoirs of a Geisha*, J.K. Rowling's *Harry Potter and the Goblet of Fire* and C.S. Lewis's *The Lion, the Witch and the Wardrobe*, the first book in his seven-volume *Chronicles of Narnia*.

The year 2006 saw film versions of Athol Fugard's *Tsotsi*, Zoe Heller's *Notes on a Scandal*, Dan Brown's *The Da Vinci Code* and Lauren Weisberger's *The Devil Wears Prada*. The year 2007 brought *There Will Be Blood* (based on Upton Sinclair's novel *Oil!* and a winner of two Oscars), Robert Ludlum's *The Bourne Ultimatum*, Neil Gaiman's fantasy *Stardust*, a version of Frank Miller's graphic novel *300* and *Away from Her*, based on Canadian writer Alice Munro's short story *The Bear Came over the Mountain*. In 2008 there were films based on Cormac McCarthy's *No Country for Old Men* (an Oscar winner for Best Picture), Stan Lee's graphic novel *Iron Man*, John Boyne's *The Boy in the Striped Pyjamas*, Philippa Gregory's *The Other Boleyn Girl*, Stephenie Meyer's vampire novel *Twilight*, and *Slumdog Millionaire*, based on Vikas Swarup's novel *Q & A* and a surprise Oscar winner for Best Picture in 2009. The year 2009 saw films of Cornelia Funke's *Inkheart*, Dan Brown's *Angels and Demons*, John Grogan's *Marley and Me*, Jodie Picoult's *My Sister's Keeper*, Audrey Niffenegger's *The Time Traveler's Wife*, Dave Gibbons's graphic novel *Watchmen*, Cormac McCarthy's *The Road*, J.M. Coetzee's *Disgrace*, Stephenie Meyer's *Twilight* sequel *New Moon*, Robert Kaplow's *Me and Orson Welles*, Christopher Isherwood's *A Single Man* and J.K. Rowling's *Harry Potter and the Half-Blood Prince* – the seventh and last novel, *Harry Potter and the Deathly Hallows*, will be produced as two films, released six months apart. Peter Jackson's film of Alice Sebold's *The Lovely Bones* is scheduled for release in 2010 and there are plans in hand to film J.R. Tolkien's *The Hobbit*, Salman Rushdie's *Midnight's Children* and Jack Kerouac's classic novel of the Beat Generation, *On the Road*. Director Ang Lee is reputed to be working on a script for Yann Martel's Booker Prize winning novel *Life of Pi*.

The majority of book-based films have tended to be based on fiction, although *A Beautiful Mind*, based on Sylvia Nassar's biography of mathematician John Nash and starring Russell Crowe, proved popular; 2003 saw a film based on Laura Hillenbrand's *Seabiscuit: An American Legend*; in 2005, *Capote* was largely based on Gerald Clarke's book on the writer, and Steven Spielberg's *Munich* was based on *Vengeance* by George Jonas. The year 2007 saw films based on Robert Graysmith's *Zodiac* and Jon Krakauer's *Into the Wild*; 2009 brought *The Soloist*, based on the book by Steve Lopez, *An Education*, based on journalist Lynn Barber's memoir, and *Julie and Julia*, based on the autobiography of chef Julia Child and Julie Powell's book on her attempts to cook her way through 524 of Child's recipes.

English-language films based on books first published in another language have included *Perfume: The Story of a Murderer*, based on Patrick Süskind's *Das Parfum*, once deemed unfilmable; *The Reader*, based on Bernhard Schlink's novel; Gabriel García Márquez's *Love in the Time of Cholera* and *The Diving Bell and the Butterfly*, based on Jean-Dominique Bauby's powerful autobiographical account of paralysis after a stroke.

Films based on the works of bestselling authors such as John Grisham, Stephen King and Michael Crichton continue; film versions of Nick Hornby's books (*High Fidelity* and *About a Boy*) and Helen Fielding's *Bridget Jones* novels have proved popular. Warner Brothers paid an undisclosed seven-figure sum for film rights to J.K. Rowling's initial work, *Harry Potter and the Philosopher's Stone* (US title *Harry Potter and the Sorcerer's Stone*), to include control of worldwide merchandising rights; the budget for the picture was believed to be £90 million. Since then, the film rights in all the *Harry Potter* novels have proved extremely lucrative; at the time of writing, three of the films based on the *Harry Potter* stories and two films from the *Lord of the Rings* trilogy feature in the top ten list of the highest-earning films of all time.

Sometimes there is a substantial delay between the publication of a book and its appearance as a film. In 2002, Martin Scorsese fulfilled a lifelong ambition in bringing to the screen Herbert Asbury's 1928 non-fiction work *The Gangs of New York*. The year 2005 brought a large-screen version of Douglas Adams's *The Hitchhiker's Guide to the Galaxy*, first conceived as a radio series in 1978, published as a book in 1979 and produced as a television series in 1981. Somewhat surprisingly, 2006 saw a version of *Tristram Shandy*, the eccentric eighteenth-century novel by Laurence Sterne, under the title of *A Cock and Bull Story*. Sometimes the works of a once well-known author have lapsed into obscurity and a film rekindles new interest, as with the 2008 version of Richard Yates's 1962 novel *Revolutionary Road* and of Winifred Watson's 1935 novel *Miss Pettigrew Lives for a Day*.

In some cases, the delay is due to the fact that some of the content was initially deemed controversial (as for E.M. Forster's *Maurice*, Patricia Highsmith's *The Talented Mr Ripley*, Bret Easton Ellis's *American Psycho* and the 2005 film version of E. Annie Proulx's short story *Brokeback Mountain* from her collection *Close Range*) or because the technology at the time of publication would not have done the book justice; 2000 saw the release of a part-animated version of the 1930s US children's classic *Stuart Little* by E.B. White (with a sequel following in 2002) and *The Grinch* (based on Dr Seuss's *How the Grinch Stole Christmas*), and recent years have seen Dreamworks produce three *Shrek* animated films based on the books of William Steig, with a fourth due in 2010. Two *Babe* films have been based on Dick King-Smith's story of *The Sheep Pig*, and 2007 saw a film of the same author's *The Water Horse*. The year 2004 saw an animated version from Studio Ghibli of *Howl's Moving Castle* by Japanese animator Hayao Miyazaki, based on the novel by Diana Wynne Jones. The same studio also produced *Tales from Earthsea*, loosely based on the stories of Ursula K. Le Guin. The year 2007 brought *The Golden Compass*, a version of *Northern Lights* from Philip Pullman's *His Dark Materials*; at the time of writing the schedule for any sequels is unclear. In 2009 there was Spike Jonze's rendering of Maurice Sendak's 1963 classic *Where the Wild Things Are* (a mix of CGI and giant monster suits) and a version of Roald Dahl's *Fantastic Mr Fox*, interestingly a return to stop-motion technique rather than CGI.

CGI has been instrumental in new films featuring the Batman and Spider-Man characters for the big screen, and this technique, together with prosthetic costuming, was seen to stunning effect in New Zealand director Peter Jackson's version of J.R.R. Tolkien's *Lord of the Rings* trilogy, released from 2001 to 2003 and a far cry from the earlier animated partial version of 1978; the trilogy has won seventeen Oscars. The first film is estimated to have taken $869 million at the box office – ironic in that Tolkien originally made arrangements for the film rights in 1969 for a sum of $250,000 after resisting approaches for fifteen years. The films are estimated to have earned $3 billion in gross revenues. *Lord of the Rings* has been followed up by Jackson's 2005 remake (at a cost of $207 million) of the 1933 film *King Kong*, itself based on a short story and screenplay by Edgar Wallace. The year 2004 saw a version of Chris Van Allsburg's *The Polar Express*, the first film to feature performance capture (where the movements of live actors are mapped on to animated characters); a film of his *Jumanji* was filmed back in 1995 and *Zathura* appeared in 2006. CGI was also a key feature in the 2005 films *Nanny McPhee* (Emma Thompson's adaptation of Christianne Brand's *Nurse Matilda* stories) and *The Lion, the Witch and the Wardrobe*, based on the first volume of C.S. Lewis's seven-volume *Chronicles of Narnia* series. A film of the second book, *Prince Caspian*, was released in 2008, with the third film, *The Voyage of the Dawn Treader*, due in 2010; however, in January 2009, Disney announced they were withdrawing from coproducing and cofinancing the series, leaving Walden Media to seek another partnership. In 2008 there was a version of *The Curious Case of Benjamin Button*, based on the 1921 short story by F. Scott Fitzgerald about a man who ages in reverse. On the technical front, the latest 'innovation' in mainstream cinema is 3D, with all the major studios coming out with 3D films in 2009 and 2010.

The last ten years have seen a number of remakes of classic films. The year 1999 saw a new version of Graham Greene's *The End of the Affair*, 2002 a remake of *The Quiet American* by the same author and plans are in hand for a remake of *Brighton Rock*, to star Helen Mirren. In 2004, remakes were issued of *The Stepford Wives* (based on the Ira Levin novel) and *The Manchurian Candidate* (based on the novel by Richard Condon) – both were considered inferior to the original film versions. The year 2005 saw a remake of H.G. Wells's 1898 novel *The War of the Worlds* and Tim Burton's version of Roald Dahl's *Charlie and the Chocolate Factory*, starring Johnny Depp, a much darker version and closer to the original book than the earlier version of 1971 starring Gene Wilder, *Willy Wonka and the Chocolate Factory*. Then 2006 brought a British remake of *Lassie Come Home*, based on the 1940 novel by Yorkshireman Eric Knight, *Poseidon* (a Paul Gallico novel) and Ian Fleming's first James Bond novel, *Casino Royale*. And 2007 saw a remake of the western *3.10 to Yuma*, based on the novel by Elmore Leonard; 2008 brought a film version of Evelyn Waugh's *Brideshead Revisited*, which was generally thought to be less successful than the much acclaimed 1981 Granada Television series; 2009 saw a creditable remake of *The Taking of Pelham One Two Three*, based on John Godey's novel and starring John Travolta and Denzel Washington – the 1974 version starred Robert Shaw and Walter Matthau.

It cannot be overemphasized that film licences are an extraordinarily complex area, and publishers with little or no experience of the medium would be well advised to obtain counsel from a media lawyer or firm specializing in such work, such as a literary agency experienced in this area. Film and television rights are the area of licensing where there is probably the most leeway for negotiation and horse-trading (conceding one or more aspects of a deal in return for concessions by the other side); a producer is likely to seek the broadest bundle of rights possible in order to secure financial backing, whilst the licensor may wish to restrict rights carefully, or at least to ensure that additional payments are forthcoming if additional rights are exploited. Another possibility may be to build in a clause so that payment is increased if a book that was not established as a bestseller at the point of negotiation later becomes a bestseller.

The appearance of a film or television version of a book can, of course, bring major benefits to the original publisher and their sublicensees, even if such rights are not controlled by the publisher. In practice, the time taken to produce a film or television version will mean that the paperback version (whether published by the original publisher or a sublicensee) is more likely to benefit directly from this form of exploitation. HarperCollins are reported to have sold ten times more copies of Tolkien's *Lord of the Rings* titles than they did prior to the film exploitation, and have also seen major increases in sales of C.S. Lewis's *Narnia* volumes; they have produced special adult paperback versions without illustrations but with added notes. Sales of J.K. Rowling's *Harry Potter* titles are now legendary (at the time of writing estimated at over 400 million copies worldwide), and Bloomsbury have also produced adult versions of the books.

A paperback licensee will require early warning of the film or television version, and will aim to reprint the paperback edition to coincide with release of the film or broadcast of the work on television, with a tie-in cover in order to maximize sales. Any publisher wishing to use stills for this purpose will normally be charged by the film or television company. A paperback contract may well provide for early release of that edition before the designated first paperback publication date if a film or television version of the book is released (see Chapter 11).

An interesting recent development has been the entry of some of the major trade publishing houses into the area of film and television. Although Penguin's TV development division was wound down in 2004, in late 2005 Random House announced a 50/50 partnership with film production company Focus Features (part of NBC Universal and known for their work on film versions of Wladyslaw Szpilman's *The Pianist*, Che Guevara's *The Motorcycle Diaries*, John Le Carré's *The Constant Gardener* and E. Annie Proulx's *Brokeback Mountain*). Random House will be able to publish screenplays, 'books of the film' and book versions of original screenplays.

In the United States, Penguin Young Readers Group announced an alliance with Walden Media to develop new books and films. In 2005 HarperCollins invested £4 million in a TV mini-series based on Bernard Cornwell's *Sharpe* novels and jointly produced by ITV and BBC America. In late 2008 HarperCollins and Sharp Independent entered into a strategic partnership to develop film projects. In a surprise move in late 2009, supermarket giant Tesco announced that it would invest in funding film production, linked to an exclusive ninety-day sales period for DVDs of the films concerned.

Chapter 22

Merchandising rights

The term 'merchandising' is applied to the exploitation of a character, personality or design from one medium by licensing its use in the context of another medium. Merchandising may take two forms: the direct reproduction of the character or design as another product such as a soft toy, or on a T-shirt, stationery, bed linen or wallpaper, where it will form the main feature; or to endorse an existing brand-name product or service such as a breakfast cereal, a yoghurt, fast food, petrol or banking. The key areas for merchandising are clothing and accessories, health and beauty, toys and games, homeware, stationery, publishing (where books are derived from characters which originated in another medium such as film or television), music, videos, DVDs, computer games (including online and interactive products) and mobile phones, and food and drink items. It is difficult to obtain precise figures for the total retail value of merchandised items worldwide but it has been estimated at over US$200 billion. In the UK, grocery items are currently estimated to hold a 30% share of the merchandising market, with clothes and other textile items holding a further 20%, toys and games 15%, and fast-moving consumer goods 10%.

This area of licensing is not of course limited to characters or designs originating from a book or other printed product such as a syndicated cartoon strip in a newspaper. Lucrative business stems from the licensing of products featuring film and television characters, pop stars and sports personalities, and books may themselves be a form of merchandising of those characters and personalities. A character that first appears in one medium may come to fame through another. Charles Schulz was reputed to earn $60 million per year from his Peanuts characters, including revenue from extensive product licensing worldwide; the characters celebrated their sixtieth anniversary in 2010.

A very early example of merchandising stemming from a book was a soft toy produced in the early years of this century based on the Golliwogg character first created by Florence Upton. The series of Golliwogg books was extremely successful, although the character is now less used in children's literature as it is perceived as having racist overtones.

Beatrix Potter agreed to arrangements for soft toys, wallpaper friezes and china objects based on the characters in her books when they first became successful between 1901 and 1913, while in 1917 she agreed to the production of items such as board games, stationery and handkerchiefs. At the time of writing there are over 450 licensees worldwide for the Potter characters, as well as the World of Beatrix Potter attraction at Bowness in Cumbria. Licensees are carefully selected to preserve the integrity of the characters. Peter Rabbit has been registered as a trademark which can be renewed every ten years, extending the life of the property. The illustrations of Kate Greenaway and of John Tenniel, the original illustrator of Lewis Carroll's *Alice* books, were also licensed for use on stationery items.

More recently, famous examples of characters that have been marketed extensively include the Peanuts characters; Garfield and Dilbert, from syndicated cartoon strips and books; Michael Bond's Paddington Bear, known from books and television; and the Beatrix Potter characters, which continue to appear on hundreds of merchandising items. On the design side, the nature illustrations from Edith Holden's *The Country Diary of an Edwardian Lady* were licensed to appear on well over a hundred different products, ranging from ceramics to toiletries and wallpaper. Designs from Jill Barklem's *Brambly Hedge* series were also widely licensed.

Success in licensing merchandising rights requires first the control of the rights in a character or design that is already well established in one form, such as a book or a series of books, and that preferably will become better known, perhaps through the medium of film or television.

The appearance of a cartoon or animated television series or a film featuring a character from a book can be the turning point as far as merchandising is concerned; an example here would be the film of Raymond Briggs's *The Snowman*. A revival of interest in the books of the Reverend Awdry followed the launch of the *Thomas the Tank Engine* series on television in 1984. Rights were initially controlled by the Britt Allcroft Company, which developed the animated series, subsequently Gullane Entertainment; in 2002, the rights were acquired by Hit Entertainment, which also handled rights in Bob the Builder, Angelina Ballerina and Pingu; in 2005, the company was bought by Apax Partners, a private equity firm. At the time of writing, thousands of Thomas products are licensed to hundreds of licensees worldwide. Japan has been a particularly successful market, with its own Thomas Land theme park. The full-length feature film *Thomas and the Magic Railway* was released in July 2000.

Rights to Enid Blyton's books (including most notably the *Noddy*, *Famous Five* and *Secret Seven* series) were acquired in 1996 from the Blyton family for £13 million by the Enid Blyton Company (now renamed as Chorion, which controls rights in a number of other literary estates, including those of Georges Simenon, Raymond Chandler and Agatha Christie, and Roger Hargeaves' Mr Men characters); in the spring of 2006, the company was acquired by venture capital company 3i. The character of Noddy was created by Blyton in 1949; the television series *Noddy in Toyland* was relaunched on Channel Five and has been accompanied by new books and a large range of merchandising products. In 2006, Entertainment Rights signed a deal with Channel Five for *Rupert and Friends*, a new CGI television series based on the adventures of Rupert Bear, who started life as a strip cartoon character in the *Daily Express* newspaper in 1920 before making the transition to books via the *Rupert* annuals; the series has generated new merchandising business.

In 1999, there was a major revival of interest in Miffy, Dutch illustrator Dick Bruna's white rabbit character. Over a hundred books have been published in the last fifty years and a wide range of merchandising items are now available. Again, Japan has been a particularly successful market for this type of illustration, as shown by gift company Sanrio's Hello Kitty merchandising phenomenon; Hello Kitty was created in 1976, and at the time of writing over 22,000 merchandising items based on the 'cute' cat are available in Japan and worldwide, ranging from inexpensive plastic purses to diamond jewellery and a platinum Hello Kitty credit card.

Many classic children's books have been brought to the screen in recent years as a result of advances in animation techniques and CGI: 2000 saw the release of the film of *Stuart Little*, based on the 1930s American classic by E.B. White, and *102 Dalmatians*, the film sequel to Dodie Smith's *101 Dalmatians*; *Stuart Little 2* followed in 2002. The first *Shrek* film, based on the book by William Steig, was released in 2001, with the fourth film in the *Shrek* franchise launched in 2010. A film of *The Cat in the Hat* by Dr Seuss (Theodore Geisel) was released in 2003. All generated hundreds of merchandising items as well as promotions for food and drink companies such as Kellogg's, Kraft, Pepsi and Burger King. The 2005 remake of the film of Roald Dahl's *Charlie and the Chocolate Factory* also generated a large number of confectionery licences. Characters that started their life in comics have also generated substantial licensing income after their move to the big screen; merchandising from the Batman films has far exceeded box-office revenue, and income from Spider-Man licensing via over 200 licensees is thought to have generated at least $100 million per film. Disney's acquisition of Marvel Entertainment in October 2009 gives them access to over 5,000 characters from the Marvel comic books (including Spider-Man, the Hulk and the X-Men), which have enormous value in merchandising terms in addition to their exploitation through the media of film and television.

Sometimes the procedure may work in reverse; the early cartoon characters of Walt Disney are perhaps the most famous examples of characters that started life in the cinema but which have subsequently appeared in books and on a huge range of merchandise. Other characters that have made the transition from film or television screen to the printed page as well as merchandising include characters from the later Disney movies *Pocahontas*, *The Lion King* and *Bolt*, Dreamworks' *The Prince of Egypt* and *Kung Fu Panda*, the Pixar films *Toy Story*, *Finding Nemo*, *Shark Story*, *Monsters Inc.*, *The Incredibles*, *Cars*, *Ratatouille*, *Wall.E* and *Up*, George Lucas's original *Star Wars* films and the three more recent prequels, the Hanna–Barbera and Warner Brothers cartoon characters, the Pink Panther, Jim Henson's Muppets, Sesame Street characters, the Teenage Mutant Ninja Turtles, Barney, the Simpsons, South Park, the Rugrats, Beavis and Butt-head, Spongebob Squarepants, Postman Pat, Basil Brush, the Teletubbies, the Tweenies, and Aardman's Wallace and Gromit, brought to the big screen in 2005 in *Wallace and Gromit and the Curse of the Were-Rabbit*. Computer games characters such as Nintendo's Mario Brothers and Sega's Sonic the Hedgehog, and dolls such as Barbie, have also made the transition to book form.

Television series such as the BBC's *Walking with Dinosaurs* and the various David Attenborough series have generated videos and books. BBC Worldwide handles licensing arrangements for products based on BBC programmes, and may also make long-term licence arrangements with individual production companies, as they did with Ragdoll Productions for the *Teletubbies*.

The publisher may not always have control of merchandising rights, even for a book-based product. These may have been retained by the author and/or artist (in many cases the same person) or an agent acting on their behalf. In some cases, an artist may have no continuing interest in merchandising arrangements if the author is the official creator of the character; the artist may have been paid a fee to illustrate a book to the author's specifications. The original contractual arrangements should clarify the situation. It is also noticeable that when there is a strong revival of interest in characters through a visual medium such as film or television, control of merchandising rights often ceases to lie with the publisher and is transferred instead to a dedicated merchandising operation.

In the case of highly illustrated children's books, it is important to remember that merchandising rights will be a key element in any film or television negotiations (see Chapter 21). An example here would be the merchandising rights to A.A. Milne's *Winnie the Pooh*, acquired along with US and Canadian film and television rights from Milne in 1930 in return for a reputed £1,000 advance and a 66% share of income by Stephen Slesinger. Merchandising rights were included in the deal he then made with Walt Disney and they are reputed to generate as much licensing revenue as merchandising for Mickey Mouse, Minnie Mouse, Donald Duck, Goofy and Pluto combined. A long-running legal dispute between the Slesinger family and Disney over the division of proceeds was settled in September 2009. In some cases, publishers themselves may be able to produce some products; these usually tend to be book-related (e.g. the

Beatrix Potter character birthday and address books produced by Frederick Warne), but some animated films and multimedia products based on the characters were also produced within the Pearson group, to which Warne belongs. However, for a publisher to successfully market merchandising items other than books presumes access to a wide range of retail outlets with which publishers may not be familiar.

In some cases, authors whose rights in this area first rested with their publishers have recovered the rights and on occasion set up their own companies to handle this side of their interests, although the publisher may continue to receive a share of the proceeds. In the case of Paddington Bear, a company entitled Paddington & Co. Ltd was set up by Michael Bond in the 1970s before the appearance of the television series, although the character is now handled by a specialist merchandising company.

The promotion of merchandising rights is a time-consuming activity, since it involves contact with a wide range of manufacturers outside the publishing industry. For this reason, many UK authors, artists and publishers have chosen to employ specialized merchandising organizations such as the Copyrights Group; this company handled licensing in properties such as the characters of Beatrix Potter, the Flower Fairies, Paddington Bear, the Wombles, Jacqueline Wilson's *Best Friends*, Eric Hill's Spot, Lucy Cousins's Maisy, characters of Raymond Briggs, as well as the licensing of Mrs Beeton and *Country Diary of an Edwardian Lady* products. It was acquired in 2007 by Chorion (see earlier in this chapter, p. 297). Copyright Promotions Ltd (www.cplg.com) represent a number of characters from film and television, including Peanuts, Dilbert, Sesame Street, the Simpsons, Rugrats, Spongebob Squarepants, Shrek, the Pink Panther and Mr Bean. In 2008 the company was acquired by a Canadian-based global entertainment and education company, the Cookie Jar Group.

These companies retain a proportion of the royalties generated from licences as their commission; this can vary from 25% to 60% depending on the agency, the territories granted and the property concerned. Merchandising specialists will probably tend to sign up properties which have already had some exposure other than in book form, e.g. as a television series, a film or through well-established toy licences. They may also act as advisers to the original creator, suggesting contacts in the publishing and media fields. Several literary agencies also now have specialist staff to handle merchandising rights.

For anyone licensing merchandising rights it is essential to monitor trends in the marketplace. This means not only studying what goods are currently available in the shops, but also attending appropriate trade events at home and abroad such as toy and games fairs, gift and stationery fairs, household goods, food manufacturing and clothing fairs, and so on. The major event Licensing International Expo is held every year in New York in June. The Brand Licensing show is held in October at London's Olympia venue.

The Bologna Book Fair is a showcase for new children's books that may also have merchandising potential. It is also necessary to monitor the relevant trade press, including specialist merchandising publications. *License! Global* magazine (www.licensemag.com) appears monthly in the USA and quarterly in Europe. Annual directories include the *Licensing Letter Sourcebook* published by EPM Communications (160 Mercer Street, 3rd Floor, New York, NY 10012-3212, USA – www.epmco.com) and *Licensing World* (www.licensingworld.co.uk). These list merchandising owners and selections of their key properties. EPM also publish the *Licensing Letter* (twenty-two issues per year). There is also the monthly publication *The Licensing Book* (Adventure Publishing Group Inc., 286 Fifth Avenue, 3rd Floor, New York, NY 10001, USA – www.adventure.com) and *The Licensing Pages* (www.licensingpages.com).

In the United Kingdom, the magazine *Licensing Today Worldwide* is published by Leman Publishing Ltd, 1 Churchgate, The Wilderness, Berkhamsted, Herts HP4 2WB (www.lemanpublishing.co.uk).

Some manufacturers are specialists in producing items in one medium (for example Royal Doulton china); others such as Hunkydory, Rainbow Designs, Mattel and Hasbro have experience in producing a range of products and hence may acquire multiple licences for the same character.

If the character or design exists only in book form, the sales figures of the book or books will be important in the promotion exercise, together with details of any plans to feature the character on television. It is inevitable that as a character receives more exposure, merchandising interest will start to snowball and requests will come in from product manufacturers. Creative licensing initiatives have included a licence for bars of Kendal Mint Cake confectionery to be produced in packaging based on the design of A. Wainwright's fell-walking guidebooks to the Lake District, and walking boots bearing the Wainwright logo. Cassell licensed the Mrs Beeton name to a pie manufacturer for a substantial fee. Unusual licences have included beer, plate, clock and postcard licences granted by the agency representing the D.H. Lawrence estate, and calendars, posters and mobiles based on the work of Heath Robinson. In 2009 Francesca Simon's characters Horrid Henry and Perfect Peter were featured on Marmite jars: the promotion provided a code for free access to a choice of audiobook downloads form Audible.co.uk (see Chapter 20).

The level of payment made for merchandising rights varies according to the resources of the licensee, expected sales of the licensed product and the popularity of the character or design that is being licensed. On occasion, a lump sum payment may be agreed for a test period of, say, a year for a product based on a character that is not yet well established. However, payment is normally made on the basis of a royalty calculated on the wholesale price of the item. The royalty might be 5–6% unless the character or design is extremely well known, in which case rates could be as high as 12–15%. Royalty rates also vary according to the nature of the product licensed; licences to the mass-market food industry could well be based on royalties as low as 1% of the wholesale price, but in the hope that the low rate will be compensated for by the volume of sales. Advance payments are usually specified in the form of a royalty on guaranteed minimum sales. Accounting is normally on a quarterly basis.

When entering into a merchandising agreement, a number of factors must be taken into account. The product on which the character or design is to appear should be appropriate. It is important to preserve the integrity of the property, and it can only be detrimental to allow it to be associated with inappropriate or shoddy products. For this reason, the licence should always define extremely carefully the nature and specifications of the product that is being licensed. If it is a greetings card, the dimensions and type should be specified. If a range of soft toys in different sizes and materials is to be produced, the size, style and materials of each should be defined (e.g. '8-inch seated figure in plush'). If different types of jigsaw are being licensed, the licence should specify if the product consists of large wood-backed pieces for young children or smaller cardboard-backed pieces for older children or adults. It is essential that these safeguards are observed in order to avoid the licensee producing different or more products than had originally been envisaged.

The licensor should require approval of both the product and any packaging at all stages of development; artwork and prototypes must be submitted for approval prior to the start of the final manufacturing process, and adequate time should be allowed for such approval and for any changes required in the product by the licensor. Once the product and packaging have been approved, no changes should be made at any stage during the life of the licence without prior approval of the licensor. This should be confirmed by the regular submission of samples of the product. The licensor should also have the right of approval of advertising for the product, and of any non-standard marketing of the product other than through standard retail outlets, for example if the product is to be given away free with another product or if it is to be 'remaindered'.

It should, however, be remembered that if merchandising rights have been included as part of a film or television deal, the contract for that deal may have required the author and/or artist to waive moral rights, and this would remove the power of approval over merchandising products licensed by the film or television company.

The licence should not be transferable to any other party, and the new copyright that will exist in the product should be acquired by the licensee and then assigned to the licensor. If, however, the nature of the exploitation requires that the licensee be able to sublicense to a third party or parties, provision must be made for the licensee to have overall responsibility for ensuring that sublicensees comply with requirements on quality control, time limits and payment.

If a character or design has already been trademarked, this should be covered in the licence so that the licensee has the status of a registered user. But it should be noted that trademark law may vary from country to country, and if merchandising rights are to be marketed extensively abroad, it may be advisable to take advice from a lawyer specializing in trademark legislation. The licence should specify the exact form in which copyright and any trademark acknowledgement appear on both product and packaging.

The markets granted to merchandising licensees should be limited to those that they can demonstrably service, and it should be remembered that not all characters or designs necessarily have international appeal; much depends on national tastes and the conditions in merchandising industries in each market. A major soft toy manufacturer might be granted world rights if it has established marketing outlets in many countries. In practice, a character or design with international appeal is usually licensed country by country, often through the medium of local licensing agents; the American market has proved particularly difficult to penetrate without such assistance. Within the European Union, all parties should be aware of the possibilities of parallel importing of competing licensed goods through the provisions of Articles 30–36 of the Treaty of Rome, providing for the free movement of goods across the borders of member states.

The contract should specify a time limit from the date of signature of the contract by which the licensee must have launched the product on the market. Merchandising licences are usually short term – perhaps two or three years – but with the provision to renew if the product proves successful; in this case it will be desirable to negotiate higher terms. If a licence comes to a natural end (rather than as a result of a dispute between the parties and cancellation) the licensee should have a defined period of time in which to dispose of their remaining stock. The licensor may, however, wish to make provision to purchase any remaining stock and to require that any specialized equipment used to manufacture the product (e.g. moulds) should be turned over to the licensor or seen to be destroyed.

While the popularity of some characters can be very long lived, others can have a short popularity span and be over-exposed through merchandising, particularly if they are linked to the appearance of a television series or cinema film; the Wombles and the Flintstones are classic examples of this. In some cases, book characters may undergo successful periodic merchandising revivals, as in the case of Enid Blyton's Noddy and Roger Hargreaves' Mr Men characters, both acquired by Chorion.

Despite some failures, revenue can be substantial; merchandising revenue from the Batman films is estimated at over $4 billion, far more than the box-office takings. At its height in 1990–1, 'Turtlemania' is said to have generated around £200 million in licensing fees from approximately 400 official Turtle products before sales began to fall off following over-exposure and piracy. The original film based on Michael Crichton's *Jurassic Park* generated a licensing boom in dinosaur items; this continued with the later sequels. As mentioned earlier, 1997 saw a massive revival of interest in *Star Wars* merchandising following the relaunch of the film trilogy; the 1999 prequel *Episode One: The Phantom Menace* had disappointing results at the box office but nevertheless generated $6 billion in merchandising revenue. An arrangement with Hasbro and Galoob for the right to produce a range of toys and other items was one of the largest in merchandising history; Galoob alone paid $140 million for the right to produce small-scale figures, vehicles and play sets, Lego acquired a first-time licence to produce construction toys and Nintendo acquired the right to produce two N64 games.

Some of the most spectacular licensing arrangements have been secured for Peter Jackson's trilogy of films based on J.R.R. Tolkien's *Lord of the Rings*, released between 2001 and 2003; these included licences for toys and games and food sponsorship deals with companies such as Kellogg's and Burger King. The films released to date of J.K. Rowling's *Harry Potter* books have also generated enormous merchandising revenue, with Warner Brothers signing deals with Mattel for toys and with Hasbro for games and confectionery; there was also a major deal with Coca-Cola. In June 2010 a theme park entitled the Wizarding Worlds of Harry Potter opened at the Orlando resort of Universal Studios. Peter Jackson's 2005 remake of *King Kong* also produced substantial licensing revenue.

Christmas 1996 saw frantic searches by parents on both sides of the Atlantic for two merchandising items for which demand had been underestimated – the Buzz Lightyear astronaut toy from the film *Toy Story* and Tickle-Me Elmo, a red furry character from television's long-running *Sesame Street*. The 1997 Christmas toy of choice was a Teletubby; £14.95 models changed hands for well over £100. In 2000, the key item was Tracy Island from TV's *Thunderbirds* series. The year 2004 saw a run on Shrek items and successive *Harry Potter* films have generated new merchandising campaigns. In 2009 Go Go Hamsters were the toys of choice, with sets reaching many times their retail price on eBay. In recent years key Christmas products have tended to be based on film and television characters rather than those derived from books, with High School Musical, Hannah Montana, Waybuloo, Bratz, Star Wars, Wall.E and Sesame Street items remaining firm favourites alongside Barbie, Transformers and Power Rangers.

Unfortunately, merchandising is an area where there is ample scope for dishonest behaviour, and there have been countless cases of piracy (replicas of legitimately licensed products) and of 'passing off', where slightly different products appear to have been endorsed by the licensor. This can occur not only in areas such as the Far East, but also within Europe and in the United Kingdom. Such items can cause substantial damage to the interests of both the licensor and their legitimate licensees. If the source of the offending articles can be identified, it will be necessary to take legal action under trademark law, if appropriate, or with a charge of copyright infringement or passing off. If there is an authorized licensee for the product in the market concerned, licensor and licensee may wish to collaborate in taking legal action against the infringement.

It is important that an overview of different merchandising licences for the same character or design is maintained; if there is any danger of an overlap of interest, the relevant licensees should be consulted before any new licences are granted.

Chapter 23

Reprographic and electronic reproduction rights

The area of reprographic reproduction rights has been greatly influenced by developments in technology. These rights were originally included in the overall category of 'mechanical and reproduction rights'; publishers attempted to cover present and future methods of reprography in contracts with wording such as 'to license the reproduction of the work ... by film micrography, reprographic reproduction ... or by means of any contrivance whether by sight or sound or a combination of both, whether now in existence or hereinafter invented'. Although some of the old technologies remain in existence, most publishers and literary agents would accept that there are now so many diverse ways of reproducing and disseminating copyright material that the old definitions are no longer adequate. The question of who should control the various rights which have developed as a result of technological advances, including those of reprography, is addressed in Chapter 2, with the proposal that verbatim electronic rights – the right to reproduce the print-on-paper product electronically – more logically lie with the publisher since they represent an alternative channel of supply for the same intellectual property, without the addition of any further value in the form of multimedia facilities.

Demand has continued to increase from the educational, academic, professional and commercial sectors for access to information selectively, speedily, with the minimum of bureaucracy and preferably by electronic means. Publishers have been forced to adapt to these market requirements to avoid the potential erosion of their rights and those of their authors.

The question of how and by whom content should be supplied to end-users has long been a topic for debate, in particular between the academic community and publishers serving that sector. Many academic users still feel that copyright is an outdated concept which hampers the free flow of information (see *The anti-copyright movement, open access and other initiatives* in Chapter 1) and some feel that publishers represent an obstacle to the availability of information which is itself produced by the academic sector. Publishers continue to maintain that they add value to academic publications via their selection process, arrangements for peer review, editing and brand value, together with their financial investment in bringing the work to market – a substantial investment given that almost all academic journals have now been digitized to facilitate electronic delivery and many academic books are available in electronic form, either as e-books directly from publishers themselves or via library aggregators. Publishers therefore feel that any onward use of published copyright material by others – some of which could erode primary sales of the original publication – should be subject to controls and also to a fair system of recompense to copyright holders and their authorized representatives.

Downstream licensing to a variety of outside information suppliers such as document delivery services or aggregators is one route; this may be done directly by the publisher or via a central licensing agency in some cases. Most major academic publishers have now become information providers direct to the end-customer via site licences. It therefore remains dangerous for rights and permissions staff operating in publishing houses to operate in isolation, as this may conflict with existing or planned company policy in the area.

Let us consider what have now become the more traditional forms of reprographic rights.

Microfilm/microfiche rights

These are the right to reproduce a copyright work in a greatly reduced type size in the medium of microfilm (a roll of film that can be accessed through a hand-held or larger viewer) or microfiche (a flat card of film which can be accessed through a hand-held or desktop viewer). The main use has been in libraries, which were able to store large amounts of material converted to these forms with a huge saving on storage space, although digital storage is now far preferred. Payment for microfilm or microfiche rights has normally been made on a royalty basis, with royalties for publications included as part of a larger fiche package calculated *pro rata* depending on the proportion of the package taken up by each work. German publisher K.G. Saur (owned by the Walter de Gruyter publishing company) still runs a microfiche as well as a digital service, with much of the material available in English.

Another service that has long employed microfilm and microfiche is University Microfilms (UMI – www.umi.com), now part of Proquest and operating on both sides of the Atlantic. For many years, UMI has acquired these rights for out-of-print titles; it is then able to provide customers with single copies on request, in either microfilm or microfiche form according to the preference of the customer. It can also provide single xerographic copies of the book. UMI pays the licensor a royalty of 10% of the sales price of the product it supplies. This was a useful service since it enabled publishers to refer on enquiries for academic books no longer in print; publishers usually supplied copies to UMI as soon as the print-on-paper edition went out of print. However, with publishers now storing their works digitally and with many able to supply customers with bound books via print-on-demand, the need for this particular service for books has been waning. However, at the time of writing UMI has a collection of some 2.2 billion page images and continues to offer thousands of period-icals and newspapers in microform and promote the service on the grounds that delivery in this form provides the user with full text together with photographs, illustrations, graphs and tables which may be absent from electronic versions for reasons of copyright clearance.

Proquest (www.proquest.com) now seeks to acquire rights to reproduce and supply material via magnetic, optical and electronic media, and to provide online services (see *Document delivery services* later in this chapter, pp. 348–50, and *Online databases* in Chapter 24).

Photocopying and scanning

Although newer methods of technology may now make photocopying seem outmoded, the area of print-on-paper reprography remains. Most office copiers are now extremely sophisticated, with technologies permitting computer files to be sent on disk or via ISDN (International Standard Digital Network) or in hard copy which can be scanned, digitally stored and then printed and bound, with a very high standard of reproduction for both text and illustrations.

At the time of the 1956 UK Copyright Act, the easy access to photo-copying machines that we now take for granted could not have been envisaged. The Act made some allowance in Section 6 for fair dealing, including the making of single copies of parts of copyright works; under the provisions for library privilege in Section 7, designated libraries were permitted to furnish a single copy of a single article from a periodical or to copy part of a book (length unspecified) for the purposes of research or private study; designated libraries were also permitted to supply copies of a whole work to other designated libraries where a copy could not be obtained in any other way. These provisions were subsequently carried over into the Copyright, Designs and Patents Act 1988 (Sections 29–30 and 37–42, respectively).

By the 1960s, the problem of large-scale photocopying of copyright material in UK schools, colleges, government institutions and industry started to become apparent; by 1977 the Whitford Committee report on the revision of copyright law had highlighted the problem as serious, and recommended its control through a central licensing scheme. The UK Copyright, Designs and Patents Act 1988 made provision in Section 116 for licensing schemes; this paved the way for the establishment of a central licensing agency to deal with *systematic* photocopying, as opposed to the limited photocopying already permitted under fair dealing and library privilege. The UK body responsible for licensing users, collecting and disbursing fees and if necessary (and with the agreement of the copyright owners) instituting legal proceedings against infringements is the Copyright Licensing Agency (CLA – www.cla.co.uk), a not-for-profit organization. The CLA was incorporated in January 1983 and issued its first licence in May 1984. It represents the interests of authors through the Authors' Licensing and Collecting Society (ALCS – www.alcs.co.uk – founded in 1977 by writers to administer various collective rights on behalf of authors) and publishers through the Publishers Licensing Society (PLS – www.pls. co.uk – founded in 1981 by the Publishers Association, the Periodical Publishers Association and the Association of Learned and Professional Society Publishers). The CLA is in effect owned by ALCS and PLS, and both of these bodies are represented on the CLA board. It also has an agency arrangement with the Designers and Artists' Copyright Society (DACS – see *The licensing of illustrations: DACS* later in this chapter, p. 318) to allow the copying of illustrations published within books and period-icals. The agency deducts a service charge from revenues prior to disburse-ment to its constituent organizations representing authors and publishers; at the time of writing, the rate is 11%. PLS deducts a further 6% from CLA revenue and on foreign non-title specific distributions before disbursing to publishers; ALCS deducts 9.5% before it disburses payments to its mem-bers. The CLA manages legal action against copyright infringements through copying on behalf of its mandating copyright holders, and has undertaken a number of well-publicized and successful test cases. It is a condition of CLA licences that the agency can conduct regular surveys of copying by its licensees.

The CLA aims to license appropriate institutions and organizations, and to tailor licences to the requirements of the users following consultation with the copyright owners and their representative bodies. Licences are in some cases issued on a blanket basis and in others transactional. Licensees receive details of the scope of their licence, and are also provided with a supply of notices to be posted next to their photocopying machines. The CLA also provides up-to-date information for licensees and rightshol-ders on its website, www.cla.co.uk. This includes the text of the licences themselves, plus relevant fees and look-up lists of excluded works.

The system of collective licensing in the United Kingdom is voluntary; this is not the case in all countries (see *Reproduction rights organizations* later in this chapter, pp. 319–20). Authors and publishers must consent (through mandates via ALCS and PLS, respectively) to their works being included in the repertoire of copyright material made available for licensing through the CLA, and head contracts with authors now normally contain a clause to cover this. The CLA's original mandate was restricted to paper-to-paper copying only, but has since been extended to include scanning and digital use of scanned copies, and more recently copying from digital originals on a separate, sector-specific, opt-in basis. The proceeds from collective licensing of material from books (not journals) are normally divided as follows: 7% of all fees received is designated for DACS; the remainder is divided equally between publisher and author, disbursements being paid out from the CLA to ALCS and PLS several times a year and thence to authors and publishers. Since 2008, the PLS-e service has enabled publishers to monitor their income online. PLS sends regular e-mail newsletters to mandating publishers as well as a quarterly *PLUS* newsletter.

In the case of journals, an arrangement was reached in June 1997 for 25% of revenue from journal copying to be paid to ALCS for contributors, unless the publisher owned or controlled the rights to 90% or more of the articles in the journals concerned over the period of a year. In November 2004, this was amended so that 15% of revenue from the copying of journals content is paid to ALCS for disbursement to contributors, with 85% payable to PLS for publishers, regardless of the copyright situation, this division being made after the deduction of 7% for DACS.

Works that are excluded from the repertoire must be notified to the CLA, which refers users to a list of such works on its website. It is also recommended in such cases that the publisher print a clear notice on the book itself that it is not available for inclusion in the collective licensing scheme. In practice, however, the majority of British authors and over 2,700 publishers have agreed that their works be included in all photocopying and scanning licences; over 1,300 have opted in to the copying of digital-original repertoire.

The scheme does not allow for unrestricted photocopying. Details of the nature and scale of copying permitted are circulated to licensees, and a notice must be displayed next to every photocopying machine. Typically, this states that up to 5% of a work or one chapter of a book licensed for inclusion in the scheme may be copied, except in the case of a short story or poem, which can be copied in its entirety provided that it does not exceed ten pages in length. The whole or part of one article from a single issue of a periodical, journal or magazine may be copied. Blanket licences do not restrict the number of copies which may be made, but some licences (e.g. to the British Library, document delivery services and press cuttings agencies) are transactional, with a fee paid for each copy produced.

It should also be stressed that certain categories of work are not included at all in the scheme: printed music (including the words); published examination papers and published tests; all UK newspapers (which are licensed separately by the Newspaper Licensing Agency Limited); maps, charts and books of tables; workbooks, workcards or assignment sheets; privately prepared testing material (such as correspondence courses, though the Open University or the National Extension College materials are included in the licence); works published outside the United Kingdom and those countries with whom the CLA has bilateral arrangements via national licensing agencies (see *Reproduction rights organizations* later in this chapter, pp. 319–20); and works that are specifically excluded from the CLA mandate. These works should be clearly identifiable from a printed notice on the work and from the lists of Excluded Categories and Excluded Works on the CLA website.

In 1999, the CLA first sought a mandate from authors and publishers to permit the digitization of limited amounts of copyright material from books and journals for licensing to various sectors. These were in the first instance the higher education sector (for the production of coursepacks); the pharmaceutical industry (to allow scanning for the purposes of regulatory submissions); licensed institutions for the visually impaired (to allow scanning for the purpose of creating Braille or Moon editions – see Chapter 18); churches; and schools (for the enlargement of text as part of the National Literacy Strategy). Although publishers have remained cautious about the extension of licences to include electronic copying and the copying of electronic originals, they have had to react to consumer demand and, following trial scanning licences in the further eduction (FE) and higher education (HE) sectors, early 2008 saw the extension of some licences (to the pharmaceutical industry, the business sector, the public administration sector, the higher education sector and the arrangements with some overseas reproduction rights organizations) to include the copying of digital originals; publishers could choose whether to mandate all their repertoire for such use, to exclude particular titles and to exclude some countries from the extended use.

The 1988 UK Copyright Act covers in considerable detail regulations for the establishment of licensing agencies to administer collective licensing in Chapter VIII, and Section 137 deals specifically with licensing to educational establishments. Since its establishment in 1981, PLS has distributed over £226 million to publishers; revenue has increased substantially over the years, with payments to publishers for the year 1 April 2008 to 31 March 2009 totalling £26.2 million.

Licensing the schools sector

In April 1986, the CLA finalized arrangements for a collective user scheme with the then 137 local education authorities (LEAs) responsible for the state school and college sector, covering approximately 30,000 institutions. Since then the licensing scheme has operated for the entire maintained school system in the United Kingdom, with rates reviewed periodically. Surveys of what is being copied are conducted by CLA's surveys team, who visit a rotating sample of 250 schools per term and collect data over the course of the term to obtain detailed bibliographic records of copyright materials copied to aid the CLA's distribution of licence fees to authors and publishers.

Until 31 March 2000, schools licences were negotiated with the Local Government Association (LGA). However, from spring 2000 a different system was necessary because of legislative changes affecting the flow of funding through the education system. Licence arrangements were agreed to cover all 24,000 state schools in England and Wales; the licence ran until 31 March 2006 and has since been converted to an annual rolling license unless either party wishes to vary the terms. Schools must now obtain an individual licence, which can be obtained through a designated CLA agent. Most LEAs have agreed to act as agents; for schools under the authority of an LEA which has not so agreed, a licence can be obtained via the Incorporated Association of Preparatory Schools, which has long been responsible for the administration of licences to independent schools on behalf of the CLA. The former grant-maintained schools were included in the main state school licence from 1 April 2000. Fees are based on numbers of full-time students or their equivalents (FTEs) rather than on usage. The rates are reviewed annually, taking into account the retail price index (RPI) and any increases in rights or repertoire available to schools under the licence.

State schools in Scotland have a separate licence, which ran until 31 March 2006 but has now been converted to an annual rolling licence. For the past year, Scottish schools have also been taking part in a pilot of a 'network' licence, allowing them to upload and copy material that includes scanned or retyped extracts from copyright works to the national GLOW network. State schools in Northern Ireland also had a licence to 31 March 2006, now converted to an annual rolling licence.

Digitization (by scanning or retyping) was introduced into the licence for state schools in April 2008 and for independent schools in April 2009, with permission to display digitized copies on interactive whiteboards and store them in course repositories or virtual learning environments (VLEs), but with no sharing between schools. Late 2009 saw consultations with mandating publishers about the possibility of extending the schools licence repertoire to include digital originals and free-to-view website content, on an opt-in basis for rightsholders. This was subsequently approved by the publishers' trade associations and PLS, and also by ALCS and DACS on behalf of creators, to be introduced during the course of 2010.

Licensing the further education sector

From 1 April 1993, following the Act of Incorporation, sixth form colleges and 450 further education and agricultural colleges that had previously been included in the LEA agreement entered into separate licensing arrangements.

In January 2005 a trial photocopying and scanning licence was negotiated with the Association of Colleges (AOC), the Association of Scottish
Colleges (ASC) and the Association of Northern Ireland Colleges, initially
to run for one year. This was introduced to enable the state FE sector to
make digital copies of copyright material within the permitted limits by
scanning from existing print copies or retyping limited extracts in digital
format; storage of scanned copies was permitted in a secure network for the
academic year, provided the original source and authorship (where known)
was credited. This has been renewed on an annual basis, while methods of
surveying scanning activity have been trailed, together with the monitoring
of impact on publishers' sales.

To date, surveys indicate that there has been no substantial impact
on publishers' primary sales, but the situation is being monitored, while a
revision of the licence to improve reporting and possibly to include digital
originals is under discussion at the time of writing.

Licensing the higher education sector

Following the establishment of licensing for schools, the CLA entered
into negotiations with the Committee of Vice-Chancellors and Principals
to cover copying in universities and the then polytechnics. After an
experimental period of licensing in selected colleges, the first three-year
licence agreement with all universities and higher education colleges commenced on 1 January 1990. In selected higher education institutions usage is
monitored by CLA-appointed staff over a four-week survey period.

The original core licence for this sector was based on the number of
FTEs multiplied by a rate agreed between the parties, which is based on a
rate per page and an agreed average amount of copying per FTE per year.

Coursepack copying was originally handled separately on a transactional
basis via CLARCS, the CLA Rapid Clearance Service; lecturers had to
apply to CLARCS and provide details of the material they wished to copy
and the number of copies to be made; publishers could set their own rates
for this usage or use the CLA default rates for book and journal material
copied. Alternatively, they could choose to have requests referred to them
for particular levels or values of copying.

However, in July 2000, Universities UK (UUK) made an application to
the UK Copyright Tribunal for a variation in the terms of the higher
education licence, seeking a substantial reduction in the rate per FTE and
for illustrations and coursepack copying to be subsumed under the blanket
licence arrangement. The tribunal procedure was lengthy and, despite
detailed submissions on the scale of copying undertaken in the sector
submitted by both the CLA and individual publishers, the final decision in
May 2002 was that all copying, including coursepack use, should be rolled
into a single blanket licence with payment set at £4 (a considerable increase

in the fee in recognition of the changed approach) per FTE per year, to be increased annually in line with the retail price index; this brought an end to the transactional CLARCS system. During the course of the action, the CLA deemed it prudent to hold back payments to ALCS and PLS pending the outcome of the tribunal; final payments were disbursed in 2004.

On 16 August 2005, the CLA reached agreement with UUK and the Standing Conference of Principals (SCOP) for a trial scanning licence for the higher education sector, with the same restrictions on the amount of material which could be copied. Scanning could be carried out by designated individuals and there is provision for full *post hoc* reporting on the material copied into course repositories. Publishers could choose to maintain their mandate for the photocopying licence but not for the scanning licence. This arrangement was superseded by a new licence negotiated with UUK and Guild HE (the successor body to SCOP) following calls from the higher education sector to include digital publications in the licence repertoire; this new licence runs from August 2008 to July 2011 and allows universities to choose between a photocopying and scanning option and a comprehensive option. At the time of writing, payment is made at the rate of £5.85 per FTE for a photocopying and scanning licence, and at £6.44 per FTE for a comprehensive licence. As for all CLA's licences, digital originals are included on a rightsholder opt-in basis.

Publishers continue to be concerned that the creation of course packs under the licence may substitute for students buying copyright works, particularly textbooks. A working group of publishers and licence coordinators supported by UUK and Guild HE and chaired by CLA is currently drawing up guidelines for good practice in the creation of coursepacks to try and eliminate this possibility.

Licensing government bodies

Although there has been some discussion of a single pan-government licence, at present licences are issued to the individual ministries. Blanket licences are issued to government departments on the same basis as those issued to business and the professions (see *Licensing business and the professions* later in this chapter, pp. 316–7); on 15 February 1994 the first such licence was signed with the Home Office, responsible for the fire, police and prison services and their respective training colleges. The Inland Revenue took out a licence in 1996. Licences have been granted in recent years to the National Health Service, the Lord Chancellor's Department, the Law Office, the British Council, the BBC, the Department for International Development, the Cabinet Office, the Child Support Agency, the Crown Prosecution Service, and the executive public bodies of the Department of Culture, Media and Sport, the Department of Health, the Ministry of Agriculture, Fisheries and Food, the Department of Education and Employment and the then Department of Trade and Industry. The licence was revised to include scanning and the use of digitized copies in 2002 and digital originals on an opt-in basis for rightsholders in April 2008. The National Health Service in Scotland, Northern Ireland and Wales has moved to the new licence, with the additional right to supply single paper copies of print works externally to patients on request. The National Health Service in England continues to have a photocopying and scanning licence only, which runs until March 2010. At the time of writing discussions are under way between CLA and the National Health Service in England for a new centrally negotiated licence to run from April 2010.

The BLDSC

The first arrangement to be finalized between the CLA and a public body was that with the British Library, under whose aegis the British Library Document Supply Centre (BLDSC) in Boston Spa falls. Revenue generated from the BLDSC service is significant, although the Library maintains that it is a not-for-profit organization.

The British Library and other non-profit libraries, including the libraries of the learned societies, have a special privilege granted to them by Parliament to supply copies for research or private study without the consent of the copyright holder and without paying any royalty. Document delivery services operated under this privilege can compete with, and in some cases undercut, commercial document delivery services. The library privilege is governed by regulations – the Copyright (Librarians and Archivists) Copying of Copyright Material Regulations 1989, SI 1989 no. 1212. Some users are prepared to pay a premium for the benefit of not complying with the detail of the regulations, and in such cases the CLA collects payments for the benefit of rightsholders. In addition, businesses and other organizations which cannot benefit from library privilege use the service under a CLA licence with the payment of a copyright fee. In the CLA's 2008–9 accounting period some £677,000 was paid out to publishers from document delivery licences, including the BLDSC arrangement. BLDSC also has direct licence arrangements with many major academic journal publishers. A substantial number of documents supplied by BLDSC to customers in the United Kingdom and Ireland are, however, still provided under library privilege, without any fees being paid to copyright holders. Supply under library privilege is not permitted to overseas customers. Negotiations are still being conducted between BLDSC and rightsholders concerning an e-library privilege service within the United Kingdom only.

The initial licence agreement signed between the CLA and BLDSC on 1 April 1991 was a transactional arrangement on the basis of a fee of £1.10 per journal article supplied by post or fax. BLDSC long pressed for a licence permitting the supply of material electronically. It introduced a service using the Ariel system, whereby BLDSC scans the print version of the publication (but does not store it); a copy is then supplied electronically to a PC in the hands of an intermediary (e.g. a library abroad), which then prints off a paper copy for the end-user. This service has been supplemented by ARTTEL and ARTEmail. A PDF is sent by secure electronic delivery; a copy of the material may then be printed off and the PDF must be deleted. Storage or retransmission of the PDF is not permitted and is prevented by DRM.

The CLA issued a new licence backdated to April 2002 which renews automatically for a twelve-month period on 1 April each year unless either side has given six months' notice of termination. Fees are either set by the rightsholder (publishers can do this via PLS-e) or carry a CLA default rate of £9 per article. BLDSC provides the CLA with quarterly usage reports together with payment of copyright fees.

In late 2003, BLDSC, in partnership with Elsevier, launched its Secure Electronic Delivery Service, currently based on Adobe Reader 6.0.1 software or later. For material licensed directly by publishers for this service, the usage permitted to customers depends on the terms of the publisher's licence to BLDSC.

Licensing business and the professions

The introduction of licensing schemes for business and the professions is crucial, and perhaps the most difficult area of all, given the diverse range of potential users. It was in relation to this sector that the 1988 Copyright Act proved disappointing from the point of view of copyright holders; it had long been known that the scale of copying by commercial companies had been increasing. The effects were being felt particularly in the area of high-level scientific journals and professional reference works. In the early stages of drafting, the Copyright Bill specified that copying for the purposes of commercial research was outside the bounds of fair dealing; however, the final text of the 1988 Act did not make copying of this kind an infringement. This was remedied by the revisions to the Act introduced in October 2003 following the implementation of the 2001 EU Directive on the Harmonization of Certain Aspects of Copyright and Related Rights in the Information Society (see Chapter 1), where it was made clear that copying for commercial purposes is not covered by fair dealing.

Between 1990 and 1993, the CLA held lengthy discussions with the Confederation of British Industry (CBI), which represents a significant proportion of British industrial concerns; it can, however, only guide rather than instruct its members. Licences for business users are normally based on a fee per professional employee (see the CLA website www.cla.co.uk for current rates; these are 'banded' depending on the class of business activity) and permit the making of copies – directly from the original – of up to one chapter of a book, one periodical article, one case law report or in other instances up to 5% of the work in question. A new business licence launched in October 2002 permitted the right to scan as well as photocopy from paper originals and in early 2008 was extended to include the copying of content from digital originals from mandating publishers on an opt-in basis for rightsholders. Licensed business users must agree to take part in sample surveys that include the provision of an information audit of the number of journals and periodicals to which they subscribe (excluding any newspapers and other works not included in the scheme), together with a list of books purchased in the previous twelve months. Also as part of a survey, selected individuals within the organization are asked to keep a copying diary for the duration of the survey and to answer a questionnaire administered face to face by a member of the CLA surveys team. They are also required to reconfirm annually the number of professional employees on which the licence fee is based.

There is now a special provision for small businesses to take out a licence for a flat annual fee based on the total number of employees rather than the number of professional employees. Current fees are shown on the CLA website.

The sectors producing the largest income are the pharmaceutical industry, the legal profession (which also has a sector-specific licence) and the financial sector. Since April 2008, arrangements have permitted the pharmaceutical industry to photocopy or scan copyright material or copy digital originals, to store copies digitally and to supply digital copies externally for the purposes of legal proceedings, regulatory submissions and patent applications, and to supply single copies externally for the purposes of medical information. A new Law Licence running from 1 November 2008 permits licensed law firms to photocopy and scan permitted amounts of content from print books, journals, magazines and law reports. Electronic storage on a case or project basis for access by relevant staff is permitted and there is a provision for employees to scan and send digitized copies to colleagues within the United Kingdom and overseas.

Other sectors now covered by licences are accounting, advertising and public relations, the chemical industry, the electronics industry, the food and drink sector, the hotel and conference sector, manufacturing industry and (last but not least) publishers themselves. An attractive element of the licence for all is that a single article (or up to 5% of a publication) can be copied digitally on to the licensee's intranet for up to thirty days.

Copyshops

A licence is available for all copyshops, whether they be independent or part of a franchise chain. If the shop is a franchisee, there may be a centrally negotiated licence document available from their head office. The licence fee is based on the actual number of machines that can produce copies within each shop or group of shops. The current annual cost of a licence is £188.50 for the first machine and £57.37 for each additional machine.

Press cuttings agencies

A licence has been available to the agencies since 2001, allowing them to photocopy extracts from newspapers and periodicals and to send them to their clients in print form in return for a per-cutting copyright fee. In 2003, the licence was extended to enable them to scan whole issues of newspapers and periodicals provided that the extracts were still sent to clients in print form. A new licence launched in 2008 permits the agencies to transmit the extracts electronically to their client companies by e-mail or via a web-based service but only with the first copy of any cutting covered by a copyright fee. For any additional copies sent or accessed by the client, a CLA business licence is required. Press cuttings agencies must provide the CLA with the names of the clients to whom they are making copies available. Any further copying of the cuttings by the client company is also only permitted if that client holds a CLA business licence. The current rates for copyright fees are set at 5p for paper copies and 10p for digital copies.

The licensing of illustrations: DACS

In 1999, the CLA reached agreement with DACS (www.dacs.org.uk) concerning the photocopying of artistic works, including graphic works and photographs included in published works. DACS has appointed the CLA as its agent, and from August 1999 licences granted to the higher and further education sectors offered this facility.

Copying of full- or part-page illustration material in published works, including the disembedding of illustrations, is now allowed provided that this falls within the maximum amount of material permitted under the licence, i.e. up to 5% of the total of any published edition, or up to one chapter of a book or one article from a journal. As explained earlier, DACS receives 7% of all CLA licensing income for distribution to relevant visual creators.

Licensing accessible copies for the visually impaired and reading disabled

Since 2003 all CLA's sector-specific licences have included provision for licensees to create accessible copies of whole works as required by the relevant course of study or work, for authorized persons within the licensee organization who have a visual impairment. As licences were updated in

2008 and 2009, this provision has been broadened to include all authorized persons who have a reading disability. In addition, CLA has a separate licence for organizations creating accessible copies for individuals external to their organization. This allows accessible copies to be sent to individuals with a registered visual impairment anywhere within the United Kingdom and the European Union. A key user is the Royal National Institute for the Blind (RNIB). Under UK law, there is no copyright fee to pay but licensees must make their catalogue of available works accessible to rightsholders and other licensees and must also keep full records of all copies sent out. At the time of writing, a revised version of this licence is due to be launched, broadening provision to all individuals with a reading disability. (See also Chapter 18.)

Reproduction rights organizations

Originally, the CLA scheme restricted photocopying to works published in the United Kingdom. The CLA now has bilateral arrangements with thirty-one other reproduction rights organizations (RROs) in Argentina, Australia, Austria, Barbados, Belgium, Canada (including Quebec), Denmark, Finland, France, Germany, Greece, Hong Kong, Iceland, Ireland, Italy, Jamaica, Japan, Luxembourg, Mexico, the Netherlands, New Zealand, Norway, Singapore, South Africa, Spain, Sweden, Switzerland, Taiwan, Trinidad and Tobago and the United States, permitting the photocopying of a range of material from those sources in the United Kingdom and in turn receiving payment for the photocopying of UK material in those markets. Some bilateral agreements (currently those with Australia, Canada, Denmark, France, Ireland, Norway, South Africa, Spain, Switzerland and the United States) also permit scanning and the copying of digital originals. Bilateral arrangements work on the basis of 'national treatment', i. e. the use of the works of international rightsholders is treated on the same basis as the works of nationals in the country concerned.

The arrangement for the United States only applies to publishers on the list of US Participating Publishers. In the last CLA financial year 2008/9, approximately £4.3 million was paid to publishers from these overseas arrangements. The CLA is a member of the International Federation of Reproduction Rights Organizations (IFRRO). Representatives of the RROs meet regularly to discuss matters of common concern, including the collective management of electronic use of copyright material. IFRRO is also available to advise when a country is planning to set up a new RRO.

The American RRO is the Copyright Clearance Center (CCC – www. copyright.com), which represents over 9,000 publishers and hundreds of thousands of authors. Schools are not covered within its remit, as they are permitted to make copies of copyright material under an educational exception of US copyright law. CCC provides an Annual Copyright

Licence transactional service to universities and colleges which permits photocopying, international e-mailing and electronic access to authorized users within the licensed site. CCC also offers Rightslink, a direct link from the websites of larger participating publishers to the CCC website which deals with the licensing of content. Another service is Rightsconnect, which links smaller rightsholders' web-based articles, book chapters and other content to its licensing price list and directly to CCC's copyright.com website, providing would-be users with automated access to licensing. Businesses are the main users of the CCC service.

It is, however, important to note that not all RROs operate on the same basis; Anne Leer, the author and media consultant, has defined the four main models:

1 *The Anglo-American model*: these RROs operate on the basis of voluntary contracts with individual rightsholders and organizations representing rightsholders. Statistical data provide title-specific information in order to determine the remuneration to rightsholders.
2 *The German–Spanish model*: these RROs operate on the basis of a statutory levy on photocopying machines, which may vary according to the type and capacity of the equipment as well as its location and use. The distribution of remuneration to rightsholders is based on statistical surveys, which involve agreed source codes relating to the type of material copied.
3 *The Dutch model*: this operates on the basis of a statutory licensing system in the area of government and education. The remuneration rates are set by regulation, except for course material and readers, which may be negotiated.
4 *The Nordic model*: here, RROs can enter into agreements only with organizations that represent a substantial proportion of rightsholders, e.g. publishers' associations or unions of authors. With the support of those organizations, the RROs' mandate can then extend to all copyright works in the relevant sector; this is termed 'extended collective licensing'. Publishers receive allocations of income according to industry statistics.

A number of former Eastern Bloc and developing countries have now also set up RROs but as yet none has a bilateral agreement with the CLA. At the time of writing, discussions are in hand with India, Russia and China. The policing and enforcement of copyright compliance are vital roles for any RRO; in late 1995, the CLA launched its campaign against illegal photocopying, Copywatch.

Over the years, a number of test cases have been undertaken against copyright infringement through photocopying, in the United Kingdom and elsewhere. These have included the successful case brought by the

Publishers Association against Manchester City Council in the early 1980s, the 1991 case against Kinko's Graphics Corporation in the United States, where the company had to pay $510,000 in damages and $1.4 million in costs to eight American publishers, and the 1992 case brought by the American Geophysical Union, Elsevier, Pergamon and Springer against Texaco for the making of single copies of articles from scientific journals. In 1994, Texaco appealed against the judgement; however, it finally agreed to settle in May 1997 for a payment of more than $1 million, retrospective licensing fees payable to CCC, together with an undertaking to enter into standard licensing arrangements in the future. The judgement in this case clearly reinforced the rights of the copyright owners and held that copying of this kind within a for-profit industrial research company is not fair use. There have been later large-scale infringement cases, including the action against the investment company Legg Mason for infringing use of Lowry's *Stock Exchange Market Analysis Reports* in 2003. In 2008 a lawsuit was brought against Georgia State University by Oxford University Press, Cambridge University Press and Sage Publications, supported by the Association of American Publishers, on the grounds of unauthorized circulation of copyright material via electronic course reserves and university websites. At the time of writing the case has not yet been resolved.

The internet and publishing

The internet is now a major feature of our everyday life; it is no longer merely a channel of communication between academics and researchers. It is used as a source of information, a quick, cheap and easy means of communication via e-mail and social networking and user-generated content (UGC) sites such as Facebook, MySpace, Twitter and YouTube (see *Social networking and user-generated content (UGC) sites* later in this chapter, pp. 330–1), as well as a channel for advertising and commerce. It is currently estimated that around 1.8 billion people worldwide have access to the internet (about 25% of the world's population), with 227 million users in the United States, 418 million in Europe (of whom 49 million are in the United Kingdom) and 738 million in Asia.

The internet was originally set up by US military and civil defence bodies in the late 1960s; in 1993, non-military functions were separated out into Arpanet (Advanced Research Projects Agency), providing a network to link communications between academic and research establishments in different areas of the United States. It is now a supranational telecommunications system that links a host of private and public networks worldwide.

By its very nature, the internet has developed rapidly and organically with no central control mechanism, no single code of conduct and with a philosophy still prevailing amongst many of its dedicated users that (apart from the initial cost of linking up and telephone time) the service is free. Users normally pay a link-up and monthly connection charge for access to the internet via an online service provider such as America Online (AOL) or British Telecom (BT), plus charges for telephone time; most providers offer a service for a fixed monthly charge. In effect, users have access to sites worldwide for the price of a local telephone call and can transfer and download digital files in perfect form and for a potentially infinite number of other users. In the last five years, more providers have offered a broadband service; this has facilitated speed of access and the ability to download even larger amounts of text and visual material. It is estimated that 400 million users currently have access to broadband and this figure is predicted to rise to 700 million by 2013.

Revenue from commercial transactions over the internet has continued to increase; websites run by conventional retailers – once considered dinosaurs by comparison with dedicated internet retailers – are growing fastest. Online sales by companies such as Walmart in the United States and Argos and Tesco in the United Kingdom are soaring. However, some customers are still reluctant to give credit card information over the net; payment fraud on credit card transactions has continued to increase despite assurances from vendors that they offer secure sites.

One very real problem with the internet is that its spectacular development over the last fifteen years has resulted in an ever-increasing morass of material with no overall system of classification, making it difficult to navigate and home in directly on relevant information. *Byte* magazine referred to 'managing infoglut', and the problem has still not been resolved. Users access material via browser systems such as Microsoft's Internet Explorer. The vast body of material has led to the establishment of numerous search engines, such as Google, Yahoo!, Ask.com and Microsoft's bing.com; Google is now predominant and since its stock flotation in August 2004 has moved into a range of other areas, including digitization of content (see *Search engines, online retailers and others: threat or opportunity?* later in this chapter, pp. 353–62).

In 1989, Tim Berners-Lee, then working at CERN Laboratories in Geneva (the European centre for research in particle physics), developed the World Wide Web (www) as a graphical interface system for the internet, and it now represents the most densely populated part of the network; it enables users to make connections between related sites at the click of a mouse. Text files are coded in Hypertext Mark-up Language (HTML). The web provides links to government and academic communications networks, bulletin boards for group discussions and websites established by companies, offering information about their products and services and providing a channel for commerce. Most publishers now have company websites on their servers, providing information to both authors and customers on their business, new publication information and ordering facilities.

A continuing problem with the internet is that there is often no way to establish the original source of the material and no hierarchy of knowledge, making it difficult to assess the accuracy of much of the information available. Everyone with access to the internet can become a 'publisher' and, in the words of a famous early internet cartoon in the *New Yorker* magazine showing a dog logging on online, 'On the internet, nobody knows you're a dog'. As the internet expands, users learn to rely on 'branded' sites for reliability of information, but a huge corpus of material is posted by individuals whose credentials cannot easily be established. A significant development has been Wikipedia, a web-based collaborative multilingual encyclopedia launched in 2001 and supported by the non-profit Wikipedia Foundation, where contributions are provided and updated by volunteers (see *Databases: the move from CD-ROM to online* in Chapter 24). It is now the most popular general reference work on the internet.

An early example of publishing on the internet was the Gutenberg Electronic Library Project, initiated in 1971 by Michael Hart at the University of Illinois. The library consists mainly of public domain works in the fields of history, literature and reference; content is posted by volunteers. At the time of writing, the Gutenberg Project has approximately 300,000 titles available online for free downloading in more than forty languages (www.gutenberg.org). Another major digitization project has been the Million Book Project, *aka* the Universal Library, at Carnegie Mellon University (www.ulib.org), which had exceeded its target in 2007, scanning books in over twenty languages; most are public domain works, but some copyright works are included with permission.

Initially a number of trade publishers experimented by placing sample chapters and entire novels online; some publications were given an interactive facility, enabling readers to obtain background material on the author, alternative plot endings, etc. This was followed by the development of e-books for downloading on to computers, personal digital assistants, smart phones or early dedicated reader devices such as the Gemstar RocketeBook; the latter devices proved less than successful. From late 2005 onwards, there have been renewed initiatives by major trade publishers to exploit their content electronically and in the last two years this activity has been spurred on by the advent of more popular dedicated reading devices such as the Sony Reader and the Amazon Kindle. This area is covered in more detail in Chapter 24.

Legislation and the internet

The question of legislative control of materials placed on the internet has surfaced on numerous occasions, most notably in relation to the transmission of violent, pornographic, racist or libellous material, or material capable of being used for terrorist purposes. Perhaps not surprisingly, one of the largest revenue streams from the internet is generated by pornography sites. A number of commercial software packages have been developed for parental use, such as Netblocker, CYBERsitter, Surfwatch, Cyberpatrol and NetNanny, and a consortium of companies with major internet interests has developed a rating service for content: Platform for Internet Content Selection (PICS). However, there has been considerable debate over the issue of government regulation of material transmitted on the internet versus the issues of free speech and freedom to publish, and on 26 June 1997 the US Supreme Court declared the 1996 US Communications Decency Act unconstitutional. Countries such as China and Singapore still continue to impose some forms of restriction on access to the internet; there is also evidence of the use of spyware to identify politically sensitive material. In early 2006, Google was widely criticized for restricting access to such material by users of its Chinese website; in March 2010, it closed its .cn site and redirected enquiries to Hong Kong following intensive hacker attacks on its Gmail service. The Chinese authorities imposed restrictions on internet sites during the 2008 Olympics; in 2009 they blocked access to YouTube, which had shown images of anti-Chinese demonstrations in Tibet and Xinjiang Province, and to Twitter and other social networking sites in June 2009 at the time of the twentieth anniversary of the 1989 demonstrations in Tiananmen Square. YouTube in particular has also been blocked in Thailand, Pakistan, Iran and Turkey.

The question of where legal liability resides for the transmission of controversial material over the internet is a vexed one; transactions cannot take place in cyberspace, and material transmitted on the internet is subject to the civil and criminal laws of over 200 countries. The main questions are which legislation should govern infringements and in which country disputes should be taken to court. Online service providers have sought immunity from responsibility; the decisions in legal cases to date have not always been consistent, since much depends on whether the provider is regarded as a mere conduit for content (such as a telephone company) or as a publisher with some knowledge of the content being disseminated. Some limitations on the liability of providers are now available under the US Digital Millennium Copyright Act (see *Copyright legislation in the United States* in Chapter 1); the UK Copyright and Related Rights Regulations 2003, SI 2003 No. 2498, gives the High Court power to grant injunctions against service providers where they have actual knowledge of another person using their service to infringe copyright (see *Copyright legislation in the United Kingdom* in Chapter 1). A valuable account of the various issues was provided by Charles Clark in *Netlaw: A Cyberspace Agenda for Publishers*, originally published by the UK Publishers Association but now available in '*The Answer to the Machine Is in the Machine*' *and Other Collected Writings* (2005, Norwegian Research Center for Computers and Law).

Action against infringing, dangerous or obscene material on the internet is normally dealt with via national legislation with provisions for 'notice and takedown'. At the time of writing, the United Kingdom has no formal legal procedures for this, but in early 2009 the UK Publishers Association established a Copyright Portal (www.publishers.org.uk.cip) where its members can log instances of online piracy of their works and initiate notice and takedown procedures; members can also see if the same infringer is using the works of fellow publishers. The portal is being made available to other trade associations, including the Association of American Publishers.

Copyright and the internet

The question of copyright control on the internet is of vital importance to content providers, including publishers, software producers, the music industry and the film and television industries. Again, the major problem is the 'sharing' philosophy of many internet users, who are often still happy to transmit material of their own and of others without expectation of payment, and to access material from others on the same basis. An early example of an infringement case was the action taken by the Church of Scientology against the posting of Church documents on the internet by ex-members of the Church. However, the most spectacular cases were those instigated by the major record companies against MP3.com and Napster.

Some lessons from the music industry?

MP3 is an algorithm which can compress digital files by a ratio of 12:1, making downloading from the internet both easy and rapid. MP3.com did not require users to copy music they owned on to their computers, but offered them a huge repertoire (more than 515,000 digitized tracks) which users could download free of charge provided they could prove that they already owned a particular CD. Five major record companies (Sony BMG, Warner Music, Bertelsmann, Universal and Warner Music) filed suit for massive copyright infringement, and in mid-2000 a federal judge ruled that MP3.com was infringing the copyright of the record companies and their artists; the company subsequently reached settlements directly with EMI ($20 million plus a fee for each EMI CD or song registered or downloaded from the MP3.com website); settlements were also reached with Bertelsmann, Sony and Time Warner. In the case of Universal, a federal judge ruled that MP3.com should pay $25,000 per infringement and estimated a total liability of around $250 million.

Also in mid-2000, the Recording Industry Association of America (RIAA) and the rock band Metallica filed suit against Napster, an ingenious service which was the brainchild of a Boston college student, Shawn Fanning.

Napster offered software which allowed users to search the directories of other users who had music stored on their hard drives and to download copies directly from those sources. Napster therefore had no repertoire on a central server; it provided an interface for searching and connecting with material held elsewhere. It claimed approximately 22 million users, and some college campuses banned its use because it was clogging vast amounts of broadband campus network capacity. Napster's contention was that it had done nothing wrong; it had no control over the content traded by its users and warned them that they must be responsible for complying with copyright requirements. The fact that Napster had no server repertoire made it far harder to tackle than MP3.com, although it did maintain lists of connected systems and the files they provided. Pressure from the major record companies was enormous and, following a court order, the original Napster service closed down in July 2001 after the company agreed to make a $26 million settlement to the record companies. A projected $8 million sale to Bertelsmann was blocked by a bankruptcy judge and Napster was forced to declare bankruptcy in 2002. Its brand was initially bought by Roxio Inc. and relaunched as Napster 2.0. In September 2008 it was bought by US electronics retailer Best Buy for $121 million. The service is available in the United Kingdom (www.napster.co.uk).

Napster was not alone; it was followed by clones such as Morpheus, KaZaA and Grokster, as well as services such as Myplay.com, eDonkey, StreamCast and Gnutella which allowed sharing of video, music and software files, whilst Freenet, originally billed as 'the new bullet-proof Napster', allowed users to share text, audio and images, offering encryption facilities so that they could not be traced. A landmark US Supreme Court ruling in June 2005 opened file-sharing operators to potential liability and was followed by notice being served on seven companies. Grokster settled its lawsuit in September 2005 for $50 million and in September 2006 eDonkey agreed to pay $30 million in order to avoid lawsuits brought by the RIAA; both have since closed their services. The courts ruled against KaZaA and in July 2006 it agreed to pay $110 million to the record labels, with further payments to be made to songwriters and music publishers.

An interesting experiment was conducted by rock band Radiohead in October 2007. Circumventing any record label, they announced they would release their seventh album, *In Rainbows*, direct from their own website and allow purchasers to choose the price they would pay. Despite this touching faith in their fan base, 400,000 illegal downloads took place on the day the album was released, with 2.3 million downloads within less than four weeks, far exceeding the number of legitimate downloads.

Further legal action taken by the RIAA in filing over 20,000 very costly lawsuits on behalf of its member record companies against individual unauthorized file sharers resulted in negative publicity, particularly in the case against a single mother in Minnesota for file sharing via KaZaA, which resulted initially in her being required to pay $220,000 in damages and at a later retrial in June 2009 to pay $1.92 million. In late 2008 the RIAA abandoned its policy of pursuing individual infringers in favour of trying to persuade internet service providers (ISPs) to become more actively involved in the battle against internet piracy. By contrast, swift and inexpensive legal provisions under German law have resulted in a drop in the level of unauthorized downloading in that country to the lowest in Europe.

The policy of involving the ISPs has been endorsed by a July 2008 memorandum of agreement between the UK government on the one hand and BPI, Virgin, BSkyB, BT, Carphone Warehouse, Orange and Tiscali on the other; this has been followed by the Digital Britain Report in January 2009 and then Peter Mandelson's Digital Economy Bill (see *Copyright legislation in the United Kingdom* in Chapter 1), which is scheduled to come into force in April 2010 and which puts the onus on ISPs to crack down on unauthorized downloading of copyright content, using the 'three strikes and you're out' mechanism of cutting off internet access to persistent offenders.

Some significant legal action did, however, continue with a major case in Sweden against an online file-sharing service called The Pirate Bay, which enabled users to download music, films, video games and other copyright content. As with Napster, no content was stored on The Pirate Bay site, but it provided a directory to assist users in locating files via the BitTorrent file-sharing network. A major court case was brought against the founders by both the music and the motion picture industry bodies, and in April 2009 the four men behind The Pirate Bay were each jailed for a year and fined a total of $3.6 million. The company was later bought in June 2009 by the Swedish company Software Gaming Factory X for approximately $7.8 million, to be run as a legitimate operation. The Swedish government has since introduced legislation requiring ISPs to reveal far more information about their subscribers, which has resulted in a 60% reduction in illegal file sharing in that country.

The major record companies formed a consortium, Secure Digital Music Initiative (SDMI), to agree digital formats for MP3 players and other digital platforms; music is available with DRM facilities (see *Commercial digital rights management (DRM) systems* later in this chapter, pp. 338–9). Thus the music industry rather belatedly recognized user demand for content over the internet after suffering a major impact on traditional record and CD sales from activities such as file sharing and the unauthorized burning of copies of CDs. This has resulted in a brutal decade for the music industry, marked by upheaval, litigation, changing business models and declining revenue. It also saw the bankruptcy of bricks-and-mortar music chains such as Tower Records and the withdrawal of stores such as HMV from overseas markets. Even surviving stores such as HMV in the United Kingdom now depend for much of their revenue on merchandise other than music.

The rise in popularity of portable MP3 devices, and of the iconic Apple iPod in particular, forced the music industry to realize it must facilitate legitimate, simple and copyright-compliant downloading facilities, with all the major companies now participating in such services. Apple first launched its iTunes service in the United States in 2003, with tracks available for download in the United Kingdom at 79p per track and around £7.99 for a whole album. A range of iPod models are now on offer and by October 2009 Apple reported sales of 220 million units, with facilities to download music and video content as well as an e-reader application (see Chapter 24). iTunes initially used DRM in the form of the Fair Play encryption system; without this it is unlikely that the record labels would have agreed to license content to Apple. However, users complained that this restricted them to downloading only content available from iTunes to their device, and also that they could not transfer iTunes content to an alternative device they owned. All the indicators were that DRM alienated users and might positively encourage illegal file sharing from other sources. Recognizing this – and alarmed by falling music revenues – the major labels reached agreement with Apple, and in January 2009 they announced they would commence removal of DRM and that by the end of 2009 all iTunes would be DRM free. Apple also altered their pricing mechanism to reflect what they had to pay to the record companies, with a range of prices for single tracks (69c, 99c and $1.29 in the United States; 59p, 79p and 99p in the United Kingdom) and with albums at $9.99 and £7.99, respectively. Amazon, which now offers its own download service, immediately took steps to undercut iTunes prices, with tracks at 59p and some albums at £3; it has also removed DRM, after reaching agreement with the major record labels. iTunes currently holds 70% of the UK music download market.

Despite the ongoing and huge popularity of the iPod, the rise of the smart phone as the 'must-have' gadget, particularly amongst the younger generation, has led to a demand for the availability of music on that platform as well. In 2008 Nokia reached agreement with the major record labels for its Comes with Music service, which gives phone purchasers access to music content for a year, after which they can continue with the service either on a subscription basis or by choosing individual tracks from the Nokia Online Music Store.

An interesting development was the launch in the United Kingdom in February 2009 of the Swedish-owned music streaming service, Spotify (www.spotify.com). After some initial problems with unauthorized content, the site has reached agreement with the major labels; 250,000 users signed up in the first month and by late 2009 it had over two million UK users and some four million more in Europe, with plans to launch in the United States during 2010. It offers several different options: a free streaming (rather than downloading) service of music tracks to computers, supported by advertising which appears every twenty minutes; alternatively, an ad-free service currently charged at 99p for 24 hours or at £9.99 per month. The service is adding 10,000 new tracks per day and enables users to create their own playlists; it has been likened to listening to the radio but with the listeners choosing what they want to hear. There is an application for the iPhone. The take-up for this service – which has far outstripped use of the UK-based Last.fm and RealPlayer (one of the first media streaming services, launched in 1995) – perhaps heralds a transition to a time when users do not feel the need to 'own' content when they can easily access it legally from a central database. Spotify has sometimes been referred to as a 'celestial jukebox' and is perhaps the musical manifestation of so-called 'cloud computing'. In July 2009 it announced the first audiobook to be available through its services: perhaps appropriately, Chris Anderson's *Free: The Future of a Radical Price*, which examines alternative business models.

Another recent development has been the entry of some ISPs into providing music services themselves, in addition to other content; Virgin and Sky have both entered into arrangements with the major labels to offer streaming and downloading services; as pay TV and broadband providers they already have a ready-made audience and billing structures in place.

All these developments give some hope that users will move to greater use of legitimate services provided that they can be seamlessly provided and remain relatively inexpensive. At the time of writing, the British Phonograph Industry (BPI) and the International Federation of Phonographic Industries (IFPI) both estimate that 95% of all downloads worldwide are still illegal. Despite this, they estimated that digital revenues would increase to provide 20% of global music revenue in 2009 (up from 15% in 2007) and that in 2012 digital revenue will represent 40% of music revenues in the United Kingdom.

The travails of the music industry are described here in some detail because they contain lessons for other industries – for the film industry, which already suffers from piracy, unauthorized copying of DVDs and now from downloading to hand-held video devices, but also for publishers in terms of the downloading of audiobooks, e-books and in some cases the full text of print titles put up on line either by enthusiasts or for profit. Whilst nobody can pretend that the illegal downloading of music is a thing of the past, there is evidence that in some ways it has resulted in free marketing for music acts and in certain cases has brought them to prominence. In some cases it appears to have resulted in an increase in legitimate sales, and there is certainly evidence that it has led to a substantial increase in paying attendance at live music events and hence revenue to the artists concerned. The illegal downloading of the whole text of books is on the increase and unfortunately authors do not have the opportunity of reaping indirect benefits from the use of their works in quite the same way.

MP3 technology has already been applied to audiobooks with services such as Audible (see Chapter 20). The area of e-books is discussed in more detail in Chapter 24.

Social networking and user-generated content (UGC) sites

With the advent of Web 2.0 came a plethora of social networking sites, based mainly on the principle of user-generated content. When the last edition of this book was in preparation, they did not perhaps merit a mention, but in the last four years the take-up has been substantial and copyright concerns have also arisen.

Collaborative, interactive and addictive, the sites have developed into substantial online communities. Some enable users to post a personal profile and to connect with 'friends'. The earliest such site was probably Friends Reunited, initially set up to enable users to re-establish contact with long-lost friends, often from their schooldays. In 2005 the site was bought by ITV for £175 million; in 2009 they put the site up for sale for £25 million as its popularity had been superseded by newer sites. At the time of writing, its sale to Brightsolid, owner of genealogy-related sites, is under scrutiny by the Office of Fair Trading (OFT). Those more popular sites include Facebook (founded by a group of Harvard graduates, now backed by Microsoft and with some 400 million users), MySpace (since 2008 owned by AOL and with some 263 million users) and the professional network LinkedIn (about 54 million users). There is also Twitter, which enables users to post a short personal profile and then to communicate news and views to a maximum of 140 characters per 'tweet'. It currently has some 445 million users and includes celebrity 'tweeters'.

There are also sites which permit the sharing of content, some user-generated and some not. Flickr (with some 32 million users) enables users to share photographs; Flixster (63 million users), for video content; and, perhaps most prominently, YouTube, which also enables users to upload and share video content, with a maximum length of ten minutes, introduced in 2006 to prevent the unauthorized upload of whole films or television shows. Founded by three former PayPal employees in 2005, YouTube was bought by Google in November 2006 for $1.65 billion. In October 2009 YouTube estimated that thirteen hours of video content were being uploaded to the site every minute and that the site was receiving over a billion views per day. There is also Second Life, owned by Linden Research Inc. and with some 1.3 million users who can enter a virtual world in the form of an avatar and lead a virtual existence there.

Although such sites may be viewed as creative, fun and free, some also have commercial potential, either indirectly through viral marketing between users or through paid advertising (as on YouTube), or directly – for example on Second Life, where virtual trading in items or property can result in real-world revenue. Many businesses, including publishers, now have a virtual presence on Second Life.

MySpace in particular has sought to monetize its activities and it hosts Fox TV and NBC's programming as well as older cult TV programmes such as *Charlie's Angels*. In September 2008 it launched its MySpace Music online service after reaching agreement with Universal Music Group, Sony BMG, Warner Music Group and EMI Music to make their catalogues available to users via streaming. However, if users wish to download content to an MP3 player, they have to purchase tracks via Amazon.

Flickr has reached an agreement with Getty Images which enables the picture agency to market selected user-generated images commercially, paying the creator a share of the resulting revenue. Alternatively, creators can choose to make their content freely available via a Creative Commons licence (see *Creative Commons* in Chapter 1).

Although much content on these sites is indeed original to those who post it, it was perhaps inevitable that copyright issues would arise as copyright images and video clips in particular were posted without permission on sites such as YouTube and MySpace, with those posting the material sometimes 'mashing' it with their own content. MySpace introduced digital fingerprint technology which checks uploads against a library of copyright-protected content. Despite a clear onscreen warning to would-be uploaders to YouTube, a great deal of copyright content found its way on to the site, some of which has been dealt with via the notice and takedown provisions of the US Digital Millennium Copyright Act (see *Copyright legislation in the United States* in Chapter 1). However, continued postings have resulted in a number of lawsuits, including one from the English Premier Football League. Following an as yet unresolved lawsuit brought by Viacom, claiming $1 billion in damages for the posting of over 150,000 clips of its material on the site, YouTube introduced a system called VideoID to try to detect copyright material and reduce the instances of lawsuits. YouTube has also faced criticism for offensive content in some of its videos.

Network communication

The academic sector has long been an enthusiastic user of network communication. In the United Kingdom, the Joint Academic Network (JANET – www.ja.net) has long linked universities, FE colleges, research councils, specialist colleges and adult and community learning providers. It currently serves over 18 million end-users across 1,000 institutions and offers video-conferencing and video-training facilities for distance learning. Network communication is particularly attractive to academics because of the ease and speed with which original material can be exchanged, reviewed by peers and in effect published without a publisher as an intermediary. Academics have often complained about the length of time taken for research papers to be reviewed and accepted for publication in academic journals.

All major journal publishers have had to take account of the requirements of both contributors and users, and almost all major scientific journals are now published in electronic as well as print-on-paper form. Some are now published in electronic form only, with *Online Clinical Trials*, launched in 1992 by the American Association for the Advancement of Science in association with Online Computer Library Catalog (OCLC), as the first peer-reviewed online medical journal. This development has had major implications for methods of subscription, as well as for the areas of abstracts, site licensing and document delivery.

Fair dealing in the digital environment

The question of fair dealing or fair use in the digital environment has long been controversial and has been a major topic for discussion in both national and international forums, most notably at the 1995 Fair Use Conference and subsequent meetings in the United States (CONFU); by the European Copyright User Platform (ECUP), consisting of thirty-seven European library associations; by the copyright committee of the International Association of Scientific, Technical and Medical Publishers (STM); and at full international level at the WIPO Diplomatic Copyright Conference in Geneva in December 1996 (see *The international copyright conventions* in Chapter 1). In the UK the topic was tackled by a joint working party of publishers and academic librarians convened by the Publishers Association and the Joint Information Systems Committee (JISC).

The main issue is again the perception of many users that access to material on networks should be free of charge. The Open Archive Initiative (OAI) encourages free access to material on web servers at universities and research institutes; this may include theses, conference proceedings, research data and courseware but also research articles in preprint or post-publication form. This view has been allied to a move on the part of some academic institutions to assert control over copyright in the work of their staff, even when it is not produced as a key element of their daily jobs. There has also been an increasing trend on the part of research institutions that have provided funding for research (most notably the Wellcome Trust and the National Institutes of Health in the United States) to make it a condition that the resulting research findings should be available as open access materials (see *The Anti-copyright movement, open access and other initiatives* in Chapter 1). All these moves have implications for traditional publishers as well as for onward providers of content such as document delivery services.

Academic publishers view network delivery as an alternative commercial channel for the supply of content to customers, in particular the supply of material from academic journals and high-level research works to users in the academic and commercial research sectors. Electronic delivery may represent an alternative method of supply for material already available in print-on-paper form, or it may be the prime method of delivering material such as electronic-only journals. It is therefore understandable that publishers who have invested time, effort and considerable financial resources in adding value to such material before bringing it to the marketplace in print-on-paper or electronic form, or both, feel that there would be very few electronic uses of the material that would not impinge directly on their ability to market the works in question commercially.

The key reason for this is that almost every electronic access to copyright material is undertaken by an individual person, but those individuals are likely to be the core readership for the material in question. Users may seek to view material online, but they may also seek to print it out as hard copy or copies, and may also retransmit a perfect copy to an unlimited number of other users. The discussion has therefore hinged on what acts of reproduction of the material can be permitted under fair dealing, and whether the same amounts of material as may be copied in the print-on-paper environment should be extended to the digital environment in the context of personal use or inter-library loan. The results of the PA/JISC working party were published in 1998 in a joint paper, *Guidelines for Fair Dealing in an Electronic Environment*, and represent notes for guidance in the UK only; the paper can be obtained from the Publishers Association or from the eLib website (www.ukoln.ac.uk/services/elib/papers/pa). Uses of material considered to be fair dealing include incidental copying involved in the viewing of part or all of an electronic publication on screen; printing onto paper of one copy of part of an electronic publication if this is done by an individual or by a librarian on behalf of an individual; copying onto disk of part of an electronic publication for permanent local storage if this is done by an individual or a librarian on behalf of an individual, and provided that the disk is either a portable medium or a fixed medium accessible to only one user at a time; transmission of part of an electronic publication for the purpose of printing a single copy with only such interim storage as is required to facilitate that printing; and transmission of part of an electronic publication to an individual at their request for permanent electronic storage (but not retransmission). Copying onto disk of all of an electronic publication, transmission of all of an electronic publication and the posting on a network or website open to the public of all or part of an electronic publication are not regarded as fair dealing and constitute acts for which permission should be sought from the copyright owner.

The issue was covered further in a booklet entitled *Joint Guidelines on Copyright and Academic Research*, published in April 2008 by the UK

Publishers Association and the British Academy (the National Academy for the Humanities and Social Sciences).

Technical systems for the management and protection of rights

Digital rights management might be defined as a set of standards and technologies that allow digital content to be distributed whilst also being protected, managed and tracked by content providers. It should therefore be seen as a transactional enabling technology to permit content such as text, music and audiovisual material to be made available to authorized users by a variety of methods – including broadband, dial-up, satellite and wireless – to a variety of platforms, including personal computers, televisions via set-top boxes, games consoles, personal digital assistants (PDAs) and mobile phones and similar devices.

There has been considerable confusion in the area of DRM, particularly between its two inherent elements – first, the management of digital rights, i.e. the use of standards and technology to identify and describe digital products and to store and express the rights associated with them; and, second, technical protection measures (TPM), the use of encryption to enforce usage conditions. These in turn are quite separate from systems designed to be used in-house for the overall business management of rights deals (see *Basic record keeping* in Chapter 6).

Managing digital rights

The UK Publishers Association has defined the management of digital rights as involving the identification and description of a piece of content, including necessary information about the rights and permissions attached to it (with payment mechanisms if appropriate), packaged in such a way as to be interoperable. In this context, interoperability has two consecutive dimensions – first, the ability of different types of content – text, music, audiovisual material – to converge or combine within a single consumer product. This requires the use of common vocabulary with a common identification and description format referred to as International Interoperable Standard – for example, ISO MPEG-21, the portfolio of standards being developed by the Motion Picture Experts Group, a subcommittee of the International Organization for Standardization (ISO) working jointly with the International Electrotechnical Commission (IEC). These provide an open framework for multimedia applications across a wide range of delivery systems and platforms, e.g. personal computers, televisions, PDAs and mobile phones. This requires 'platform-independent standards' enabling different types of machine to receive or exchange the same content packages. Elements of MPEG-21 include Digital Item

Identification and Description, a Rights Data Dictionary and a Rights Expression Language.

ACAP (Automated Content Access Protocol – www.the-acap.org) is a joint initiative by the European Publishers Council, the World Association of Newspapers and the International Publishers Association, working with publishers, search engines and other technical and commercial partners. ACAP is an open, non-proprietary protocol (originally pioneered by the newspaper industry as it took its content online) which has been extended to the book industry with the aim that it should become a universal standard for online publishing.

The initial focus of ACAP has been to devise a simple communication language which can be recognized by search engine crawlers and which enables rightsholders to specify clear details of who can exploit their content and how. The project is supported by the European Commission and publishers are being encouraged to adopt ACAP at its basic level; the system is simple and free to implement. Publishers can also choose to become members of ACAP on the basis of an annual subscription, and can then work with the organization to develop specific business solutions.

Technical protection measures

The other aspect of DRM – perhaps more accurately the digital management of rights dimension – involves TPMs, encryption and access control mechanisms, with which rightsholders in the publishing and other copyright industries may seek to protect their content, to maintain control of copyright material and to prevent unauthorized access to that material – the philosophy of Charles Clark's maxim that the answer to the machine is in the machine. It is unlikely that all such mechanisms can be completely standardized and it is this aspect which is viewed by some would-be consumers as an attempt by the copyright industries to 'lock up' their content. There is, however, an increasing need for compatibility, given the range of content which is now being delivered electronically and the fact that the digital world knows no geographical boundaries.

There have been many developments in both aspects of DRM technologies, such as encryption, the watermarking of material to indicate ownership, the fingerprinting of material to indicate the identity of the transmitter, and unique identifier systems for designated units of copyright material and payment systems, be they transactional or otherwise. There has also been considerable debate on whether electronic copyright management systems should be run on the basis of watermarking and fingerprinting or via encryption, i.e. whether they should be access driven or protection driven. The question of whether any electronic copyright management system can be run entirely on a transactional basis has also been discussed, since the cost of collecting some payments – as in the print-on-paper environment – could exceed the expected income.

Identifiers

Much work has been done in the field of identifiers in recent years. The publishing industry has long employed identifiers with formal standard status in the form of the ISBN (International Standard Book Number) for individual books and, more recently, e-books, the ISSN (International Standard Serial Number) for individual journals, and the SICI (Serial Item Contribution Identifier) for individual journal issues and articles. The music industry has employed standard identifiers that facilitate the management of rights and flow of royalties, such as the ISWC (International Standard Work Code) for the identification of musical works. The publishing industry has now developed the ISTC (International Standard Text Code) for the unique identification of textual works. The ISTC identifies the underlying work and will link to the various editions and other manifestations of that work, with clear implications for rights management. There are also plans to introduce the ISNI (International Standard Name Indicator), which would distinguish between authors with similar names.

In the internet environment, identifiers are generically referred to as URIs (Uniform Resource Identifiers); the main identifier is the URL (Uniform Resource Locator). However, since the URL identifies a location on the web, it can become inoperative, returning an error message if sites close down or change their structure.

A widely adopted solution to the problem of persistent identification is the DOI (Digital Object Identifier), originally developed by the Association of American Publishers but now administered by the International DOI Foundation. The DOI has been referred to as a 'digital licence plate', a dumb identifier but with a routing system to facilitate trading in copyright material on the internet with a potentially fine degree of granularity. The DOI Foundation defines it as 'a managed system for persistent identification of content-related entities on digital networks'. The system leads users to a constantly updated database that links the DOI to the URL containing the material required. The DOI is a permanently assigned number consisting of two parts: a prefix assigned by the agency which administers the system and which identifies the agency and the current copyright owner, and a suffix assigned by the copyright owner which could incorporate existing identifiers such as an ISBN, ISSN or a special number devised by the owner to tag a designated piece of material. The user simply clicks an onscreen button, which sends a message to the directory and thence to the owner's database. This may display details of the digital product itself or the owner's charging mechanism, or it may require the would-be user to contact the owner for further details.

The main companies to register with the DOI have been the major academic publishers, particularly those with a large journal repertoire where there is a need for granular identification of content. By 2009 over 40 million DOIs had been assigned by DOI registration agencies in the United States, Europe and Australasia. Frankfurt 1999 saw the announcement of CrossRef (www.crossref.org), a project for reference-linking between journal articles; the service provides a cross-publisher citation linking system for millions of articles. CrossRef is a DOI registration agency for scholarly and professional journals.

Metadata

The need to develop a consistent system of description for content and types of use is a prerequisite for trading intellectual property electronically, and the last ten years have seen much activity in the area of metadata. The <indecs> project was established in November 1998 with backing from the European Commission and ran for some eighteen months; its partners and affiliates represented a broad cross-section of interest groups (including the publishing and music industries) since it was recognized that it was no longer practical for different sectors to develop different solutions to the same problem. The task of <indecs> was to develop an open standards framework for the metadata required to support automated commerce in intellectual property in the network environment. The outcome included a Rights Data Dictionary and a structured approach to metadata which has been adopted as baseline technology for the ISO-MPEG-21 Rights Data Dictionary standard.

There have been a number of other groups active in the area of metadata, in particular the librarian-driven Dublin Core Metadata Initiative, aimed at building international consensus for developing a common core of semantics for resource description, with support from OCLC (for more information, see www.purl.org/dc/). The ONIX (International Online Information Exchange) system has been developed by Book Industry Communication (BIC), EDItEUR (the Europe-based international trade standards body for global book and serial supply chains) and the Book Industry Study Group as a new international standard for transmitting product information (www.editeur.org.onix.html). ONIX for Books has been adopted as a trade standard in Australia, Canada, France, Germany, Italy, the Netherlands, Norway, Spain, Russia and Korea as well as the United Kingdom and the United States. Release 3.0 was launched in April 2009 and will be in general use by 2010. ONIX for Licensing Terms is the generic name for services offered by ONIX; ONIX for Publications Licences (ONIX-PL) is intended to support the communication of licence terms for electronic resources from a publisher to a user institute to enable the licence terms to be loaded into the institute's electronic resource management system and linked to the actual digital resources. The same underlying standards could also be used to link usage terms to products in a publisher's digital repository. Further information is available from the EDItEUR website (www.editeur.org).

The ARROW project

Chapter 1 highlighted the current focus of governments and copyright authorities on the need to deal with the use of orphan works (works for which the current rightsholder is unknown). One proposed solution to the problem is the ARROW (Accessible Register of Rights Information on Orphan Works) initiative. Supported by the European Commission under its project eContent*plus*, ARROW has been developed by a public–private partnership including the UK Publishers Association, the Copyright Licensing Agency, the Authors' Licensing and Collecting Society, the Publishers Licensing Society, EDItEUR, as well as a number of overseas publishers associations, libraries and reproduction rights organizations. The project aims to provide would-be users of copyright content with a technical infrastructure where existing databases of content and rights information around Europe can be coordinated, accessed and searched via a single portal, with the aim of creating a European registry of out-of-print and orphan works. This raises issues in connection with the establishment of a Book Rights Registry under the US Google Settlement (see *The Google Settlement* later in this chapter, pp. 356–61) which plans to include titles of UK origin. The ARROW project is scheduled for completion in 2011.

Commercial digital rights management systems

One of the most interesting early developments in the area of DRM was the launch of the ContentGuard system in September 1999. Originally developed by Xerox's Palo Alto Rights Management Group with backing from Microsoft, the software includes units that check for copyright clearance automatically and allow publishers to define categories of rights, licences and fees. The system can tie in with other software with encryption and delivery facilities, such as Adobe Acrobat, and can track and report usage back to the publisher. It is fully integrated with e-commerce programs to approve credit and remit payment to the publisher. ContentGuard is format independent, allowing publishers to create content in, for example, Adobe PDF format or in HTML or XML; it also pioneered the development of several DRM technologies, including XrML (Extensible Rights Mark-up Language), which formed the basis of the ISO MPEG-21 Rights Expression Language. Other DRM providers include InterTrust (www.intertrust.com), SealedMedia (www.sealedmedia.com) and DocuRights (www.docurights.com).

DRM technology was much vaunted in the 1999–2001 period, but when the dotcom bubble burst, some providers either went out of business completely or retrenched. Adobe's ContentServer was initially heralded as the main DRM application in the e-book market for desktop PCs but sales discontinued in November 2004 after limited take-up. In April 2004, ContentGuard employees, Microsoft and Time Warner (a major content provider with film, television, music and publishing interests) acquired the majority of shares in ContentGuard, leaving Xerox with a small minority shareholding. In November 2004, the French electronics group Thomson acquired a 33% voting stake, reducing Microsoft's holding to 33% and deflecting a potential EU enquiry into that company's potentially dominant interest in the technology. Microsoft has incorporated DRM components into its Windows programs and Internet Explorer and promotes its Windows Media DRM system. The question of whether DRM should be applied to e-books remains under discussion, especially given the move of the music industry away from DRM on the grounds that it was felt to encourage piracy.

Access and payment

There are a number of possible models for granting authorized users access to online material and for charging for such use. These include controlled access to databases via passwords or PINs, issued either to subscribers to an online service or in some cases to purchasers of a related fixed-medium product – for example, some publishers of CD-ROM products are providing a supplementary online information service on the internet, which is accessible to purchasers of the CD-ROM and updated regularly. A number of major academic textbook publishers now offer supplementary websites to accompany many of their books, accessed by a PIN and updated regularly.

An alternative possibility is access via site licences, a form of subscription giving subscribers at a designated site or sites access to a corpus of material in electronic form, supplied either directly from the publisher's own server or via an intermediate service.

As an alternative to payment by subscription, there is credit card billing, although, as mentioned earlier, there remains a perception that to send details of credit cards over the internet is not always secure, and many customers still prefer instead to fax or post their credit card details to the publisher. A further alternative comes in the form of the electronic commerce systems which have been developed by alliances of software companies, banks and credit card companies; an early example was CyberCash, founded in 1994 and now owned by PayPal; other examples are PayPoint and Cybersource.

For any electronic copyright management system to operate effectively, there must be a clear underlying legal acceptance of the validity of reproduction rights in the electronic environment; of what constitutes the concept of fair dealing in that environment; of the liabilities of online service providers; and a guarantee that the rights of copyright holders to encrypt their material will be upheld. Achievement of all these aims is now far nearer as many countries have implemented the provisions of the 1996 WIPO Copyright Treaty (WCT) into their domestic legislation (see *The international copyright conventions* in Chapter 1). The need to establish voluntary licensing systems which provide users with access to content whilst protecting the rights of copyright owners is paramount if statutory licensing schemes are to be avoided.

The last five years have seen an increase in debate in both legal and governmental forums over the balance between the interests of creators and content providers, on the one hand, and of consumers on the other. The WIPO Copyright Treaty provided for legal protection against the circumvention of technological protection measures for copyright material, and this was endorsed by Article 6 of the EU Directive on the Harmonization of Certain Rights in the Electronic Environment (see *National, multinational and international copyright initiatives* in Chapter 1). In February 2005, the EU advisory body on data protection and privacy released a draft document on the implications of DRM systems with digital watermarking facilities being used to identify and track users online, with subsequent implications for their right of privacy. In the United Kingdom, late 2005 saw the launch of an All-Party Parliamentary Internet Group enquiry into DRM; the British Publishers Association was amongst sixty organizations which made submissions to that enquiry. A topic under the spotlight since as long ago as 2002 (with particular reference to the music industry) has been the need for interoperability and compatibility to provide a seamless service for users as a key prerequisite for consumer acceptance of DRM; against this must be set the fact that the development of standards is time consuming, given the natural competition between rival technologies and standards.

The content industries would of course prefer to avoid any mandatory imposition of standards; it may well be the case that the market will force providers to react to consumer demand for compatibility, or a dominant technology may emerge to set the standard. In the meantime, there are already individual initiatives; in August 2005, Sun Microsystems launched its Open Media Commons, an open source, royalty-free DRM standard. Sun's Project DReaM technology is available for sharing, including DRM-OPeRA, an integrated DRM technology which is independent of specific hardware and operating systems and not restricted to specific media formats. There are also content-sharing licences available through the medium of movements such as Creative Commons and CopyLeft (see *The anti-copyright movement, open access and other initiatives* in Chapter 1).

Electronic reproduction rights

The demarcation lines between reprography, electronic copying or digitization of copyright material and electronic delivery of that material have become increasingly blurred, and the aim of this section is to cover areas involving the electronic equivalent of photocopying, where users may seek to scan, store, view, download and possibly print out in hard copy form extracts of copyright material originally available in print-on-paper form, rather than whole works. These include the areas of customized publishing, coursepacks, the use of abstracts, document delivery and digital libraries, whether these are libraries established by traditional libraries or services offered by commercial providers.

Several key copyright points must be addressed in relation to electronic copying. First, do the publishers who wish to grant permission for copying in this form themselves have the right to utilize or to authorize others to utilize the material electronically? Whilst head contracts drawn up in recent years will almost certainly make reference to these rights, older contracts almost certainly do not, although the subsidiary rights clause may make reference to authorizing others to use the material by a variety of means either existing or yet to be invented. If there is any element of doubt on this score, these rights should be clearly negotiated with the authors or their representatives – the 'upstream' aspect of electronic licensing. The rights involved here are 'verbatim' electronic rights for the straightforward reproduction of extracts from the printed material, rather than any plans for more complex use such as the addition of multimedia facilities.

Second, if the material to be supplied electronically includes textual or illustrative material drawn from outside copyright sources, did the permission secured for original publication include the right to scan, digitize, store and reuse that material electronically, or (more likely) was it restricted to use in print-on-paper form only? Again, if it did not, such permission should be secured from the external copyright holders. In the STM sector, the STM 'exchange' guidelines recommend that member publishers should include electronic rights as well as print-on-paper rights when permissions are granted (see *Anthology and quotation rights* in Chapter 17).

Third, can there be any form of fair dealing (in American terminology, 'fair use') in the electronic environment? This topic was addressed earlier in this chapter (see pp. 332–4). Publishers generally remain of the view that 'digital is different', and that there is justification for only very limited fair dealing in this environment. This is because the act of copying electronically produces a copy that is identical both in content and quality to that of the original, rather than an inferior copy such as is produced through the medium of photocopying. In addition to this, the electronic copy can potentially be copied and transmitted to an infinite number of recipients, and the whole concept of differentiating between private and public usage breaks down in the digital environment.

There is still a view in much of the user community, in particular in the academic sector, that content should be easily and freely available, and that copyright represents an obstacle to this – hence the rise of the open access movement (see *The anti-copyright movement, open access and other initiatives* in Chapter 1). The area of electronic copying is of particular significance to publishers of journals and high-level reference works in the STM area, who are usually themselves the copyright owners in the works through assignment of copyright from individual contributors. Their view is that electronic use is an exercise of primary publishing rights rather than secondary or subsidiary rights, and such use therefore needs to be carefully assessed in view of the impact on sales of the primary product. There is certainly a view that if permission is to be granted, publishers should be able to set their own fees according to the value of the material and the nature of the usage, and should also have the right to refuse permission if the proposed use is detrimental to their legitimate interests.

Many in the user community – in particular academic librarians – feel that library privilege should be extended to the electronic environment, with the electronic media simply providing an alternative channel for supplying material for the purposes of private study or inter-library loan. The issues of fair dealing and inter-library loan were addressed in the United Kingdom by PA/JISC working parties that developed a set of guidelines for UK use.

Electronic copying is now a simple process; it may be as simple as scanning the document concerned to produce a bit-mapped digital representation of the original page so that it can be stored in an electronic database in character-encoded form. The text can then be searched and viewed onscreen and reproduced on demand in hard-copy form. The equipment is now very inexpensive and the electronic copy, unlike a photocopy, is identical to the original. The need for clear recognition of digitization, storage (temporary or permanent), display, transmission, downloading and printing out of hard copies as restricted acts both in national copyright legislation and in international copyright directives and treaties has already been covered in Chapter 1. In terms of copyright law, unauthorized electronic copying constitutes an infringement both of the author's primary right to control the reproduction of a work (which may in turn have been assigned to the publisher by contract) and of the publisher's own right in the typographical layout of the work. Manipulation of the text (see below, p. 343) may also result in an infringement of the author's right of integrity, while inclusion of material as part of a larger work without adequate acknowledgement may infringe the author's right of paternity, both aspects of moral rights introduced in the 1988 UK Copyright, Designs and Patents Act. It is the view of publishers that whilst clear legislation on copyright in the electronic environment is vital, they cannot

rely entirely on the law, but must rely rather on the negotiation of commercial contracts with users and on compliance with these contracts.

Usage is not necessarily restricted to simple reproduction. Once in electronic form, the text may then be manipulated through word-processing,
and alterations can be introduced, selections can be made, other material
merged and notes added. In addition to this, the material can be disseminated either in its original form or in adapted form to multiple users
through local or wide area networks. This makes it a highly attractive
medium for educational or academic use, since it can be used to customize
material for a course or for specific class use.

One of the main problems inherent in electronic copying and network use
lies in the fact that the copyright owner cannot 'track' the use of the material
easily in the same way as for physical copies; indeed, the copying is no longer
restricted to physical form, but may be ephemeral copying in the form of
temporary display on a screen or transmission via a network. One solution
to this problem may be the development of a reliable identifier system
which would code copyright material in more granular units than the ISBN,
the ISSN or even the SICI (see *Identifiers* earlier in this chapter, pp. 336–7).

A central question has been whether electronic copying is best
administered by individual publishers themselves or through collective
licensing arrangements. The International Federation of Reproduction
Rights Organizations (see *Reproduction rights organizations* earlier in this
chapter, pp. 319–20) has spoken in favour of collective licensing schemes
for the new technologies, partly on the grounds that if publishers are
perceived to be placing obstacles in the way of meeting the needs of would-
be users, it is possible that provisions for compulsory licensing could be
introduced at both national and international levels.

Many larger multinational publishers undertake some of their licensing
direct; in the United States, some have chosen to use the Copyright
Clearance Center (CCC) services (see *Reproduction rights organizations* earlier
in this chapter, pp. 319–20). In the United Kingdom, after lengthy consultations with CLA and PLS (see *Photocopying and scanning* earlier in this
chapter, pp. 308–21) publishers have extended some of their mandates (e.g.
to the pharmaceutical, law, public administration, higher education and
further education sectors) to permit specified electronic copying uses,
although in the education sectors licensees are currently required to report
on their scanning activities so that publishers can monitor whether there is
a resultant effect on primary sales.

Customized publishing and coursepacks

Customized publishing escalated significantly in the United States from 1993
onwards, although it had appeared somewhat earlier in the Netherlands.
Campus bookstores and nearby copyshops provide shrink-wrapped

coursepacks and customized bound textbooks or 'collegiate texts' for specific college courses; these may consist entirely of published materials selected from books and journals, or may be augmented with material written by faculty members.

The University of Stanford, the University of Southern California and Cornell University were all early producers of material in this form. Copyright clearance for this type of use can be undertaken via the American RRO, the Copyright Clearance Center, at a standard charge per page, or via direct contact with the original publishers, also on a per-page basis. The CCC also launched a blanket digitization licence in return for a surcharge on its photocopying licence to pharmaceutical companies; this allows for intranet use, temporary storage, storage for back-up purposes and internal digital copies, as well as for regulatory submissions.

In the United Kingdom, the issue of coursepacks and their impact on sales of the original printed edition remains the subject of much debate. Publishers have defined a coursepack as 'a collection of material planned and systematically copied to support a module or course of study'; this could include material copied and made available as a single coursepack, or a series of sequentially copied materials which eventually build up into a coursepack. In the print-on-paper environment, such use was originally covered by a separate part of the higher education licence, which was then transactional and processed via the CLARCS system. However, coursepack use was rolled into the blanket higher education licence as a result of the judgement of the Copyright Tribunal in 2002 (see *Licensing the higher education sector* earlier in this chapter, pp. 313–4). The impact on primary sales is still being monitored and, as mentioned earlier in this chapter (p. 314), publishers are developing guidelines for best practice in order to avoid substitution.

Some publishers have sought to enter the custom publishing market themselves. As long ago as 1989, McGraw-Hill launched its PRIMIS project, working with Eastman Kodak and R.R. Donnelley & Sons, as an on-demand printing unit. Teachers could order material customized from McGraw-Hill books and journals, with delivery of printed stock within a few weeks of the order. The next stage was to implement delivery via an electronic network linked to designated campus bookstores, where customers could select and order the combination of material they required; copies could then be printed and bound on site. In 1992, McGraw-Hill offered to license the software to other publishers, but the take-up was limited. More recently, customized publishing for specific courses has been undertaken on a large scale on both sides of the Atlantic by Wiley Blackwell and by Pearson Education, but to date this has been done in bound print-on-paper form.

In the United Kingdom, an early customized publishing project was SCOPE (Scottish Collaborative On-Demand Publishing Enterprise). Administered from Stirling University, the project covered thirteen

Scottish universities. It was established under the aegis of the Follett Implementation Group on Information Technology (FIGIT) and funded by the Joint Information Systems Committee of the Higher Education Funding Council as part of the Electronic Libraries Programme (eLib).

A later development was HERON (Higher Education Resources ON-Demand). HERON was set up as a consortium of the universities of Stirling, Napier and Southbank and Blackwell Retail Ltd. The aim of the project was to develop a national database and resource bank of digitized texts for the higher and further education sectors (including published material and unpublished higher education material) to enable the provision of coursepacks in paper or (if the publisher agreed) in electronic form. Digitization could be undertaken by HERON or by the higher education institutes using the scheme; alternatively, the material may be provided to HERON in digitized form by the publisher where this is available, for inclusion in the HERON resource bank. The scheme was considered particularly useful for distance learning. To some extent, HERON represented an experimental scheme to test take-up in the higher education sector at a slightly lower rate per page than the CLA digitization licence. In March 2002, HERON was acquired by Ingenta; more details of the project can be found at www.heronweb.ingenta.com.

Another development was the launch in July 2000 of Knovel.com, a subscription-based web publishing venture based in the United States, which currently offers online access to over 2000 scientific and technical reference works from major publishers such as Wiley Blackwell, McGraw-Hill and Elsevier (www.knovel.com). Its proprietary software technology allows the site to offer online text with tables that are interactive, allowing users to add figures into 'live' equations and graphs and obtain immediate computations and to customize content.

Site licences

The expansion of academic networks and the pervasive use of the internet have led academic journal publishers to rethink the means whereby they supply their product to their customers in the higher education sector, particularly as journal subscriptions continue to fall, subscription prices rise and customers may be affected by fluctuating exchange rates for non-UK journals. Despite this, in 2009 Research Libraries UK reported that research-based institutions currently spend some 75% of their library acquisition budgets on journals.

In late 1995, three publishing groups – Academic Press, Institute of Physics Publishing and a consortium of the Blackwell publishing companies – entered into site licensing agreements covering the entire higher education sector in England, Scotland, Wales and Northern Ireland. Arrangements were negotiated by the Higher Education Funding Council of England

(HEFCE) on behalf of all four regions, and were initially established during a three-year pilot scheme commencing on 1 January 1996.

The terms of the licence varied very slightly from publisher to publisher, but in practice the licence permitted users in higher education institutions – students, faculty and librarians – to use the material licensed in either print-on-paper or electronic form for educational and academic research purposes; this included multiple photocopying for coursepack use without the need to seek separate permission from the publisher. Depending on the terms of the licence, material was made available in electronic form either via the publisher's own server or via an HEFCE facility, and substantial discounts were given off the price of print-on-paper subscriptions, with HEFCE reimbursing the difference. This scheme represented an interesting way of tackling the blanket versus the transactional licence, in that it ensured that the publishers concerned received a negotiated financial return for the use of their material, while relieving users of the need to apply on a case-by-case basis for electronic use or print-on-paper use that fell outside the realms of fair dealing.

The National Electronic Site Licence (NESLi) commenced with a three-year project established in close consultation with the Publishers Association and JISC, running from 1995 to 1997 and managed by an appointed managing agent (initially a consortium of the University of Manchester, Blackwell and Swets); NESLi2 is its successor (www.nesli2.ac.uk). The aim is to make academic journal content available electronically to all UK higher education institutions. University libraries are offered the opportunity to purchase electronic journal subscriptions separately from their print-on-paper equivalents. The model licence contract is based on the PA/JISC model (see later in this chapter, p. 347) and is available from www.nesli2.ac.uk/model.htm. Participating publishers may set different prices and access terms.

In the United States, the CCC has administered many site licences on behalf of academic publishers, and a number of major journal publishers in both the United States and Europe have set up programmes for site licences directly with academic institutes, consortia of such institutes and commercial research companies.

A number of key points should be taken into account when negotiating a site licence, and great care should be taken to define precisely the rights that are being granted. The publication or range of publications to be licensed must be specified clearly (e.g. the years of issue of journals included in the licence), together with details of any additional material or changes to be included. The site must be clearly defined (e.g. a single geographical site, a single institution or organization, a group of institutions or organizations, and whether remote access is permitted). It must also be clear whether the licence is for use on an individual designated terminal, a local area network or a wide area network.

The licence should state whether users are named individuals, specific groups of users (e.g. students, faculty and librarians in an academic institution), all employees of the institution or organization, the users of designated authorized terminals, or walk-in users – the latter should be restricted to on-site access only. The contract will almost certainly be non-exclusive (as other licences may be granted elsewhere for use of the same body of material); it should state clearly the date of commencement, its duration and any provisions for negotiating an extension. The contract should state whether the publisher will supply the licensee with any physical materials to facilitate use of the content (e.g. print-on-paper originals for digitization, or electronic files in designated form) and whether the publisher will be involved in instalment or back-up services, including the supply of updates or corrections to the licensed material. The contract should specify the financial terms of the licence and the accounting dates, together with a clear definition of the use that may be made of the material and of any restrictions on such use. It should be specified clearly whether the material must be used as it stands or whether it can be modified in any way (licensors should bear in mind that this may impinge on the moral rights of the contributors whose work is included in the licence arrangement). The contract should also include the usual provisions, such as warranties and indemnities, conditions of termination and prevailing legislation. Provision should also be made for the licensee to submit to inspection and enforcement procedures, and it may also be wise to include a confidentiality clause.

A very useful model site licence for the use of material supplied in electronic form was developed by another PA/JISC working party in 1999 and is amongst model licences for electronic use included in Owen (general editor), *Clark's Publishing Agreements* (7th edition). See also the NESli2 licence mentioned earlier in this chapter (p. 346).

An increasing number of publishers and learned societies on both sides of the Atlantic have established arrangements for the online delivery of their journals to academic institutions and other customers, including Elsevier's ScienceDirect project and the SpringerLink service, as well as initiatives from John Wiley, Harcourt, Wolters Kluwer and many of the university presses.

Abstracts

Although abstracts of journal articles are entitled to copyright protection, certain types of abstracts can currently be used in the United Kingdom without permission or payment. Section 60 of the 1988 UK Copyright, Designs and Patents Act states:

> When an article on a scientific or technical subject is published accompanied by an abstract indicating the contents of the article, it is

not an infringement of copyright in the abstract, or in the article, to copy the abstract, or issue copies of it to the public.

However, this is not the case if an authorized licensing scheme for abstracts is in place. The section does not apply to medical abstracts or to abstracts on subjects such as law, the humanities or the social sciences. It does, however, apply to abstracts in any medium and permits use in any medium; it also applies to abstracts regardless of the country of original publication.

Abstracts are perceived by journal publishers as having significant value, since they act as a gateway for potential users of the complete article to which they relate, particularly in the digital environment, where users seek a rapid and convenient one-stop shop for articles of particular interest to them without necessarily investing in print-on-paper subscriptions to all the journals concerned. If the above loophole did not exist, publishers would be able, if they chose, to license the use of their abstracts by abstracting and indexing services or indeed by academics, librarians and commercial research organizations.

Document delivery services

Recent years have seen a continuing demand for document delivery services. Libraries, institutes and commercial enterprises seek access to selected material in either paper or electronic form rather than relying on the purchase of books and journals. This trend has been due to a number of factors: pressure on library acquisition budgets, the increasing number of journals, the rising cost of journal subscriptions and the wish to pay only for material that has specifically been identified as necessary. Individual users in both the academic and the commercial research environments have specified that their main need is for speedy access to relevant high-level research material (preferably peer reviewed) at their desktop via a one-stop shop, with the facility to search for the material they require by topic rather than by journal title or publisher.

The global document delivery service is worth millions of pounds per year, only a small proportion of which is channelled to the original publishers of the material that is being supplied. The British Library Document Supply Centre is still able to undertake a significant proportion of its copying activities under library privilege (see *The BLDSC* earlier in this chapter, pp. 315–6).

The implications of document delivery services for academic and professional publishers have been significant, particularly as print-on-paper subscriptions fell in the 1990s at a rate of about 5% per year. A number of commercial companies provide data on journals and contents lists, with author and title indexing (CAS-IAS – current awareness services and individual article supply) via online services such as Uncover, originally a joint project of CARL (Colorado Alliance of Research Libraries) and B.H. Blackwell Ltd but bought in February 2000 and now offered as UnCover2 by the UK company Ingenta (www.ingentaconnect.com), which already offered information on thousands of journals through its existing services. These enable users to select articles of interest which can then be obtained from a variety of services. Initially, document provision was in paper form or by fax, but nowadays such services are able to supply material electronically. IngentaConnect's InTouch provides an e-mail alert service. Full-text supply services include e-mail tables of contents of selected journals to subscribers. Supply services include the ISI (Institute of Scientific Information) and the various services run by Ingenta (www.ingenta.com), the various services offered by ProQuest (purchased in February 2007 by the Cambridge Information Group, and specializing mainly in the humanities and social sciences), EBSCO and Knovel.

In the 1990s, a range of model contracts was supported by the major journal subscription agents (dubbed the 'John Cox' models after the consultancy which developed them); these are available to cover arrangements with a single academic institution, for academic consortia, for public libraries, and for corporate, government and other research libraries. Details are available at www.LicensingModels.org.

ISI belongs to Thomson Scientific (www.webofknowledge.com); the ISI Web of Knowledge offers a broad range of information services, including alerting services and current awareness services, through to full-text delivery where publishers have permitted ISI to do this. It maintains a database of many thousands of international journals, books and proceedings in all subject areas. Its services are available in a variety of forms, including online. Publishers can set the base subscription rates for their material, with additional charges for printing off designated quantities of hard copies if the publisher wishes to permit this. Publishers may also set charges for document delivery via ISI.

Another service is Elsevier's Scopus, launched in November 2004 as a full text-linking and indexing database covering thousands of scientific titles from a large range of STM publishers and promoted as the largest collection of abstracts collected online. The full text of the article is only one click away from the search results list and is only displayed if the user's library is authorized to access it.

All these developments have forced publishers to address a number of questions: whether they wish to license material direct on a non-exclusive basis to commercial document delivery services (and, if so, at rates which provide adequate compensation for the effect on journal subscriptions); whether authorization should be granted in electronic form as well as in traditional paper and fax form now that the market so clearly demands this;

or whether they seek to enter the document delivery market directly themselves.

An alternative to dealing direct with the various document delivery services – perhaps more useful for smaller publishers – is to channel all such requests via an RRO such as the Copyright Clearance Center in the United States or the Copyright Licensing Agency in the United Kingdom. The CLA offers a transactional document delivery licence which allows for payment to be set by the publisher or to operate on the default rates set by the CLA (currently £9 per journal article), with provision for referral to the publisher in the case of applications in excess of the publisher's specified mandate.

Another possibility is for publishers to view document delivery as an opportunity rather than a threat, and to undertake it directly themselves rather than allowing the commercial services to dominate the market. Only the largest publishers have the resources to tackle this.

On the document delivery front, publishers were forced into defensive mode when a German library consortium under the name of Subito set up a document supply service to academic institutions within Germany and elsewhere, claiming that their activities were legitimate under an agreement with the German RRO VG Wort, and charging €4 per document with no payment to the original copyright owners. Legal action was taken against Subito by the International Association of Scientific, Technical and Medical Publishers (STM); a preliminary ruling by the Munich Regional Court validating Subito's actions was overturned in May 2007 by the Munich Higher Regional Court, which held that the supply of documents by electronic means was illegal. Subito has reached agreement with individual publishers for the supply of documents to German-speaking countries.

Digital libraries

While commercial document delivery services are in effect building up electronic libraries of their own, the library sector has also entered the field. In the United States, the Library of Congress established its Digital Library Visitors' Center in October 1994. In partnership with other large US libraries, it embarked on a major digitization programme of American historical collections and is participating in the National Digital Library Project. Details of the Library of Congress project are available on their website (www.lcweb.loc.gov). The majority of major university libraries have established projects giving electronic access to their holdings via the internet; permission is obtained from copyright holders before digitizing copyright works as opposed to older material.

The Koninklijke Bibliotheek (the Royal Dutch Library) and the Bibliothèque Nationale Française are working on the digitization of their holdings and are linking up with similar projects being undertaken by libraries in other countries.

In the United Kingdom, an early small-scale electronic library project, ELINOR (Electronic Information Online Retrieval) was set up at the multi-site De Montfort University; materials were scanned and available for access via thirty-two terminals. The project was initially funded by the British Library, IBM and the Milton Keynes Development Corporation.

The 1993 Follett Report stressed the opportunities offered by information technology to meet the information needs of the academic sector and, on the recommendation of the Follett Implementation Group in Information Technology, the Electronic Libraries Programme was established by JISC. Its objectives include the use of information technology to implement services in digitization, on-demand publishing, electronic journals and electronic document delivery. Information on current projects can be obtained on the eLib website (www.ukoln.ac.uk/services/elib).

Of key interest to academic publishers are the plans of the British Library, announced as long ago as 1993, to establish a digital library as a means of storage, conservation and access to its holdings. It established a Digital Library Programme to seek a proportion of the necessary funding for this huge venture through private finance partnerships, since the entire cost of the programme cannot be met from government funds. In November 2009 the Library announced the addition of the 500,000th item to its long-term digital storage facility (a December 1864 issue of the *Birmingham Daily Post* newspaper). A separate but related digital initiative has been the Library's move to extend legal deposit to electronic products to ensure a comprehensive national archive. The Legal Deposit Libraries Act 2003 received royal assent on 30 October 2003 and came into force in January 2004, and by November 2009 the Library reported 386,000 items deposited via the scheme. As an interim arrangement, publishers may choose to deposit electronic publications under the terms of the Voluntary Code of Practice 2000, while the Library reviews its procedures and facilities for acquiring electronic publications in both offline and online form. Publishers will wish to ensure that a balance is struck between the public interest in adding to the scope of the published national archive and their own commercial interests.

In January 1997, the British Library and Elsevier Science, the world's largest publisher of scientific journals, launched an arrangement to make bibliographical data available electronically for Elsevier journals as part of the British Library's inside service, an integrated current awareness, document ordering and delivery service. The service can be accessed via the Library's website (www.bl.uk). This experiment was followed by making the full text of Elsevier journals available to the Library electronically for document delivery, with payment made direct to Elsevier rather than via the CLA. The Library has direct licences with a number of major journal publishers for electronic document delivery (see *The BLDSC* earlier in this chapter, pp. 315–6).

The British Library has stated its intention to provide access to its copyright-cleared holdings electronically, and it is expected that users seeking to access materials from remote sites will be charged for this use. It is also the intention of the Library that there will be links providing access to the holdings of other copyright, national and academic libraries. Publishers remain concerned that if their materials are to be included in the service they should receive a fair reward for use of this material, whether by individuals, academic or commercial institutions or public libraries.

In March 2006, the European Commission announced plans to help set up an online digital library (originally named e2010, later Europeana) to provide internet users with access to millions of books, photographs, films, manuscripts and other cultural works held by European libraries, including the British Library. Launched on 20 November 2009 with over five million items in its collection, the site crashed almost immediately as it was bombarded by more than 10 million hits per hour. Works included in the project are currently in the public domain; the venture will expand during 2010.

In the United States, there is the Open Library (www.openlibrary.org), a project of the non-profit Internet Archive and funded in part by a grant from the California State Library. The goal is to create a single page on the web for every book that has ever been published in order to produce a searchable catalogue: at the time of writing, approximately 30 million records have been gathered from nineteen major libraries and some 20 million records are accessible on the site, with links to the full text of approximately one million out of copyright works.

In April 2009 UNESCO launched the World Digital Library (www.wdl. org), an ambitious project managed by the US Library of Congress. The aim is to make available, free of charge and in multilingual format, significant primary materials from cultures around the world. The search engine Google (see *The rise of Google* later in this chapter, pp. 353–4) contributed an initial sum of $3 million towards developing the project. The materials available are in the public domain and have been sourced from major libraries both within the United States and from many national libraries.

It is worth flagging in this section that commercial initiatives by electronic aggregators such as Questia, NetLibrary, MyiLibrary and eBrary (see *Electronic digitization services, e-book publishers and aggregators* in Chapter 24) are, in effect, offering a form of digital library service. Models set up by companies specializing in providing e-books to the academic and professional sector include provision for users wishing to search and access only part of the content, whilst users in the trade sector are probably more likely to wish to download the whole work for reading purposes.

Search engines, online retailers and others: threat or opportunity?

The rise of Google

Few initiatives have caused as much debate in the publishing community or commanded as many column inches in both the trade and the general press as the entry of the technology company Google into the area of digitization of printed material, and its ambitions for expansion in this area. At that time it would have been difficult to predict what has since ensued.

Founded in 1998 by Larry Page and Sergey Brin as a search engine for use on the web with the corporate motto 'Don't be evil', Google has attracted users worldwide and is currently estimated to control 65% of the search engine market in the United States and over 70% of the world market; it operates services in a number of languages other than English. In August 2004, the company went public; its share price soared, and it has become one of the most successful technology companies in the world. It has at times come under heavy fire for blocking access to politically sensitive topics in countries such as China.

In late 2003, Google developed what was originally termed the Google Print programme and approached publishers with a view to securing permission to digitize the complete text of books as part of its mission 'to organize the world's information and make it universally accessible and useful'. Publishers who signed up to the arrangement sent hard copies or PDFs of books to be included in the programme to Google, who undertook the scanning where necessary and put the texts up on their site, enabling users to undertake a keyword search. Also appearing on screen was advertising in the form of AdWords related to products and services; publishers would receive a share of revenue generated from contextual advertising sales if the ads were clicked on by users accessing the text. Publishers have chosen to deal with this revenue stream in different ways, some viewing it as subsidiary rights income to be shared with authors according to contract, whilst others viewed it as marketing income. The majority of publishers on both sides of the Atlantic have signed up for this service on the grounds that it is essential to gain product visibility via Google's powerful search engine.

Users of this Google service can browse the text of works in copyright five pages at a time, with a total viewing capacity set by the publisher but with a maximum default rate of 20% of the whole work. Text is shown as a low-resolution jpeg image which is adequate to give a flavour of the text but not comfortable to work with for any length of time; users are not permitted to download or print out the material they access. The site then refers users via a 'Buy this book' button to the website of the publisher and of online retailers such as Amazon. Google's main argument has been that the service provides publishers with publicity for their wares and facilitates purchase of the book in print form. In November 2005, the service became Google Partner under the general umbrella of Google Book Search (www. books.google.com) after feedback that users were mistakenly thinking that the site provided facilities for them to print off material.

In late 2004, Google launched its Google Scholar programme (www. scholar.google.com) with a view to scanning the content of scholarly journals; it stated that material would only be available to all users if it had been made available on the open access model, and that other material would only be accessible to authorized subscribers to that journal content. This programme understandably posed a threat to the direct supply of journal content electronically, and most of the major publishers in this area refused to participate.

The Google Library Project

Even more controversial was the Google Library Project (www.print.google. com/googleprint/library.html), also launched in late 2004, when Google announced that it had reached agreement to digitize the entire holdings of the university libraries of Harvard, Stanford, the University of Michigan, the New York Public Library and the University of Oxford via the Bodleian Library; in turn, they would supply the libraries concerned with digitized files of the scanned works. The aim was to scan some 15 million works over a period of ten years, with a budget of $100 million: a hugely attractive arrangement for the universities concerned in terms of cost and labour. The exact arrangements with each institution differed, but the overall plan was to scan the full texts of works considered to be out of copyright, which would be fully browsable and downloadable by users; for copyright works, users would have access to what Google termed 'snippets' of text, which Google claimed they were entitled to provide under the terms of the fair use provision under US copyright law. Further problems arose when Google stated that they would consider all works published pre-1923 in the United States and pre-1900 in the United Kingdom to be in the public domain; they initially stated that they would also consider out-of-print works to be in the public domain. Quite apart from the copyright issues this raised, the resulting archive of books and journals would be in direct competition with publishers' own electronic offerings as well as those of licensed digital aggregators such as Proquest, MyiLibrary, Questia and NetLibrary (see Chapter 24).

This initiative provoked protests from individual publishers and from a range of publishing organizations, including the American Association of Publishers, the Association of American University Presses, PEN USA, the Authors Guild in the USA, the British Publishers Association, the Association of Learned, Professional and Scholarly Publishers, the Society of Authors and the Association of Authors' Agents in the United Kingdom, the International Publishers Association, STM and IFRRO. Nigel Newton of Bloomsbury spoke out strongly against the Google initiatives, saying that a Pandora's box had been opened and could result in a technology company ending up in control of digital files of a vast range of copyright work; author Antony Beevor was also fiercely critical.

In August 2005, Google altered its stance to state that publishers could remove specific titles from inclusion in the programme and imposed a temporary moratorium on its scanning activities until November 2005. However, rightsholders stressed that copyright is an opt-in rather than an opt-out regime, and in September 2005 three US authors and the Authors Guild filed a class action suit against Google in the United States, seeking an injunction against any copyright infringement and damages for any copyright violations to date. This was followed in October 2005 by the AAP filing suit on behalf of publishers McGraw-Hill, Pearson Education, Penguin, Simon & Schuster and John Wiley. In the United Kingdom, the Publishers Association sought assurance from the Bodleian Library that copyright would be respected and also that legal deposit copies would not be used as the basis for digitization. Google then stated that only out-of-copyright works would be digitized in the United Kingdom under this programme; the Bodleian, Harvard and Stanford all confirmed they would not permit the scanning of in-copyright works, although it is arguable how that status can always be clearly established.

On the general issue of fair use, in February 2006 the California District Court had ruled that the display of thumbnail-size photographs on Google's Image Search service was not covered by fair use and could infringe copyright. A lawsuit had already been brought against Google by a publisher of adult magazines and websites.

Google had planned to extend its Library Project to the digitization of materials from European libraries, although it stated that only out-of-copyright works would be involved as 'We fully acknowledge that copyright laws in the US and Europe are different. We have no intention of breaking copyright law'. However, in 2006 French publisher La Martinière filed suit against Google for unauthorized scanning of its publications and by November 2006 it was backed by a further suit from the Syndicat National de l'Edition (SNE, the French publishers' association); it became apparent that the scanning exercise in US libraries included many non-English-language titles.

With an increasing number of lawsuits underway or planned, Google mounted major PR exercises at the London Book Fair and BookExpo in 2006 to allay publishers' concerns. The company also announced that its planned and quite separate Google Publisher programme would allow publishers to sell their complete books online, with publishers setting a download price per title and also specifying the range of use permitted.

Book publishers have undoubtedly been conscious of the spectre of what has happened in the music industry (see *Some lessons from the music industry?* earlier in this chapter, pp. 325–30) and there was a very real fear of Napsterization of published content and also concerns that Google is a technology rather than a publishing-related company, with aims of its own in capturing data on its users and whose ownership could change in the future. There was also concern that, once in control of electronic files on a large scale, Google could in the future seek to compete with publishers themselves.

The Google Settlement

October 28th 2008 saw the announcement of a settlement between Google and the authors and publishers who had taken legal action in the United States. The terms are complex; the main document is 134 pages long and with appendices runs to over 300 pages, and required approval by the US District Court of the Southern District of New York, with a Fairness Hearing set for 11 June 2009. The full text of the Settlement is available at www.googlebooksettlement.com/agreement.html. The Settlement administration site is available at www.book.google.com/booksrightsholders.

Under the Settlement, Google agreed to pay the sum of $125 million, of which $30 million would cover legal fees, $45 million would fund minimum 'cash payments' of up to $60 per title or $15 per full insert (defined as text such as forewords or afterwords, epilogues, children's book illustrations, poems, quotations, song lyrics, tables, graphs or charts) for works which Google had scanned, and $34.5 million would establish a not-for-profit Book Rights Registry to administer payments to authors and publishers and represent rightsholders in negotiating future uses Google might wish to make of content.

By that stage Google had scanned some seven million works, of which one million were believed to be out of copyright, five million in copyright but out of print, and one million in print and still commercially available. Under the Settlement Google could only continue to display commercially available works in the programme if the rightsholder permitted them to do so, with 63% of revenue generated by Google to be paid to the Registry for onward transmission to publishers after deduction of administrative costs; publishers would then divide the income with their authors as per their contractual obligations.

Going forward, Google would be permitted to exploit a number of new 'revenue models', including print-on-demand, per-page pricing for custom publishing of coursepacks, the publishing of summaries, abstracts and compilations of books, revenue from a public access licence, allowing extracts printed out at public viewing points such as libraries, as well as offering various 'display uses'. These would include 'snippets' (only three or four lines of a book would be viewable, with no more than three snippets from the same book to be displayed); a preview service, where customers could view up to 20% of a work, of which no more than five pages are consecutive, with users able to print off copies; and lastly online access on a 'institutional Licence' subscription basis and via a 'consumer licence' to individual customers (for viewing, but not for downloading) at prices set by Google, ranging from $1.99 to $29.99 (prices which could be over-ridden by authors or publishers). It was expected that institutional licensing would be likely to generate the most revenue. For works remaining in the scheme which are not commercially available, payments to rightsholders would be made on a varying scale: 100% to authors whose rights have reverted to them; 100% to publishers for works 'made for hire' under that provision of US legislation; for works published pre-1987 where rights have not reverted to the author, a division of 65% to the author and 35% to the publisher; and a 50/50 division between author and publisher for works published from 1987 onwards. For individual use, advertising would appear on the pages and any revenue generated would be divided with the rightsholder. For institutional subscriptions they would pay rightsholders a one-off fee of $200 per title; subscriptions would be calculated on the basis of FTE numbers.

The question of how payment would be made for orphan works (works which are still in copyright but where the current rightsholder cannot be found – see Copyright legislation in the United Kingdom and Copyright legislation in the United States in Chapter 1) is as yet unclear and there have been suggestions that this might best be handled through national RROs (see Reproduction rights organizations earlier in this chapter, pp. 319–20) since they have access to rightsholder databases.

The Settlement provided a deadline of 5 May 2009 by which any objections to the Settlement should be lodged, and a deadline of 5 January 2010 by which rightsholders must submit claims to Google for any of their titles digitized by Google before 5 May 2009; applications must state whether the work is still commercially available. Once claims have been lodged, rightsholders can then 'manage' their titles and can choose to issue notice that commercially available titles should no longer remain in the project.

The Settlement made it clear that it applied to titles scanned in the United States and applied only to works 'with a US copyright interest', and there has been considerable debate over this definition since many of the titles scanned might have been first published outside the United States, not registered with the US Library of Congress but nevertheless covered by copyright in the United States by virtue of the country of origin belonging to a common copyright convention with the United States (see Copyright recognition between countries in Chapter 1). Also queried was the definition of 'commercially available' and whether this would include titles available as print-on-demand or available for sale in some form outside the United States.

Excluded from the Settlement were magazines, journals, serials and newspapers, e-books of works which do not exist in print form, sheet music, unpublished personal material, public domain US government-published works, and in most cases pictorial works such as photographs, illustrations, maps and paintings unless these are fully controlled by the publisher. Also excluded were works or inserts published after 5 January 2009 and works or inserts scanned or digitized by Google after 5 May 2009.

Rightsholders had a number of choices in reacting to the Settlement: (1) to do nothing, which would mean agreeing to the terms of the Settlement by default but not claiming any share of the payment; (2) to opt out, which would mean deciding whether to take a separate legal action against Google; or (3) to file a claim for a share of the payment for titles digitized before 5 May 2009, and then 'manage' the inclusion of future titles in the programme.

The deadline for opting out or objecting to the Settlement was set at 5 May 2009, and the deadline for requiring the removal of digitized titles from the programme at 5 April 2011.

Reaction to the Settlement by interested parties – e.g. authors, publishers and rival e-content providers – was mixed, and has been described by the press as ranging from euphoria to desperation. Some potential users greeted the news with what has been described as Utopian enthusiasm, envisaging that millions of long-unavailable titles would once again become accessible. Some commentators felt that for relatively little outlay Google had achieved many of its original aims (the company's annual turnover is currently estimated at $20 billion) and had also secured something of a monopoly over access to vast amounts of orphan work content which could be monetized without danger of prosecution. The *Library Journal* referred to the sum as 'pocket change to the well-capitalized search giant'. An *Economist* article on the topic of Google was headed 'Tome raider'. Literary agent Piers Blofeld has publicly referred to the Settlement as 'the greatest intellectual land grab in history'. Other commentators questioned what would happen if Google's future pricing policy impacted on library budgets and hence on sales by existing e-book suppliers such as aggregators, or by publishers themselves.

In April 2009 Google requested a sixty-day extension to the 5 May 2009 deadline for opting out of the Settlement. The presiding judge extended the deadline to 4 September 2009 and the June Fairness Hearing to 7 October 2009. In the meantime over 400 objections to the Settlement were lodged, including from the French and German governments, the Canadian Standards Association, the Japan PEN Club, DC Comics, the Federation of European Publishers, the Syndicat National de l'Editions and the Open Book Alliance (including Amazon, Microsoft and Yahoo!). By contrast, Sony (manufacturers of the main e-reader rival to the Amazon Kindle) filed in support of the Settlement, as did several US civil rights groups and a number of prominent US authors, including Garrison Keillor and Judy Blume.

On 18 September the US Department of Justice submitted a filing to the New York court objecting to a number of aspects of the Settlement. A status conference took place between Judge Denny Chin and the parties to the Settlement on 7 October 2009. In the run-up to the opening of the Frankfurt Book Fair, German Chancellor Angela Merkel weighed in on the debate, confirming Germany's objection to the Settlement and appealing for more international cooperation on copyright protection; there was considerable debate over the Settlement during the Fair itself. In December 2009, the German government announced the Deutsche Digitale Bibliothek, a project which would connect the databases of 30,000 German cultural and academic organizations, which would also be linked to Europeana (see *Digital libraries* earlier in this chapter, pp. 350–52).

In France, publishers La Martinière and author group La Société des Gens de Lettres (SGDL) had taken out a separate lawsuit against Google in Paris, seeking a €15 million fine and a further penalty of €100,000 for each further day Google scanned their works. In December 2009 a Paris court imposed a €300,000 fine and a penalty of €10,000 per day until French material was removed by Google. A more recent backlash has come from the publishing authorities in China.

On 13 November 2009 the parties to the Settlement filed revisions which were intended to address the objections filed with the court. The terms of the Settlement would now apply only to works published in the United States and registered with the US Copyright Office, plus books published in the United Kingdom, Australia and Canada, thus removing some 95% of foreign-language books from the Settlement and hence some 50% of the titles originally included. 'Commercial availability' was defined as 'for sale new, from sellers anywhere in the world, through one or more then-customary channels of trade to purchasers within the United States, the United Kingdom, Canada or Australia'. The date for claiming cash payments under the Settlement was extended from 5 January 2010 to 31 March 2011. Other changes included a provision for some revenue generated from the use of orphan works to be held and after five years used to try and locate the rightsholders. There were also limitations on future activities to be undertaken by Google, removing any provisions for custom publishing and limiting any print-on-demand exploitation to titles which are not commercially available. Rightsholders may request renegotiation of the 63/37% division of revenue for commercially available titles, and if agreement cannot be reached may remove the titles concerned. Google committed to making the content available to other retailers.

The board of the Registry is to include at least one author and one publisher from each of the countries concerned and also to include a court-approved fiduciary to represent the interests of rightsholders of unclaimed titles. Google also undertook to use a pricing algorithm to simulate prices in a competitive market and to remove any title subject to an exclusion request promptly and in any case no later than thirty days from receipt of such notice. A provision in the original Settlement which would have prevented rights being made available to competitors at better terms than those available to Google was removed.

On 19 November 2009 Judge Chin gave preliminary approval to the Settlement and required supplemental notices to be sent by 14 December 2009. A deadline for opting in, opting out or objecting to the revised Settlement was set for 28 January 2010 and a Final Settlement Fairness Hearing set for 18 February 2010. Amongst the objections filed to the revised Settlement were submissions from the Open Book Alliance and the Hachette publishing group; a number of major authors (including J.K. Rowling) have also opted not to have their works included. On 4 February 2010 the US Justice Department filed a thirty-one page document stressing that the proposed revisions still did not fully address author concerns over their copyrights and would grant Google a monopoly over millions of orphan works. Judge Chin has not made a final ruling.

In the United Kingdom the Publishers Association and ALCS have generally endorsed the revisions, although the Booksellers Association has continued to voice some concerns and the opinions from literary agents have been mixed. Whilst news of the revised Settlement addressed the fears of some objectors, at the time of writing the Writers' Union of Canada has rejected the deal and the Federation of European Publishers has continued to express some 'serious concerns'. The Open Book Alliance was expected to lodge a formal appeal against the revised Settlement. On 20 November 2009 Amazon filed a request for the judge to reconsider his preliminary approval and for more time to be allotted to renegotiating the Settlement.

The complications of the Settlement did not deter Google from proceeding with other plans; at BookExpo America in May 2009 it promoted its planned Google Publisher programme (now renamed Google Editions), whereby publishers could sell digital versions of their latest titles to customers via Google, competing with Amazon's e-book programme for the Kindle, where they contract directly with publishers. A more detailed programme was rolled out at the Tools of Change conference at Frankfurt in October 2009, with Google promoting content as being available to 'buy anywhere, read anywhere' from a 'cloud library'; this is therefore not a download service but rather an online access service, with provision to access in offline mode if the user is in an area with a low signal. The service will offer facilities for bookmarking, marginal notes, copy and paste of up to 20% of the work and printing off content, but not the whole work, via a single click. Once purchased, the work can be accessed via the user's account on any device they own, either directly from Google, via a partner retailer or from a publisher's own website in partnership with Google, with varying models for division of revenue. Content will be offered with or without DRM, depending on the requirements of the publisher. If the licence granted to Google ends – or if Google should cease its service or cease to exist – users will be supplied with a downloadable PDF. Google envisages that a bundling option could be offered with a purchase of a hard copy of the book plus the e-book version. Google Editions is scheduled to launch in 2010 with approximately half a million titles.

Amazon

The issue of Google has been covered at some length and is ongoing, but Google is of course not the only player to enter this field. In October 2003, the online retailer Amazon (mission statement 'to be the earth's most customer-centric company') launched its Search Inside! service in the United States, extending this to the United Kingdom in 2004. The initial service enabled users to view the front and back covers of a book, the table of contents and the index. The service was then extended to enable users to search by keyword and then access a list of books and then sentences from those books containing the keywords. Users can view up to 20% of the total work but the right-click function has been disabled to prevent extracts being printed out; they can use a link to purchase a copy of the book. Publishers have been more sympathetic to this type of service, particularly since Amazon was careful to enter into early consultations with publishers on the scheme; many have now signed up to the service.

In November 2005, Amazon announced plans to launch two new services: Amazon Pages, which allows users to purchase online access to scanned material (either full or partial text) at a rate per page set by the publisher, who can also specify whether storage and printing out is permitted; and Amazon Upgrade, whereby users can pay an extra fee to access electronically books which they have purchased from Amazon in print form. Users have the facilities to bookmark and annotate the e-book version. Also in 2005, Amazon acquired Mobipocket, the e-book platform which facilitates delivery to mobile devices including smart phones. They also acquired a small print-on-demand operation, BookSurge, in the United States, and in May 2006 launched a service to supply out-of-print and lower-volume titles. For Amazon's Kindle device, see pp. 380–3.

Yahoo! and Microsoft

In October 2005, search engine company Yahoo! announced that it was joining forces with Adobe Systems, Hewlett-Packard and the libraries of the universities of California and Toronto in an Open Content Alliance consortium (OCA – www.opencontentalliance.org), in an initiative to create a digital archive of printed material, audio and audiovisual works from publishers, libraries and archives, but subject to the permission of the copyright holders for those works still protected by copyright. Microsoft has since joined this alliance with its own MSN Book Search service in mind; plans were to concentrate initially on out-of-copyright titles and Microsoft reached agreement with the British Library, with an initial investment of $2.5 million to digitize 100,000 public domain titles from the Library's holdings. In 2005 it launched its Live Search Books and Live Search Academic programmes in the United States as a competitor to the Google programme. In April 2008 it launched the Live Search programmes in the United Kingdom; the proportion of the book available to view could be set by the publisher, with a default percentage of 20%. However, after reportedly scanning some 750,000 books and indexing 80 million journal articles in May 2008 came Microsoft's shock announcement that it would close down the services in order to concentrate on other aspects of digital search, and that it would donate its scanning equipment to libraries and digital partners. In the aftermath of the announcement Ingram Digital, formerly Microsoft's scanning partner (www.ingramdigital.com) offered publishers who had participated in the Live Search programme the opportunity to move to its own Search and Discover platform free of charge with books which had already been scanned. Microsoft has since launched its Bing general search engine, in May 2009; in July of the same year it announced a ten-year deal with Yahoo! whereby Bing would power Yahoo!'s search facility, with Yahoo! retaining a substantial share of resulting advertising revenue.

Are publishers keeping pace?

Previous editions of this book have queried whether publishers are up to speed in the electronic environment. The publishing industry was long accused by user groups such as librarians and academics of having a 'head in the sand' attitude towards digital development, and warnings were issued that publishers ran the risk of being overtaken by events. In the last fifteen years substantial progress has been made by publishers; the delay was perhaps understandable given the scale and complexity of the issues involved: the danger of erosion of copyright protection for authors and publishers; the difficulty of tracking and controlling usage in the electronic environment; the dilemma of whether direct control, central administration via RROs or a mixture of both policies is the best route given the disparity of user groups and the uses to which copyright material can be put; the difficulty of setting appropriate rates of payment for varying types of material and usage; and the major question of whether certain categories of publication, in particular high-level scientific journals, should still be published in print-on-paper form as well as electronic form. Almost all academic publishers now offer journals either with a subscription to include both formats or as electronic only.

In recent years, publishers have been forced to take action through a variety of means, some experimental, and with varying degrees of success. Users expect to have swift access to content electronically and publishers have been forced to reach pragmatic solutions, particularly in the light of the anti-copyright movement and the open access lobbies mentioned in Chapter 1 and the expectation (particularly amongst the younger generation) that content should be free (see *Some lessons from the music industry?* earlier in this chapter, pp. 325–30). STM and academic publishers, by virtue of the nature of their content and the demands from their market, have progressed further and faster in this area than their trade counterparts, but the last four years have seen a flurry of activity in the trade sector to make content available electronically, driven in particular by the advent of more popular dedicated reading devices such as the Sony and the Kindle, and by e-reader applications for smart phones (see Chapter 24). However, the nature of the two sides of the publishing business still differ, with academic content lending itself more towards delivery in partial form, and trade publishers tending more towards delivery of the complete work in e-book form, although some non-fiction publishers in areas such as cookery and travel have developed models for the supply of partial content.

The entry into the field of digital supply of content of newer and less traditional players such as Google, Amazon and Microsoft has undoubtedly galvanized publishers into focusing more intently on this side of the business. The Google Settlement in particular has highlighted what is perhaps a lost opportunity by governments, publishers and libraries themselves in creating what could be viewed as a twenty-first-century equivalent of the great Library of Alexandria. It has also caused authors and authors' agents to raise the question of who should control these rights and to warn that publishers should not assume that control lies in their hands unless the rights concerned are clearly spelled out in the original head contract or granted by the author at a later date if the head contract antedates the advent of the rights concerned (see Chapter 2).

Chapter 24

Electronic publishing and multimedia rights

Chapter 23 has provided coverage of some aspects of electronic publishing, as there is increasing pressure from users, particularly in the academic and commercial research sectors, for fast and easy access to selected extracts of copyright material electronically rather than through the medium of photocopying. This chapter is devoted to full-scale electronic publishing and multimedia licensing, although there is inevitably some area of overlap with certain aspects covered in Chapter 23, in particular electronic libraries and digital aggregators.

Electronic publishing has now become a significant feature of the publishing industry and there have been significant technological and commercial developments during that time. The old maxim 'content is king' has been superseded by the realization that in reality 'the consumer is king', which has forced content providers across the creative industries to make major changes and investments to facilitate access to their wares as a result of user demands; however, they still face considerable opposition from some consumers who feel that copyright requirements impede access to material they expect to be provided free of charge (see *The anti-copyright movement, open access and other initiatives* in Chapter 1), and this has resulted in copyright being put under the microscope at international, multinational and national levels.

It had been predicted that the so-called information superhighway in the form of a full-scale multimedia network would be with us by the year 2000, providing homes and workplaces with telecommunications services, television (including interactive television, e.g. participation in game shows and panel discussion programmes), computer services, shopping services, entertainment and access to information on demand via a single fibre-optic pathway.

At the time of writing we have moved much closer to the scenario envisaged. Few could have imagined the pervasive influence of the internet; in particular, e-mail is now a standard means of communication both for business and for personal purposes; the internet provides a major source of information for the educational, academic and professional sectors as well as for the general public, with e-commerce over the net taken for granted. The initial obstacles to the information superhighway dream were the limitations on access to telecommunication networks, combined with inadequate bandwidth to provide full-scale fast delivery of multimedia facilities via the internet. This situation has changed radically with the introduction of broadband services by providers such as BT, Virgin and Tiscali; by the end of 2009, there were estimated to be 1.8 billion internet users worldwide, with 17.6 million subscribers to broadband services in the United Kingdom and 70 million in households in the United States. By December 2009, it was estimated that 87% of households in the United Kingdom had access to digital television services via satellite, cable or a set-top box: UK television services will transfer completely to digital services by 2012; the major migration to digital took place in the United States by mid-2009.

The convergence of a wide range of players from different industries has continued, with telecommunication companies, cable service providers, internet service providers, television and satellite broadcasting services, electronic hardware and software producers and content providers sealing alliances.

There has also been convergence within the film industry itself, with Paramount (part of Viacom) acquiring Steven Spielberg's DreamWorks in late 2005 at a price of $1.7 billion and Disney acquiring the animation studio Pixar in early 2006 for $7.4 billion. At the time of writing, Comcast, a major provider of cable television, telephone and internet services, is looking to acquire NBC Universal, one of the largest film and television companies. Many publishing companies are themselves part of conglomerates that may include film, television, newspaper, telecommunication and cable interests. The concept of cross-fertilization in terms of maximizing revenue from IP rights 'within the family' is still mooted as an ideal, but to date it has still not proved completely successful. Despite this, 2009 saw Disney acquire Marvel Entertainment and Warner Brothers bought DC Comics.

The development of video-on-demand (VOD) services was initially slow as the service depended on adequate band width, but this has improved and there are now numerous services on both sides of the Atlantic for the delivery of film and television content on demand to customers' homes and also to devices including laptops and mobile phones; full-scale delivery of films by this method inevitably impacts on the video rental business (see Chapter 21).

Have publishers been able to keep pace with technological developments? Initially, some maintained a waiting brief; others formed strategic alliances with electronic producers (e.g. Dorling Kindersley's early alliance with Microsoft); some of the larger companies, particularly those which were par of media conglomerates, entered the field to produce electronic products, the majority in CD-ROM form and based on existing print-on-paper products. Some projects were developed completely in-house, while others were developed together with software houses, sometimes on a joint venture basis.

The year 1996 was notable for the number of publishers on both sides of the Atlantic who announced that they were either downsizing or with-drawing completely from the multimedia publishing area; these included Simon & Schuster, Reed Interactive and Penguin. In 1997, Random House and HarperCollins both sold their multimedia publishing operations to full-scale electronic producers. Reasons quoted included the high cost of multimedia development, the time and cost involved in clearing rights in copyright material from a wide range of outside sources, strong competi-tion from other more established new media producers, problems with marketing and distribution, and disappointing sales growth. Perhaps the main lesson learned was that a bestselling book does not necessarily translate into a successful multimedia product.

Some publishers had more impact in the market. Helicon (founded in 1992 as a buy-out from the reference division of Random House but in 2002 acquired by Research Machines) published a number of successful multimedia encyclopaedias. Encyclopaedia Britannica launched a CD-ROM version and now delivers online. Dorling Kindersley were initially successful with publications such as *The Way Things Work*, *The Ultimate Human Body*, *Children's Multimedia Dictionary* and *My First Amazing World Explorer*, but the operation ultimately proved unprofitable and was rolled into Pearson's Digital Media Division following the acquisition of Dorling Kindersley by that company in early 2000. From the non-publisher sector, Microsoft launched its *Encarta* encyclopaedia with some initial success, but closed down the service in both disc and online format in March 2009.

A significant development in the mid-1990s was the launch of the hybrid product – CD-ROMs backed up by material on websites accessible to purchasers of the CD-ROM. These services can provide additional information which is regularly updated. Outside the trade sector, most academic publishers now offer supplementary websites to accompany their major textbooks and these 'added value' features are now deemed essential in what is a highly competitive market.

In 2000, the advent of the e-book was seen as a significant development which could have a considerable impact on traditional book sales – the supply of an entire book electronically for downloading to a desktop computer, laptop, palmtop device or dedicated reading device. Various aspects of e-books will be covered later in this chapter; their initial impact proved disappointing, but in the academic sector they are now a significant presence (often supplied via aggregators – see *Electronic digitization services, e-book publishers and aggregators* later in this chapter, pp. 387–90). The advent of a new and more popular generation of dedicated e-reading devices such as the Sony Reader and the Amazon Kindle have had a significant impact on the e-book publishing policy of trade publishers. E-books are generally viewed as an alternative platform for delivery to the end-user and hence as a sale rather than as a subsidiary right.

In view of these various developments, it is crucial to consider the range of rights which should be sought by publishers when contracting with authors and illustrators, and to consider whether any electronic publishing rights acquired should be for exploitation by the publishers themselves, via a joint venture with an electronic producer or via full-scale licensing, or with provisions in the contract for all those possibilities.

The question of who should control electronic and multimedia publishing rights is addressed in Chapter 2. As authors and their representatives such as agents and publishers have gained more exposure to electronic publishing, there has generally been more acceptance that verbatim electronic rights – the electronic storage and retrieval of text and illustrations as they appear in a print-on-paper version of the work – fall logically within the realm of volume rights granted to the publisher and the concern has been to reach agreement on a reasonable level of author royalties for e-book sales. By contrast, full-scale multimedia rights, with the addition of other elements such as sound or an interactive facility, should be the subject of negotiation between author and publisher, and could include enhanced e-book rights (see *Mobile phones* pp. 384–6). A plethora of recent initiatives, often instigated by new players such as Google and Amazon (see *Search engines, online retailers and others: threat or opportunity?* in Chapter 23), have caused agents to question whether this form of electronic publication should form part of the publisher's bundle of rights unless they are specifically covered by contract. One thing is sure – control of such rights should never be simply assumed. In addition to the landmark 1999 Tasini case (see *Who should control electronic and multimedia rights?* in Chapter 2), 2000 saw a number of lawsuits filed by authors against publishers for the inclusion of their works on databases; these included five suits filed by the American Authors Guild against Reed Elsevier (LEXIS/NEXIS – see *Online databases* later in this chapter, pp. 370–2), Westlaw, Dialog, Dow Jones Reuters and Proquest Databases. Separately, a number of prominent Canadian authors, including Margaret Atwood, lodged complaints against the US-based website Contentville.com, which sold copies of articles from more than 1,800 magazines, academic journals and newspapers; this site was closed down in October 2001. Then 2002 saw a lawsuit between Random House and e-book publisher Rosetta Books after Rosetta claimed that e-book rights did not form part of the publisher's package for pre-1994 titles; the suit was eventually settled in favour of Rosetta Books.

Care should be taken not to create a conflict of rights; for example, licensing rights to produce an animated multimedia product could conflict with rights granted to a film or television company for the same book (see *Television* and *Cinematographic film rights* in Chapter 21). Many film and television companies now seek multimedia rights as part of their own licence.

It is difficult to produce neat definitions for the terms 'electronic publishing' and 'multimedia'; both involve the exploitation of material in a variety of electronic forms and for a variety of 'platforms', the term used to describe the technical device on which the material will be utilized. At its simplest, electronic publishing falls into two broad categories: first, the loading of copyright material on to an electronic database so that this body of information (either a single work, or more commonly a collection of different works) can be accessed by the user; to date, this type of product continues to be more commonly used in the educational, academic, professional and research sectors. The advent of the e-book was expected to open significant possibilities in the trade sector, and the new e-reader devices are starting to fulfil those expectations. In the meantime the development of smart phone technology providing access to the internet has opened up other possibilities (see *Mobile phones* later in this chapter, pp. 384–6). The rapid development of the internet provided a medium for basic electronic publication, and the introduction of wider broadband facilities now makes it more appropriate as a channel for full-scale multimedia publication. The second category is the publication of copyright material in the form of offline fixed-medium software which can be used for educational, leisure or business purposes (e.g. on CD-ROM, although this medium is now less popular).

The term 'multimedia' encompasses the exploitation of copyright material on a range of platforms, but implies the presence of a variety of elements. Electronic publishing consultant Tony Feldman defined it thus: 'Multimedia is the seamless integration of text, sound, images of all kinds and control software within a single digital environment.' A multimedia product may include text, graphics (perhaps animated), sound effects, video clips and perhaps an interactive facility, which will enable the user to browse and home in on particular features of the system through a series of choices offered. The degree of user control is determined by the computer software providing the interactive facility.

Multimedia products remain extremely expensive and complex to develop; it is perhaps not surprising that many traditional print publishers have withdrawn from large-scale investment in the area, although educational publishers have started to develop products for interactive whiteboard use in recent years. These have tended to be original products rather than electronic versions of material previously published in print form.

Software

Much computer software is developed as an original product by both hardware and specialist software manufacturers, but there are other instances where it is based on existing copyright material licensed for use in this form.

The field of lexicography remains particularly fruitful in this context. A number of dictionary publishers have licensed their databases to hardware or software manufacturers as the basis of spellchecker software or definition dictionaries for word-processing software. Payment is normally made on the basis of a royalty per copy sold, based on the price received by the manufacturer of the software rather than the retail price paid by the user. Royalties may range from as low as 7% to as high as 30%, depending on the perceived value of the data to the licensee. Licences are usually short (three or four years) and may specify a guaranteed level of royalty income, escalating for each year of the licence. Another development was that employed by Houghton Mifflin, which developed software based on their *American Heritage Dictionary of the English Language*, allowing the reader of an e-book with this facility to double-click on any word and obtain an instant definition, with full credit given to the dictionary and the publishers.

On the lighter side, manufacturers of games software may seek to produce adventure games based on a book, as with Terry Pratchett's *Discworld* titles, or on books subsequently developed as films, such as J.K. Rowling's *Harry Potter* series – in such cases, the electronic games rights will be included as part of the package acquired by the film company. The games manufacturer will normally make licence payments on an advance and royalty basis. In some cases, there may be opportunities for deals that involve packaging a copy of the book with the software. (See *Video games* later in this chapter, pp. 375–7).

It is essential to tie up software licensing arrangements very tightly, and to include the form in which the material will be produced and the hardware for which it is intended. As with many types of electronic publishing, it is possible to make separate arrangements for the same material to be used on different hardware.

A number of publishing houses publish software themselves. Initial ventures into educational software for school use generally proved unsuccessful; schools are now more inclined to purchase CD-ROM-based or online multimedia material. Publishers needed to deal with the problem of unauthorized copying of their products, despite the introduction of copyright protection for software in domestic legislation. Most software producers are prepared to permit the making of a single back-up copy of a program, and both commercial and educational producers print details of copyright restrictions on the packaging of the materials. These are referred to as 'shrink-wrap contracts' on the understanding that once the packaging is opened the user is considered to be bound by copyright restrictions.

Those publishers still producing educational software have sought to deal with the problem of multiple copying by issuing site licences for individual software programs to individual schools. When such a licence is granted, the publisher will supply the school with an unprotected disk, which can then either be copied or used on a network within the school. A site licence permits copies to be made of the software program and any accompanying material up to an agreed number of copies within a specified period of time. For an extension of the licence and the right to make further copies, the licence would have to be renewed. Payment for the term of the licence is normally made on the basis of a lump sum, which may be in the region of £300–500 for secondary schools and lower for primary schools, which tend to have fewer computers.

Publishers maintain a register of the schools licensed; a debugging service is offered to registered licensees to deal with any faults which may arise. Licensees are restricted to using the material for educational purposes only within their own schools and may not pass on copies to third parties. If the contract is terminated, the licensor can require the destruction of copies of the software and any written materials produced while the licence was in force.

Software licences may also be granted on a commercial basis to other companies, for example for translation into another language. It is important to remember here that a number of levels of translation may be involved – from one human language to another, but possibly also from one computer language to another and for use on different hardware ('versioning'). Any changes of this kind must be established during the course of the licensing negotiations, and the licensors must define very carefully what rights are being granted.

Licences of this kind are normally negotiated on the basis of an advance payment against royalties, with royalties ranging from 10% to 20% based on the actual price received by the licensee rather than on the retail price paid by the end-user. Licences should be limited by quantity, geographical sales territory and time; licence periods should be short, with provision for renewal if the arrangements are satisfactory. The licensor should specify that full copyright acknowledgement appears on the screen, on the software label, on any external packaging and on any printed material that accompanies the software.

Electronic databases

These can exist in a variety of forms: accessible online via desktop computers, laptops or via hand-held devices, including mobile phones, offline in the form of CD-ROM products, or as databases on chip memories in hand-held products.

Online databases

An online system consists of a central computer system with a large, usually predominantly textual database, which enables users of the system to access data remotely via a modem facility linked to a telephone or perhaps directly via the internet. Payment is usually made in the form of a subscription charge paid to the information provider, the online service provider and payment for online time.

A well-established example of an online database that employs published copyright material is LEXIS, which since early 1997 has been part of Reed Elsevier's LEXIS/NEXIS service, which also provides news and financial information to subscribers. LEXIS is a giant database of primary source material, giving the full text of case law; legal publishers have licensed material for inclusion on the database and LEXIS is responsible for digitizing the material.

Subscribers to the service are members of the legal profession, who have access to the service through terminals in their own offices. They can feed in key terms to retrieve relevant legal precedents; accessing the database in this way can save many hours of searching through volumes of legal reports when they are preparing a case. LEXIS subscribers pay a monthly subscription charge to Reed Elsevier, a fee to the online service provider and an additional fee for each search of the database that they instigate. The exact material accessed is not known to LEXIS. Copyright holders whose work is licensed for inclusion on the database are paid by one of two methods, either a small fee per annum for each case included, or, for the major sources that provide a large proportion of the material on the database, a *pro rata* percentage of the annual income received by LEXIS from access fees, that percentage linked to the proportion of the database formed by their material. Subscribers to LEXIS can print off hard copies of the text they require, but experience indicates that for detailed study they often return to the traditional printed book once the material they require has been located and its source identified. Payment arrangements for information in hard copy form vary according to arrangements with individual subscribers.

In January 1997, Sweet & Maxwell, another major legal publisher, launched its Current Legal Information abstracts and indexing service on CD and also online on a subscription basis; it currently offers this services via the Legal Journals Index on Westlaw UK and the Articles Index from Lawtel.

The industry has grown quickly since the late 1980s; databases of this kind have proved ideal for subscribers wishing to search large amounts of material quickly, and many exist which incorporate bodies of information such as the full text of newspapers, scientific journals and abstracts (see *Abstracts* in Chapter 23). Subscribers are often companies undertaking commercial research and development, such as pharmaceutical firms. A wide range of databases are available worldwide, many of them (e.g. Bloomberg, Reuters, the *Wall Street Journal* and the *Financial Times*) providing regularly updated news and financial information to subscribers.

Access to material online can pose problems in terms of copyright, in particular the question of how to track use of material and deal with the question of payment for that use (see also *Access and payment* in Chapter 23). Although it is comparatively easy to track the use of material by direct subscribers to an online service, the linking of many databases via the internet continues to give some reason for concern, particularly as many internet users expect to obtain information free of charge. It is therefore vital to have adequate systems for tracking usage and ensuring payment for copyright material (see *Commercial digital rights management systems* in Chapter 23).

Optical disc media

Optical discs remain the dominant platform for storing and disseminating multimedia materials. The most common form of optical disc is the CD-ROM (Compact Disc Read-Only Memory), with its upgraded version, the CD-ROM XA (Extended Architecture) developed by Sony, Philips and Microsoft, which is most commonly used in multimedia publishing. Similar in appearance to CD audio discs, they carry data that can be accessed by a computer fitted with a suitable CD drive.

Databases: the move from CD-ROM to online

In the 1980s, CD-ROMS were largely textual, making them the ideal medium for offline databases, primarily for the academic, professional and business sectors. The storage potential of this system was particularly attractive to libraries, which are the single biggest user group. A CD-ROM provides a capacity equivalent to about 250,000 pages of text, in fully searchable form.

An early example of a CD-ROM database was ADONIS, launched in 1992 by a consortium of high-level publishers, in particular Elsevier, Springer and Blackwell Science. ADONIS provided access to the text of about 750 journals, mainly in the area of biomedical science; the contents of the journals were indexed. ADONIS users were mainly pharmaceutical companies; each subscriber paid an annual fee. The service was then folded into the ScienceDirect online service (see *Site licences* in Chapter 23).

Another example of a CD-ROM database was the *English Poetry Full-Text Database* originally produced by Chadwyck-Healey, now owned by Proquest. The CD-ROM version was launched on four discs at a price of £22,000; since it contained the full-text works of 1,350 poets from AD 600 to 1900, it represented a cost-effective way for libraries to build a collection. Almost all such large database services are now available in online form; Proquest offers the *Literature Online* database as well as *History Online*.

A number of book publishers embarked on publishing their own data-base-type products in CD-ROM form. Lexicographical material lends itself well to this medium; the *Oxford English Dictionary* (OED) is available in this form at a price considerably lower than that of the multi-volume print-on-paper edition. In March 2000 Oxford University Press (OUP) launched an online version of the *OED* (www.oed.com) on a subscription basis and in 2004 it launched an online version of the *Oxford Dictionary of National Biography* (www.oup.com/oxforddnb.com), which offers links to portraits of many of the subjects from the collection of the National Portrait Gallery. In 2002, OUP launched *Oxford Reference Online*, which offers content from hundreds of Oxford encyclopaedias, dictionaries and companion volumes; this was followed by *Oxford Scholarship Online*, containing the complete texts of over 1,350 OUP monographs with a search facility and links to external online content such as journal articles. The *New Grove Dictionary of Music and Musicians* and the *Grove Dictionary of Art* were originally published by Macmillan but are now published by Oxford University Press; the online edition of the *Grove* music dictionary was launched in January 2001 and has links to digital sound; the online version of the art dictionary has links to museum and art gallery websites. Cambridge University Press offers access to a major collection of its publications through *Cambridge Online*.

The dissemination of information through databases raises particular questions of copyright and hence concern in the minds of copyright holders that material may be put to uses that were not intended when the licence was first granted. It is therefore important when granting such licences to try to ensure that the facilities permitted to end-users are speci-fied as clearly as possible, whether the material is available to subscribers through an online database or in the form of CD-ROM material purchased outright. Licences are usually very short – perhaps two or three years – and renewable only if the arrangement proves satisfactory.

The development of major reference works is by definition an expen-sive exercise. An interesting development in 2001 was the advent of the online encyclopedia *Wikipedia* (www.wikipedia.org), an open source refer-ence work with the ambitious aim of creating a world where 'every single human being can freely share in the sum of all knowledge'. At the time of writing Wikipedia offers more than 14.3 million articles in 270 languages. The name is derived from the Hawaiian '*wiki wiki*', meaning 'quick'. The Wikipedia Foundation is funded by public donations; material is provided by over 100,000 volunteer writers and editors and it is currently the fifth most visited website in the world and the most popular online reference work. It also has a sister site, Wiktionary (www.wiktionary.org), with dictionary databases in several languages. Wikipedia generally maintains stubborn independence on political content, which has led to the Chinese authorities closing access to the site on numerous occasions.

Multimedia products on CD-ROM and online

Because CD-ROM is a relatively slow medium, it has been used primarily for textual data. However, as the technology developed, images and sound could be incorporated as well. This has led to the extension of the market beyond that of professional users and into the education and home entertainment markets with interactive versions of books such as Douglas Adams' *A Hitchhiker's Guide to the Galaxy*. The medium lent itself well to encyclopaedia-type products and to topics which benefit from a mix of text, images and sound, such as Penguin's *Viking Opera Guide* and many of the Dorling Kindersley multimedia products based on materials previously published in print-on-paper form. Multimedia products also lend themselves to educational use, and the market expanded when computers with CD-ROM drives became available in classrooms. CD-ROM products with supplementary web-based materials have proved popular, although in recent years CD-ROMs have lost ground to online products.

The main problem encountered by producers of multimedia products is the sheer investment of time and money necessary to develop the product and to re-clear rights for the use of any external copyright material such as film clips, music and images, particularly since the different industries involved utilize significantly different mechanisms for payment. The advantages of full ownership of content are apparent.

Other CD technology

A number of other CD technologies have been launched, only to fall by the wayside. CD-I (Compact Disc Interactive) was developed by a consortium of Philips, Sony and Matsushita in 1991; the player was designed to be plugged into a television set and was also able to play CD audio discs and Eastman Kodak photo CDs. Despite high initial hopes for the platform, it never secured a viable market. The same fate befell CD-TV, launched by the computer manufacturer Commodore at about the same time. Both platforms suffered from a lack of high-quality content.

Compression technologies are now sufficiently developed to enable full-length motion pictures to be stored on a CD. Since the last edition of this book appeared, DVDs (originally Digital Video Discs, now Digital Versatile Discs) have come to dominate the market over VHS videotapes. The DVD was developed by two separate consortia, one consisting of an alliance between Sony and Philips and the other a grouping of Toshiba, Time Warner, Thomson, Matsushita and MGM. To avoid the VHS/Betamax videotape scenario, agreement was reached on a common standard in December 1995. However, at the time of writing Sony's BluRay format (backed by Philips, Apple, Dell and Hewlett-Packard) is overtaking

Toshiba's HD format (backed by Microsoft and Intel) to become the next DVD standard.

A DVD can carry approximately 4.7 gigabytes of digitized information, as opposed to the 700 megabytes of a CD-ROM. A DVD can carry a full-length film and may also include out-takes, additional information about the making of the film, interviews with the stars, etc. Players were first launched on the market in 1997 at a price of between £500 and £600, but have now fallen to well below £100, with BlueRay players at between £200 and £300; the machines can also play standard DVDs. Machines that can record to DVD remain slightly more expensive than basic players at prices between £100 and £300.

The launch of the DVD was initially delayed by the Hollywood film industry, which lobbied for a worldwide protection system that would involve different encoding formats for each of six geographical areas. The film industry also lobbied strongly for a read-only format, fearing that DVDs with a recording facility would impact on their interests.

Video games

Other contenders in the CD and DVD field include Sega and Nintendo, together with Sony the three largest manufacturers of video games. The three main players in the games console market are Sony, Nintendo and Microsoft, and 'console wars' tend to take place every five to six years. Sony launched its PlayStation 2 (PS2) in Japan in March 2000; it was promoted as a 'miracle machine' that could become the future platform for home entertainment, with cinema-quality graphics and facilities to play DVDs and audio CDs, and at the time of writing it is still the all-time bestselling games console, with sales of over 136 million. The launch of the much-vaunted PlayStation 3 (PS3) was delayed due to technical problems but it was finally rolled out in November 2006. It features an HD BlueRay optical drive for superior graphics and can also play normal DVDs. The latest model has a 60GB hard drive with wifi, giving users free access to the Playstation Network to meet and play other gamers, plus the facility to buy and download new games.

Microsoft first entered this market with its Xbox in 2001; it launched the Xbox 360 console in November 2005. By mid-2006 it was interoperable with PCs and mobile phones using the Windows operating system, with access to Xbox Live Marketplace to purchase and download games. It also offers a Video on Demand (VOD) service for music videos and films.

Nintendo launched its Gamecube console in early 2001 but it did not prove very successful. The Nintendo Wii was launched in late 2006, priced considerably lower than the PS3 and the Xbox 360; its main feature is a wand-like remote control device which enables players to simulate action on screen (e.g. with a sword or a tennis racket). The Wii offers internet access for the purchase and downloading of games, as well as access to news and weather information. Nintendo offer a number of shorter and cheaper games for the console to attract family users and more 'casual' gamers – these include its Sports Suite and its Big Brain Academy range of mental agility exercises.

At the time of writing, the Wii has far outsold the PS3 and the Xbox 360 (some 56 million units sold), despite the fact that it does not offer HD graphics. Nintendo has also launched a handheld touchscreen console, the DS; apart from its gaming facilities, in December 2008 it offered a Classic Books collection cartridge for £17.99, with further plans for books to be available for download.

September 2009 brought a cheaper version of the Sony PS3, the Slim, with a 120GB hard drive. In October 2009 Sony launched its handheld PSP Go, with 16GB memory, integrated Bluetooth and a slot for memory cards. There is also a facility for users to download books and comics using its Digital Reader service.

In 2009 there were several significant changes in the games industry: more games produced for hand-held consoles and a move to developing games for use on mobile phones. Games for hand-held devices are usually more complex and more expensive at around £30, but with multiplayer facilities. Warner Bothers has licensed an application (app – see *Mobile phones* later in this chapter, pp. 384–6) for the Apple iPhone, *Harry Potter Spells*, which uses Bluetooth short-range wireless connectivity to enable two players to duel; this costs only £2.99. The downloading of games to mobile phones has overtaken the purchase of ringtones, music and video content.

Video games can take 18–25 months to develop; the development costs are very high but some games can prove extremely lucrative: *Grand Theft Auto IV* took over $500 million in sales during its launch week. The majority of them are original, but in the last two years there has been a move towards developing games based directly on books, as well as games based on films which originated as books. The year 2009 saw the launch of games based on the *Horrid Henry* books for the Nintendo Wii and the hand-held DS. There are a number of different games based on J.R.R. Tolkien's *Lord of the Rings* trilogy – those published by Black Label Games (part of Vivendi Universal Active), which are based directly on the books, and others published by Electronic Arts, which are based on the Peter Jackson films.

It is currently estimated that the games industry was worth some US $25 billion in 2009, excluding the sales of consoles, advertising revenue and sales of other merchandise derived from onscreen advertising.

Recent years have seen a boom in 'massively multiplayer online games' (MMOG), many of which are set in Tolkien-style virtual worlds and which can attract hundreds of thousands of players. *World of Warcraft* is reputed to have over 10 million subscribers worldwide. Participants control individual characters who may or may not be human as they fight monsters, embark on quests and acquire money, skills and special powers. These games can prove addictive, with players spending dozens of hours a month in effect living in a parallel world and interacting with a community of other players. There have been increasing instances of crime (in particular identity theft) taking place in the MMOG environment.

Hand-held electronic devices

As a result of the general drive towards portability in computer products, developments in microchip technology have made it possible to produce a range of devices in palm-top sizes. It is important to make a distinction between multipurpose products such as personal digital assistants (PDAs), products specifically designed for reading purposes but accessing content via ROM-cards or cartridges or by downloading from a website, and dedicated products containing a specific body of text which may be derived from an existing book or database.

Dedicated chip-based electronic devices

Material suitable for licensing in this form includes popular reference materials such as encyclopaedias and almanacs, bibles and concordances and guidebooks. The other main sources of material are linguistic products such as dictionaries and their derivatives, including spellcheckers and language teaching materials for business and tourist use.

The text cannot be manipulated, but the user can search and access it onscreen via the keyboard. Examples of this would be the hand-held electronic bibles, dictionaries, crossword solvers, medical and other reference works published by the American company Franklin Electronic Publishers; prices currently range from around $30 to $100. Seiko has produced products such as the hand-held *Britannica Concise Encyclopedia*, which contains the *EB Concise Encyclopedia*, the *Concise Oxford English Dictionary*, the *Concise Oxford Thesaurus* and the *Concise Oxford Dictionary of Quotations*; at the time of writing, the UK price is £97.86.

If a work is licensed for use in such a form, the royalty is likely to be modest – perhaps between 2% and 5%, based on the price received by the manufacturer of the product rather than the full retail price paid by the end-user. This is because the main cost of the product lies in the dedicated technology rather than in the content element.

Hand-held e-book readers

In 1993, Franklin diversified into the medical and business sectors and also launched its Bookman platform. Franklin still produces a wide range of

ROM-cards for the Bookman; these include dictionaries, thesauruses, language teaching materials, encyclopaedias and titles for leisure use, such as cookbooks and wine guides. Franklin has also developed products for professional use, including medical reference works under licence from publishers.

An early platform for which there were high expectations was the Sony Data Discman, launched in Japan in 1990 and in the United Kingdom in 1992. The Discman weighed just over 15 ounces, with a backlit LCD screen measuring 3.5 inches diagonally and a QWERTY keyboard enabling users to search and display data. Software for the Discman was in the form of three-inch optical discs storing 200,000 megabytes of information, 100,000 pages of text or 32,000 graphic images. *Thomson Directories*, the *Hutchinson Encyclopedic Dictionary* and a multilingual dictionary were bundled with the Discman for its UK launch. However, take-up of the product was disappointing and the platform failed.

In July 2000, Franklin launched its eBookman, approximately equivalent in size and weight to a PalmPilot (see *Personal organizers and personal digital assistants* later in this chapter, pp. 383–4) but with a larger screen. At prices of up to $290, the devices are designed for downloading content from e-retailing sites (e-books currently cost from $3.95 to $39.95) and come with a slot for plugging in cards with extra memory or further content. They can also download MP3 files for music or audiobooks and have organizer facilities. The usual model is for publishers to supply digital files and for revenue from the price of the e-book version to be shared between Franklin and the originating publisher in agreed proportions.

In 1997, Nuvomedia launched the RocketeBook, a hand-held dedicated reading device designed for the downloading of e-books from the websites of online retailers. The company was acquired in early 2000 by Gemstar, a Pasadena-based company best known for its VCR-programming technology. Initially launched at $300, the price of the RocketeBook then fell to $199, with hardware available only in the United States. The RocketeBook was about the same size as a trade paperback and could store approximately 3,200 pages of text with a clear display on a mono-chrome screen; turning pages was achieved by the press of a button, and backlighting and type size could be adjusted.

The RocketeBookPro could store about 15,000 pages. The devices had touch-sensitive screens with facilities for users to bookmark and annotate pages. A speaker was available for reproduction of any embedded sound files, but the devices were more suitable for text reproduction than for the downloading of sophisticated graphics. Content for the initial models of RocketeBooks could be downloaded to a desktop and then loaded into the device.

Gemstar also acquired ownership of SoftBook, a slightly larger hand-held device which concentrated more on providing electronic content to business and professional users. In September 2000, new models of the RocketeBook (REB1100, $300 with monochrome screen) and the SoftBook (REB1200, $700 with colour screen) were launched. Weighing in at 17 ounces and 33 ounces respectively, each had a modem facility enabling users to download encrypted content directly from the Gemstar website on to the readers, with facilities to store 150 titles. Despite considerable publicity, the devices did not attract a sufficient market – perhaps because at that time there was still a resistance to reading whole books on screen, albeit in portable form. Gemstar closed down this part of its operation in July 2003.

Despite these disappointing experiences, Sony remained keen to establish a new hand-held reading device, working with Philips and E-Ink (see *E-paper and E-Ink* later in this chapter, p. 386). The device was launched under the name of the Librié in 2004 in Japan; it used an E-Ink rather than an LCD display and could store up to 10,000 pages and run on a set of four AAA batteries, holding up to 100 e-books in a 10 megabyte memory. Sony launched the device in the United States in September 2006 at a price of $349.99; files were available only in Sony's own format and users had to download e-books from Sony's e-bookstore, Connect.com, first to a PC and then on to the device. In October 2007 the device was replaced by the Sony Reader PRS 505 model, with a six-inch screen (this was made available in the United Kingdom in September 2008 at a price of £299), and followed by the Sony Reader Touch ($299 in the United States, £249 in the United Kingdom) and by the smaller Sony Reader Pocket ($199 in the United States, £179 in the United Kingdom). In October 2008 Sony launched the PRS 700 in the United States, priced at $400; this model had an LED backlight, a stylus and facilities for annotation. Sony currently offers over 600,000 titles for downloading from its website. By late 2008 Sony had started to move to the.ePub format and had completed the process by 11 December 2009, using ADEPT, Adobe's digital rights management (DRM) software. The device can also handle PDFs.

At the time of writing, no Sony models available in the United Kingdom enable users to download content directly to the device via a wifi facility; the Sony Reader Daily Edition, with a seven-inch screen and 3G connectivity, was launched in the United States in December 2009 and can store up to 1,000 titles; no release date has yet been announced for the United Kingdom.

In 2006, iRex Technologies, in partnership with Dutch electronics company Philips, launched the Irex iLiad device at a price of £433. In May 2008 the device was relaunched at a price of £399 through the Borders bookstore chain, with facilities to download e-books from the Borders website. The device has an 8.1 inch screen and comes preloaded with fifty public domain classic titles. It can handle e-books on the Mobipocket platform and PDFs, with content downloadable direct to the device.

By March 2009 the device was also available through the W.H. Smith website; at that point Borders, already in financial trouble, abandoned marketing the device as it was felt that the price was unsustainable in the face of competition from other devices. In September 2008 iRex launched the iRex Reader 1000; aimed at business users, it has a 10.2 inch screen.

At the time of writing, the dominant device is the Amazon Kindle. Launched in its first version in the United States in November 2007 at $399, it was replaced in February 2009 by the Kindle 2, at a price of $359. Its key feature is the facility to download e-books direct from the Amazon website (www.amazon.com/kindlepublishing). Jeff Bezos has said that Amazon's aim is to supply 'every book ever printed in any language available in less than sixty seconds'. With a six-inch screen, a QWERTY keyboard and wireless connectivity through a system called Whispernet via the EUDO network, the device also offers free access to Wikipedia and facilities for searching, highlighting and bookmarking. This version also offers a text-to-speech feature with an automated voice; this raised concerns from a number of publishers who felt that audio rights were not part of the package granted. Amazon has since stated that this facility will only be provided where it has been authorized by the publishers concerned.

E-books are provided for the device in a bespoke format (criticized by some as as limitation compared with Sony's more open platform), although non-DRM protected e-books on the Mobipocket platform can also be supplied. Most e-books were initially priced in the United States at $9.99 and over 300,000 are currently available from the Amazon website. In July 2009 Amazon was heavily criticized for acting in Big Brother mode when it deleted copies of George Orwell's *1984* and *Animal Farm* from users' devices, apparently in the aftermath of the books being uploaded by a publisher who did not control the rights in those titles. Amazon have since stated that they will block the initial downloading of illegal copies but will not delete copies downloaded by customers in good faith.

There was a considerable delay in launching the Kindle 2 outside the United States because of the complications in reaching agreement with mobile phone operators to enable the wifi facility for direct download of content; agreement was planned with AT&T and its roaming partners. The device was finally launched in the United Kingdom in early October 2009, but with devices being shipped from Amazon in the United States and an initial requirement that content must be downloaded from Amazon.com rather than from Amazon.co.uk. This raised issues of territoriality on many titles which had different publishers on each side of the Atlantic; Amazon aims to facilitate downloading from local sites by mid-2010. From Spring 2010 UK users will have access to over 65,000 nineteenth-century public domain works of fiction, made available as part of the British Library's e-book project.

In May 2009 Amazon launched the Kindle DX, a device enabling wireless downloads and aimed at the college textbook market. Priced at $489 and with a 9.7-inch screen, the device supports PDFs, and a pilot programme was run with US college students, featuring a range of textbooks from Pearson Education, Cengage and Wiley Blackwell. The DX was launched internationally in January 2010, with the capacity to hold 3,500 e-books and with an auto-rotate function. Although academic publishers have been producing e-books far longer than trade publishers – and Springer in particular has made many of its books available for the Kindle – most viewing tends to be on desktops, laptops or netbooks rather than dedicated devices. The college market has been reluctant to move to e-readers for a number of reasons; the screen size has been considered too small to do justice to complex layouts, they are currently available in black and white only and have limited facilities for interactivity. Apart from the availability of books from aggregators (see *Electronic digitization services, e-book publishers and aggregators* later in this chapter, pp. 387–90), a popular college option has been CourseSmart.com, a site which works with twelve major textbook publishers and which enables students to download content for a limited period of time (usually 180 days); they can copy and paste extracts into a word-processing application. Over 2,000 textbooks are currently available from the site at less than half the price of the print versions. One crucial factor may be that students will be reluctant to purchase a separate device only for reading; the launch of Apple's much vaunted and more versatile tablet laptop, the iPad, with a 10.7 inch LCD screen may prove more attractive to this market. Previewed in January 2010 and with its initial launch in April 2010, the iPad resembles a giant iPhone (see *Mobile phones* later in this chapter, pp. 384–6). All models will have a high speed wifi connection; the basic model is priced at $499. More expensive models will follow with3G mobile broadband facilities. The iPad offers a touch screen with full-colour reproduction and e-books can be downloaded from Apple's iBookstore, providing direct competition with the Amazon Kindle and indeed with Google Editions (see *The rise of* Google in Chapter 23, pp. 353–61). Access is available initially only for US users, until arrangements are in place for national iBookstore sites which will comply with territorial restrictions. Most of the large trade houses have confirmed arrangements with Apple, and major textbook publishers are working with software company ScrollMotion Inc. to ensure that the complex layouts of their books can be adapted for the iPad. The advent of the device provided an opportunity for a new pricing model which gives publishers more control over e-book prices (see later in this section, p. 383).

Whilst Sony and Kindle have dominated the dedicated e-reader market to date, there are other players. In October 2009, booksellers Barnes & Noble launched their Nook e-reader at a price of $259. With a six-inch screen, the device uses the Google Android facility for wifi downloading from the Barnes & Noble website, which currently offers over 750,000 titles. The device uses E-Ink with a full-colour backlit touch control screen below; e-books can be in.ePub or PDF format or the Fictionwise e-reader format (Barnes & Noble acquired the Fictionwise e-book retailer in March 2009). The books have DRM protection. The device can store up to 1,500 titles and has facilities for highlighting and annotation. There is also a facility to 'lend' books to friends and family for up to fourteen days.

Other devices include Spring Designs' Alex Reader (available only in the United States), the Bookeen Cybook at £200 and Interead Ltd's Cool-er at £199.95, which offers a choice of over 700,000 titles (including 500,000 public domain titles from Google); it is sold in the United Kingdom via Argos. In June 2009 Borders, having abandoned the iRex iLiad as too expensive, launched the Elanex at £189; it features a six-inch screen and comes preloaded with 100 public domain classics. It supports e-books in ePub and PDF format, but its future is at present unclear, with Borders announcing bankruptcy in December 2009. Plastic Logic is due to launch its Que ProRead in 2010 at a price of around £300, with a 10.5-inch screen and wifi download facilities; it is aimed mainly at business users.

The Consumer Electronics Show in January 2010 saw the launch of the Skiff Reader, based on a flexible sheet of stainless steel and with an 11.5-inch touch screen. Also featured were the Samsung E6 and E101 readers (six-inch and 10-inch screens, respectively) and the Entourage edge double-screen device, with a 9.7-inch e-paper display on one side and a 10.1-inch LCD screen on the other; this uses Google's Android technology. Also announced were the wifi-enabled Cool-er Connect, the Cool-er 3G and the Cool-er Compact.

The research company Forrester has predicted that sales of e-reader devices will rise from some three million in 2009 to 13 million in 2013 and that by that time the e-book market will be worth $1.4 billion. A survey conducted at the 2009 Frankfurt Book Fair predicted that digital sales will overtake print sales by 2018. Such figures can be notoriously unreliable, and what is also unpredictable is the cannibalizing effect e-book sales may have on print sales. Whilst at the time of writing they remain a relatively small proportion of publishers' turnover, some major trade publishers (in particular Simon & Schuster, HarperCollins and the Hachette Book Group) have taken deliberate steps to delay the release of e-book versions of major trade titles by up to four months to avoid damaging hardback sales. By contrast, the e-book version of Dan Brown's bestselling *The Lost Symbol*, published in September 2009 with an initial hardback run of 6.5 million copies, was published simultaneously with the hardback. The question of delaying the release of e-book versions has led to debate on whether this will encourage piracy and may also drive authors to separate out e-book rights and deal direct with e-book publishers. In December 2009, bestselling business author Stephen Covey made arrangements for e-book rights in two of his titles direct with dedicated digital publisher Rosetta Books, with the e-books to be made available via Amazon. In January 2010 Ian McEwan made a deal direct with Rosetta for five of his titles, with a guarantee of at least 50% of all resulting income.

The model for content acquisition for e-readers, or more recently mobile phones, has normally been for the e-book supplier to seek a contract directly with the publisher for rights to distribute works on the platform concerned, with the publisher to store digitized versions of the works on its own server and to set prices for the electronic version, such versions then to be 'supplied' to the e-book company at a discount off that price which could be as high as 60%. The company may itself be the supplier of the e-reader device, with its own website to supply content (e.g. Sony or Amazon), or an independent company. The question of whether this is a licence or rather a sale analogous with distribution of a print-on-paper edition was the subject of much debate, but at the time of writing most publishers would classify such arrangements as sales and would provide in their head contracts for payment of a royalty to the author based on the net receipts from such sales. In January 2010 Amazon had announced that from 30 June 2010 it would increase its US royalty rate for publishers and authors who contract directly to them for e-book rights for the Kindle, on condition that an e-book must be priced at least 20% below the lowest price for any physical edition of the same title and not sold cheaper anywhere else; Amazon would then pay 70% of proceeds.

However, the advent of the iPad has triggered a new payment model: Apple is understood to have reached agreement on an 'agency' model, with major publishers setting e-book prices and Apple retaining a share of the revenue. The move by Amazon to price almost all e-books at a standard $9.99 in the United States had resulted in increasingly negative reactions from trade houses; a well-publicized dispute with Macmillan US in February 2010 initially resulted in Amazon suspending the 'buy' button for Macmillan's print and e-book offerings on Amazon. An 'agency' agreement was eventually reached, with Macmillan setting e-book prices (likely to be $14.99) and Amazon retaining 30% of the revenue. Other major trade houses plan to follow suit, including HarperCollins and Hachette.

It is perhaps worth noting here that some public libraries in the United Kingdom are now offering online borrowing facilities. The user enters his or her library membership number online and can download an e-book to his or her computer. The contents will be deleted after fourteen days.

Personal organizers and personal digital assistants

Other products that may utilize copyright material are pocket organizers, such as those still produced by Sharp and Casio. Into these are inserted memory cards carrying data, which could include material from encyclopaedias and dictionaries (e.g. a mini-dictionary, phrase book or spellchecker). The information is accessed via the keyboard of the organizer. Here royalty rates can be as high as 15–20%, again based on the price for the card or cartridge received by the manufacturer rather than the retail price paid by the end-user.

Another platform for the use of copyright material has been the personal digital assistant, originally introduced as the electronic version of the Filofax but later with more sophisticated facilities. PDAs have standard functions such as diary, address book and word-processing facilities; they have been manufactured by a number of companies, including Psion, Palm (which in 2003 acquired its rival Handspring) and Apple, an early entrant to the market with its Newton, now discontinued. PDAs are either operated with a QWERTY keyboard or rely on digital recognition of the user's handwriting with a stylus. A number of PDAs also provide internet access, allowing users e-mail and web-browsing facilities. This enabled them to be a vehicle for the downloading of e-books. By 2002, Palm dominated the PDA market, but by mid-2003 this market was severely eroded by the advent of smart phones and Palm has now diversified into that area.

Mobile phones

The British government auctions for 3G licences were hotly contested but the phones were not launched until late 2004. The introduction of WAP (Wireless Area Protocol) technology facilitated the development of mobile phones with internet access. This enables users to browse the web and receive e-mail messages. Smart phones from companies such as Motorola and Sony Ericsson and those with Symbian operating systems from Nokia are now combined with many of the functions of PDAs, in particular a keyboard enabling the user to send text messages. An innovative device with major take-up has been the BlackBerry, a wireless phone and e-mail device developed by Canadian company Research in Motion (RIM) with a current user base of over 21 million people.

Since the initial launch of the BlackBerry the market has seen a host of smart phones, the most iconic of which has been the Apple iPhone. It has touchscreen technology and uses a Mac OS X operating system; in addition to e-mail facilities, users can display photos and videos and download music. Apple's App Store enables users to download a wide range of applications ('apps'), some of which are free and some of which are charged for. By February 2010 over 140,000 apps were available, including maps, recipes, games and the free Stanza e-reader app, which is also available for the iPod Touch. At the time of writing, over 12 million e-books had been downloaded in the first year since Stanza was launched. It was developed by Lexcycle, a software company bought by Amazon in April 2009. There are currently over 27,000 e-books available for sale on this platform, together with access to over 50,000 out-of-copyright classics. Late 2009 saw a flurry of e-book activity on the iPhone, overtaking the downloading of games for the first time. Amazon has a free Kindle e-book reader app available for the iPhone. A wide range of publishers have made apps available for the iPhone, including Oxford University Press, with over seventy apps for reference titles, and Haynes for its car maintenance manuals; some commentators have said that reference titles, where users wish to access relatively small amounts of content, are likely to be more successful given the small size of the screen. An innovative approach was Canongate's 'enhanced' app for the e-book version of rock star Nick Cave's novel *The Death of Bunny Munro*, which includes audio and video versions of the author reading the novel, background music and a newsfeed on the author.

Apple normally retains 30% of the price of the app, with the remainder divided between the developer and the content owner. A number of other phone manufacturers have produced rival devices, including the BlackBerry Storm, the Palm Pre and the Nokia E72. The most publicized new device, heralded as a 'superphone', is the Google Nexus One, manufactured by Taiwanese firm HTC, utilizing Google's Android software and providing direct links to Google's Gmail service on sites such as FaceBook and Twitter.

The delivery of e-books to mobile phones was pioneered in Japan, where romantic novels have proved particularly popular with young female commuters on the Tokyo metro system; the trend is also growing strongly in Korea and in mainland China, which at the time of writing has over 703 million mobile users. In Japan, the market for *keitai shosetsu* (mobile phone novels) is estimated to be worth over $100 million per year. The novels are normally original rather than based on a previously published print title, but can go on to sell one to two million copies in print once the writer has become popular.

Companies specializing in producing e-books for mobile phones include Fictionwise (now owned by Barnes & Noble) and GoSpoken, which offers books in audio as well as in text form. In October 2005, iCue launched a programme in the United Kingdom for downloading books to mobile phones with appropriate technology, aimed particularly at children and teenagers; it already has arrangements with a number of publishers. ShortCovers, a Canadian company with the Indigo bookstore chain as its major shareholder, rebranded itself as Kobo in January 2010 and sells e-books in ePub and PDF format which can be read on virtually any device except the Kindle. It also offers 1.8 million public domain titles.

Although dedicated reading devices such as the Kindle have had a significant take-up, particularly in the United States, and may be more suitable for reading complete works such as novels, the mobile phone has emerged as a popular multi-function platform of choice, reflecting customer demand for text, audio and video content whilst 'on the move'. The number of 3G users is expected to rise from 100 million worldwide in 2006 to 2.4 billion by 2010.

E-paper and E-Ink

E-paper is a project developed by the MIT MediaLab and Xerox PARC. The plan is for a book consisting of 'digital paper'; words flow on to the pages by means of transparent electrodes controlled by microchips in the spine. The 'book' would be infinitely reusable, but with current costs per sheet of paper the product is not yet available commercially. The E-Ink Corporation expects to demonstrate a colour version of e-paper in May 2010 and related products should become available by the end of 2010.

E-Ink is a technology and also the name of the company which has developed it. Founded in 1997, its investors include Philips and Toppan, the Japanese printing company. The aim was to create a new type of electronic display which looks like paper; liquid ink is held within a very thin film. The ink consists of a clear liquid containing particles known as 'paint chips', which are either black (positively charged) or white (negatively charged). The film is laid on top of a grid of conductive pixels; when an electric field is applied, the chips move either to the top or the bottom of the particle depending on whether the charge is positive or negative. The display then shows as black or white and contains areas representing text and pictures. An E-Ink display is very high resolution and hence easy to read; E-Ink devices are also cheap to run as they use less energy than LCD and can run on short bursts of power to charge the display screen. Content can be transferred to E-Ink devices by connecting them to a PC and inserting a memory card. E-Ink is the medium used in the new generation of dedicated reading devices (see *Hand-held readers* earlier in this chapter, pp. 377–83).

Technology and standards for e-books

To avoid the problem of competing formats similar to that of VHS/Betamax in the video domain, Microsoft and others pressed for an open e-book standard (OeB), which is XML based. The Association of American Publishers supported this initiative, which would enable users to download an e-book from any authorized site and use it on any authorized platform. While PDF has proved ideal for usage requiring an exact image of the printed page (e.g. for scientific journals), XML-based format allows for the reflowing necessary for display on hand-held devices.

In September 1999, Microsoft announced its Microsoft Reader software, designed to enable users to display e-books on desktop and laptop PCs.

Apart from Microsoft Reader, the main software applications used for e-books are Mobipocket Reader (developed by a French company acquired by Amazon in April 2005), Palm eReader and Adobe Acrobat eBook Reader. The International Digital Publishing Forum (IDPF), the trade standards organization, is encouraging the wider adoption of the open source.ePub format; this is XML based and compatible with many mobile devices. A number of e-reader devices use Adobe Content Server 4 (ACS4) for DRM to protect.ePub and PDF files, and it is expected that ACS4 will be supported by an increasing number of mobile phones.

However, an interesting question will be whether there will be a move to make e-books DRM free, a trend initiated within the music industry when Apple removed DRM from its iTunes store in January 2009 (see *Some lessons from the music industry?* in Chapter 23). DRM was felt to have encouraged rather then deterred piracy, and e-book readers may well feel that having paid for an e-book they should be able to transfer and read it on the device of their choice. This debate continues.

Electronic digitization services, e-book publishers and aggregators

The e-book sector of the industry has expanded considerably since the last edition of this book appeared, and a variety of models have emerged to bring content to end-users. These include publishers digitizing and supplying their own material direct (a model favoured by many STM journal publishers, see *Site licences* in Chapter 23) and publishers who have sought the services of external digitization providers such as Overdrive who may offer them digital warehousing services for their content. Others have made arrangements with companies which offer digitization and e-distribution services, either direct or via online retailers such as Amazon. This has led to a range of complex alliances, investments and acquisitions.

A report by JISC (the Joint Information Systems Committee, which drives and in some cases funds the provision of electronic content to UK universities), published in September 2003, identified a perceived gap between the demand from university librarians and academics for e-books and the provision of book content in electronic form by publishers (as opposed to journal content, where academic publishers have been providing electronic content since the mid-1990s). This need has to some extent been addressed by 'bundled' projects such as *Oxford Reference Online* and *Oxford Scholarship Online* (see *Databases: the move from CD-ROM to online* earlier in this chapter, pp. 372–3) and similar initiatives by publishers such as Wiley Blackwell, Cambridge University Press, Sage and Taylor & Francis, available on the basis of institutional licences with the help of some deals via JISC. A later 2009 JISC *E-book Observatory Report* confirmed that e-books are now a part of academic life, with 65% of students and faculty having used e-books, relieving pressure on short-term loan collections at times of peak demand. The report also implies that there is no impact on core print sales.

On the textbook front, multinationals such as McGraw-Hill and Pearson Education have launched their own e-publishing programmes, with content delivered in Adobe Acrobat format directly from their own websites and at prices comparable to or lower than those of the print-on-paper editions. Versions are also available for downloading on to hand-held devices. In the UK, Taylor & Francis announced plans for the supply of its entire backlist electronically, and initially reached agreement with Versaware to digitize and provide digital warehousing for some 17,000 titles, to be sold at about 20% less than the price of print-on-paper versions. Smaller academic publishers such as Cavendish (since acquired in early 2006 by Taylor & Francis) have also made content available in PDF format, both to individuals and bundled for institutional use.

On the trade side, Penguin Putnam announced arrangements with Lightning Source, the Ingram-owned print-on-demand supplier for digitization and supply. Simon & Schuster also announced a link with Lightning Source for the provision of digitization services for onward sale of e-books for platforms such as e-book readers and PDAs. In early 2001, Time Warner and Random House launched e-publishing ventures for platforms such as the RocketeBook and the GlassBook, but by 2003 both platforms had failed and in December of the same year retailer Barnes & Noble withdrew from selling e-books via its website. By 2009 there was a resurgence of electronic activity by trade publishers, spurred on by the availability of more popular e-reader devices and facilities for downloading content to mobile phones; Barnes & Noble has re-entered the e-book market supplying content for its own device, the Nook (see earlier in this chapter, pp. 381–2).

Electronic libraries and aggregators

NetLibrary is based in Boulder, Colorado, and launched with the slogan 'Unbound books. Boundless possibilities'; it is now part of the content division of OCLC (Online Content Library Center). The service provides electronic versions of complete texts online by means of site licences to academic and research libraries as well as to corporations. Access allows viewing of pages one by one, with software to prevent full copying, cut and paste and redistribution. The service provides facilities for full text search and enables resource sharing by library consortia and support for distance learning. Subscription access expires at the end of the relevant course. Users are allocated a 'checkout time' by the library.

At the time of writing netLibrary claims to have over 200,000 titles available, with content in English, Spanish, French, German and Chinese (see www.netlibrary.com for further details). Publishers receive payment in the form of a *pro rata* share of subscription revenue plus 50% of access fees for their material. Libraries purchasing one 'copy' secure access for a single concurrent user and must pay more for multiple access.

Questia Media bills itself as 'the world's largest online library'; the company is based in Houston and was launched in early 2000 with a reported $45 million in venture capital support. The initial aim was to provide full-text access to books and journal articles directly online to humanities students, rather than via site licences to academic libraries. The service is primarily subscription based and allows users to view a page at a time. There are facilities to annotate and highlight texts and print single pages as they view them. Over 250 publishers have licensed content to Questia, with digitization being undertaken by Questia; currently access is offered to over 70,000 books and over two million journal, newspaper and magazine articles. Payment to publishers is a royalty based on a *pro rata* share of subscription revenue, a share of page viewing revenue and also of 'electronic sales of access', i.e. access to licensed material, accessed outside the body of material available on subscription. (See www.questia.com for more information.)

In October 2000, Random House, McGraw-Hill and the Pearson publishing group announced joint investment in eBrary, to build a collection of books and journals online. Libraries can choose whether to purchase perpetual access or to pay on an annual subscription basis; there are single- and multiple-user options. Participating publishers can determine the degree of access and set fees for their own material. They are paid on the basis of an algorithm which takes into account the proportion of their material making up part of the total database and the number of times their material is accessed. (See www.ebrary.com for further information.)

Proquest offers a wide range of databases to libraries and specializes in the humanities and social sciences. Publishers are paid a share of subscription revenue (www.proquest.com).

Books 24x7 specialize in providing collections of publications in the fields of business, management, finance, computing and engineering; their main subscribers are commercial companies but they also supply collections to the libraries of higher education institutions. Corporate subscriptions enable named users to have unlimited access to the content; royalties are paid to publishers based on usage (www.books24x7.com).

Safari Books Online is a joint venture between publisher O'Reilly and the Pearson Technology Group; it offers an online reference library of titles in the area of computing on a monthly or yearly subscription basis (www.safaribooksonline.com).

Knovel offers online libraries of titles in the fields of engineering and hard sciences, primarily to corporate libraries (www.knovel.com).

MyiLibrary, a Coutts company, offers a library of over 175,000 academic titles for use in university libraries; publishers receive a share of subscription revenue (www.myilibrary.com).

Credo (formerly called CrossRefer) offers a database of reference titles to university and professional libraries; publishers receive a share of subscription revenue (www.credoreference.com).

Other players include Ingram Digital (which also offers services to publishers as a digital warehouse) and book wholesalers Blackwells and Dawsons.

It can be seen that a wide range of players are involved in the area of e-publishing; most recently, the entry of technology companies such as Google into the arena of active online whole-book supply is significant (see *Search engines, online retailers and others: threat or opportunity?* in Chapter 23).

Electronic publishing: have initial expectations been fulfilled?

The death of the traditional book has been forecast for some time by many, but despite these predictions the book in print form can still justifiably be championed as an efficient device, portable, requiring no power source and enabling its user to read, annotate and enjoy it in a wide range of circumstances. John Updike has written: 'Our notion of a book is often as a physical object, precious even if no longer hand-copied on sheepskin by carrel-bound monks ... that books endure suggests we endure, our inner tale not writ in the water of E-ink.' However, it cannot be denied that speed of delivery, the possibilities for portability of a large body of content and search facilities have proved attractive to an increasing number of users, many of whom are of an age to perceive electronic delivery of content as the norm. It is important to flag that there are still some key differences in requirements between the trade market on the one hand and the educational, academic and professional markets on the other. The majority of purchasers of trade e-books will normally wish to acquire the whole book, whilst many users in the academic and professional sectors are likely to wish to search large bodies of material and then home in on specific content via a desktop or laptop rather than a hand-held device, although the medical profession has found the portability of the latter such devices invaluable and the increased versatility of mobile phones has opened up new possibilities.

Some commentators predicted that there would be substantial losses by some e-publishers along the way; this indeed proved to be the case, with 2001–3 proving a very negative time for e-publishing which saw retrenching by many traditional publishers, downsizing by some electronic companies and the demise of a number of platforms and providers.

Microsoft predicted that by 2004 hand-held electronic readers would weigh less than 16 ounces, would be priced at less than $100 and would reach 28 million consumers. To date, this has failed to occur, although the introduction of improved technology to facilitate reading onscreen, the convergence of PDAs and mobile phones and the advent of new dedicated e-book readers together with a wider range of titles for these formats could well bring these predictions nearer to reality. Certainly publishers in all sectors of the industry are undertaking a broad range of digital initiatives driven by consumer demand.

Checks before contracting

As with any area of licensing, publishers must be sure that they themselves have control of the appropriate rights in the first place. The golden rule remains to acquire rights broadly and to license rights narrowly; any publishers with serious intentions of exploiting electronic rights in a work (either themselves or in a joint venture via the medium of licensing) will therefore need to negotiate the inclusion of such rights in the initial contract with the author. If the head contract was drawn up at a time when no such rights were envisaged, it is always wiser to return to the author for approval and specific agreement on financial arrangements, and many academic publishers are doing so when large-scale electronic delivery programmes for their backlists are envisaged.

The dangers of assuming that e-book rights are automatically part of the publisher's right to publish 'in book form' were demonstrated in the case of *Random House v. Rosetta Books*, where Rosetta had produced e-book versions of eight pre-1994 Random House titles under direct licence from the authors' agents and the publisher contested their right to do so. The case was settled in December 2002 in favour of Rosetta, who then went on to acquire a range of later titles under licence from Random House.

Agents and authors' societies have recommended that authors should restrict the granting of electronic rights to a defined option period, unless the publisher can demonstrate clear plans for electronic exploitation from the start. This highlights again the question of differentiation between verbatim electronic rights – the direct reproduction of a book as it stands, where electronic distribution is seen by most publishers as an alternative platform for delivery rather than a sublicensing arrangement – and full-scale electronic multimedia rights, where value is added to the product by the enhancement of the book with sound, images and so on. Payment arrangements for authors will need to be clearly differentiated in the head contract and are likely to be in the form of a royalty on net receipts if an electronic version is classed as a sale (e.g. the supply of an e-book version direct to a customer or via an e-book retailer or an aggregator) and as a share of subsidiary rights income if the arrangement is a true licence to a third party.

It is also important to check (even if electronic rights have been included in the head contract) whether there are any restrictions on duration which might affect contractual arrangements for onward use. For example, if the head contract grants the publisher the right to publish and license the work for a period of ten years and eight of those years have already passed, it will not be possible to grant an electronic or multimedia licence for even a three-year period without negotiating an extension of the head contract.

Other aspects to check will be the terms on which permission was granted to use third party copyright material – illustrations or text – in the content of the original print-on-paper work. Some illustrations may have been commissioned by the publisher, who may have acquired full copyright in return for an outright fee. In other cases, an illustrator may have an ongoing interest in the work in the form of a royalty and a share of any licence income (this will be common with well-established illustrators of children's books). If illustrations have been obtained from external sources such as picture agencies, museums or art galleries, it is vital to check whether permission was cleared only for use in the original print-on-paper book and also whether such permission was restricted in terms of publication in the original language or territory, or for a designated print run. In most cases it will probably be necessary to reclear permission and pay fees for the reuse of such illustrations in the context of an electronic product, whether produced by the publisher or via a licensee; the alternative (common with some STM publications in electronic form) is to omit the illustrations concerned and to replace them with a statement that they are excluded for copyright reasons.

Attention should also be paid when works include text quoted from external sources. While some material may have been used under the provisions of fair dealing or under the 'exchange' system introduced by STM publishers (see *Anthology and quotation rights* in Chapter 17 and *Fair dealing in the digital environment* in Chapter 23), it cannot always be assumed automatically that this use can be extended to the electronic environment, and if there is any element of doubt it will be wise to return to the original copyright holder to reclear rights in the required context.

Contractual considerations

It should be remembered that some areas of electronic exploitation are relatively recent – new models for use are emerging daily, and for some types of deal there may be no clear extant model; negotiations will therefore inevitably include some degree of improvisation and concessions on both sides if workable agreements are to be reached.

A number of features will have to be taken into account when negotiating deals for electronic or multimedia exploitation of a literary work. It is essential to define what material is being licensed (e.g. the whole work or only some elements of it) as well as the platform for which the license is being granted (e.g. for a CD-ROM product, the licensee's website or for use on a particular version of Sony's PlayStation) and the use to which the product will be put (e.g. use in the home, educational or business sector). It will also be necessary to establish how the end-user will receive and access the product, whether the licensor's material is to be incorporated in a product with other material, and whether the licence will permit users to download, store, print off material or manipulate material in hard copy form. Other important questions will be the estimated time for development of the product, the expected release date, the licensee's previous experience of producing product for that platform, their resources in terms of sales staff and distribution channels, the expected price of the product and the licensee's marketing plans. Licensees should also be asked what technical protection measures will be put in place to deter copyright infringement.

It is technically possible to license the same material separately for use on different platforms, and this reinforces the need for tight contractual definitions and short licence periods – three to four years has been common, and licences are often linked to sales levels and revenue generated. The duration of the licence should be tied to a fixed calendar date, such as the date of the licence contract, rather than the launch of the product, which could well be delayed. There should be provision for rights to revert if the product does not appear on the market in reasonable time (a non-performance clause), if the platform fails (common in this area, as evidenced earlier in this chapter regarding the failure of various hand-held devices – see pp. 377–9) or if the revenue generated falls below a specified level.

As well as defining the format on which the material will run, it is vital to specify the human language in which the material will be exploited and to ensure that any additional exploitation (e.g. versioning into foreign languages) is covered by separate payment arrangements. It should be remembered that there may already be existing licensees for print-on-paper versions of the text in some languages. The geographical territory in which the product will be sold must also be clearly defined, bearing in mind regulations aimed at preventing distribution restrictions within the single European market. There should also be provisions for how the material will be adapted for electronic use and for quality control over the product, particularly if it is based entirely on an existing book and if the publisher's brand is involved; multimedia producers may be reluctant to agree to straightforward product approval, but regular consultation throughout the period of product development (including on packaging) may be an acceptable compromise. For books with individual authors (as opposed to compilation works such as dictionaries or encyclopaedias) there is a strong case for involving the author in the consultation process. Publishers should insist on clear acknowledgement of the source of the material, both onscreen, on the packaging of any offline product and on any printed material accompanying the product. Termination clauses are particularly important in a field where the life of some licences may be short.

The question of payment for the right to use material in the context of a multimedia product is a particularly complex area. The overall nature of the deal may vary considerably – perhaps the publisher is developing the product but needs to reach agreement with a range of parties, from the author through to picture suppliers, record companies and film companies; perhaps it is a joint venture between the publisher and an outside company such as a software house, or a straightforward licence arrangement between a publisher and an outside company. Even if the deal is a licence, much will depend on the nature of the title and the way in which it is to be used as part of a multimedia product. A key task will be to try to establish the importance of the title as an element of the overall product, which will in effect be an anthology or compilation of many elements in addition to the underlying text – sound effects, music, animation or film clips could all be added, as well as the software aspect, which may provide an interactive facility. If the multimedia product is heavily dependent on the literary work – perhaps an illustrated children's book, or a branded product such as an encyclopaedia – then there will be justification for requiring a higher level of payment for the use of that work.

In addition to considering the relative 'value' of the title as part of an electronic or multimedia product, it is important to establish the way in which the material is to be used and the projected sales of the end product, which can be difficult to predict if the product is intended for a new platform. The usual method of payment for an offline product will be an up-front fee, with subsequent royalty payments (usually paid quarterly) based on the price of the end product from the manufacturer to the retailer rather than on the price paid by the end-purchaser. If royalty payments are to be calculated on net receipts, it is essential to obtain from the potential licensee a clear definition of what will constitute net receipts; this may involve obtaining details of distribution channels and discount policies. It is dangerous to attempt to give specific guidelines on royalty percentages since these could range from as low as 1% to over 10%, depending on the importance of the title that is being licensed in the context of the final electronic product. If the title is a branded product such as an encyclopaedia, directory or guidebook, and there is a possibility that the multimedia title might be 'bundled' – included in the price of the hardware product on which it will run – it will be wise to include a contractual provision that the exact arrangements for such use will be agreed at the time. Bundling can provide excellent product visibility, but it does not guarantee long-term success since the platform itself may fail; it may be advisable to make bundling arrangements subject to the approval of the licensor.

It is less common to receive payment in the form of a lump sum or on the basis of a royalty without any advance payment, unless of course the material in question forms only a tiny part of the electronic product. The general aims should be for some up-front payment, a royalty interest that will continue if the product becomes established, the facility to extend the licence on negotiated terms or to cancel the licence if the product (or the platform on which it is intended to run) fails to appear within an agreed period of time or if revenue fails to meet expectations. Licensees have often complained that licensors have unrealistic expectations of licence income and that they fail to recognize the high costs inherent in developing multimedia products. If the material is being licensed for use in a product which will be paid for on a subscription basis, much will depend on what proportion of the end product depends on the underlying copyright work, in order to arrive at a fair share of the subscription revenue.

Joint venturing between a publisher and an electronic producer for key projects has been a common model in the area of multimedia; in any such arrangement it must be very clear who will be responsible for aspects such as clearance of rights, control of the design of the end product, financing, revenue accounting, marketing and distribution, and ownership of the final product. If it is felt that the partners in the joint venture have provided equal input to the development process, the ownership of copyright in the end product could be joint; if, however, the balance is in favour of the publisher in terms of provision of the underlying title, work in 'adding value' to produce a multimedia product, or the provision of development finance, then copyright in the final product should be in the name of the publisher. It will, however, be important to establish whether any existing operating software belonging to the electronic producer can be used in the development process free of charge, or whether payment may be required for the use of this or any new software architecture developed.

If the product is to be licensed on (e.g. versioned for foreign editions), an experienced electronic producer can provide localization kits to facilitate adaptation work, and may require the first option on undertaking development work for the licensees. When licensing on, it is vital to ensure that appropriate rights have been cleared in any material derived from outside sources, e.g. film clips, animation and music.

An important aspect of multimedia publishing – and indeed of electronic publishing in general – is that of the author's moral rights; those of illustrators may also be involved. Many of the products will be interactive in nature and some allow for manipulation of material. The question of the right of integrity will arise, and it may be that the electronic producer seeks a waiver of those rights. It should be remembered that although waiver is currently permitted under UK copyright legislation, it is not permitted in European countries with the *droit moral* tradition.

Several useful contract models for use in the multimedia area can be found in Alan Williams, Duncan Calow and Nicholas Higham, *Digital Media Contracts, Rights and Licensing* (2nd edition, Sweet & Maxwell, 1998) and Ingrid Winternitz, *Electronic Publishing Agreements* (Oxford University Press, 2000).

Figures for the value of the multimedia industry vary enormously; the cost of developing such products remains high and rights clearance for intellectual property in a wide variety of forms remains complex. A discussion panel at the MILIA fair as long ago as 1997, under the heading 'Shouldn't we be rich by now?', emphasized the fact that income growth had not been as rapid as might have been expected and this remains the case for many players, with the possible exception of the games industry. Several years later, it remains a significant question which industries will be in a position to control and benefit from growth in the multimedia market; to date, the most successful products have tended to be fixed-medium products developed by the software industry, although the picture is changing as broader bandwidth facilitates the fast delivery of multimedia material over the internet. The last ten years have seen book and journal publishers concentrating their efforts more in the area of various models of electronic text delivery, without the complications of the added components required for multimedia development.

Verbatim electronic content delivery

Many of the same considerations apply concerning the need for control of electronic rights, clearance for permission for the reuse of copyright material drawn from external sources and short-term contracts for carefully defined usage.

It remains difficult to provide firm guidelines on financial terms and contractual documentation for licences covering the supply of verbatim electronic content since much depends on the parties involved, the method and chain of supply, the identity of the end-users, what usage of the material is to be permitted and the financial model employed when charging end-users.

A number of companies operating in the field offer publishers supplying content either a *pro rata* share of subscriptions paid by end-users to what is in effect a digital library or a share of the price of the e-book, which with discount could be some 20–30% lower than the price of the equivalent print-on-paper edition. Publishers will need to reach agreement with authors and agents on the appropriate division of revenue. Some authors and agents are of the view that publishers do not have the costs of materials and warehousing associated with publication in print-on-paper form, and that this justifies payment of a higher percentage of revenue from electronic publications. After a number of initiatives by individual trade publishers, the Society of Authors has argued that authors should receive at least 25% of net receipts from e-book sales and preferably higher – a figure of 75% has been mentioned; also that the royalty rate should escalate. At the time of writing, some of the major trade houses have settled at 25% of net receipts, although others offer less (20% from Macmillan USA and 15% from Random House UK). Publishers have contested paying higher rates on the grounds that the argument that they have lower costs is invalid and that e-book sales will inevitably have some cannibalizing effect on print sales. Academic publishers, who embarked much earlier than their trade counterparts on major investment in digitizing and tagging backlists consisting of many thousands of titles, may have a different perspective; some offer royalty rates on net receipts for e-book sales at rates comparable with those paid for print sales.

Publishers need to question electronic 'middle men' closely on what access will be permitted to users, and whether facilities such as permanent storage, hard-copy printouts and manipulation facilities such as cut and paste are envisaged. Models may vary considerably between the trade sector, where users are more likely to wish to download complete e-books for reading on laptops, dedicated e-readers or mobile phones, and the academic and professional sectors, where users are more likely to use desktops or laptops to search for specific parts of works of use to them for educational or business purposes. It is particularly important if a licence is terminated that the contract provides for prompt deletion of the material concerned and the return of any electronic files provided by the licensor.

Teletext and audiotex

The last section of this chapter deals with two forms of electronic publishing for which publishers may on occasion become content providers.

Teletext

Teletext services include the BBC's Ceefax service and ITV's Teletext service; at the time of writing, over half the televisions in the UK are equipped to view teletext and it remains a popular source of information despite its rather dated look.

Ceefax (launched by the BBC in 1973 and the oldest teletext service in the world) and Teletext are information services that are transmitted through encoded television signals and accessed via television sets that are designed to receive such services. Information includes news, television listings, subtitles to television programmes for the hard of hearing, weather information, recipes, selected share price information and supplementary information relating to specific television programmes. Teletext also provides more popular services such as daily horoscopes and quizzes.

A casualty in this field was Prestel, a view-data service originally developed by the Post Office, then commercially launched and run through British Telecom but since superseded by the wide range of information in effect available free of charge via the internet. It was accessed via a telephone line through the use of a modem, with information then displayed on a television or computer screen. It provided a wider and more commercial range of information than Ceefax or Teletext, with many of the pages of information compiled by outside bodies. Information ranged from share prices to flight schedules and business data, and some publishers were able to license appropriate content to this service, receiving a share of the revenue when their information was accessed. Subscribers to Prestel paid a quarterly charge to BT, together with charges for the time they spent accessing the information. The subscriber base remained limited and in 1994 the Prestel name and equipment were sold to the *Financial Times*; Prestel Online, an internet service provider (ISP) spin-off, was sold to Scottish Telecom and from 2002 was merged into that company's other ISP activities. By contrast with Prestel, the French Teletel system has remained very successful.

Audiotex

These are voice databases accessed by telephone on premium rate telephone lines. The caller rings the appropriate telephone number in order to obtain information, which may be factual or which may feature advertising promotions for a commercial product. Some services are passive, consisting of linear pre-recorded messages. Others are interactive, using voice- or tone-detection systems to control the interactivity. Examples of services which could involve the use of published copyright material are those covering areas such as family health, pet care, sport and encyclopaedias. Services are offered by BT and other telecoms providers. BT charges special rates per minute for these services, depending on the specific service. Of these rates, approximately half of the income is passed on to the organization running the service, which may in turn have acquired a licence for the use of material from the copyright holder. Payment for copyright material should be made on the basis of a royalty for each call accessing the relevant material; the proportion passed on to the copyright holder could vary from 25% to 50% of the fee received by the organization running the service. In some cases, it could be worthwhile for the copyright holder to link up with a commercial sponsor whose name might be used in conjunction with the information service, for example a pet food manufacturer for an audiotex service line on pet care.

Chapter 25

Supply of duplicate production material to licensees

Chapter 6 referred to the possibility of supplying potential licensees with electronic files for review purposes only. These would normally be supplied free of charge, but careful consideration should be given to the supply of full files of a title to potential licensees in markets which may be subject to piracy problems, or where the track record of the potential licensee is unknown – partial files may be preferable. Watermarking files may be of help to deter unauthorized reproduction, but will not prevent unauthorized translation. When supplying files to potential licensees in more reliable markets, it may still be wise to consider asking the recipient to sign a brief confidentiality agreement confirming that the files are for review purposes only and that they will be destroyed if licence arrangements do not go ahead.

There are many occasions when a deal is finalized and the licensee wishes to acquire duplicate production material in order to produce the licensed edition. Examples might include the sale of English-language territorial rights where the licensee is manufacturing its own edition (see Chapter 9), book club rights where the club manufactures its own copies (Chapter 10), paperback rights where the licensee is independent of the licensor (Chapter 11), low-price reprint rights (Chapter 12), other reprint rights (Chapter 13), serial rights (Chapter 14), translation rights (Chapter 16) and electronic licences (Chapters 23 and 24). The material may be for the whole book (in the case of an English-language reprint edition) or for some or all of the illustrations (in the case of serial rights or a translation).

Traditionally, publishers supplied licensees with duplicate film, but today the majority of material is supplied in the form of electronic files, either for the whole book or perhaps for the illustrations only, depending on what type of edition the licensee will be producing. It should, however, be remembered that the supply of production material to a licensee removes control over print quantities from the licensor; this may be significant in the case of mass-market illustrated books which have been licensed to particular markets on the basis of restricted print runs (e.g. central and eastern Europe, Russia and China). In such cases, it may be wise to consider a contractual requirement to see copies of all printer's documentation to verify the size of printing undertaken, as there have been many cases of unauthorized excess printings being undertaken in these markets.

It is important to establish exactly what the licensee requires before obtaining a quotation from the printer. If it is production material for the whole book, will cover material also be required, or will the licensee want to produce a different cover design, either from choice or because there may be copyright issues with allowing the original cover image to be used? It is always preferable to specify these items separately. If only illustration material is required, will it be all illustrations or only certain types: colour plates, black and white halftones or line drawings? Again, it may be wise to specify the elements separately unless the licensee has clearly specified that production material is required for all illustrations in the book. It may be cheaper to supply material for all pages containing illustrations, leaving the licensee to remove the original text if the book is to be translated. Consideration should also be given to whether the licensee may require the removal of English-language lettering from the illustrations themselves, and whether this will be simple to achieve (a book designed for coedition sales should normally have the lettering on a separate black plate).

Specifications

If a licensee still requires production material in the form of duplicate film, it is essential to obtain very precise technical specifications from the licensee in order to avoid confusion or error. The specification should not be given simply as 'duplicate positive film' or 'duplicate negative film' but as 'duplicate positive film, right-reading, emulsion side down' so that an accurate price can be obtained from the printer. Different specifications may be required for the interior of the book and for the cover film if the licensee requires this. Inadequate specifications could mean that film is supplied which may then require an additional stage of duplication by the licensee, with consequent extra costs.

It is always wise to check with the printer or the in-house production department whether the licensee's required type of film will produce adequate results; it may be that an alternative and more satisfactory specification can be recommended. For example, if film is held in positive form and the licensee also requires film in positive form, two stages of duplication are involved which may involve some loss of quality, while the supply of duplicate negative film will require only one stage of duplication.

If material is required by the licensee in electronic form, it is advisable to check what can be supplied and whether this format is acceptable to the licensee. Publishers usually now store material on CDs, which currently have a capacity of 700 megabytes, or DVDs, with a capacity of 4.7 gigabytes.

The most common software tool used for typesetting and pre-press work is currently QuarkXpress, usually used in the Mac version. However, it is not particularly suitable for technical typesetting (e.g. text containing significant numbers of mathematical or chemical formulae); here the most common format is 3B2, which is in common use in the United Kingdom and increasingly in the United States and Germany. It may, however, be problematic for users in other countries. At the time of writing, InDesign and FrameMaker are also used, particularly for books containing a significant proportion of illustrations.

Photoshop is the most common software package in use for photographs; for drawings, the most common packages are Adobe Illustrator, Macromedia Freehand and CorelDraw. Files created in these tools can easily be exported as EPS (Encapsulated Postscript) files for vector graphics and as TIFFs (Tagged Image File Format) for scanning images. While the former can still be edited, the latter are bitmaps and cannot be altered significantly. Again, it is important to check with the licensee whether they require electronic files for the whole book or only for certain categories of illustration. Licensees seeking to acquire electronic rights (for example aggregators such as ProQuest or Credo) ideally require files in XML format, although if these are not available they may be prepared to accept PDFs, Word files or work from print copies of the books concerned. XML files are also the preferred format for producing a range of editions for the reading impaired (see Chapter 18).

Quotation

Once the required specifications are established, a quotation should be obtained from the typesetter or printer holding the material. If material is to be supplied in the form of film, it is advisable for cover film and interior film to be specified separately, and it will also be helpful to establish in what form the material will be supplied, whether it will be in large imposed sheets or cut to page size. Exact specifications should be given for electronic material. Some publishers may hold electronic files in-house and may be prepared to supply copies free of any charge for physical duplication costs, although they may still wish to make a charge for the supply of material in convenient usable form as a contribution towards their origination costs.

The supplier should be asked to ensure that the quotation will be valid until a specified date by which the licensee could be expected to have placed a firm order. If the material is to be produced in the United Kingdom, the supplier should make it clear whether VAT is included in the price quoted; for material manufactured abroad, the relevant exchange rate should be quoted, which should hold for the duration of the quotation.

When quoting a price for duplicate production material to the licensee, a decision must be taken on whether to supply 'at cost' – which might include the addition of a handling charge of, say, 10% – or whether a mark-up will be applied to provide a contribution towards the cost of origination. This is particularly important in the case of heavily illustrated books, where it could well be reasonable to mark up the price of the material substantially; there is also a considerable benefit if a licensee orders material containing complex design layouts or mathematical setting. The price could also be constructed to include an element to cover the reclearance of picture permissions for the licensee's market if this work is being undertaken by the original publisher, and here the exact figure could be quoted; it is less common to specify the exact contribution towards origination costs. It is advisable to highlight the fact that these additional elements are being included in the price quoted.

The question of setting prices for the supply of duplicate production material in electronic form can be more complex. Although the principle is the same (the licensee benefits from the provision of material in which the licensor has invested time and effort), there is often an expectation on the part of the licensee that a copy of the work in electronic form costs almost nothing to produce, and there can sometimes be resistance to high charges which reflect a contribution towards the origination costs. The situation may vary greatly from title to title; for example, the author of a computer title may be prepared to supply a copy on disk or CD at no charge, whereas a typesetter will almost certainly specify a retrieval and copying charge which the licensor will wish to recover from the licensee, regardless of whether or not they also decide to add a mark-up on the price. The real point here is the value of receiving material in this form to the licensee; for books which have involved heavy investment by the licensor and where the licensee is spared time and expense by receiving duplicate material, there is good justification for setting a price which reflects that benefit, regardless of the method of supply.

An alternative to supplying electronic files in disk form would be to upload them to the FTP (File Transfer Protocol) site of the licensee if they have one, or to the licensor's own FTP site, perhaps to a dedicated rights site on a particular server. The latter course is more complex in terms of ensuring that only the authorized licensee can access the designated file, with a user name and password provided by the licensor. This could be done either by organizing the site so that licensees can access their own 'folders', or by uploading individual files to a dedicated rights site for collection via a password on or by a specific date, after which the file would then be taken down, but this latter procedure is less secure and more complicated to administer in terms of knowing when the file has been collected by the appropriate licensee. Again, since the licensee is receiving production material in usable form, there is a strong argument for charging for supply by this method.

Copyright in fonts

It is often overlooked that there is copyright in printing fonts themselves; typefaces are the intellectual property of their designers and manufacturers, and that right was reinforced in the United Kingdom by the Copyright (Computer Programs) Regulations 1992, which amended the UK Copyright, Designs and Patents Act 1988.

Duplicate film or electronic files are often supplied to licensees, who will produce their licensed editions in other languages, and may well use characters other than Roman ones (e.g. for languages such as Russian, Chinese, Japanese and Arabic). Their requirement for duplicate production material is usually to facilitate the reproduction of photographs or diagrams rather than the original text, so the issue of font copyright will not be relevant. However, when duplicate film or electronic files are required by licensees for reproduction in the English language (e.g. for a UK book club, for an American publisher or for the production of a low-price reprint edition in markets such as India or China) the licensor should check whether the licensee holds a valid licence for the use of the font or fonts concerned. The same situation applies if the licensee wishes to pay an offset fee for reproducing the typesetting of the original edition without acquiring duplicate production material. Licensors may wish to consider including a clause to cover this in the licence contract itself or to deal with the requirement in separate correspondence covering the supply of duplicate production material.

A useful pamphlet, *Guide to Legal Typeface Use*, is available from Fontworks UK Ltd (New North House, 202–208 New North Road, London N1 7BJ; tel. 020 7226 4411; www.type.co.uk), the UK partner in the Fontshop International network, the world's largest font retailer, representing over thirty font manufacturers.

Payment

The timing of payment for production material is important. Duplicate film of a large book heavily illustrated in colour can be extremely expensive in itself, and it would be unwise to order such film on behalf of a relatively unknown licensee without some form of guarantee on how payment will be made. The safest method of dealing is to request full prepayment for the material before placing a firm order, and some publishers maintain this policy when dealing with a new customer for the first time, whether material is supplied in film or in electronic form. Alternatively, payment for very expensive material could be made against a letter of credit, although this will involve additional charges for the licensee. A compromise arrangement might be to require part payment in advance of placing an order, with the balance payable on delivery of the material. As a general principle, it is always unwise to place an order for duplicate production material if the licence contract itself has not yet been signed, nor the advance payment safely received.

Often the licensee will not be ready to order duplicate production material at the time the licence contract is negotiated, and may not at that stage know the exact technical specifications required. In such cases, it would be preferable not to cover the purchase of production material in the contract itself, but to deal with this by correspondence or by an addendum to the contract at the stage when exact specifications and prices are known. If publication of the book depends on the supply of duplicate production material, it would nevertheless be wise for the licensee to have at least an estimated cost prior to signing the contract.

Documentation

It is vital to obtain exact instructions from the licensee on what documentation is required in order for the material to be safely despatched and received at the other end without importation problems. The documentation required may vary according to the material, the method of despatch, the country of manufacture and the destination country; it may include documents other than an invoice, such as a certificate of origin. Importation into some countries requires an import licence.

The onus should be on the licensee to specify how the production material is to be described and whether it is to be declared accurately in terms of its nature and value. Licensors should bear in mind that it may constitute an offence to misrepresent the value of the material. If the value is under-declared to avoid or reduce customs duty, it will not be possible to insure the material for its true value, and this should be pointed out to the licensee; if there is any loss or damage to the material in transit, the licensor could not then be expected to arrange for the supply of replacement material free of charge.

Delivery

The method of delivery of the material to the licensee may not have been decided at the point the quotation is received, but it should be remembered that while the cost of sending a few pages of film or a CD by airmail post may be modest, the cost of sending a heavy set of film for a large illustrated book by courier can be substantial, although this scenario is less common today. It is therefore wise to quote the price of any production material exclusive of packing, insurance and shipping charges, making it clear that these will be charged separately when the preferred method of delivery and the packed weight of the material are known.

The provision of production material to publishers in some countries can cause considerable problems in terms of pricing, documentation require- ments and physical delivery. Some countries pose significant problems with administrative obstacles to prepayment and importation; this is still a feature of some former socialist countries. It is sometimes simpler to deliver film in person if this is practical; if not, air freight or courier services should be used in preference to ordinary mail. Publishers in some countries prefer to avoid the use of the words 'film' or 'disk' in documentation and may instead prefer the film to be described as 'book material' or 'illustration material'. If CDs are being shipped for production purposes, it would be wise to specify that they are for book production use, otherwise they may be treated as commercial audio or audiovisual disks and incur VAT charges. Delivery via an FTP site may be preferable.

If material is subsequently impounded by customs authorities in the country of the licensee, it should be made clear that it is the licensee rather than the licensor who will be liable for any attendant costs or delays caused by the description of the goods. If a subagent is involved in a licence deal, they should not be permitted to deduct commission from the price agreed for the sale of production material, since this is a technical supply of goods and separate from the licence arrangement. The author does not normally receive any share of this income either, as it represents a contribution towards the original publisher's origination costs. This may be a reason for covering the supply of production material to a licensee by separate correspondence rather than including details in the licence contract, to avoid any administrative confusion when paying the author's share of licence revenue.

Useful names and addresses

Authors Licensing and Collecting
Society
The Writers' House
13 Haydon Street
London EC3N 1DB
Tel. 0207 264 5700
Fax 0207 264 5755
e-mail alcs@alcs.co.uk
www.alcs.co.uk

Book Industry Communication
39–41 North Road
London N7 9DP
Tel. 0207 607 0021
Fax 0207 607 0415
e-mail info@bic.org.uk
www.bic.org.uk

Bradbury Phillips International Ltd
29 Aubert Park
London N5 1TP
Tel. 0208 202 9192
e-mail info@bradburyphillips.co.uk
www.bradburyphillips.co.uk

Brighteye Ltd
21 Weedon Lane
Amersham
Bucks HP6 5OT
Tel. 01494 726069
Fax 01494 726069
e-mail enquiries@brighteyeltd.com
www.brighteyeltd.com

British Copyright Council
Copyright House
29–33 Berners Street
London W1P 4AA
Tel. 01986 788 122
Fax 01986 788 847
e-mail secretary@britishcopyright.org
www.britishcopyright.org

Copyright Licensing Agency Ltd
Saffron House
6–10 Kirby Street
London EC1N 8TS
Tel. 0207 400 3100
Fax 0207 400 3101
e-mail cla@cla.co.uk
www.cla.co.uk

Design and Artists Copyright Society
33 Great Sutton Street
London EC1V 0DX
Tel. 0207 336 8811
Fax 0207 336 8822
e-mail info@dacs.org.uk
www.dacs.org.uk

Inland Revenue
Centre for Non-Residents
Fitzroy House
P.O. Box 46
Nottingham NG2 1BD
Tel. 0115 974 2000
Fax 0115 974 1919

International Association of Scientific,
Technical and Medical Publishers
(STM)
Prins Willem Alexanderhof 5
2595 BE The Hague
Netherlands
Tel. 31 70314 09303
Fax 31 70314 0940

UK address:
Prama House
267 Banbury Road
Oxford OX2 7HT
Tel. 01865 339321
Fax 01865 339325
www.stm-assoc.org

International Publishers Association
3 avenue de Miremont
CH1206 Geneva
Switzerland
Tel. 22 3463018
Fax 22 3475717
e-mail secretariat@
internationalpublishers.org
www.internationalpublishers.org

Klopotek UK ltd
90 Long Acre
London WC2E 9RZ
Tel. 0207 716 5500
Fax 0207 716 5595
www.klopotek.co.uk

Public Lending Right
PLR Office
Richard House
Sorbonne Close
Stockton on Tees TS17 6DA
Tel. 01642 604699
Fax 01642 615641
www.plr.uk.com

Publishers Association
29B Montague Street
London WC1B 5BW
Tel. 0207 691 9191
Fax 0207 691 9199
www.publishers.org.uk

Publishers Licensing Society Ltd
37–41 Gower Street
London WC1E 6HH
Tel. 0207 299 7730
Fax 0207 299 7780
www.pls.org.uk

The Publishing Training Centre at
Book House
45 East Hill
London SW18 2QZ
Tel. 0208 874 2718
Fax 0208 870 8985
e-mail publishing.training@
bookhouse.co.uk
www.train4publishing.co.uk

Society of Authors
84 Drayton Gardens
London SW10 9SB
Tel. 0207 373 6642
Fax 0207 373 5768
www.societyofauthors.org

That's Rights!
JDC Software
29 Harley Street
London W1G 9QR
Tel. 0207 681 2014
Fax 0207 681 2031
e-mail info@thatsrights.com
www.thatsrights.com

Index

Related titles from Routledge

Comparative Media Law and Ethics
Tim Crook

Providing practical and theoretical resources on media law and ethics for the UK and USA and referencing other legal jurisdictions such as France, Japan, India, China and Saudi Arabia, Comparative Media Law and Ethics is suitable for upper undergraduate and postgraduate study, and for media professionals who need to work internationally.

The book focuses on the law of the UK, the source of common law, which has dominated the English-speaking world, and on the law of the USA, the most powerful cultural, economic, political and military power in the world. Media law and ethics have evolved differently in the USA from the UK. This book investigates why this is the case. Tim Crook also considers other media law jurisdictions:

- **Common law: A focus on India** – the biggest democracy in the world and largest middle class.
- **Civil law: A focus on France** – the influential founder of the European Union and host country for ECHR at Strasbourg.
- **Socialist law: A focus on China** – the country with the highest economic growth and largest population.
- **Islamic law: A focus on Saudi Arabia** – one of the most influential sources of legal religiosity

Tim Crook analyses media law, as it exists, the ethical debates concerning what the law ought to be, and the historical development of legal and regulatory controls of communication. Underlying concepts discussed include media jurisprudence – the study of the philosophy of media law; media ethicology – the study of the knowledge of ethics/morality in media communication; and media ethicism – the belief systems in the political context that influence journalistic conduct and content. Throughout, media law and regulation is evaluated in terms of its social and cultural context.

The book has a companion website at **www.ma-radio.gold.ac.uk/cmle** providing complementary resources and updated developments on the topics explored. If you need to compare different law and ethics systems, are studying international journalism or want to understand the legalities of working in the media in different jurisdictions, then you will find this an important and useful guide.

ISBN13: 978-0-415-55157-1 (hbk)
ISBN13: 978-0-415-55161-8 (pbk)
ISBN13: 978-0-203-86596-5 (ebk)

Available at all good bookshops
For ordering and further information please visit:
www.routledge.com

Related titles from Routledge

Inside Book Publishing
Fourth Edition
Giles Clark and Angus Phillips

How do publishers work and make money? Why do they exist?

This expanded and thoroughly revised fourth edition of *Inside Book Publishing* is designed for students of publishing, authors needing to find out publishing secrets, and those wanting to get in or get on in the industry. It addresses the big issues – globalization of publishing, the impact of the internet – and explains publishing from the author contract to the bookshop shelf.

It covers:

- how the present industry has evolved
- publishing functions – editorial, design and production, marketing, sales and distribution, and rights
- the role of the author
- copyright and contracts
- the sales channels for books in the UK, from the high street to e-books
- getting a job in publishing.

It features:

- topic boxes written by expert contributors
- a glossary of publishing terms
- suggestions for further reading
- a directory of publishing organizations
- a companion website (www.insidebookpublishing.com).

It is an essential tool for anyone embarking on a career in publishing, and a useful handbook for those who are in the industry and for authors.

978-0-415-44156-8 (hbk)
978-0-415-44157-5 (pbk)
978-0-203-34154-4 (ebk)

Available at all good bookshops
For ordering and further information please visit:
www.routledge.com

An Introduction to Book History

David Finkelstein and Alistair McCleery

An Introduction to Book History provides a comprehensive critical introduction to the development of the book and print culture. David Finkelstein and Alistair McCleery chart the move from spoken word to written texts, the coming of print, the book as commodity, the power and profile of readers, and the future of the book in the electronic age. Each section begins with a summary of the chapter's aims and contents, followed by a detailed discussion of the relevant issues, concluding with a summary of the chapter and suggestions for further reading.

Sections include:

- The History of the Book
- Orality to Literacy
- Literacy to Printing
- Authors, authorship and authority
- Printers, Booksellers, Publishers, Agents
- Readers and reading
- The Future of the Book

An Introduction to Book History will be an ideal introduction to this exciting field of study, and is designed as a companion text to *The Book History Reader*.

978-0-415-31442-8 (hbk)
978-0-203-31443-5 (ebk)

Available at all good bookshops
For ordering and further information please visit:
www.routledge.com